DAILY LIFE IN

THE COLONIAL SOUTH

Recent Titles in
The Greenwood Press Daily Life Through History Series

The Reformation
James M. Anderson

The Aztecs, Second Edition
Davíd Carrasco and Scott Sessions

The Progressive Era
Steven L. Piott

Women during the Civil Rights Era
Danelle Moon

Colonial Latin America
Ann Jefferson and Paul Lokken

The Ottoman Empire
Mehrdad Kia

Pirates
David F. Marley

Arab Americans in the 21st Century
Anan Ameri and Holly Arida, Editors

African American Migrations
Kimberley L. Phillips

The Salem Witch Trials
K. David Goss

Behind the Iron Curtain
Jim Willis

Trade: Buying and Selling in World History
James M. Anderson

DAILY LIFE IN

THE COLONIAL SOUTH

JOHN T. SCHLOTTERBECK

The Greenwood Press Daily Life Through
History Series: Daily Life in the United States

AN IMPRINT OF ABC-CLIO, LLC
Santa Barbara, California • Denver, Colorado • Oxford, England

Library of Congress Cataloging-in-Publication Data

Schlotterbeck, John T.
Daily life in the colonial South / John T. Schlotterbeck.
pages cm — (The Greenwood Press daily life through history series. Daily life in the United States)
Includes index.
ISBN 978-0-313-34069-7 (hardback) — ISBN 978-1-57356-743-5 (ebook)
1. Southern States—Social life and customs—To 1775. I. Title.
F212.S45 2013
975′.01—dc23 2012047330

ISBN: 978-0-313-34069-7
EISBN: 978-1-57356-743-5

17 16 15 14 13 1 2 3 4 5

This book is also available on the World Wide Web as an eBook.
Visit www.abc-clio.com for details.

Greenwood
An Imprint of ABC-CLIO, LLC

ABC-CLIO, LLC
130 Cremona Drive, P.O. Box 1911
Santa Barbara, California 93116-1911

This book is printed on acid-free paper ∞

Manufactured in the United States of America

For Barbara, Jesse, and Marian

CONTENTS

PREFACE: SOUTHS BEFORE THE SOUTH

Daily Life in the Colonial South describes how Native Americans, Europeans, and Africans created new societies in the South Atlantic from initial European contacts in the early 1500s to the eve of the American Revolution in the 1760s. Through frequent interactions, new patterns of living, behaving, and believing developed across diverse and changing physical, demographic, economic, and social environments from the Chesapeake Bay to the Lower Mississippi River as people adapted inherited cultures, institutions, and social patterns in new settings. This book examines patterns of everyday life in the colonial South, how they developed and changed over time, and differences across lines of nationality, ethnicity, religion, race, gender, and class.

Historians of daily life examine routine activities and popular beliefs of ordinary people in the past: how they made a living, lived in families, used material objects, prepared meals, had fun, displayed bodies, understood the spiritual world, engaged in disorderly behavior, and constructed social identities. Historians study daily life because, as sociologist Alfred Schutz observed, "The everyday world of common-sense objects and practical acts is the paramount reality in human experience."[1] By studying everyday life, historians seek answers to mundane, but elusive, questions. How did people spend their day? What were common beliefs and collective actions? How did lived experiences affect public behavior and cultural values? How did particular historical contexts (e.g., Southerners' colonial status) shape daily life? In what ways did daily life vary between men and women, between the enslaved and the free, between Native Americans and Euro-Americans, between members of different ethnic groups, and between the wealthy and the poor? How did ordinary people's lives change over time and why?

The study of daily life in the United States began with museum curators, who used material objects to teach about the past, and with social historians, who utilized social science methods pioneered by historians of early modern Europe to tell a new history "from the bottom up." Beginning in the 1970s with studies of Puritan communities in colonial New England, social historians exploited abundant local records to examine settlement and population patterns, family life, material culture, work routines, social and geographic mobility, popular religious beliefs, and community politics. Their purview expanded to other localities, the 17th-century Chesapeake (principally, tidewater Virginia and Maryland) and 18th-century rural Pennsylvania, and to overlooked groups: women, slaves, laborers, the poor, and Native Americans. Ordinary people, many of whom were illiterate, left far fewer written or material records of their lives than members of elite groups. By asking new questions of traditional sources such as letters, diaries, travel narratives, newspapers, and legislative debates, and by developing new analytical techniques to exploit neglected sources like court records, shipping lists, and newspaper advertisements, one can learn how ordinary people behaved and why. We now have a much richer palette of colonial America where all segments of the population, not just elite males, are historical actors and where private lives have as much historical significance as public action.

Historians of everyday life make assumptions about the human condition that shape how they study the past. They seek to link "material circumstances" of daily life to the "inner world of popular experience" by paying careful attention to patterns of behavior and action, to modes of thought and belief, and to underlying but often-unarticulated "taken for granted" rules that govern day-to-day life.[2] People in the past engaged in many of the same activities we do today; yet, historians of daily life emphasize differences between the colonial world of our ancestors and modern-day life. Much about the past remains unknown: actual sexual behavior as opposed to norms of sexual conduct or popular knowledge and work skills that remained within conversations between family members and friends. On the other hand, we understand lives of colonial people in ways they could not. Patriarchy, a belief in women's innate inferiority to men, profoundly affected women's everyday lives, but for most colonial women, their subordination was so culturally ingrained they barely understood its impact. In tracing racism's origins, we are the ones who see race as a problem in the colonial South. By focusing on ordinary peoples' experiences, historians of everyday life emphasize the costs of historical change that provided opportunities for a few at the expense of many. Colonization hardly improved the lives of most Native Americans, indentured servants, or African slaves. Still, it is important to see individuals at the bottom of society as actors making their own history and not merely as victims of oppression. Some European women had sex with African men, challenging both gender and racial norms. Trade with Europeans provided new material and political opportunities for some Native men. Slaves established families, formed communities, and created new cultures despite the shackles of their enslavement.[3]

Study of daily life encompasses both the impress of culture on day-to-day behavior and resistance to and renegotiation of cultural norms. The colonial South provides an ideal laboratory for studying these processes. Colonial societies' newness with weakened social and political institutions and diverse populations made them unusually fluid places. Responses of colonial Southerners, especially charter groups of early settlers, to the novelty of their situation richly reveal processes of constructing new societies and negotiating new identities. Unlike traditional historical narratives, this book does not foreground powerful men, major events, or great ideas. Nor does it begin in Europe and move westward as explorers discovered new worlds, and Europeans settled frontier areas. Instead, it envisions the southeast as a vast stage filled with many actors in plays they scripted from scene to scene. Stories emerge, none preordained, in the course of action and change as actors enter and exit and unseen directors add unanticipated elements. Three aspects of the colonial South's set are most telling: the diverse mix of characters, the connections to the Atlantic world, and the geographic variety.

The arrival of Spanish, English, and French explorers and settlers to the South Atlantic and the Gulf of Mexico coasts added to the mix of already diverse indigenous peoples. Later immigrants from England, Scotland, Ireland, and Europe especially Germans, Jews, and

French Huguenots, and slaves from the West Indies and from Africa added to this diversity. New ways of living arose from daily interactions between new arrivals and older settlers, between women and men, and between individuals of different classes, ethnicities, and races. These new societies in the colonial South were unlike anything in Britain, Europe, Africa, or precontact America. European and African newcomers so altered southeastern environments that for Native Americans, their ancient homelands became a "new world" for them as well. Everyday life arose from this constantly changing mix of inherited traditions and New World experiences. Daily life in the colonial South offers perspectives for understanding the formation of new societies and how they changed over time.

Historians have expanded the colonial South's boundaries beyond English settlements on the South Atlantic coast to include Spanish Florida, French Louisiana, the backcountry, and interior Native American communities. Although early European settlers were geographically separated from each other as well as from their homelands across the ocean, they were part of an imperial and expanding Atlantic world. Over time, ties of empire, trade, and migration strengthened connections colonial Southerners had with other North American settlements and with England, Western Europe, Caribbean colonies, and Africa. Greater integration into the Atlantic world brought new people, new ideas, new conflicts, and new material goods into daily life. Through these ties, English settlers experienced similar trajectories in economic growth, race relations, class formation, political evolution, and social institutions that later made nationhood possible. Imperial policies pursued by Spain and by France, in contrast, kept their colonial outposts of Florida and Louisiana, respectively, weak and underdeveloped. Expanding the geography of the colonial South provides comparative contexts for connecting patterns of daily life to broader economic, political, cultural, and imperial changes over the course of the 17th- and 18th-century Atlantic world.

The earliest settlements sprawling across the colonial South—Saint Augustine, Florida (1565); Jamestown, Virginia (1607); Saint Mary's City, Maryland (1634); Charles Town, South Carolina (1670); New Bern, North Carolina (1711); New Orleans, Louisiana (1718); and Savannah, Georgia (1734)—developed long before anyone was conscious of "the South" or of being "Southerners." Founded over almost two centuries and for different purposes, encountering varied environments and indigenous peoples, developing different economies, attracting varied populations, and expanding significantly beyond initial settlements, early southern communities were too isolated from each other and too diverse to forge a common identity. Even features often cited as distinctively southern—plantations, landed elites, and enslaved laborers—were also present in some parts of the middle and northern colonies and even truer of West Indies colonies but absent in the early southeastern backcountry. Important aspects of everyday life in the colonial South like subsistence farming, ethnic and religious diversity, subordination of women, or patterns of Indian–white relations existed elsewhere in colonial America. Settlers identified first with their ethnic group or as overseas Europeans, then as Protestants or Catholics, and only later as Virginians or as Carolinians, but never as Southerners. Ironically, awareness of significant regional differences and of conflicting sectional interests first emerged during the American Revolution, as political leaders from New Hampshire to Georgia learned to work together for the first time to make a nation.

Still, specific aspects of daily life, which would later define southern nationality in the antebellum era, began in the colonial period. These include market agriculture, planter domination, slave labor, distinct African American cultures, white supremacy, continued Native presence, absence of cities, evangelical religion, and disparities of wealth, power, and status that shaped social relations across lines of gender, race, and class. Examining daily lives of ordinary southern people in the colonial period is one of the best ways to understand the origins of these southern traits, their variations across time and space, and formation of a "southern way of life."

This book examines daily life in the 17th and 18th centuries with brief coverage of the pre-1600 period in five regions of the colonial South: the Chesapeake (tidewater Maryland, Virginia, and northern North Carolina), the Lowcountry (coastal southern North Carolina, South Carolina, and Georgia), the backcountry (interior Maryland, Virginia, the Carolinas, and Georgia), Spanish Florida, French Louisiana, and native interior. Daily life encompasses private lives and public actions of all members of society: women and men, blacks and whites, Native Americans and Europeans, and common folk and gentry. The first chapter provides a historical survey in 50-year intervals with profiles of early settlements, major events, and important developments between 1500 and 1750. Eight topical chapters explore aspects of daily life: labor, families, possessions, food, leisure, bodies, beliefs, and disorder. The final chapter interprets the origins of southern distinctiveness as arising from daily life in the colonial era. Each chapter begins with a thematic overview followed by sections on specific topics organized by region, group, and/or time. Some chapters emphasize historians' writings and debates about important developments like the origins of slavery or importance of religion. Other chapters rely more heavily on historical actors' voices to capture their observations on the colonial South's newness and variability. Most chapters note differences within Native, European, and African groups, but occasionally (in Chapter 7, for instance), I create composite personalities to encapsulate broadly shared experiences. Chapter 9 is written as imaginary newspaper stories about real events. I retained most original spellings in quoted texts but added punctuation for clarity. Images provide visual evidence for major themes or details to extend the analysis. A chronology, maps, population tables, and bibliography provide additional aids for understanding and learning more about the colonial South.

As a work of synthesis, I have benefitted from several decades of exciting new scholarship, which has broadened the colonial South's geographic reach and deepened our understanding of the lives of previously overlooked groups. The conclusions, however, are my own.

ACKNOWLEDGMENTS

Historians research and write in isolation but are sustained by intellectual and personal networks. Long ago, Jack Greene insisted that understanding the colonial South required looking beyond British settlements, and Bill Freehling modeled using lean prose to convey ideas with clarity. Susan Schreiber opened up the world of material culture as providing new avenues to examine everyday life. My history companions at DePauw University especially Julia Bruggemann, James Cooper, John Dittmer, David Gellman, and Barbara Steinson, provide daily examples of the creative synergies between scholarship and teaching. Their sustained moral support, great humor, inspired creativity, and lively conversations make them the best colleagues and friends one could ever hope to have. This book is a culmination of several decades of teaching early American history and material culture to DePauw University students, whose intellectual curiosity and insightful observations over the years honed my thinking on small details as well as broad patterns about the nature of the colonial South.

DePauw University generously supported this project with grants from the Fisher Fund that provided sabbatical assistance in the initial phase and from the Professional Development Fund to defray some permission costs. David Harvey, vice president for Academic Affairs, adjusted my teaching load that allowed me to complete the project. Jamie Knapp cheerfully fulfilled numerous requests to borrow materials, and librarians at Hope College and Randolph College made available their resources. Dana Ferguson and Wes Wilson provided invaluable assistance in preparing the manuscript, and Beth Wilkerson created the maps. I am grateful to the many institutions that allowed me to include images from their collections.

Randall Miller is an editor most scholars can only dream of having. A chance meeting led to his recruiting me for this project, and only his unflagging enthusiasm, unwavering patience, and unstinted feedback made completing this book possible. Michael Millman and Erin Ryan, ABC-CLIO-Greenwood Press, facilitated final stages of manuscript preparation.

Jesse and Marian have launched their own academic careers over the course of writing this book. They are an inspiration and unending source of pride. Barbara's constant presence and loving faithfulness in my personal and professional life, my own special lodestar, is the reason for this book.

NOTES

1. Alfred Schutz, *The Problem of Social Reality* (The Hague: M. Nijhoff, 1962), cited in Michael Barton, "The Study of American Everyday Life," *American Quarterly* 34, no. 3 (1982): 219.

2. Geoff Eley, "Forward," in *The History of Everyday Life: Reconstructing Historical Experiences and Ways of Life,* ed. by Alf Lüdtke (Princeton, NJ: Princeton University Press, 1989), viii and Jack Larkin, "The View from New England: Notes on Everyday Life in Rural American to 1850," *American Quarterly* 34, no. 3 (1982): 245.

3. For excellent introductions to theoretical issues in writing histories of everyday life, see Alf Lüdtke, "Introduction: What Is the History of Everyday Life and Who Are Its Practitioners?" Dorothee Wierling, "The History of Everyday Life and Gender Relations: On Historical and Historiographical Relationships," and Wolfgang Kuschuba, "Popular Culture and Workers' Culture as Symbolic Orders: Comments on the Debate about the History of Culture and Everyday Life," in Lüdtke, *History of Everyday Life,* 3–40, 149–68, and 169–97; and Ben Highmore, "Introduction: Questioning Everyday Life," *The Everyday Life Reader* (London: Routledge, 2002), 1–38.

CHRONOLOGY

1000 BCE Beginnings of agriculture along river courses with planting of seed crops. Hunting and gathering still remained the most important food sources for Natives.

200 BCE Natives plant tropical flint corn, squashes, and gourds expanding their repertoire of food resources.

900–1500 Beans, squash, and eastern flint corn cultivated in the Southeast. Population growth allowed urban mound-building cultures to develop near major river systems.

1513 Juan Ponce de León failed to find healing springs, "a fountain of youth," but names the peninsula, Florida.

1526 Lucas Vázquez de Ayllón established the first Spanish settlement in the colonial South. Meeting resistance from the Guale, the surviving one quarter of original settlers abandoned the colony the next year.

1528 Alvar Núñez Cabeza de Vaca started his expedition along the Gulf Coast.

1533 Henry VIII divorced Catherine of Aragon breaking England's alliance with Spain and fealty to the Roman Catholic Church. The Church of England became the established church and the Protestant Reformation spread to Britain.

1539–1543 Hernando de Soto rampaged throughout the Southeast attacking villages, capturing chieftains, commandeering foodstuffs and Native porters, and spreading epidemic diseases. Most paramount chiefdoms collapsed and devolved into smaller loosely confederated village societies.

1560s English conquest of Ireland began under Elizabeth I. English landlords recruited Highland Scots as tenants to work seized lands. They became the Scots-Irish or Ulster Scots in the colonial South.

1564 French Huguenots established a settlement, Fort Caroline, on the Saint John's River. Jacque Le Moyne, naturalist and illustrator, documented Timucun culture. His watercolors were lost in a Spanish attack, and images attributed to Le Moyne are engravings made by Theodore de Bry, a Belgian printer.

1565 Pedro Menéndez de Avilés established Saint Augustine, the first permanent settlement in Florida. He quickly attacked and destroyed the Huguenot outpost.

1570 Jesuits arrived in the Chesapeake Bay with Paquinquineo, aka Don Lois, who had been abducted by the Spanish in 1561 and had converted to Catholicism. Renouncing his baptism, he returned with Powhatan warriors and destroyed the mission. Powhatan became paramount chief of six villages in eastern Virginia. Over the next 30 years, he expanded his rule to 30 villages with 14,000 settlers. Tribute payments and warfare supported his paramount chieftaincy.

1585–1587 Two expeditions of English colonists settled at Roanoke Island off the coast of modern-day North Carolina. A relief expedition arrived in 1590 and found the settlement abandoned. Known as the "Lost Colony," survivors were either killed or adopted by local natives. Thomas Hariot, naturalist, and John White, artist, recorded Carolina Algonquian culture.

1595 Franciscans began successful mission work with Guale and Timucua villagers on the Atlantic coast from Saint Augustine to present-day Savannah and in Apalachee villages in northwestern Florida.

1607 The Virginia Company, a joint-stock trading firm, sent 144 men and boys to establish a colony in the Chesapeake Bay. Jamestown was the first permanent English settlement in the colonial South. Expecting immediate riches, settlers depended on local Powhatan Indians for food.

1609–1614 First Anglo-Powhatan War, a low-intensity conflict, began as Paramount Chief Powhatan limited food supplies to colonists, who retaliated by attacking villages and seizing Native food reserves. War ended when John Rolfe, a Virginia planter, married Pocahontas, a daughter of Powhatan.

1616 John Rolfe sent the first commercial tobacco crop to England launching a tobacco boom. By 1624, over 200,000 pounds of tobacco was exported annually and more than 3 million pounds by 1638. Tobacco became a mainstay of Virginia's economy for three centuries. Virginia shifted from company to private landowning. Each shareholder received 100 acres; company workers were promised 50 acres after completing their indentures; and 50-acre "headright" claims were given for each person who immigrated to the colony.

1617 Pocahontas died in England during a publicity tour for the Virginia Company. She became an Anglican, a rare example of Native conversion in the English colonies.

1619 A Dutch ship arrived from the West Indies with "20 odd Negars," who originally were from Angola or the Congo. They were probably held as indentured servants. Virginia Company sent first shipment of 100 London children and poor women as indentured servants to work in tobacco fields.

1622–1632 Opechancanough launched Second Anglo-Powhatan War to drive the English from Virginia. Almost one-third of colonists died in initial attacks; they retaliated with a war of extermination. War ended in 1632 as Powhatans ceded most of their homeland, which allowed for rapid expansion of tobacco cultivation. The Virginia Company lost its charter in 1624, and Virginia became a royal colony.

1630s High mortality in Virginia from epidemic diseases reduced life expectancy. A 20-year-old male could expect to live until 43, about 10 years less than his English counterpart.

1632 George Calvert, Lord Baltimore, received a charter as proprietor that gave him title to land in Maryland, a trade monopoly, and governing powers limited only by requiring settlers' "advise and consent." In 1634, Saint Mary's City, the first settlement, became the capital. Intended as a haven for Catholics, Maryland Protestants quickly formed a majority of the population.

1640 Africans were barred from carrying arms or serving in Virginia militias.

1643 Head or "poll" taxes levied on all field workers defined as all males (white and black) and all black females over age 16. This law distinguished black women presumed to be field workers from white women laboring in their own households.

1644–1646 Third Anglo-Powhatan War began with surprise attacks by Opechancanough. About 400 colonists were killed; Virginia militiamen retaliated by destroying most Powhatan villages. A 1646 treaty confined Powhatans to a small reservation, and Native population declined to 2,000 by 1669.

1649 "Act Concerning Religion" blocked creation of any religious establishment in Maryland. Its purpose was to protect Catholics from Protestant persecution.

1650 About 300 blacks lived in the Chesapeake; some were free, but most were held as servants or as slaves-for-life.

1653 Virginia settlers began moving into northeastern Carolina along Albemarle Sound as family farmers raising tobacco and trading with Indians for deerskins.

1662–1669 Virginia and Maryland codified black slavery by decreeing enslaved women's children were slaves for life, increasing penalties for interracial sexual liaisons, banning interracial marriages, denying emancipation to baptized slaves, and giving owners immunity from prosecution if a slave died during corporal punishment.

1670 Colonists recruited from New England, Virginia, and the Barbados settled coastal Carolina. The early economy was based on cattle, provision crops, and forest products sold to West Indies sugar planters. Virginia had over 50 Anglican parish churches.

1672 Royal African Company, founded in 1663, secured a monopoly on the English slave trade expanding supplies of African slaves to southern planters.

1672–1696 Castillo de San Marcos was built outside Saint Augustine.

1675–1676 Bacon's Rebellion, the largest settler uprising against colonial authority before the American Revolution, began with skirmishes between settlers and Natives on the Virginia frontier. Nathaniel Bacon, upstart leader, alternated between challenging Governor William Berkeley's authority and attacking peaceful Native villages. His army burned Jamestown in September 1676, but the uprising ended with Bacon's death in October. Florida mission system expanded to 36 villages north from Saint Augustine and west to Florida's Gulf Coast with perhaps 15,000 Native converts.

1680 Charles Town was founded, which became the Lowcountry's economic, political, social, and cultural center. To deter slave insurrections, slaves in Virginia were barred from carrying arms and required written permission to leave plantations. Slave runaways who resisted capture could be killed. Armed with guns from Carolina traders, the Savannahs attacked the Westos to divert the lucrative trade in deerskins and in Indian slaves from Virginia to Carolina merchants.

1682 French established Fort Saint Louis on Texas coast.

1684 Scotsmen established Stuart's Town, Port Royal, Carolina, to challenge Spanish Florida.

1686 Spanish forces from Florida failed to dislodge English settlements on Edisto Island, Carolina, but seized several slaves, who were freed after becoming Catholics. Carolina militiamen and Yamasee warriors retaliated by attacking Guale mission villages and Native converts fled south to Saint Augustine.

1685 King Louis XIV issued *The Code Noir,* a comprehensive slave code that, in theory, encouraged slave baptisms, recognized slave marriages, and allowed for manumitting slaves. Provisions stipulating physical care and limiting corporal punishments were widely ignored.

1689–1695 Rebellion by Protestant Association in Maryland ousted the Catholic proprietary governor after settlers learned about the Glorious Revolution in England. William and Mary had seized the throne from Catholic Charles II in a Protestant coup. Maryland became a royal province in 1691; Church of England was established in 1692; and in 1695, the capital moved from Saint Mary's City to Annapolis.

1690s Free population in the Chesapeake in the 1690s and in Carolina 20 years later began to grow more through natural reproduction than from immigration making stable family life possible. Carolina adopted Barbados' harsh slave laws to control growing slave population.

1691–1692 Rebellious settlers in northern Carolina secured their own representative assembly and deputy governor from proprietors. Virginia banned miscegenation. Owners received compensation from the state if their slaves were killed while resisting arrest. Special county courts of "oyer and terminer" were established to try slaves accused of crimes, including felonies.

1693 Spanish Crown promised freedom to any slave fugitive who fled to Florida and converted to Catholicism.

1698 Ending of Royal African Company's monopoly on the slave trade opened trade to independent merchants. Slave prices fell as supplies expanded.

1699 Spanish established a fort in Pensacola Bay to block French expansion eastward.

1700 Population of the colonial South reached 210,200: 34 percent whites, 4 percent blacks, and 62 percent Indians.

1700–1710 Virginia planters imported 7,700 slaves and Carolina planters 3,000 slaves. African slaves displaced white indentured servants in the Chesapeake labor force and outnumbered whites in Carolina. Rice revolution in Carolina shifted the economy from provisioning and Indian trade in deerskins and slaves to rice and indigo (beginning in the 1740s) cultivated by enslaved Africans.

1701 Society for the Propagation of the Gospel in Foreign Parts was founded in London to fund Anglican ministers and missionaries in the colonies to proselytize the unchurched.

1702 Governor James Moore of South Carolina attacked and burned Saint Augustine but failed to capture Castillo de San Marcos. Pierre Le Moyne, Sieur d'Iberville, established three French outposts on the Gulf of Mexico in Biloxi Bay, Mobile Bay, and at the mouth of the Mississippi River.

1702–1704 Indian–Carolina militia attacked Timucua and Apalachee villages, seized 4,000 Indian slaves, and destroyed the mission system in central Florida.

1705 Robert Beverley published *The History and Present State of Virginia* (London), the first history of a southern colony by a native.

1706–1711 French Huguenots from Virginia established Bath in 1706, and Swiss and Palatine Germans settlers founded New Bern in 1710, which became North Carolina's capital the next year.

1706–1722 Governor's Mansion constructed in Williamsburg, Virginia's new planned capital that replaced Jamestown in 1699. The mansion's size, positioning, flanking dependencies, symmetry, multiple windows, and richly paneled interior became the prototype for wealthy planters' great houses.

1706–1732 Church of England was established in Carolina (1706), North Carolina (1715), and Georgia (1732) strengthening Anglicanism's influence in the colonial South.

1707–1709 Isaac Watts, English theologian, published *Hymns and Spiritual Songs, in Three Books* (London), a compilation of Psalms and original sacred songs. His collection became the basis of American Protestant hymnody.

1711–1712 Tuscarora uprising in the North Carolina frontier. Carolina militiamen and Indian warriors defeated them and most Tuscarora left Carolina to join their Iroquois kinsmen in New York.

1715–1716 Pan-Indian rebellion led by the Yamasee in South Carolina, who repudiated their old alliance with Carolina traders because of their abusive and arrogant behavior. A joint Carolina–Native force defeated the Yamasee who fled to Spanish Florida.

1716 Spanish missions and settlements established in East Texas. First theater in the colonies was constructed in Williamsburg but disbanded in 1745.

1717 French established Fort Toulouse on the Upper Alabama River to secure Choctaw trade against encroaching Carolina traders.

1718 The Company of the Indies, a French joint-stock company, established New Orleans as headquarters to revitalize Louisiana. By 1730, the company imported 6,000 slaves and 5,400 settlers, including Le Page Du Pratz, to develop tobacco and indigo plantations. De Pratz's *Histoire de la Louisiane* was based on his time with the Natchez in the 1720s. Edward Teach, aka. "Blackbeard," was captured off Ocracoke Inlet, North Carolina, shutting down a pirate haven in the Outer Banks.

1720s Slaves in the tidewater Chesapeake began to establish families. Population increasingly grew more through natural increase than from slave imports. By mid-century, Native-born Creoles outnumbered saltwater Africans on tidewater plantations. Land rushes by tidewater planters rapidly settled the Virginia and Carolina piedmont and expanded tobacco plantations worked by slaves.

1722 First public market opened in Charles Town. Enslaved women sold country produce and handicrafts from stalls.

1723 Free blacks in Virginia were excluded from militias and denied voting rights.

1725 Louis Congo, a slave from Angola, was appointed public executioner for Louisiana to control the unruly population of French servants, criminals, soldiers, and paupers in exchange for his freedom and land.

1727 Ursuline Order, a confraternity of nuns, was established in New Orleans. The order emphasized women's religious devotion and personal piety and opened a girls' school and a women's shelter. *Maryland Gazette,* first newspaper in the colonial South, began, but suspended publication from 1734 to 1745. *South Carolina Gazette* (1732–) and *Virginia Gazette* (1734–) were the first continuously published newspapers.

1729–1731 Natchez–Bambara uprising began north of New Orleans against French land encroachments on native land and enslavement of recently arrived Bambara warriors from Senegambia. Over 200 settlers and soldiers were killed. Choctaw warriors and French militiamen destroyed the Natchez settlement; survivors were enslaved and sold to West Indies planters.

1730 Population of the colonial South reached 292,000: 50 percent whites, 27 percent blacks, and 23 percent Indians.

1730–1740 Slave imports peaked with 15,700 slaves arriving in Virginia and 21,210 in Charles Town.

1730s–1750s German and Scots-Irish settlers traveled south from Pennsylvania down the Great Wagon Road to backcountry Maryland in the 1730s, Virginia in the 1740s, and Carolina and Georgia in the 1750s. They developed family farms, ethnic neighborhoods, diversified agriculture, artisan shops, and small towns, prototypes for settlement patterns in the Upland South and Lower Midwest.

1733 Georgia was founded as a haven for London's poor and to challenge Spanish Florida with Savannah as the capital. German Lutherans established Ebenezer on the Savannah River. Florida governor reaffirmed offer of freedom to fugitive slaves converting to Catholicism.

1733–1741 Highland Scots settled in Cape Fear River Valley and in Wilmington, North Carolina, and in the Altamaha River Valley and Darien, Georgia.

1734 *Every Man His Own Doctor: Or, The Poor Planter's Physician* was published in Williamsburg, a popular treatise for curing common ailments with local medicines.

1738 Gracia Real de Santa Teresa de Mose, a free-black town, was established north of Saint Augustine as a buffer against Georgia settlers.

1739 Stono uprising in South Carolina was led by recently arrived slaves from Angola and Kongo. Many were soldiers and Catholics. Before it was suppressed, 21 whites and over 75 blacks were killed.

1740 Itinerant evangelist George Whitefield arrived in Charles Town, condemned planters' materialism, and preached a faith of emotional vitality and new birth.

1740–1742 War between Georgia and Florida began. An English–Indian force led by Georgia Governor James Oglethorpe laid siege to Saint Augustine; black militiamen assisted the Spanish in saving the city. Governor Manuel de Montiano failed to take Saint Simons Island, Georgia.

1745 The Ancient and Honourable Tuesday Club of Annapolis was established as a gentlemen's drinking and social organization.

1747 *The Art of Cookery Made Plain and Easy . . . by a Lady* was published in London and became a popular cookbook in the colonial South.

1749 Georgia Trustees lifted ban on slavery. Carolina planters quickly expanded rice and indigo cultivation in Georgia with slave laborers.

1751 George Washington led Virginia militia from Winchester, Virginia, to reconnoiter the French at the forks of the Ohio near modern-day Pittsburgh. A skirmish there began the Seven Years War between Great Britain and France and, later, Spain.

1753 Moravians established a communal religious settlement, Wachovia, in North Carolina Piedmont.

1754 Nine-year-old Olaudah Equiano, an Igbo from modern-day Nigeria, arrived in Virginia, but was purchased by a British captain. Teenage-Equiano learned English and seamanship and was baptized an Anglican in 1759. Seven years later, he purchased his freedom, and in 1789 published *The Interesting Narrative of the Life of Olaudah Equiano,* one of the earliest autobiographies by an ex-slave.

1760 Population of the colonial South reached 614,000: 54 percent whites, 37 percent slaves, and 9 percent Indians.

1760–1761 Carolina–Cherokee war began when a Cherokee siege forced surrender of British troops at Fort Loudon in Overhill Cherokee Country. An expedition comprised of regular British forces, Carolina militiamen, and Indian warriors failed to defeat the Cherokee but laid waste to villages and fields and forced their surrender. Carolina militiamen resented British contempt of their fighting abilities.

1760s Carolina slaves established families and population began to increase naturally. Planters imported 9,700 slaves to Virginia and 21,850 to South Carolina.

1762 Saint Cecilia Society, the first musical society in the colonial South, was founded in Charles Town and presented a regular series of subscription concerts.

1763 Treaty of Paris ended Seven Years War. The British acquired Canada and Louisiana from the French and transferred Louisiana to the Spanish in exchange for East and West Floridas. George Whitefield converted John Marrant, a free black living in Charles Town.

1765–1771 Separate Baptist insurgency spread to Virginia as itinerant preachers attracted large crowds and preached sermons denouncing Anglican ministers' hypocrisy and planter gentry's worldliness.

1768–1771 Discontented backcountry farmers in North Carolina initiated the Regulator Movement to protest corrupt officials and unfair taxes. Governor William Tyron's forces defeated the Regulators at the Battle of Alamance in May 1771.

1770 Population of the backcountry reached about 250,000; Charles Town had 10,000 residents making it the colonial South's largest city.

1775 Population of the colonial South reached 972,500: 56 percent whites, 38 percent slaves, and 6 percent Indians.

1

NEW SOCIETIES

This survey of the historical context of daily life in the colonial South comprises a series of snapshots starting in 1500, just before Native American contact with Europeans, then every 50 years up to 1750, when conflicts flared over who would control North America. Written documents provide European perspectives on colonization, while oral traditions—often recorded more than a century later—incorporate Indian and African voices into these stories. Spanish, English, and French explorers and settlers of 16th, 17th, and 18th centuries encountered hundreds of different Native American communities whose day-to-day lives varied across diverse environments from the Chesapeake Bay south to the Gulf of Mexico and west to the Appalachian Mountains and across the Mississippi River. Europeans profoundly transformed Indians' worlds, while New World conditions altered colonizers' initial plans. Settlers' daily lives mixed European ways with significant Indian and African influences, and vice versa, but the precise nature of this hybrid varied from place to place and changed over time depending on environmental conditions; economic development and trade patterns; voluntary and forced migration streams from Britain, Europe, and Africa; imperial policies; and degrees of political and social development. By the mid-18th century, regional differences within the colonial South waned in favor of broadly shared patterns of daily life among whites' property-owning households, black slaves' newly forged almost autonomous African American cultures, and Native Americans' new material culture and political confederations.

1500

According to Natchez tradition, when First Man and First Woman (his wife) descended from the Sun to the Theloel (the Natchez), they ordered the people to move to a land beyond the great river safe from their enemies. The first Great Sun promised to teach us to live better and in peace among ourselves but only if we constructed a temple and preserved the sun's eternal fire, the source of life itself. The people prospered, cultivating abundant corn, beans, and squash on cleared fields of rich alluvial soils. They built villages on river bluffs convenient for trade and safe from floods and enemy attacks. Men hunted deer and game and fished, while women and children gathered wild plants, nuts, and berries. The people became numerous and powerful conquering neighbors who made tribute and labor payments. The Great Sun's successors, descendants of First Woman and the Suns' earthly relatives, protected the people. The Sun lived at the Grand Village of Natchez on a plaza atop a pyramid-shaped mound 10 feet high in a grand house 45 by 25 feet. Opposite was the temple with the sacred eternal fire, a direct link between the sun and the people. The people honored the Great Sun with gifts of deer, corn, and food, which he stored in the temple and redistributed in times of need. They gathered on the Great Plaza to bless sacred corn seeds and arrivals of first green corn in the spring, and renew the temple roof. Men tested their strength in ball games. When a Great Sun or a noble person died, his spouse and servants honored him by sacrificing themselves to accompany and serve him in the next world. The Great Sun, male nobles, and distinguished men mixed their seed with common people, and by joining nobles and commoners and the sacred and the ordinary in this way, they assured the sun's continued blessings. It was not always so. Once, a guardian let the sacred fire extinguish; sickness spread and many Suns died. Only after confessing and bringing fire from a second temple at the far end of the country did the Suns live and harmony was restored.

The Timucua related their origins this way: We were people of the sea and the forest too numerous to count, but scholars have numbered us over 150,000. Some said we came from the southern

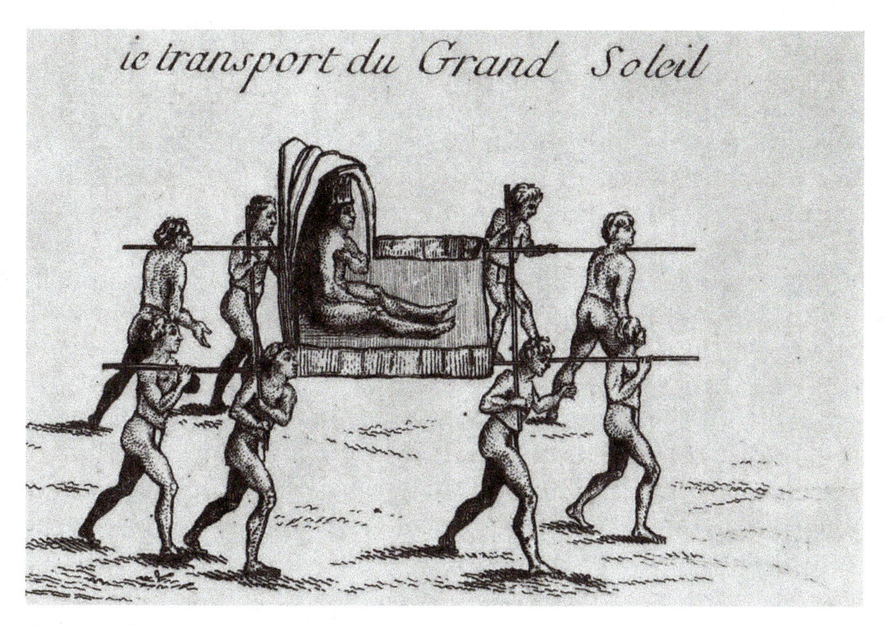

The Natchez Great Sun. Although wearing a common breechclout, Mississippian societies' sacred rulers were accorded great deference and carried on litters to ceremonies. The bow and quiver of arrows represented men's hunting prowess. Etching from Le Page Du Pratz, *Histoire de la Louisiane* (Paris, 1758). (Library of Congress.)

islands across the sea long ago, but most believed we have always lived here, time out of mind. Strangers named our country "Florida" and called us "Timucua" because we speak the same language. We were never united as one people, and our many dialects were so different we have difficulty understanding each other. Families of eight or nine people occupied each of the two-dozen or so houses that constitute our villages. Women were expert horticulturalists, tilling corn, beans, and squash on cleared fields and gathering acorns, berries, and wild plants from woods and riverbanks. Men dressed in deerskins hunt turkeys, birds, raccoons, alligators, and rabbits and caught fish and shellfish from rivers, estuaries, and the sea. We set fires to fertilize planting ground, reduce undergrowth, and increase game herds. Village leaders collected surplus food for winter storage and as security from poor harvests and sent tribute to chiefs whose warriors defended us from enemies and whose priests maintained spiritual harmony. Men and women shared political and spiritual authority. While men held leadership positions, they could only acquire them through relationships to women whose relatives united many villages into loose federations. Even chiefs honored for war prowess, decorated with exotic copper ornaments, and carried on men's shoulders accompanied by flute players, wielded limited power. Village leaders, priests, healers, warriors, and orators made major decisions in council houses. Deliberations started by consuming large drafts of the "white drink," a sacred tea that women made from yaupon holly leaves, to purify the body and clear the mind. Europeans called this the "black drink" from its dark color and marveled at its wondrous properties and powerful effects.[1]

A town of 500 people on the bluffs of the Coosawattee River in modern-day northwestern Georgia was the capital of the paramount chiefdom of Coosa. Their oral histories recounted tributes of food, exotic trade goods, and warriors arriving from 6 towns only a day's walk away and from chiefs more than 20 miles away who recognized our chief's authority. You entered our town through a defensive palisade to a central plaza where dances, ceremonies, and games were held; marveled at a 10-feet high platform mound where our chief lived; and visited communal houses of adults and their children and unmarried siblings. We lived with our ancestors, who were buried in our homes and work sheds with daily necessities such as flint-making tools and blades for men and fine articles like "copper earspools and headdresses, painted and modeled pottery, and conch shell cups" for chiefly ancestors.[2] Subsistence activities filled most days. Rich planting grounds on floodplains provided abundant corn, beans, and squash. Women and children gathered seasonal wild plants, nuts, and fruits. Men caught sucker, drum, and catfish in nearby rivers and hunt deer, black bears, turkeys, and passenger pigeons in uninhabited forests between chiefdoms. Our houses were about 20-feet square and, like the town, had central hearths and four posts that held up roofs and marked off squares for food preparation. Partitions between posts and the outer wall created sleeping and work spaces. Depressed floors; framed walls covered with clay, thatch, and bark; and thatched peaked roofs provided comfort in winter and summer. In fair weather, we worked outside under covered platforms. Our story was not a happy one. Dietary deficiencies and infectious diseases shortened life expectancies to 26 years, and only one-third of infants survived to age five. European epidemic diseases appeared in the 1540s, decimated our village, and caused our chiefdom's collapse. We moved downstream to Alabama and joined the Upper Creek Confederacy.

When we were few in numbers and lived in high valleys of the Appalachian Mountains, stories recounted the Cherokee world's origins. Then, the earth was an island floating in a vast sea suspended at four cardinal points by cords hanging from the sky vault. At the behest of the animals, which were crowded in the upperworld, Water Beetle dove down into the water world and returned with soft mud that he gradually spread to form land. When the earth island was still soft, Great Buzzard "reached the Cherokee country, [but] he was very tired, and his wings began to flap and strike the ground, and whenever they struck the earth there was a valley, and where they turned up again there was a mountain." Animals and plants were ordered to watch and keep awake for seven nights, but only owl, cougar, cedar, pine, spruce, holly, and laurel did so. These animals received powers to see and hunt at night, and only these trees remain green all year. The people rarely attained their purity, but this was why we admired and feared owls and cougars and used evergreens in sacred ceremonies. In ancient times, when humans had became numerous and destructive, the animals held council and decided to send sickness and bad dreams to people in retaliation. Little Deer, the most hunted animal of all, gave humans a reprieve: If they asked pardon for killing one of them, he promised to forgive them. Plants, humans' friends but animals' enemies, took pity and agreed to "furnish the remedy to counteract the evil wrought by the revengeful animals."[3] The world, we believed, presents two contrasting faces: upperworld and underworld, sun and moon, east and west, north and south, fire and water, summer and winter, men and women, young and old, animals and plants, sickness and health, war and peace, farming and hunting. Peace and prosperity required maintaining clear boundaries between these opposites through balancing their attributes. It was not always easy to do this.

1550

In 1540, according to old stories, runners brought news of approaching strangers with extraordinary powers. They rode large four-legged beasts with manes and tails, carried weapons that harnessed thunder and lightning, and possessed rare metal objects. Whether they were men or spirits in human form no one could say, but everyone noted their hairy faces, braying voices, and rude manners. Death accompanied them, but, miraculously, left them unharmed. Were they the same strangers who appeared from time to time on floating islands and took people away? In 1513, Juan Ponce de León "named" their land "Florida" after landing on Easter day and performed a strange ritual of planting a cross and a banner and declaring oaths to god and king accompanied by trumpet flourishes and gunfire. The Ais on the Atlantic coast and Calusas on the Gulf of Mexico quickly sent them scurrying. Thirteen years later, Lucas Vázquez de Allyón arrived in present-day South Carolina with six hundred colonists, some men wearing black robes, others with black skins, including Francisco de Chicora, an Indian from Winyah Bay, captured in 1521 and taken to Spain where he filled eager Spanish ears with tales of a land of almonds, olives, and figs: a new Andalusia. Francisco's stories carried him home, and he and his companions fled into the swamps. Undeterred, Allyón moved south and settled in Sapelo Sound among the Guale in present-day Georgia. Settlers of the colony, San Miguel de Gualdape, the first Spanish settlement in the southeast, quarreled and many died. When the Guale withheld food and water, surviving colonists, a quarter of the original group, returned to Española the next year.

More fantastic were tales of Alvar Núñez Cabeza de Vaca, leader of a 400-man expedition that landed on Florida's gulf coast in 1528 searching for gold and slaves. They too were inhospitable guests. After seizing an Apalachee chief, a leader of a wealthy and powerful people near present-day Tallahassee, his warriors unleashed powerful arrows that pierced Spanish armor. The intruders fled on makeshift rafts and landed by Galveston Island, Texas. The Karankawas enslaved and scattered the survivors. One captive, Cabeza de Vaca, it is said, possessed unusual powers. He and his three companions—including Esteban, a black Moorish slave—traveled from community to community healing, trading, and attracting an entourage. In spring 1536, they encountered a Spanish slaving expedition in present-day Sinoloa, Mexico. The Spanish were "dumbfounded at the sight of me, strangely undressed and in company with Indians," Cabeza de Vaca recalled, and he prevented his rescuers from enslaving his Pima followers. How could these strangers be of the same people as Cabeza de Vaca? "We healed the sick, they killed the sound," the Pima wondered, "we came naked and barefoot, they clothed, horsed and lanced; we coveted nothing but gave whatever we were given, while they robbed whomever they found."[4] Strangers were not all alike: There were good Spaniards with healing powers and wondrous objects and evil Spaniards who seized men and brought death. One must deal with them cautiously lest spiritual powers become unbalanced and bring destruction.

Hernando de Soto, who landed near present-day Tampa Bay in May 1539 with 600 Europeans and numerous horses, mules, pigs, and dogs, cared little about upsetting the spiritual harmony that sustained life. Convinced southeastern North America was another Peru that would secure fame and fortune, he pillaged for gold and slaves among village farmers and urban chiefdoms. Holding chiefs as hostages; plundering reserves of corn, beans, and squash; seizing women for servants and for sexual pleasure; enslaving Indian men with iron collars and chains as porters; murdering or mutilating resisters; and burning villages, de Soto presented a grisly visage. Natives fled, gave him presents to curry favor, told stories of treasures farther off in another county, or fought back with guerrilla tactics and assaults on Spanish camps. Nothing stopped

Fortified Timucuan village. Palisades and guardhouses protected against enemy raids like the one being repelled on the lower right. River locations, central council houses, and circular thatched houses were typical of native villages in coastal Florida. Engraving by Theodor de Bry, 1591, of a watercolor by Jacques Le Moyne, 1564. (Library of Congress.)

the Spanish marauders. Their four-year rampage coursed along Indian trails northward through Florida's gulf coast to the Apalachee, then across central Georgia to the Cofitachequi in western South Carolina, to the southern Appalachian Mountains in western North Carolina and the Chiaha in eastern Tennessee, south through Coosa country in central Alabama and the Tascaloosa in Mississippi, then across the Mississippi River through Arkansas to Caddo country on the Great Plains, finally returning to the Mississippi River and the powerful Natchez. Finding nothing they valued and understanding even less of their native hosts, the survivors—about half, including de Soto, were dead—stumbled back to Mexico in September 1543. They left behind, concludes historian David J. Weber, "a trail of shattered lives, broken bodies, ravaged fields, empty storehouses, and charred villages."[5]

The Spanish left the southeast for 20 years, but their intermittent presence had already transformed daily life even for indigenous people without physical contact with the uninvited intruders. Spanish hogs multiplied in the rich mast of southeastern forests, became feral ancestors of the south's famed razorbacks, and introduced pork into southerners' diet. Spanish material culture—gold coins, rosaries, axes, and other items—obtained from plundered shipwrecks along Florida's treacherous coast or from war casualties circulated as prized objects traded over long distances. Spanish diseases, especially smallpox and measles, carried by unseen pathogens were the most disruptive of all. Native Americans' physical isolation from the Old World and lack of exposure to animal-borne diseases left them vulnerable and created ideal conditions for "virgin soil epidemics," according to historian Alfred Crosby. Death was Europeans' constant companion. After initial contact, native populations fell precipitously. "Half the natives" on an island off the coast of Texas, Cabeza de Vaca reported, "died from a disease of the bowels and blamed us."[6] Densely populated farming peoples along river courses were the most vulnerable to infectious diseases, and as people fled disease-ridden towns, they unknowingly spread contagion. Shamans' powers waned, as they were helpless in stopping death's march. Chiefs no longer collected surplus corn and their domains collapsed. The old and the young, struck especially hard, robbed people of memories of the past and certainties of a future. As riverine Mississippian societies fell into disarray, upland peoples—less exposed to disease—gained power, absorbed refugees, and created new peoples Europeans later called Chickasaws, Choctaws, Creeks, and Cherokees.

1600

Pedro Menéndez de Avilés, governor of Florida, feared his French adversaries more than his Timucuan neighbors. For decades, French pirates and corsairs had menaced Spanish convoys heavy with Mexican silver for the king's treasury after they left the Caribbean and sailed close to the south Atlantic coast on their way to Spain. In a final insult, Protestant French Huguenots, infidels to the Spanish no better than Moors or Indians, erected Fort Caroline on the Saint John's River in 1564 on land claimed by Spain but now a base for plundering Spanish ships. Menéndez arrived on September 8, 1565, the feast day of Saint Augustine, and so named the settlement. Relying on Timucuan guides and Indian trails, he and his men marched 40 miles north, attacked unsuspecting soldiers at the French fort, and then turned south to surprise French survivors of an earlier ill-fated attack on Menéndez's fleet. It was one of the largest military engagements in the early south with perhaps 300 men slaughtered. "To chastise them in this way," Menéndez reported to Felipe II, "would serve God Our Lord, as well as Your Majesty" by advancing the Counter-Reformation against dangerous heretics, strengthening imperial claims against rivals, protecting Spanish ships, and providing refuge and a salvage center for shipwreck survivors.[7] Enjoying royal support, Menéndez came—as had earlier *adelantados*, or military proprietors—to explore, conquer, settle, and become wealthy from Indian labor and New World resources. With over 700 settlers, 300 soldiers, several priests, and ample supplies, he established a network of seven forts from Tampa Bay on the Gulf of Mexico to Santa Elena in present-day South Carolina, the first capital, and recruited Spanish settlers. Accompanied by Don Luis, an Algonquian convert, Jesuits in 1570 even opened a mission near Bahía de Santa María, what the English later called the Chesapeake Bay.

By 1600, Menéndez's Florida empire was reduced to a single settlement, Saint Augustine, and its garrison, Castillo de San Marcos, with a mere 500 settlers and 27 slaves. Luis soon abandoned Catholicism, his baptismal name, and Spanish lifestyle to live with his people. Tired of Jesuits's demands for food when harvests were poor and insults to their sacred beliefs and blaming them for disease outbreaks, Powhatans dispatched these nettlesome intruders within a year. Florida almost suffered a similar fate. Lacking gold or silver, easy passages to northern Mexico or across the North American continent, a population of sedentary Indians to exploit,

Castillo de San Marcos, Saint Augustine, Florida. Following English and native attacks on Spain's vulnerable outpost this extensive stone fortification replaced an earlier wooden structure. Construction continued from 1672 to 1756. (Library of Congress.)

or Christian converts, Florida's scarce resources, exposed location, and hostile natives attracted few settlers from Spain or her colonies. The Spanish repaid natives' hospitality with unruly soldiers and haranguing priests. Indian hostility prompted harsher Spanish reprisals. Coastal Floridians were an "infamous people, Sodomites, sacrificers to the devil . . . ," a frustrated Menéndez wrote to Felipe II in 1573, and added "it would greatly serve God Our Lord and your majesty if these were dead, or given as slaves."[8] Spanish Florida barely survived as a fledgling mission frontier and military outpost on the fringes of Spain's valuable Caribbean and Mexican colonies.

The English had even less success as colonizers. Courtiers and empire builders gasped at Spain's growing wealth and military power from gold and silver mined by conscripted Indians and grasped for their piece of New World wealth. The South Atlantic coast most attracted their gaze: so near to Spanish treasure-laden fleets ripe for plucking John Hawkins and Francis Drake had proved; so peopled with Indians eager to exchange Protestant civility for savagery and Catholic idolatry Anglican clergymen preached; so rich in exotic Mediterranean crops filling every need propagandists prophesized; and yet so empty to provide for homes for England's unemployed explorers promised. In 1584, Sir Walter Raleigh obtained Sir Humphrey Gilbert's patent making him *adelantados* of North America, including title to all land, towns, castles, and palaces, and promised to defend it from Catholic Spain and France. He named his princely domain "Virginia" to honor the queen and attract royal patronage, but Queen Elizabeth—preoccupied with conflicts in Ireland and with Spain—provided but one ship and few supplies.

The English knew little about the South Atlantic, but their conquest of Ireland provided models for early Virginia. During the 1570s and 1580s, that restless province erupted in bitter civil war between the armies of English Protestant overlords and Irish Catholics. English officers, including Gilbert and Raleigh, demanded the Irish convert to Protestantism or face destruction and deemed anyone defying their rule ungrateful barbarians incapable of English civility and unworthy occupants of undeveloped land. Ireland provided techniques, rhetoric, and personnel for early colonial ventures in the South. To no one's surprise, Raleigh and Gilbert chose Ralph Lane, a hardened veteran from the Irish wars, to lead the first settlement in Virginia.

Promising beginnings yielded bitter fruit. A 1584 expedition that included Thomas Hariot, an astronomer and scientist, and John White, an artist, landed on the treacherous Outer Banks off the North Carolina coast and befriended Wingina, chief of the Roanoke people. They returned with Hariot's favorable accounts, White's watercolors, and two native specimens, Manteo and Wanchese, supposedly eager to learn England ways. The Roanoke youths became Raleigh's prized trophies at fundraisers and cultural brokers between English and southern Algonquian worlds. Encouraged, promoters recruited 600 colonists under Lane's leadership, who sailed on seven ships the next year. The captains found plundering the Spanish Main more lucrative than supplying a struggling settlement and delayed settlers' arrival until late July, too late to plant crops. Only 100 men stayed behind to construct a fort and cottages. Settlers, unable to feed themselves on the edge of an unknown land, bickered. The Roanokes—tired of their new neighbors' unpredictable behavior—cut off supplies, attacked the village, and either tortured or adopted survivors. Some individuals likely became Algonquians but perished as English people, surviving only in legend as the "lost colony."

Despite advancing age, Powhatan, mamanatowick, or paramount chief of Tsenacomoco, the land the English called Virginia, impressed the much-traveled John Smith when they met in 1607. He ruled some 30 dependent tribes with 14,000 subjects including 3,200 warriors. Smith greeted Powhatan, Wahunsenacawh to his people, seated on a raised platform in his meeting house attended by 40-long bowmen bodyguards, several of his many young wives, councilors, and orators. A man with "such Majestie as I cannot expresse," Smith recounted, "not yet have often seene, either in Pagan or Christian [lands]."[9] Powhatan had inherited six district chiefdoms from his mother around 1570 when he was about 30 during a time of change and danger. Like other southern Algonquians, Powhatan's people were village-dwelling farmers, hunters, and gatherers. Their main town was just east of the "fall line" near the modern city of Richmond, where the piedmont escarpment suddenly drops to the level coastal plain, an area not only rich in subsistence and other resources but also within striking distance of the Monacans, the Powhatan's Siouan-speaking enemies who lived in the hilly interior. Algonquian population growth strained corn reserves, and people died from unknown diseases. Massawomecks, Iroquoian speakers from the north, periodically made lightning raids against southern Algonquians. Men spoke of strange men in black robes arriving in 1570 accompanied by Paquinquineo, aka Don Luis, a young man from a chiefly Paspahegh family, who had disappeared nine years earlier. How he had changed! New clothes covered his body, his speech was unintelligible, and he spoke of Jesus, a paramount god. Reunited with relatives, he led an attack that wiped out the strangers.

Through war, alliances, intimidation, negotiation, and trade, Powhatan extended his rule to create the largest political confederation in the southeast. By the early 1600s, his chiefdom included all of tidewater Virginia between the James and Potomac rivers—except the Chickahominies, independent allies—and brought order to Tsenacommacah and great prestige to its paramount chief. Powhatan commanded many warriors; obtained wealth from tribute payments or taxes of corn that he redistributed in times of need and from exotic trade items like freshwater pearls, shell jewelry, copper, and puccoon (a red dye); and gained access to the holy temple Uttamussak in Pamunkey. He cemented his authority through personal networks of district and village chiefs by installing relatives, brothers, and adult sons as *weroances* and at least one wife as a *weroansqua* over lesser chiefdoms; selecting wives from tribute villages;

and resettling people in occupied lands. He moved his capital to Werowocomoco on the lower York River to provide river and land access to his chiefdom. When priests prophesied, "from the Chesapeake Bay a nation should arise which should dissolve and give end to his empire," Powhatan's warriors wiped out the Chesapeakes and repopulated their territory with loyal Nansemonds.[10] They would not be the Powhatans' last threat from the east.

1650

London merchants' promises were irresistible: a few years' labor in the Garden of Eden, a share of company profits, and land of one's own—a new start in a New World. Richard Frethorne, an educated young man, signed on and arrived in Virginia in 1621 during the tobacco boom. How different seemed Virginia's prospects from the troubled times 14 years earlier, when most doubted settlers' very survival. In 1607, they located Jamestown, the initial settlement, on an easily defended peninsula on the James River, 60 miles from the mouth of Chesapeake Bay. There the English found few resources, inconstant natives, illness, and starvation. After a decade of experiments, John Rolfe mastered tobacco cultivation's intricacies, and the colony's economic success seemed assured. Planters sent 40,000 pounds of tobacco to England in 1620, and exports rose almost 40-fold by decade's end. To repay Frethorne's passage costs to Virginia, the ship captain sold his labor for four or five years to William Harward, director of the Society of Martin's Hundred, a joint-stock company owning an 80,000-acre plantation, 10 miles downriver from Jamestown. Frethorne labored alongside several hundred other indentured servants, mostly single young men like himself from England's middling social ranks, sons of small farmers, tenants, or artisans, who had earlier left their villages for opportunities in England's port towns. At the end of his term, Frethorne was likely promised land, provisions, tools, and a new suit of clothes.

Anticipating paradise, Frethorne found instead a world of labor, illness, and death. Eager to cash in on high tobacco prices, planters imported many servants, as they received 100 acres of land for each one, and located claims along river courses. They extracted as much labor from their servants as possible. In theory, indentures were legal contracts that protected servants' lives and welfare. In reality, planters used their power to impose harsh discipline. Servants toiled in fields 10 to 14 hours a day, 7 days a week. After Frethorne rowed goods upriver to Jamestown, landing at night, only the kindness of Goodman Jackson, a gunsmith, provided shelter and food. We "must Worke hard both earelie, and late for a messe of water gruel," Frethorne wrote home in 1623, "and a mouthfull of breade for a pennie loafe must serve for 4 men which is most pitiful . . . , when people crie out day, and night, 'Oh, that they were in England without their lymbes and would not care to loose anie lymbe to bee in England againe.'" Most servants did not suffer long. Overworked, underfed, unacclimated to a new environment, they proved all too vulnerable to "agues and fevers" of miasmic swamps, dysentery, and typhoid fever. Dangers lurked in forests as well. Some men ran off never to be seen again; others fell victim to escalating English–Powhatan violence. In 1622, Powhatans sought to drive the English from their homeland and killed almost 350 settlers, including eight people at Martin's Hundred. Who knew when the Powhatans would return? Who would help them? "Wee are but 32 to fight against 3000 if they should Come," Frethorne wrote to his parents despairingly, "and the nighest helpe that Wee have is ten miles of us."[11]

Opechcancanough, mamanatowick after Powhatan's death in 1618, had his fill of the strangers. At first, they were weak and too ignorant to live off the land's bounty. Yet, they possessed metal objects that made daily life easier: hooks to catch fish, knives to dress venison, needles to sew skin clothing, pots to cook stew or to be cut up to make arrowheads and implements, mirrors to aid in beautifying bodies, and, most wondrous, guns that made enemies run. Welcoming the bearded strangers (so many men and so few women!) with gifts, Powhatans eagerly traded trifles of surplus corn and venison for rare metal goods and offered an alliance of permanent protection for occasional assistance against their enemies. Little did they know the strangers would become so numerous, their thirst for material possessions so insatiable, denunciations of *kwiokos* (the Powhatans' god) so shrill, demands for land so unrelenting, and determination to remain so persistent. Neither withholding food (the "starving time" of 1609–1610), nor adopting John Smith, the English leader, nor marriage between Pocahontas (Powhatan's daughter) to Rolfe, nor forest skirmishes secured peaceful relations. In 1622, the Powhatans attacked outlaying settlements to defend their land, way of life, and very survival. They killed a third of the English, and almost won the ensuing war of attrition, before being repulsed. English survivors used the attacks as pretexts for justifying systematic appropriation of native lands and slaughter of native foes. The

Powhatans tried again in 1644, met defeat, and had no choice but to sue for peace. No longer masters of eastern Virginia, the Powhatans and their allies were confined to small reservations and forced to make annual tributes of deer and fowl to the governor.

In 1655, Anthony Johnson, a small planter on Virginia's Eastern Shore, sued Robert and George Parker, his wealthy neighbors,

Chesapeake Bay. The English first settled along numerous rivers, bays, and estuaries on both shores of the Chesapeake Bay. It took almost a hundred years to breach the "Fall Line," or limit of river navigation by large vessels, into the Piedmont and west to the Appalachian Mountains shown in the upper left corner. (NASA/Goddard Space Flight Center.)

to secure the return of John Casar, Johnson's slave, who claimed he was free and had sought sanctuary with the Parkers. Johnson, like other litigious planters, relied on county courts to protect his property and secure control over scare labor that made personal independence possible during Virginia's booming tobacco economy. Johnson, however, was a black man, sold in 1621 at Jamestown as "Antonio a negro" to a Mr. Bennett, a planter. Johnson's first name suggests Portuguese and Christian associations. Perhaps Portuguese traders acquired him in Ndongo or Kongo on the modern-day Congo/Angolan coast, whose peoples had converted to Catholicism in 1490. Like most blacks in the Chesapeake before the late 17th century, he likely arrived as part of an odd lot and may have lived for a while in the Caribbean where he learned to speak English and adopt English mores. Antonio certainly possessed the resourcefulness of cosmopolitan Atlantic Creoles—blacks from the ports of Africa, Europe, and the New World—who historian Ira Berlin describes as "familiar with the commerce of the Atlantic, fluent in its new languages, and intimate with its trade and cultures."[12] One of only 5 out of 56 laborers to survive the 1622 Powhatan attack on Bennett's plantation, his service defending the settlement earned official praise. Bennett also recognized Antonio's talents and allowed him to farm on his own, marry an African woman, and baptize his children in the local parish church. Antonio's independent labor enabled him to purchase his freedom. Now "Anthony Johnson," he moved with Bennett to Virginia's Eastern Shore, where by 1651, he acquired at least 250 acres of land, raised tobacco, owned slaves, and defended his family's reputation before neighbors.

Johnson's independence and modest prosperity were unusual. There were only about 20 free black families on the Eastern Shore and, at most, only 20 percent of the 1,700 blacks in the entire Chesapeake had escaped servitude by mid-century. Slavery was not yet codified into law, but most blacks were held as quasi-slaves. Even so, historian Ira Berlin observes, Chesapeake Virginia was still a society with slaves, where "slavery was just one form of labor among many," and not a slave society, where "slavery stood at the center of economic production."[13] Lines between freedom and slavery were permeable with wide variations in individual experiences under servitude. Laws banning blacks from possessing arms or prohibiting interracial sex often went unenforced. In the early decades, most blacks worked along white indentured servants and even Indians. Many enjoyed some free time to provision themselves, raise tobacco patches, or work for themselves. Powhatan resistance to land dispossession and servant rebellions against abusive treatment posed far greater threats to planters' security and well-being than the small number of blacks, who comprised less than 5 percent of the population. Within a few decades, even these tentative possibilities of participation and acceptance in Chesapeake society disappeared as tobacco planters turned to enslaved Africans to expand production and establish themselves as provincial grandees.

George Calvert, the first Lord Baltimore, dreamed of a New World haven where Catholics and Protestants lived harmoniously. In 1632, Catholic-leaning King Charles I granted Calvert and his heirs the upper Chesapeake Bay north of Virginia as "the true and absolute Lords and Proprietaries" with exclusive rights to lands, taxation, and trade and "free, full, and absolute Power . . . to Ordain, Make, and Enact Laws, of what Kind so ever . . . of and with the Advice, Assent, and Approbation of the Free-Men."[14] After Calvert's sudden death, sons Cecilius and Leonard, the first governor, sought to realize his vision. They recruited settlers with generous land grants, 100 acres for every arriving adult and 50 for each child, and religious toleration even for Quakers, Puritans, and Jews. Some 200 colonists arrived in February 1634 and constructed Saint Mary City, named for Henrietta Maria, the king's Catholic wife, near the confluence of the Potomac River with the Chesapeake Bay, a site as stunning then as today. Economically, Maryland succeeded greatly. Replicating Virginia's tobacco economy and attracting experienced Virginia colonists, ordinary planters exploited servant labor and initially enjoyed modest prosperity and social mobility. Politically, Maryland failed stunningly. Most settlers were Protestants, including radical Puritans and Quakers from Virginia and England, who carried their Catholic bigotry to Maryland and chafed at the proprietor's privileges. England's religious conflicts, which culminated in civil war in 1642, spilled over into Maryland politics, and the Calvert family spent much time defending antiproprietary settlers' challenges to their authority and Protestants' attacks on their charter in England.

On his second visit to the Florida missions in 1616, Visitor General Fray Luis Gerónimo de Oré was pleased with Franciscans' progress in spreading the true Catholic faith among heathen Indians, which vindicated earlier opposition to shutting down the expensive backwater colony. Over the past 20 years, friars extended their work north from Saint Augustine to the Guale along the Atlantic coast in present-day Georgia and South Carolina and inland to the Timucua in central Florida. Oré approved Franciscans' methods of living in

Indian villages, learning native languages, teaching European skills and crops, mixing rewards and punishments, encouraging converted children to mock their pagan parents, incorporating native ceremonies into Catholic rituals, and suppressing heathen social practices like polygamy and ball games. The fruits were new communities of Christian Indians, who understood the faith, assisted in mass, received communion, served as catechists, and made confession. By mid-century, there were 70 Franciscan missionaries who claimed some 26,000 converts (actual numbers were half that), and the number of missions continued to grow for another quarter century to 36 churches stretching westward to the Chattahoochee River, 250 miles from Saint Augustine, among the Apalachees and Apalachicolas or Lower Creeks.

Missions were fragile communities dependent on natives' cooperation and labor for survival. Spanish Florida, in truth, was a thin chain of military posts. The largest, Saint Augustine, the capital, had only 200 to 300 residents. Governors, administrators, and soldiers competed with priests for Indian labor and corrupted natives with drink and loose living. In 1657, Governor Diego de Rebolledo asserted civilian control over Indians and priests, claimed sole authority to punish Indians for crimes and determine market prices, required approval before requisitioning Indian men as porters, and restored Indian ball games and other ceremonies. The objects of civilians and friars' concerns, however, continued to decline in numbers from smallpox and other epidemic diseases. The Apalachees fell from about 25,000 in the early 1600s to some 10,000 by the 1680s, and the eastern Timucuans numbered just 1,370 in 1675. Florida never became a self-sustaining colony and lived off native labor and foodstuffs and the crown's *situado* or annual subsidy, which in theory paid, clothed, and supplied soldiers, friars, governors, and other royal officials. Since the 1640s, the Guale and Apalachee chafed under Spain's heavy-handed rule.

1700

In 1700, Carolina poised between an economy that was based on Indian trade in deerskins and Native American slaves and one built on rice plantations worked by enslaved Africans. It was the only non-Indian settlement between distant Chesapeake outposts and near Florida missions. Six thousand residents clustered among low marshy islands north and south of Charles Town, the principal settlement. Founded almost 30 years earlier by 8 proprietors, powerful allies of King Charles II with prior experience as West Indian planters, slave traders, colonial governors, or policy makers, they hoped to challenge Spanish power in Florida and the Caribbean, produce agricultural commodities benefitting the English economy, and enrich themselves. A 1663 royal charter granted exclusive rights to settle the area between Currituck Inlet and Spanish Florida and, modeled on the Maryland Charter, generous powers of government, subject to the "advice, assent, and approbation of the freemen," including collecting land taxes and controlling trade. The proprietors offered generous "concessions and agreements" to attract settlers: free land, low quitrent or land tax payments, religious toleration including Jews but not atheists, English rights to anyone swearing loyalty to the king, and a representative assembly. To jump-start the project, proprietors recruited experienced colonists from New England, Virginia, and the Barbados, a Caribbean island. From the beginning. Carolina had a polyglot population of blacks and whites from the West Indies alongside English, Dutch, French Huguenot, Scots, and Ulster Scots immigrants.

Land and governance were the heart of colonial planning. In 1669, Sir Anthony Ashley Cooper with John Locke's assistance developed an elaborate plan, the Fundamental Constitution of Carolina, to create social order with a hierarchy of proprietors, landed elites, and ordinary planters. They proposed surveying land into counties each with forty 12,000-acre squares. Proprietors received one square with another eight sections reserved for hereditary nobles with fancy titles like "landgrave" and "cicaque." The remaining two-dozen parcels were headright grants to settlers: 150 acres for every free person and male servant above age 15 and 100 acres per female servant and boy under 15. Colonial government modeled class hierarchy. Proprietors or their representatives, colonial nobles, and deputies elected by settlers met as one body, but all laws required the proprietors' assent. The constitution guaranteed owners absolute authority over slaves, even Christian Africans. Proprietors started an experimental farm with semitropical crops, silk, wine, citrus trees, olives, indigo, and the like to spur economic development. From the start, Carolina was a slave society, and, as in the Chesapeake, aggrandizing land and accumulating wealth were settlers' primary aspirations.

Other parts of the proprietors' plans proved unworkable. Instead of orderly development, it took a decade to establish Charles Town in 1680 at the junction of the Ashley and Cooper rivers, which Charlestonians declare form the Atlantic Ocean. Under the headright system, settlers claimed scattered tracts of fertile soil along numerous rivers and streams. No Mediterranean crops suited coastal Carolina's semitropical environment. Conflict, not harmony, characterized public life. Settlers chafed at proprietors' privileges, and in 1691, elected deputies met as a separate body and secured rights to initiate legislation. They promptly ended proprietors' monopoly over the Indian trade in deerskins and slaves.

Carolina began as a Barbadian outpost, a "colony of a colony," according to historian Peter Wood, as many black and white settlers arrived from there, and the island was the largest consumer of Carolina exports. Over the previous half century, sugar had displaced tobacco on Barbados as large planters, including several Carolina proprietors, expanded operations, replaced indentured servants with African slaves, and squeezed out small landowners. Promises of free land in Carolina were irresistible to small Barbadian tobacco planters and freemen. Early Carolina settlers raised corn, hogs, and cattle to feed themselves; sold provisions to West Indian planters; and turned pine forests into lumber, shingles, and barrel staves for the Caribbean trade. Most laborers were white indentured servants who looked forward to receiving freedom dues from masters and 100 acres of land from the proprietors. Large landowners brought small numbers of acculturated black slaves from the Barbados and other Caribbean islands. Small gangs of white servants and African and Indian slaves worked together in fields, cow pens, and forests sharing skills, culture, camaraderie, and distrust of their masters.

Search for a profitable staple crop continued. Under West African slaves' tutelage, planters cultivated rice on dry land, and by 1700, they were exporting 400,000 pounds of rice annually and earning enormous profits. Within a decade, rice transformed black and white lives, as planters acquired huge plantation tracts, built fine houses in the countryside and in Charles Town, imported thousands of slaves directly from Africa, and sent them to the brutal tasks of clearing land and cultivating rice. Enslaved Africans already outnumbered indentured servants and Indian slaves in the fields, and by 1708, they comprised a majority of Lowcountry Carolina's population.

Early lucrative trade in deerskins and Indian slaves provided capital to invest in African slaves and rice cultivation. A century of contact with Spanish settlers spawned Carolina Indians' desires for European metal goods, especially guns. Coastal peoples, who were rebuilding populations lost to European diseases, initially welcomed Carolina settlers as new sources for trade goods and as

Charles Town from the harbor. Rice, indigo, and slaves made South Carolina's capital the wealthiest city in British North America. The prominence of the ship and the Exchange (1771), the large building in the center, attest to the Atlantic trade's importance. Wealthy planters' homes line the harbor, while three African American figures in the lower left allude to the sources of Carolina's prosperity. Engraving by Samuel Smith, 1776, of a painting by Thomas Leitch, 1774. (Library of Congress.)

valuable allies against the Westos, recently arrived Iroquoian speakers, who were armed with guns from Virginia traders and attacked local residents. Carolina merchants exploited densely populated but politically divided native communities to establish trade partnerships with favored groups. Warriors with guns swept through forests killing deer that wives processed into skins for trade. By 1700, Indians exchanged over 50,000 deerskins annually, about a third of the value of all Carolina exports, for metal goods, textiles, ammunition, guns, and rum.

Expanding Carolina–Indian trade revolutionized geopolitics south to Florida and west to the Mississippi River. As local deer herds declined, hunters traveled greater distances, encroached on rival peoples' hunting preserves, and escalated forest wars. Merchants prized captive women and children even more than deerskins as plantation laborers or as commodities to trade for African slaves from the West Indies. Merchants encouraged Indian trade partners to attack their enemies by promising ready markets for captives. The southeast descended into an orgy of violence and slave trafficking, as thousands of native men became slave raiders selling tens of thousands of captives. Men from the tiny Saint Augustine garrison, including black militiamen, failed to dislodge Carolinians on Edisto Island in 1686 and could not protect unarmed Florida mission villages with their tempting populations of acculturated Indians. In the 1680s and 1690s, Carolinians and Yamasees attacked the Guale and pushed friars southward. James Moore, governor of South Carolina, burned Saint Augustine in 1702. Two years later, his army of 50 whites and 1,000 Creek Indians attacked the Timucua and Apalachee with devastating effect, capturing over 4,000 slaves. A century of Franciscan mission work lay in ruins and reduced Florida to the garrisons of Saint Augustine, San Marcos de Apalachee, and Pensacola. The once prosperous Apalachee were extinguished as a people. For most Florida Indians, it was, as historian Jerald Milanich describes, "the end of time."[15]

French efforts to extend trade south from the Great Lakes to the Gulf of Mexico challenged Spanish Florida and northern Mexico and provided interior native communities new outlets for acquiring trade goods and allies. Three years after René-Robert Cavelier, Sieur de La Salle, traveled down the Mississippi River to the Gulf of Mexico in 1682, the French established Fort Saint Louis on the Texas coast to press their claims to the Mississippi River delta and Gulf of Mexico. The French antagonized the locals, the Karankawa, who beat the Spanish in wiping out the struggling settlement. Twenty years later, French-Canadian Pierre Le Moyne, Sieur d'Iberville, established three gulf posts: Fort Maurepas in Biloxi Bay, Fort Conde in Mobile Bay, and Fort Mississippi near the river's mouth. By the early 1720s, a network of trading posts expanded French trade and influence: Fort Rosalie at modern-day Natchez and the Arkansas Post on the Mississippi River, Fort Toulouse in central Alabama to secure Choctaw trade and block Carolina traders, and Natchitoches at the center of the Caddo Confederacy in northwestern Louisiana on Mexico's border. Spain responded to French incursions into territory long claimed but never occupied by reinforcing Presidio de San Marcos at Saint Augustine, constructing San Carlos de Austria in Pensacola Bay in Western Florida in 1699, and 20 years later rebuilding San Marcos de Apalachee on Apalachee Bay to reinforce Pensacola and reclaim West Florida. Mexican officials rushed solders eastward, who built a presidio, San Francisco de los Delores, and a wooden fort, Nuestra Señora del Pilar de Los Adaes, just 12 miles from Natchitoches. Franciscans established Texas missions near the Sabine River.

French control of the Mississippi River expanded their influence from the Gulf of Mexico to the Great Lakes. Like Spanish Florida, Louisiana attracted few European settlers (there were less than 300 in 1708), and far longer than in Virginia or Carolina colonists depended on native peoples for food, protection, and economic survival. Trade and diplomacy preoccupied French officials, as it did for the Spanish and Carolinians. Everyone wooed Choctaws, Creeks, Cherokees, Chickasaws, and others with presents, trade goods, and promises of protection. With few settlers and remote from supply bases, the French won over the Choctaws with generous gifts and promises to end slave raids. These interior Indian confederacies—rebounding from epidemic diseases and absorbing refugees from shattered coastal and riverine communities—outnumbered the small European outposts, controlled sources of deerskins and Indian captives, and held the region's military balance of power. By strategically restraining warriors, threatening to overrun isolated European settlements, or attacking Europeans' Indian allies, confederacy leaders played one European power off against another to maintain their autonomy and increase their economic and political influence.

Meanwhile, the Chesapeake entered a period of stability and expansion. Gradually falling mortality made family life possible, and emerging planter elites strengthened political and social institutions. With low prices since mid-century, tobacco became a mass consumer item in England and Europe, but profitable cultivation required an expanding scale of operations. Greatest rewards went to the largest planters whose political connections ensured acquiring huge tracts of fresh land now cleared of Powhatans and who possessed capital or credit to buy slaves and servants. Tobacco planters dominated the House of Burgesses, the provincial legislature, county courts, and Anglican parish vestries. They used political power to advance their economic interests: minimal interference from London, favorable trade with English merchants, protection of private property, control over African slaves, and domination over social inferiors. Astute governors learned working with not against great planters brought political peace and personal fortunes. Ordinary planters relied on wealthier neighbors for work, services, food, and credit essential for their survival. African slaves solved Virginia's chronic labor shortage, made worse as England's growing economy and other English colonies lured potential emigrant servants elsewhere. Labor scarcity grew just as English merchants became involved in the slave trade. Soon ships from Africa plied Chesapeake waters, disposing their human cargoes in small parcels to great planters along Virginia's rivers.

The gentry's rise came at ordinary planters' and indentured servants' expense. They accused planters of acquiring the best land, seizing property to repay debts defaulted because of low tobacco prices, and monopolizing the Indian trade that blocked expansion westward. The explosion came in 1676 when Nathaniel Bacon, a recently arrived, well-connected gentleman—who resented his exclusion from Governor William Berkeley's inner circle—recruited followers from small planters, laborers, indentured servants, and black slaves. Bacon's army alternated between attacking peaceful Indian villages, scapegoats for lower-class frustrations, and threatening the governor. Forcing Berkeley to flee and burning Jamestown, Bacon suddenly died and the rebellion collapsed. Fewer Indians decreased the Indian trade's economic importance, and by 1700, English settlement had spread along both shores of the Chesapeake Bay, to high ground between rivers, and to the fall lines of the Potomac, Rappahannock, York, and James rivers. As African slaves replaced indentured servants, there were fewer freed workers to challenge the gentry's power. Harsh slave codes placed blacks under owners' firmer control and made extending economic and political opportunities to ordinary whites less threatening. Virginia secured social peace by exchanging fears of class war for threats of slave rebellion.

Settlement spread across Virginia's southern border to eastern North Carolina. Although officially part of Carolina, offshore barrier islands eliminated natural harbors, sand bars made sea travel treacherous, and swamps and pine forests isolated residents from Charles Town. In 1655, Nathaniel Bates settled on the Albemarle Sound's western shore raising tobacco and trading with Indians for deerskins. In the 1660s, a second settlement along the Cape Fear River extended the Carolina Lowcountry northward. Ex-servants and small planters with a few slaves drifted south from Virginia to escape gentry control and squat on unclaimed land. Food crops and livestock met family and farm needs or were traded locally, and market crops of tobacco, salted meat, and naval stores were sent to Norfolk, Virginia, for store goods. Isolation increased settler suspiciousness of outside authority. John Culpeper led a rebellion in 1691 that secured a separate representative assembly, a deputy governor from Charles Town, and the right to form local governments. Settlements became more diverse when Palatine Germans established New Bern in 1705 and French Huguenots laid out Bath in 1706. Despite the colony's small population, North Carolina's family labor, mixed economy, and ethnic diversity would become prototypes for 18th-century backcountry settlements across the south.

1750

If Alexander Hamilton, a Maryland doctor, had traveled south instead of north from his Maryland home in 1744, he would have been equally surprised by the colonial South's expansiveness, prosperity, variety, and complexity. Societal change intensified after 1700. Then, Indians still outnumbered white settlers by almost 2 to 1 and blacks comprised just 4 percent of the south's estimated 210,000 people. Over the next 60 years, population almost tripled to 614,000, and the racial balance transformed: only 9 percent were Indians, over 54 percent were white, and blacks (almost all slaves) mushroomed to almost 37 percent.[16] Rapid population growth pushed colonial settlements beyond the Chesapeake and the Low-country to upcountry Virginia, North Carolina, and South Carolina after 1720; East Texas in 1716; Louisiana in 1718; and coastal Georgia in 1732. Each regional society had distinct economies, ethnic and racial compositions, labor systems, social classes, Indian relations, and ways of living. Agricultural surpluses and raw materials strengthened trade and market relations as planters shipped more and more tobacco, rice, indigo, naval stores, and deerskins to Europe; wheat, corn, and salted meat entered the growing intercoastal and Caribbean trade; and producers traded surpluses and labor locally. Colonial participation in the African slave trade increased merchant and planter ties to Africa, other North American colonies, and the West Indies. Family and enslaved labor improved new ground, generating sustained economic growth and raising the free population's living standards. Members of independent households, whose heads owned land and tools or possessed skills to provide sufficiency, embraced a consumer revolution as cheap English manufactured goods filled storekeepers' shelves.

Like most wealthy provincials, our imaginary traveler was unperturbed about deepening social divisions. He enjoyed the company of elite families, notable for their substantial fortunes, political influence, social prominence, and cultural patronage. He ranked gentlemen's English education, enlightened leadership, metropolitan tastes, sumptuous homes, and generous hospitality among the colonial South's greatest achievements and their wives charming ornaments for fine living. Dependents, especially indentured servants and enslaved Africans, merited indifference not concern. Servants, most believed, enjoyed opportunities for new starts after completing labor contracts. Slavery, everyone acknowledged, was essential for growing staple crops that generated colonial wealth, and, the thinking went, slaves—marked by capture, divine judgment, and color—were ideal plantation laborers. Our traveler often encountered Indians but carefully denoted military allies and trade partners from odd-job laborers living in European settlements or mission Indians worthy of contempt. Startled, occasionally disturbed, by the variety of living patterns and languages among European immigrants, he scarcely recognized that slaves, drawn from even more diverse cultures, created independent communities or that Indians adjusted in different ways to rapid change. Celebrating the colonial South's enlightened and prosperous society, he scarcely recognized how English settlers' growing ties to the mother country and intermarriage among elite family members created a provincial aristocracy or how interactions between people from Scotland, Ireland, Europe, Africa, and Indians and endemic violence shaped colonial southerners' sense of self and their new societies' identities.

Expansion dispersed settlements and broadened slave ownership. Increased African imports and natural growth among American-born Creoles darkened the colonial South's population. By the 1750s, 40 percent of all Virginians were enslaved and blacks comprised 60 percent of the Lowcountry. The gentry, a mere 1 or 2 percent of white families, were at the pinnacle of southern society. In one Virginia county, 7 out of every 10 taxpayers in 1716 owned slaves, but only 4 held more than 20, and the richest man, Robert Carter, possessed 126! When he died in 1732, his estate was valued at £100,000, worth over $6 million today, and included over 1,000 slaves, 300,000 acres of land, and £10,000 in cash. Farther south, rice profits made a few men very rich. They displayed their wealth by financing mansion houses on their estates and in Charles Town and Savannah, the political, commercial, and cultural hubs of Carolina and Georgia, respectively, and by impressive rounds of conspicuous consumption. Even Georgia—founded as a haven for the poor, wayward youth, and English debtors; planned as a colony of small farmers with land grants restricted to under 500 acres; and slaves and rum prohibited—succumbed to rice's allure. Attracting only a few English, Germans, and Highland Scots, Georgia proprietors lifted the slavery ban in 1750. Carolina planters with political connections acquired huge land tracts, amassed large slave holdings, and quickly extended the rice revolution southward.

Chesapeake planters especially imagined themselves as patriarchs presiding over ordered communities of many dependent slaves, children, and wives. "Besides the advantage of a pure air, we abound in all kinds of provisions without expense," William Byrd of Virginia wrote to an English friend:

> I have my flocks and my herds, my bond-men and bond-women, and every soart of trade amongst my own servants, so that I live in a kind of independence on every one but Providence. However this soart of life is without expense, yet is attended with a great deal of trouble. I must take care to keep all my people to their duty, to set all the springs in motion and to make every one draw his equal share to carry the machine forward. But then 'tis an amusement in this silent country and a continual exercise of our patience and economy.[17]

Large plantations became manorial estates with mansion houses, slave quarters, shops, mills, and surrounding fields. Thus was born the quintessential southern landscape.

Large plantations were complex operations that depended on international and colonial markets, slaves' uncompensated labor, and wives' fulfillment of domestic duties. Virginia planters assembled tobacco shipments (their own and those of small planters), sent them to British merchants, ordered manufactured goods, and distributed imports to neighbors. Few fortunes rested on tobacco alone. Virginia planters personally managed their operations and engaged in many economic activities: land speculation, loaning money, law or medical practices, and invested in slave trading, iron forges, gristmills, distilleries, and stores. Old settled areas around the Chesapeake Bay shifted from tobacco to grain cultivation. Planters' wealth grew from growing armies of enslaved field workers organized into small gangs in tobacco and family work teams in rice and on many skilled male slaves to cultivate, process, support, and transport crops. Slaveowners learned to balance corporal punishment enjoined by harsh slave codes with ceding some control over work processes, encouraging slave families, allowing garden and provisioning rights, and time off as the price of slaves' labor. Plantation mistresses' enjoyment of class privilege required deferring to their husbands' authority, supervising domestic slaves, and organizing social events, which made southern hospitality famous and enhanced their families' prestige.

Planter patriarchs distinguished themselves from ordinary folk by building great brick houses in the latest Georgian styles filled with imported English furnishings, china, and silver; sending sons to England for education and polishing; and enjoying the latest English fashions, entertainments, and dances. They displayed their prominence at church by promenading to front-row pews just before services began, at race courses with large bets on pedigreed horseflesh, and at county courts by dispensing justice from raised benches. They expected social interiors to give way before gentlemen's carriages, doff caps when greeting men in wigs, and obey the written word in the Bible and in the Law. Public ceremonies, the opening of colonial assemblies or anniversaries of royal births, reenacted social hierarchy with processions headed by bearing the royal seal and followed by ranks of the governor, council members, and assemblymen.

Landownership positioned men in white society's middling ranks and included small planters with under 10 slaves and 200 to 500 acres of land, craftsmen, lawyers, and teachers. Land, tools, and skills and labor of wives, older children, and a convict servant or slave or two provided self-sufficiency and modest living standards, and qualified men for political participation. Farmers without slaves, a third of the white population, rented land and owned personal property, but were often indebted to the gentry and only a failed harvest away from falling into poverty. Economic opportunities were declining in old settled areas. Skilled slave carpenters, blacksmiths, millers, shoemakers, watermen, and teamsters reduced openings for white men. Except for Charles Town with roughly 8,000 inhabitants in 1750, there were no cities in the colonial South. Williamsburg had fewer than 1,800 people, and Annapolis, New Bern, and Savannah (capitals of Maryland, North Carolina, Georgia, respectively) were even smaller. An urban middle class of lawyers, doctors, craftsmen, and shopkeepers, so conspicuous in northern colonial cities, remained small. Intermarriages between elite family members consolidated wealth, power, and prestige. Powerful Indian confederations limited westward expansion, and the gentry monopolized opportunities in old settlements and blocked young men's aspirations. No wonder ordinary folk welcomed evangelicals' condemnations of gentry pride, display, and consumption. No wonder they followed evangelists' calls for new awakenings and creating moral communities of "brothers and sisters," who were redeemed by Christ and nurtured one another. Baptist and Methodist itinerants founded numerous churches among the colonial South's humble folk. It was the beginnings of the southern Bible Belt.

Changing demography, new crops, and repressive laws defined blacks' outer lives, while slave resistance and accommodation shaped interior meanings. Africans from different regions and ethnic groups arrived in the colonial South to a mix of saltwater slaves, acculturated English speakers, and American-born Creoles. Newcomers did backbreaking work, clearing woodland for tobacco and cornfields or digging ditches to drain marshes and putting up levees and gates for rice. Larger slaveholdings and routinized production processes diversified slaves' work roles, structured slaves' personal lives, and created distinct regional black cultures.

In the Chesapeake, small gangs of women and older children worked fields from dawn to dusk in all weather or performed domestic labor for owners. Many slave men became skilled craftsmen, watermen, teamsters, and valets and learned about a world beyond the plantation. Falling mortality meant more slaves survived to adulthood, found partners, and had children. Owners encouraged slave population growth by moving slaves into family cabins in quarters away from mansion houses. Marrying and socializing with slaves on adjoining plantations and quarters created neighborhood slave communities.

Slaves from the West African rice coast brought technical knowledge of rice cultivation to the Lowcountry. Organized under a task system, once workers met daily labor stints, the rest of their time was their own to raise provisions and engage in petty trade. Because men outnumbered women and the swampy countryside was notoriously unhealthy, family life was only just beginning by mid-century. Limited contact with owners—who fled the countryside for Charles Town to escape malaria and other miseries—large slaveholdings, and an African majority enabled reworking of African traditions in basketry, net fishing, language, female marketing, and child naming. Black life in Charles Town was very different, as slaves' small numbers speeded acculturation to English ways. They became dockworkers, boatmen, domestics, artisans, and concubines. Mingling with countrywomen in Charles Town's markets, urban slaves remained aloof from their rural compatriots.

In their struggles to create some personal and family lives of their own, slaves faced repressive laws that closed opportunities for freedom, empowered owners to discipline their human property without restraint (killing an unruly slave was no crime), restricted slaves' opportunities to gather, and created slave patrols to police quarters at night. Slaves retaliated when and where they could. Groups of Africans ran away seeking refuge in the mountains, swamps, Spanish Florida, or Indian villages. Mysterious fires destroyed tobacco houses, broken dams flooded rice fields, and rumors spread about slaves who allegedly poisoned whites. More often, slaves took (not stealing in their eyes) foodstuffs and garments raised or purchased from their labor as compensation for meager food and clothing allowances or for personal adornment. Between the interstices of planters' power and slaves' labor, blacks wrested some time and space for themselves to create enduring—if fragile—personal, familial, and collective lives.

In the 1730s, a very different society was developing in the frontier or backcountry, a large region of hills and fertile valleys running from Maryland's Mason and Dixon Line south through the Great Valley of Virginia to the Carolina Piedmont and west to the Smoky Mountains.[18] Poor men from seaboard communities moved here, but even more numerous were Highland Scots, Ulster Scots from Northern Ireland, and Germans, who arrived in Philadelphia and migrated south along the Great Wagon Road through the Shenandoah Valley of Virginia or passed through Charles Town to frontier Carolina and Georgia. Highlanders and Ulster Scots fled deteriorating conditions from grasping landlords, weak markets, and British political repression. Arriving as indentures, family groups, or in the case of Ulster Scots, entire Presbyterian congregations, they gravitated to the frontier where speculators offered cheap land and they could settle in groups and retain much of their customs and language. Antiauthoritarian attitudes and toughness from fighting the British in Scotland or Catholics in Ireland made them ideal frontier settlers. Germans from the Rhine Valley in southwestern Germany and northern Switzerland fled overpopulation, heavy taxes, religious repression, military conscription, and wars, and usually arrived in groups. Some families indentured themselves for four to five years as redemptioners. Others came as congregants from many sects: Lutherans, Reformed, Baptists, Moravians, and pietists of various kinds. Like the Scots, Germans sought cheap land where they could settle near one another, establish churches and schools, and maintain German language, religion, and customs.

Community self-sufficiency was high in the new country, as every household member—wives, older children, and wealthy farmers'

Backcountry landscape. Rail fences, horse-drawn plows, and tilled fields typified backcountry farms in Virginia, the Carolinas, and Georgia. Salem, founded by Moravians in 1765, rises on the horizon with an outlying tavern for entertaining strangers in the upper right. (Watercolor by Ludwid Gottfried von Redeken, "A View of Salem in N. Carolina," 1787. Collection of the Wachovia Historical Society; photograph courtesy of Old Salem Museums & Garden, Winston-Salem, North Carolina.)

servants—labored to turn woodlands into farms. Within a generation, farmers shipped surplus wheat, flour, corn whiskey, hemp, flax, tobacco, naval stores, and timber eastward. Drovers arrived in Philadelphia, Charleston, and Savannah with herds of backcountry cattle and hogs. Farmers traded with artisans and town merchants in Frederick, Maryland; Winchester and Stanton, Virginia; Salem, North Carolina; Camden, South Carolina; and Augusta, Georgia. In older backcountry areas, large landowners began arriving with gangs of slaves to create grain and tobacco plantations. After the American Revolution, settlers carried Upland South landscapes of dispersed neighborhood settlements with households related by kinship, ethnicity, and religion and dotted with churches, shops, stores, mills, and market towns to the Upland South and Lower Midwest.

The vast area from the Appalachian Mountains south to the Gulf of Mexico and west to Texas was a borderland of political and economic conflicts. Spanish, French, and English trade posts and settlements asserted imperial claims, but they lacked settlers or soldiers to dominate natives or European rivals. Diplomacy was essential for survival, trade, and securing proxy Indian armies.

Pressuring Spanish Florida in 1733, the English granted land between the Savannah and the Altamaha rivers to a group of trustees, led by James Oglethorpe, who promised to set up a colony to help relieve England of its debtors and provide a free-labor experiment producing "exotic" items such as silk.[19] More important, Georgia settlers, imperialists hoped, would shield Carolina settlers from Indian attacks and close down the slave runaway haven in Saint Augustine.

The French made ambitious plans to turn Louisiana into a plantation colony. The Company of the Indies, a private trading firm, founded New Orleans in 1718 as the principal settlement and imported 5,400 European colonists, mostly convicts, and 6,000 Africans to develop tobacco and indigo plantations along the Lower Mississippi River Valley. Crops failed in Louisiana's humid subtropical climate, and by 1731, only a third of Europeans had survived the unhealthy environment. Corrupt officials found the Indian deerskin trade and embezzling government coffers more lucrative than effective leadership. While officials courted trade partners with diplomacy, they killed and enslaved weak dependent tribes along the Gulf Coast and Mississippi Delta. Settlers turned to petty trade with Indians and Africans for survival and brutally treated soldiers seeking sanctuary in Indian villages or in Spanish or English territory. Determined to maintain class and race control, Louisiana officials employed Indians and slaves to track down deserting soldiers, turned convicted settlers over to Indians for torture, hired blacks as executioners (Louis Congo was notorious in this regard), employed Indians as slave catchers, and armed slaves to attack defenseless Indian villages.

European wars and trade rivalries sparked violence in borders between English Georgia and Spanish Florida, Carolina and Louisiana traders, and French Louisiana and Spanish Texas. Alliances between European powers shifted unpredictably, and diplomats an ocean away yielded territory soldiers had won on the ground. Indian warriors changed loyalties on raids against exposed European settlements and enemy villages in their quest for male honor, guns, rum, trade goods, and slaves to sell or adopt to rebuild populations devastated by disease and warfare. In 1711, the Tuscarora attacked whites in northern Carolina who had encroached on their land for decades without payment. The Yamasee joined Carolina militiamen to defeat them. French–Spanish cooperation preserved gulf posts from falling to an army of Carolinians and Alabamans, Creeks, and Choctaws. Four years later, the Yamasee rebelled, killing hundreds of whites. Carolinians retaliated by making a trade alliance with the Cherokee, who then attacked the Lower Creeks (the Yamasee's allies) and defeated them. In 1729, the Natchez rebelled against French appropriation of their planting grounds and joined by 200 slaves killed over 200 soldiers and settlers. Fearing a simultaneous slave rebellion and an Indian war, the French convinced their Choctaw allies to attack the Natchez. Within a year, most Natchez villages were burned out and over 500 Natchez slaves were shipped to the West Indies. In 1733, Saint Augustine's governor promised freedom to slave runaways from Carolina and Georgia who converted to Catholicism. Six years later, 20 recently arrived slaves from Angola—likely Catholics from the Kingdom of the Kongo—sought sanctuary. In what became known as the Stono rebellion, they attracted over 100 slaves and killed some 20 whites on their march southward before Carolina militiamen defeated them. Georgia governor James Oglethorpe led an army of over 2,000 men into Florida in 1740, seeking runaway slaves and Spanish blood; soldiers, free black militiamen, and reinforcements from Cuba turned them back.

No one could eliminate all rivals, but colonials' gains came at natives' losses. Carolina traders and Louisiana officials' cynical divide-and-conquer policies crushed coastal Indian resistance before 1750, reduced native populations east and south of the Appalachian Mountains, and opened up the backcountry for European settlers. Economic rivalries and ethnic cleansings came at frightful costs as hundreds of colonists were killed and tens of thousands of Indians died from warfare, enslavement, or want. Even after Indian slave markets waned, violence remained traders' handmaiden. With neither captives nor deerskins to offer for sale, Carolina merchants imposed themselves on native communities, offering shoddy goods, ignoring trade protocols, forcing men to serve as unpaid porters, and raping women with impunity.

New times required new survival strategies. Creek villagers welcomed refugees, formed confederations, and strengthened central political authority to maintain autonomy. Choctaws, strategically poised between Louisiana and Carolina, became slave catchers and demanded extravagant presents for their loyalty. Survivors of Carolina wars, collapsed Spanish missions, and slave runaways found independence deep in the Florida peninsula became the Seminole, an ethnically and linguistically mixed people. The Catawba, encapsulated in the Carolina Piedmont between European settlers and Cherokee enemies, adopted remnant peoples and pursued an accommodation policy. Catawba women sold baskets, and men worked as day laborers and as slave catchers. In each case, by playing off different European groups and native communities, Indian groups sought to maintain their independence in an increasingly violent world.

TOWARD REVOLUTIONS?

George Washington's 1751 march from Winchester, Virginia, to reconnoiter French intensions in the forks of the Ohio River near modern-day Pittsburgh reverberated in chain reactions that remapped European empires, eroded Indian independence, acerbated social tensions, and created a new nation. Washington's militia represented one of many competing interests: French and British imperialists' resolve to control the North American interior, Pennsylvania and Virginia land speculators' dreams of profits from western settlement, and western Indians' determination to preserve their autonomy by exploiting European divisions. Drawn into international conflict, war's impact was decidedly local. Militiamen marched off to battle, some never to return. New levies and military appropriations created economic hardships for many and profits for a favored few. Competing factions within Indian nations debated remaining neutral or aiding one of the combatants. Indians, some France's allies and others as revenge for colonial encroachments, attacked backcountry settlements from Maryland to Georgia. Colonials in-vaded Cherokee country, burned villages, and collected scalps as bounties. In 1763, peace redrew colonial boundaries and created new problems. Canada and Florida became English, and France transferred Louisiana to Spain. Britain's larger empire required new taxes, permanent frontier posts, and added British troops and administrators. Cherokees and Creeks, internally divided during the war, lost their ability to negotiate between French and British traders to get the best deals. Political leaders chafed against new imperial policies that challenged long-standing practices of colonial autonomy. Backcountry settlers protested local governments' failure to protect them or provide justice and demanded access to frontier land. It was a new world for all.

By 1770, as conflict escalated over Britain's new colonial policies, colonial southerners faced divergent paths to the future. Was the colonial South an enlightened society of widespread opportunity for personal independence based on abundant land, frontier expansion, economic growth, rising living standards, and male political participation? Alternatively, was the colonial South an anglicized provincial society of growing economic inequality with an entrenched planter aristocracy and assertive government officials who looked to England for social values, order, and taste and for implementing new imperial policies? Or, was the colonial South's future a redeemed society as Baptist and Indian preachers called for personal accountability not passive deference to authority and envisioned a country of moral communities of believers, not individuals aggrandizing and displaying wealth? What futures and dreams did slaves and Native Americans have in this increasingly uncertain and volatile colonial world?

NOTES

1. See illustration on p. 289.
2. David J. Hally, "The Chiefdom of Coosa," in *The Forgotten Centuries: Indians and Europeans in the American South, 1521–1704,* ed. by Charles Hudson and Carmen Chaves Tesser (Athens: University of Georgia Press, 1994), 244.
3. James Mooney, "Myths of the Cherokee," *Nineteenth Annual Report of the Bureau of American Ethnology* (Washington, D.C., 1900), cited in Charles Hudson, *The Southeastern Indians* (Knoxville: University of Tennessee Press, 1976), 133, 159. The full texts of these two stories are on pp. 133, 134 and 157–59.
4. Alvar Núñez Cabeza de Vaca, *Cabeza de Vaca's Adventures in the Unknown Interior of America,* ed. and trans. by Cyclone Convey (New York: Crowell-Collier, 1961), 125, 128, cited in David J. Weber, *The Spanish Frontier in North America* (New Haven, CT: Yale University Press, 1992), 42, 44.
5. Weber, *Spanish Frontier,* 52; see map on p. 388.
6. Cabeza de Vaca, *Adventures,* cited in Weber, *Spanish Frontier,* 58.
7. Menéndez to Felipe II, Saint Augustine, October 15, 1565, in *New American World: A Documentary History of North America to 1612,* 5 vols., ed. by David Beers Quinn (New York: Arno Press, 1979), cited in Weber, *Spanish Frontier,* 63; see illustration on p. 375.
8. Menéndez to the king [1573] in *Colonial Records of Spanish Florida, Vol. 1: 1570–1577,* ed. by Jeanette Connor (Deland: Florida State Historical Society, 1925), cited in Weber, *Spanish Frontier,* 75.
9. John Smith, cited by Frances Mossiker, *Pocahontas: The Life and Legend* (New York: De Capo Press, 1996), 243.
10. Cited by Helen C. Rountree, *Pocahontas, Powhatan, Opechancanough: Three Indian Lives Changed by Jamestown* (Charlottesville: University of Virginia Press, 2005), 45.
11. Richard Frethorne, "Letter to His Father and Mother from Jamestown" [1623], in *The Records of the Virginia Company of London,* 4 vols.,

ed. by Susan Myra Kingsbury (Washington, D.C.: Government Printing Office, 1906–1935), 4: 58.

12. Ira Berlin, *Many Thousands Gone: The First Two Centuries of Slavery in North America* (Cambridge, MA: Harvard University Press, 1998), 17.

13. Ibid., 8.

14. Maryland Charter, June 20, 1623, in *Settlements to Society, 1607–1763: A Documentary History of Colonial America* ed. by Jack P. Greene (New York: W.W. Norton and Co., 1975 [1966]), 26.

15. Jerald T. Milanich, *Florida Indians and the Invasion from Europe* (Gainesville: University Press of Florida, 1995), 231.

16. Table 2.1 and map on p. 390. Population figures from Peter Wood, "The Changing Population of the Colonial South: An Overview by Race and Region, 1685–1790," in *Powhatan's Mantle: Indians in the Colonial Southeast*, rev. ed., ed. by Gregory A. Waselkov, Peter Wood, and Tom Hatley (Lincoln: University of Nebraska Press, 2006 [1989]), 60, 61.

17. William Byrd II to the Earl of Orrery, Virginia, July 5, 1726, in *American Negro Slavery: A Documentary History*, ed. by Michael Mullin (New York: Harper and Row, 1976), 57, 58; see illustration on p. 142.

18. See map on p. 390.

19. See illustration on p. 380.

2

LABOR

Colonial Southerners spent most waking hours laboring to feed, house, and clothe themselves and produce goods for exchange.[1] The colonial South's varied natural resources abundantly supported human life. Native Americans' expertise as cultivators, hunters, gatherers, and fishermen acquired from centuries of occupation provided ample subsistence, reserves for lean years, tribute payments to political leaders, and items for trade. Indians taught Europeans how to plant New World crops of corns, beans, squash, and tobacco, and Indian foods exchanged for European goods sustained most early settlements. European crops, small grains, weeds, other plants, and domestic animals like horses, cattle, swine, and sheep spread across the colonial South changing Native American subsistence labor and fostering commercial ties with Europeans. West Indian broadleaf tobacco and African rice made plantations sites of unremitting toil and contributed to the transatlantic economy's growth. Europeans' ideas that land and labor were market commodities for personal profit rationalized dispossessing Native Americans and importing many servants and slaves whose labor made a few men very wealthy.

Daily routines, labor force compositions, and work experiences varied depending on each settlement's economic base. The English sought profits by trading with Indians, plundering Spanish galleons sailing up the Atlantic coast, or exporting forest products or agricultural commodities. The search for viable staple crops dominated the early Chesapeake and Carolina Lowcountry. Within 10 years, English Virginians mastered tobacco cultivation, which became the Chesapeake's economic mainstay for the next century and a half. White indentured servants labored alongside a handful of blacks, but soon after 1700, imported African slaves dominated plantation labor forces. The Carolina Lowcountry developed more slowly. Forest products, meat, deerskins, and Indian slaves were primary exports for the first 30 years after the English established a foothold there. White and black workers enjoyed much independence in this underdeveloped extractive economy, and hunting and raiding pulled native men into the Atlantic economy. After 1700, rice became Carolina's gold, and Lowcountry planters imported thousands of African slaves whose labor and expertise made their owners the richest men in English North America.

Labor in Spanish Florida and French Louisiana reflected their status as missionary, military, and/or trade outposts. European settlers were sparse: only 7,000 in both colonies in 1760 compared to over 350,000 in the English southern colonies, but European plants, animals, diseases, manufactured goods, and the deerskin and Indian slave trade altered Native American labor. Hybrid economies developed around Florida mission villages until Carolina traders' Indian allies destroyed them in the early 1700s. Louisiana was the southern terminus of France's vast trade empire extending up the Mississippi River to the "middle ground" of the Ohio River Valley and Great Lakes. Briefly in the 18th century, the French imported African slaves to introduce plantation agriculture, but lack of profits created a subsistence exchange economy instead.

By the mid-18th century, patterns of daily work reflected the colonial South's economic diversity, maturity, and integration into the Atlantic economy. In this overwhelming agricultural society—some 90 percent of the working population made their living from the soil—market and subsistence labor intermixed. In the interior, Native American women maintained traditional horticulture but spent more hours processing deerskins for trade. Self-sufficient backcountry farmers relied on wives' and children's labor and exchanged small surpluses for store goods. Large planters' enslaved minions not only produced export crops of tobacco and wheat in the Chesapeake and rice and indigo in the Lowcountry, but also raised foodstuffs, herded animals, produced domestic manufactures, and developed craft skills that made plantations economically independent and more profitable. Road networks, country stores, and warehouse landings facilitated local and long-distance trade as port towns teamed with artisan shops, export merchants, and professional offices. With 10,000 people in 1770, Charles Town was the largest city in the southern colonies and fourth largest in all of British North America. The colonial South's growing wealth and economic maturity rested on the backs of tens of thousands of servants and slaves, who toiled without compensation from dawn to dusk (and often beyond) in fields, shops, and homes. The world of work is fundamental to understanding daily life in the colonial South.

NATIVE AMERICANS BEFORE EUROPEAN CONTACT

Through centuries of living in the land, indigenous peoples in the southeast acquired intimate knowledge of their particular environments and developed effective techniques for utilizing natural resources. The mix of horticulture, hunting, gathering, and fishing varied over place and changed over time as people migrated to new areas or acquired new skills. Human ingenuity provided abundance in most years, surpluses for lean times, and goods to exchange with outsiders. In village societies, some individuals acquired expertise in fashioning tools: axes and hoes for clearing land and cultivating plants, bows and arrows for hunting, weirs for fishing, wooden canoes for traveling, woven fiber baskets and ceramic pots for storing food and preparing meals, and decorated matchcoats and jewelry for adorning bodies. Some men and women became full-time priests revered for their knowledge of plants' healing powers or ability to appease the spirits who ruled all things. Other men had special gifts of endurance in hunts, bravery in war, or eloquence in speech and became respected leaders. Specialized labor most characterized political confederations like the Natchez on the lower Mississippi River or the Cofitachequi in what became South Carolina, where divine rulers lived on large artificial mounds and abundant food supplies from riverine agriculture and trade brought wealth and power. Everywhere, labor differed between men and women, followed seasonal patterns, and left distinct imprints on the land.

Gender divisions were a fundamental principle in organizing work in native communities. Men cleared land for farming; hunted large and small game; fished rivers and bays; constructed houses, buildings, and furnishings; and made bows, arrows, fishing gear, various tools, and dugout canoes. Women tended gardens and fields; gathered wild plants, berries, seeds, roots, nuts, shellfish, and firewood; preserved food and prepared meals; made clothes, pottery, and baskets; and reared small children. Men's labor alternated between periods of rest and intense physical exertion that required distant travel, endurance, discomfort, and strength. Women's work was more constant and repetitious but communal and closer to villages. Women and men spent most work time apart, yet cooperated on some tasks. Men cleared new ground for crops, helped women with corn planting, and skinned animals. Women processed venison carcasses and cured animal skins for clothing. Men and women acquired different but finely honed complementary skills. Male hunters intimately learned the ways of animals: their habits and movements, their strengths and vulnerabilities, and propitious times for hunting and fishing. Female horticulturalists and gatherers intimately understood the ways of plants: tending varieties of corns, beans, and squashes to check soil exhaustion and ensure successful harvests; fashioning fine baskets from plant fibers; discovering powers of different plants and nuts as foods or medicines; and learning propitious times for collecting them.

Work varied with the seasons. During the cold months from mid-October to mid-March, men hunted and fished, and women gathered wild foods, especially nuts. In the warm season from mid-March to mid-October, women tended fields and gathered wild plants, while men fished and rested. Native peoples' intricate knowledge of and resourcefulness in utilizing their environment impressed Europeans. As one Englishman observed in the early 17th century:

> In March and April they [Virginia Powhatans] live much upon their [fishing] Weeres, and feed on Fish, Turkeys, and Squirrells and than as also sometimes in May . . . they plant their Fields and sett their Corne, and live after those Monethes most[ly] of[f] Acrons, Wallnutts, Chesnutts, Chechinquamyns and Fish, but to mend their dyett, some disperse themselves in smale Companies, and live upon such beasts as they can kill, with their bowes and arrows. Upon Crabbs, Oysters, Land Tortoyses, Strawberries, Mulberries and such like; In June, July, and August they feed upon the rootes of Tockohowberryes [wild potatoes], Grownd-nuts, Fish, and greene Wheat [corn], and sometime upon a kind of Serpent, or great snake of which our people likewise use to eate.[2]

For native peoples, time was cyclical with no sharp divisions between time spent on subsistence, ceremonies, or warfare. Nor were subsistence activities sharply segmented or specialized, but overlapped to create multiple safety nets and reduce the impact of harvest failures or poor hunts.

Algonquian Indians fishing. Coastal natives devised many ways of securing food from their diverse environments including dip nets, dugout canoes, fires for night fishing, spears, weirs, and fish traps. Numerous varieties of fish, turtles, sharks, and crabs indicate Europeans' wonder at the New World's abundance. Engraving by Theodor de Bry, 1590, of a watercolor by John White, 1584. (Library of Congress.)

Horticulture was a relatively recent addition to much older hunting–gathering activities. Maize agriculture originated in Mesoamerica and spread to the southeast in successive waves of new plants and cultivation skills. Around 1000 BCE, seed crop plants, sunflower, sump weed, and chenopodium were sown along riverbanks and crossbred to create hybrid varieties. Tropical flint corn arrived around 200 BCE along with squashes and bottle gourds. Beans and eastern flint corn (the latter a hardier variety adapted for cool, moist climates) appeared in the southeast by 1200 CE and allowed for successful horticulture in the Ohio and Mississippi river valleys and in Virginia. Horticulture's importance in the total subsistence systems varied depending on local resources. Natchez's extensive maize fields on rich alluvial soils in the Lower Mississippi River Valley supported large villages, centralized political organization, and extensive trade. Calusas in South Florida lived mostly on fish, shellfish, fowls, and wild plants. The Caddo in East Texas ate more buffalo than corn, while Algonquians on the Delmarva Peninsula lacked deer and relied on fish, fowls, and horticulture. In the 1530s, marooned Spanish explorer Cabeza de Vaca lived among hunter-gatherers on Galveston Island subsisting on fish and roots.

We can begin the work year with spring planting of corn, beans, and squash and fishing. Men cleared new planting ground with stone axes, "girdling" trees, or removing circles of bark, which eventually killed them. Trees were left to rot or burned after they died. Women and men removed roots and weeds with hoes, made of short wooden handles with flint, shell, or animal-bone blades. Southeastern native peoples cultivated many varieties of corn, beans, and squash. Women planted two crops of early corn that matured in only 10 or 12 weeks in garden plots near villages, and men assisted in planting late corn in large alluvial fields on riverbanks. Women used hoes to work the soil into hills about a foot in diameter and spaced three or 4 feet apart and digging sticks to plant four to six seeds in each hill and pile dirt around them. Contrary to popular belief, Indians did not plant fish to fertilize corn seeds. Women planted pole beans whose vines grew up corn stalks; various bush, kidney, snap, and pinto beans; gourds; squashes; pumpkins; and sunflower between corn hills.

Men moved to camps along the Atlantic and Gulf coasts and inland streams for spring fish runs. They prized large fish (e.g., catfish, paddlefish, sturgeon, and gar pikes; some weighed over 100 pounds) and smaller fish (e.g., shad, bass, perch, sunfish, and mullet), which are storied in southern cuisine. Fishing techniques were as numerous as fish varieties. Men constructed weirs across tidal channels made of small poles and interwoven reeds or oak splints and baskets that caught fish at low tide. Rock traps aligned in V-formations partially dammed swift-flowing streams and captured spawning fish swimming upriver. Other methods included dip nets, cane spears, trot lines stretched across the water with dangling lines and hooks made from deer or turkey bones, and night fishing in dugout canoes with fires to lure fish.

In early summer, women harvested green corn that marked the end of fasting and planted a second corn crop. Women and children tended large fields chopping weeds, mounding dirt around corn stalks for improved support and drainage, and shooing away animal and bird predators. Women aided by children and old men gathered seasonal wild vegetables, berries, fruits, nuts, and seeds in succession. They picked blackberries, gooseberries, raspberries, wild strawberries, huckleberries, black gum berries, mulberries, palmetto berries from trees, and wild grapes. Women gathered seeds of cockspur grass, water lily, chenopodium, and cane, and parched and pounded them into meal. They collected grasses, canes, reeds, and pine straw to make baskets. Women assisted men in catching crabs, gathering oysters, and digging clams.

Early fall was women's busiest time as they harvested late corn in baskets carried on their backs that was stored in raised cribs to reduce losses from mice and other animals. Men returned to fishing camps and hunted migrating birdlike passenger pigeons, whose enormous flocks darkened the sky, and waterfowl heading south along the Mississippi flyway. Women and children gathered chestnuts, pecans, hickory, acorns, black walnuts and the roots and tubers of red and white coontie, groundnuts or Indian potatoes, wild sweet potatoes, morning glories, swamp potatoes from arrowhead, and Jerusalem artichoke. Late fall was best for gathering persimmons, wild cherries, papaws, crab apples, wild plums, and prickly pears.

Winter was hunting time. From late October until early March, able-bodied people moved to camps sometimes several hundred miles away. White-tailed deer, fat from acorns and thick with winter coats, were especially prized. Armed with bows made from black locust, ash, and Osage orange; buckskin strings; and arrows made from cane or red dogwood and tipped with sharp bone points, hunters were accurate from only 40 yards. Except during fall rutting seasons, when bucks become more aggressive, getting close to animals required great skill—as deer, anthropologist Charles Hudson notes, "have sharp senses, are frightened easily, and are extraordinarily swift and agile."[3] The best way to catch a deer was to become like one. Hunters wrapped themselves in deer-head decoys and imitated deer motions and calls. Large groups of hunters trapped deer herds by burning circles of dry leaves, making U-shaped formations, or forcing them into rivers or ravines where they were easily

An Algonquian village. This composite drawing of an open village includes bark-covered pole dwellings (a), green (e) and mature (g) corn, a "scare crow" platform (f), tobacco (h), pumpkins, deer hunting, and communal spaces for feasts (d), prayers (b), and dances (c). Natives planted corn, beans, and squashes together and not in separate fields as shown here. Engraving by Theodor de Bry, 1590, of a watercolor by John White, 1584. (Library of Congress.)

shot. Bear, valued more for oil extracted from fat than for meat, were even more dangerous prey, and hunters drove females from hollow treetops with fires. Small game was an important part of winter diet. Young men and boys shot wild turkeys with bows and arrows; set snares to trap rabbits, raccoons, beaver, otters, muskrats, and opossums; and used blowguns made from hollowed cane to kill squirrels. Florida Timucuas bravely impaled alligators with long poles jammed down their throats. Meanwhile, women and children gathered nuts and tuberous plants. Women's most laborious winter work was scraping, drying, soaking, and smoking skins to prevent decay; pounding and stretching them into soft leather; and fashioning clothing and other items.

Native Americans thrived in the southeast not only from abundant natural resources but also by carefully maintaining delicate balances between humans, plants, and animals. Maize, a domesticated plant, cannot survive without human intervention. Women prayed to Corn Mother for successful harvests and sang corn songs to remind them of their special relationship. Men prepared for hunts with rituals and prayed to deer spirits to sacrifice individuals so the people could live. Corn thrives in well-drained soils but quickly exhausts soil nutrients. Indians chose planting grounds near rivers with easily tilled alluvial soils to take advantage of spring floods that deposited enriching silt. Planting beans, a nitrogen-rich legume, replenished cornfields, and late winter burnings added nutrients to the soil. Intercropping beans, squashes, and other plants with corn made Indian fields messy to European eyes, but covered exposed soils, reduced erosion, and checked weed growth. Gatherers weeded out inedible plants to encourage growth of edible ones. Hunters set fires to clear underbrush, seedlings, and saplings that allowed larger tree growth and created grassy meadows. By nurturing edge environments, hunters increased deer herds and turkey flocks. Improved hunting prevented animal overpopulation. Europeans marveled at extensive park-like southern woodlands, and the southeast's abundant biodiversity seemed a Garden of Eden. They rarely recognized their origins in Indians' subsistence activities.

Native Americans were not natural ecologists. Armed with European guns, Indian men exterminated beaver and deer to acquire European trade goods, and there is evidence of massive game kills in the precontact era. Overfarming and harvest failures contributed to the decline of Mississippian Mound Builders centuries before Columbus. But native people lacked metal technology to dominate and transform their environment. More importantly, they saw themselves as part of the natural world. Life required maintaining proper relationships with plants and animals that sustained them. Unless propitiated with prayers and rituals, these powerful spirits might withhold nature's gifts from the people.

Trade, like subsistence labor, was a social as well as an economic activity. Men from interior hunting societies followed trail networks that connected the Chesapeake Bay to the lower Mississippi River and the Florida coast to the Great Lakes to exchange upcountry flint, hard cane, feather cloaks, and animal skins for lowcountry salt, dried fish, and seashells from coastal people. Even more valued were exotic items (mica, soapstone, copper, and grizzly bear teeth) that came from hundreds even thousands of miles away. Fashioned into personal adornment items (such as gorgets or necklaces worn around the neck and wrist bracelets), these rare objects gave owners spiritual power and superior status. Lacking currency, Indians extended village reciprocity by trading with outsiders. Ritualized hospitality was essential for establishing friendship ties between individuals and groups before bargaining could begin. Honored guests, male traders brought gifts and news and expected refreshments, entertainments, and female companions. Most Indians welcomed European trade, as they exchanged easily produced items (maize or deerskins) for fantastic objects like mirrors, gold coins, fish hooks, iron kettles, hatchets, knives, guns, and powder, which lightened daily work, beautified bodies, and defeated enemies. As long as natives were numerous and Europeans scarce, trade followed Indian protocols and served Indian needs. Once Europeans learned to support themselves in the colonial South and trade goods became necessities of daily life, native communities' autonomy was compromised and Indians' ability to resist land dispossession weakened.

17TH-CENTURY CHESAPEAKE

England's leaders believed labor was a moral as well as an economic necessary that was sharply delineated by class and by gender and regulated by households and communities. Unremitting arduous work was humanity's fate and obligation after Adam and Eve's expulsion from the Garden of Eden. Idleness was the Devil's handmaiden unless one belonged to the gentry who enjoyed leisure for self-cultivation and refinement. Gender defined tasks. Men prepared fields; cultivated grain crops; tended livestock; fabricated metal and leather goods; cut timber; constructed buildings, ditches, and fences; and handled market trade. Women's labor was domestic: tending gardens, dairy, and poultry; processing and preserving food; making cloth and clothing; preparing meals; washing and cleaning; and bearing and rearing children. Women only did field work during busy sowing and harvest times. Households were primary economic units of society, and household heads—husbands, fathers, and masters—supervised day-to-day labor conditions and oversaw dependents' welfare. Youths and young adults spent several years living in other households as bound apprentices to learn crafts, farm skills, or housewifery or were employed as farm laborers, domestics, or journeymen until they acquired the wherewithal to marry and form their own households. Unless they were orphans, apprentices retained legal rights with relatives nearby to protect them from abusive masters. Wage labors were free to leave unsatisfactory employers. Frequent village festivals, holidays, and communal rituals provided welcome respites from work's drudgery.

Demographic and economic changes that underlay early colonial ventures also loosened traditional controls over labor. England's population growth from 3 million people in 1500 to 4 and 5 million in 1600 and 1650, respectively; land-enclosing landlords, who shifted from grain cultivation to sheep pastures and evicted tenants from lands they had farmed for generations; and boom-and-bust cycles of overseas woolen trade, all left tens of thousands of people without work or livelihoods. Armies of the landless and unemployed roamed the countryside and migrated to towns seeking work, became vagabonds and robbers, or swelled the urban poor's ranks. Fearing society was out of joint, authorities used courts to force the idle to work, sanctioned corporal punishments against recalcitrant laborers, attacked the unemployed as vicious and lazy, and advocated sending England's poor and wayward youth to New World plantations. Men and women dreamed of new worlds of abundance and opportunity. Seagull, a character in the 1605 play *Eastward Hoe,* proclaimed that in Virginia: "Golde is more plentifull than copper is with us; . . . and for rubies and diamonds they goe forth on holydayes and gather 'hem by the sea-shore to hand on their children's coates, and sticke in their children's caps. . . . [and] You shall live freely there, without sergeants, or courtiers, or lawyers, or intellegencers."[4]

Merchants' calculated search for profits founded Jamestown in 1607. Over the previous half-century, merchants had used joint-stock companies to pool resources for overseas ventures and secured government charters that awarded them trade monopolies. Since personal losses were limited to the size of one's investment, these commercial enterprises' greater resources financed ambitious projects and fostered risk-taking and material striving. The Virginia Company, a joint-stock company chartered in 1606, promised investors handsome dividends and settlers future shares of company profits, land, and higher social standing. The first settlers included gentlemen eager to lead but shunning physical labor; specialized craftsmen like blacksmiths, carpenters, bricklayers, masons, and goldsmiths and perfumers to refine precious commodities; and common workers, mostly young men from port towns. Completing a fort, storehouses, church, and shelter and planting provision crops, colonists then searched for gold, silver, and precious stones and experimented with wine, silk, sugar, fish, or iron as profitable exports. John Smith, one of the few experienced leaders, lamented there was "no talke, no hope, nor worke, but dig gold, wash gold, refine gold load gold."[5] They sent naval stores of pitch and tar, salt, fine timber, sassafras, and animal hides traded from the Powhatans to England, but no gold, silver, or Spanish plunder.

Anticipating a Garden of Eden and docile natives, settlers expected riches without work. They survived only through Powhatan generosity. With abundant resources but scarce labor, Jamestown needed jacks-of-all-trades willing to devote themselves to unremitting toil of extracting marketable commodities from Virginia's environment. Men with hunting skills were in short supply; in England, deer hunting was a gentlemen's pastime not a subsistence activity. "Though there be fish in the Sea, foules in the ayre, and Beasts in the woods," Smith confessed, "their bounds are so large, they so wild, and we so weake, and ignorant, we cannot much trouble them."[6] With everyone a company employee, the colony's leaders marshaled labor along military lines. Overseers marched work gangs to company fields at 6:00 A.M., to mandatory chapels and communal meals at noon, back to the fields from 2:00 to 4:00 P.M., and later to required evening prayers. At other times, men worked their own provision grounds. With little personal stake in the colony's commercial success and demoralized by illness and mortality, men resented regimented labor. Draconian measures under Sir Thomas Dale's *Lawes Divine, Morall and Martiall* (1612) sparked only more resistance.

In the 1610s, John Rolfe experimented with tobacco, a crop the Spanish had introduced to Europeans, whose smoke was believed to have medicinal value. Settlers found Virginia's local variety to have a harsh "biting taste," but Rolfe combined Powhatan expertise with purloined seeds from the Spanish West Indies and within a few years mastered tobacco cultivation. In 1617, colonists sent 20,000 pounds of tobacco to England. As a luxury item commanding high prices, tobacco profits were enormous. During boom years that lasted until 1630, a laborer annually raised tobacco selling for £200. Virginia went tobacco mad: production soared from 500,000 pounds in 1626 to 10 million pounds annually by the 1660s. For the next two centuries, the Chesapeake's economy rested on tobacco.

The tobacco boom coincided with changes in company policies to reduce expenses and attract settlers. In 1617, stockholders received 100 acres of land and company workers were promised the same after completing their indentures. Anyone paying transportation costs to Virginia received a 50-acre "headright" grant for each person including family members and servants. Some servants attained headright grants at the end of their terms as part of their freedom dues. Promises of land and economic mobility sparked immigration. Private landowning rewarded planters whose tobacco profits paid for importing more servants who awarded planters more land grants to expand tobacco production even more. Planters sought the choicest tobacco grounds near river landings and scattered their holdings along Virginia's numerous eastward-flowing rivers. For the rest of the 17th century, at least 75 percent of English immigrants arrived as indentured servants, bound to masters for four to seven years to repay their passage costs and maintenance during their time of service.

Personal wealth came from extracting maximum labor from indentured servants. Most were single young men in their teens and early 20s; men outnumbered women 5 to 1. Servants came from England's middling and lower ranks—sons and daughters of small farmers, tenants, or journeymen artisans—who had left home seeking work in rural villages and port towns. Enticed by merchants' glowing promises of better lives in Virginia or swept off alleys in urban slums, servants' lives in Virginia were far worse than bound orphans in England. Planters inspected each cargo of new arrivals: "Some view'd our limbs, and other's turn'ed us round," a servant recounted in verse, "Examening [us] like Horses, if we're sound."[7] Indentures were property to be bought, sold, and gambled away. Women and men worked in fields 10 to 14 hours a day 7 days a week and in foul weather, lived in flimsy shelters, ate monotonous corn gruel, and enjoyed few holidays. In theory, indentures were legal contracts that promised sufficient food, clothing, and shelter; protection of servants' welfare; and freedom dues of corn and clothes. In reality, planters used their control over the Virginia General Assembly and local county courts to uphold corporal punishment and extend contracts of servants who stole goods or ran away. Few planters feared suits for raping female servants (by law, the child was placed in servitude) or even for causing a recalcitrant's servant's death. After treating English servants' labor as commodities, exploiting them to the point of endurance, and denying effective legal rights, planters had few scruples enslaving Africans later in the century.

Plantation making was brutal work. Less than half of indentured servants possessed agricultural skills; most were unfamiliar with cultivating tobacco or corn or clearing forests. Plows, draft animals, gardens, poultry, and dairies were scarce in early Virginia, and servants labored with simple hand tools: axes, hatchets, hoes, saws, adzes, and froes. Despite a scarcity of women servants, planters in their rush for profits bent traditional gender labor divisions. Men performed the heaviest work, cutting down small trees and removing rings of bark from large trees to kill them, but women joined them in the tedious physically exhausting tasks of grubbing roots and stumps, burning brush, setting out tobacco seedlings, weeding tobacco stalks, in addition to cooking and washing clothes. Tobacco exhausted soils after three or four years of continual planting. Forest clearing resumed unabated during winters.

As a labor-intensive crop, tobacco required closely supervised labor throughout the annual cultivation cycle. In late January or February, gangs of four to ten male and female workers cleared planting ground, then sowed tobacco seed mixed with ash in specially prepared beds. After spring showers, they transplanted tender seedlings to wet fields, which had been raked into square hills 3 to 5 feet apart with hilling hoes. Tobacco required constant attention until mid-August to replant dead plants, weed hills with hoes, cut off plants' tops to prevent flowering, prune "succors" or inferior ground stalks, and pluck off voracious tobacco worms. Successful harvesting and curing required utmost judgment, as ill-timed or improper handling ruined even the most promising crops. Just at the right moment, workers cut mature stalks, hauled them to curing sheds, and hung them on scaffolds for two weeks to dry. In November, workers completed final processing: "stemming" or stripping leaves from stalks; twisting them into bundles; packing them tight into hogsheads with a mechanical "prizer" or press to keep out air; and, finally, a year after setting out seedlings, hauling

Processing tobacco. Raising a successful tobacco crop required closely supervised small gangs of indentured servants or slaves. Illustrated are "curing" tobacco in special barns (a) and (d), sun drying (b), tying leaves stripped from stalks, "prizing," or tight packing (c), rolling one-thousand pound tobacco hogsheads (e), and government inspection (f). William Tatham, *An Historical and Practical Essay on the Culture of Tobacco* (London, 1800). (Library of Congress.)

the processed tobacco to nearby wharves for shipment and sale in England.

Secure subsistence and falling mortality after the mid-17th century enlarged labor forces, encouraged specialized labor, and reasserted traditional gendered labor divisions on large estates. Some servant women were domestics assisting planters' wives and daughters, and men became skilled blacksmiths, carpenters, leatherworkers, teamsters, and watermen. Tobacco always had priority; no one escaped the fields at pressing times. Adapting Powhatan cultivation techniques, servants planted corn in the spring between tree stumps in partially cleared fields or in hills 4 or 5 feet apart in old tobacco fields. Corn required occasional chopping of weeds during summer and harvesting in the fall after housing tobacco. Workers stored picked ears until winter husking bees when they stripped leaves from ears and shelled kernels from cobs to be ground into meal at night with hand mills. English apple, peach, and cherry trees bore fruit after a few years that female servants pressed into hard cider and peach brandy. Women kept ducks, chickens, geese, and bees; tended vegetable gardens; turned milk into butter and cheese; and processed flax and hemp that they spun into thread and wove to make coarse linen clothes. Cattle roamed freely and thrived from abundant forest, marsh, and meadow forage. Men rounded up animals for winter slaughter, fattening them with fruit, meadow grass, corn fodder (corn blades and tops), and corn shucks, before killing and cutting up carcasses. Women assisted in preserving meat and processing cuts for bacon, roasts, and hams.

A small number of Africans labored along white male and female servants. Debates over early blacks' legal status, slavery's origins, and the relationship between slavery and racism have preoccupied historians for decades. Scant evidence yields inconclusive answers.[8] In 1619, a Dutch ship from the West Indies arrived with " twenty odd" Africans originally from Angola or the Congo. By 1650, no more than 300 blacks lived in the Chesapeake, most were imported from other New World colonies and at least partially acculturated to European ways. They worked alongside English servants in fields, but early distinctions between white and black servants reveal worsening labor conditions. In 1640, black male servants were barred from carrying arms or serving in militias against Powhatan warriors. Three years later, males of both races over age 16 but only black female servants were taxed as laborers, presumably because the latter worked in fields while white women performed domestic work. Estate appraisers placed higher values on black than on white servants suggesting the former served longer terms. Courts punished white runaways with additional time but ordered absconding blacks to serve for their remaining lives.

The early Chesapeake was no racial Utopia, yet little distinguished black and white workers' daily labor or material lives.

Free emigrants and servants who survived onerous work and diseases enjoyed much opportunity until mid-century. Servants' freedom dues included a bushel of corn and a suit of new clothes and, perhaps, tools and a headright grant. Undeveloped tracts were available to rent. Many African servants were freed at the end of their terms or earned money to purchase their freedom. Crushing victories over the Powhatans in the 1620s and 1640s opened up land along the Chesapeake Bay for settlement. Tobacco cultivation required much sweat equity but modest capital, and large plantations were scarce until the 17th century's end. Ordinary planters, like Robert Cole of Maryland, relied on the labor of wives, children, and a few servants, and on neighboring planters to sell his tobacco to pay taxes and purchase store goods. He measured success by independence acquired through owning land and indentured servants, profits from rising land values and larger livestock herds, and having wives who worked inside homes but not in fields. Ordinary settlers delighted in the abundance of forests and estuaries. They hunted deer, turkeys, wild hogs, and small game; gathered maple sugar, sassafras roots, nuts, berries, and persimmons (made into beer); caught fish in rebuilt Indian traps; and gathered shellfish, crabs, oysters, and clams from the Chesapeake Bay.

After 1660, falling tobacco prices brought hard times to small planters and ex-servants. Planter-merchants with the largest labor forces, the most fertile lands by river landings, personal ties with London merchants, and connections to colonial governors dominated Chesapeake society by century's end. Former servants became wage laborers or tenant farmers clearing new land for planters, while small tobacco farmers were a single harvest failure away from joining their ranks. The gentry's rise coincided with a shift from servant to slave labor. White servants became scarcer and more expensive just as English merchants increased supplies of African slaves. Falling mortality after mid-17th century made paying more to acquire slaves for life more profitable than hiring servants for short terms. Unlike whites, slaves enjoyed no English legal rights and could be driven harder and longer, and their skin color marked their servile status. Work assignments were divided along the color line with black women and men working fields, free and servant white women in households, and white men monopolizing skilled labor. By 1700, blacks comprised 13 percent of the Chesapeake population, marking a shift in the labor system from racially mixed indentured servants to enslaved Africans and sealing the Chesapeake's future as a slave society.

FLORIDA

As the Spanish came to the southeast to explore, conquer, convert, and trade, Florida attracted far fewer European settlers than British North America's agricultural colonies. Adventurers, soldiers, traders, and priests in Spain's northern outpost of her vast New World empire expected riches in gold and silver, profitable export commodities, or soul harvests for Christ. All assumed Indians would satisfy Spanish labor needs. Pedro Menéndez de Avilés, *adelentado* (or governor) of Florida, occupied land near villages, demanded tribute payments of corn and other foods, and drafted Indian laborers as porters and workmen. Overlooking the seasonality of native subsistence networks, Europeans rarely moderated food demands to accommodate periods of scarcity. Eventually tiring of their intruders' continued demands for food and labor, native generosity turned to withdrawal and hostility. Coastal peoples relocated into the interior to avoid contact, withheld food to starve the Europeans out, or attacked settlers to drive them away.

In 1585, Menéndez recruited 50 Spanish families to Santa Elena on the South Carolina coast and to Saint Augustine with promises of land and cattle to raise provisions for soldiers and staple products and protection against hostile natives. Menéndez envisioned an export economy of rice, pearls, sugar, fruit, grains, wine, silver, naval stores, dried fish and beef, hides, wool, and bacon. Success proved elusive. Located near coastal swamps with limited cropland, settlers poorly understood corn, beans, and squash cultivation or which European crops could prosper in this semitropical country. They ignored Native Americans' reliance on multiple food sources, and when European monoculture failed, they cursed their poverty. Difficulties adapting to new environments and eliminating Indian resistance to Spanish occupation forced settlers to abandon rural areas and concentrate near military and administrative posts of Saint Augustine, Pensacola, and Natchitoches. By 1700, Saint Augustine, with just 200 people, was the sole European settlement in Spanish Florida and survived as a salvage and refuge center for shipwreck survivors, a feeble assertion of Spanish claims to North America. In the 18th century, a few African slaves and Indians worked as herders on governors' cattle and wheat *haciendas* (or large estates), in Central and West Florida. Most residents supported themselves as soldiers or officials and lived off the *situado*, the oft-delayed annual subsidy from Mexico that sustained Spain's North American backwater.

Everywhere the Spanish settled or founded missions, they introduced European wheat, small grains, fruit trees, horses, cattle, pigs, and metal tools that transformed land and altered Indian subsistence labor. Cultivated plants and weeds spread faster than Spanish settlers and when Europeans first encountered some Indians, they were surprised to find them already growing European vegetables and fruits. Spanish hogs became feral razorbacks and multiplied rapidly feasting on the southeastern forests' rich mast and uprooting Indian corn. Cattle from governors' *haciendas* trampled Apalachee fields. Spanish cattle preceded Spanish missionaries and soldiers in East Texas, and Creek men had become expert herders before extensive contact with Europeans. Horses pastured on rich savannas and migrated to the Great Plains where they transformed native peoples into fierce nomadic hunters and warriors and created florescent equestrian cultures. Agriculture and herding enriched diets of some natives and reduced importance of male hunts. Guale men and women on the coast, however, spent more time raising foodstuffs for missionaries and less on fishing, hunting, and gathering, thus reducing the nutritional quality of their diet. The Calusas became wealthier from salvaging shipwrecks along southern Florida's treacherous waters and acquiring captives for enslavement or adoption, metal objects for daily subsistence, gold and silver for adornment, and prized exotic trade items.

Waning as a settlement frontier, Florida waxed as a mission frontier transforming Indian labor. By 1675, Franciscans claimed over 15,000 converts in 36 mission villages north from Saint Augustine to Port Royal Sound in South Carolina among the Guale, west through Central Florida among the Timucua and Apalachee to the Apalachicola on the Chattahoochee River. Friars relied on Indian labor to create new Christian communities apart from Spanish settlements and military posts. Priests with soldiers commandeered Indian men to construct churches and houses and native women to feed them. Franciscans expected neophytes' assistance in daily routines, like ringing mission bells, preparing meals, and helping with masses. Male and female converts added European wheat, grapes, and watermelons; orange, peach, fig, and pomegranate trees; and hogs, cattle, sheep, goats, and chickens to traditional farming, hunting, fishing, and gathering. They acquired new skills and crafts learning to use wheels, saws, and chisels, and some men became proficient blacksmiths fabricating iron tools, nails, and church bells.

Spaniards squabbled over control of Indian labor. Governors denounced parasitic priests who lived off Indians; ate Indian-produced food; demanded "gifts" of food at masses and for performing weddings and burials; forced men to be unpaid porters and servants; and sold Indian-produced deerskins, tobacco, swine, fowls, vegetables, and corn in Saint Augustine and in port towns. Priests attacked the *repartimiento de indios*, the drafting of Indian men to work on public works projects (like the 15-year rebuilding of Castillo de San Marcos) and to unload ships, repair roads, build bridges, and operate ferries. They condemned soldiers' and settlers' appropriation of native men as porters, farmers, herders, servants, and laborers, and claimed bans on attending mass and abusive mistreatment hindered their soul-saving work. Indian men resented laboring as unpaid or underpaid porters, abused human beasts of burden, who hauled goods where horses and mules were scarce that separated them from their families for long periods. Settlers easily evaded laws protecting Indian workers from abuse.

In the late 17th century, Carolina opened up new opportunities for Indian men outside demeaning mission labor. Hunting deerskins to sell to merchants avoided agricultural work and provided access to desired trade goods. Florida Indians "get along so well with the English . . . ," a friar wrote to the Spanish king in 1700, because they "do not oblige them to live under the bell in law and righteousness, but rather, only as they wish. . . . The English bring them guns, powder, balls, glass beads, knives, hatchets, iron tools, woolen blankets and other goods."[9] Unconverted Indians—who desired cheaper and higher quality English goods and resented Spanish labor drafts, suppression of religious ceremonies and ball games, and denial of guns and ammunition—joined slave-raiding expeditions into Florida, where alienated mission Indians participated in destroying Christian villages. Seeking steady supplies of English goods, Creek men became professional hunters and slavers sweeping down the Florida peninsula as far as Tampa Bay.

By the early 18th century, English and French merchants' domination of the Indian trade and alliances with the Lower Creeks, Cherokees, Choctaws, and Chickasaws threatened Spanish Florida's survival. With little to attract settlers, the mission system destroyed, few goods to trade, and dependent on the Crown's annual subsidies for food and supplies, Florida survived as a backwater outpost with some 2,000 settlers in 1745, less than a tenth of the white population of Carolina and Georgia. In the late 1750s, several hundred Canary Islanders settled just north of Saint Augustine to supply food for the military garrison and discourage further English encroachment. Spain's restrictive trade policies, which limited colonial trade to a few New World ports and to Spanish goods carried on Spanish ships, made imported goods scarce and expensive. Smuggling became an important livelihood that was facilitated by Florida's numerous harbors along a long unprotected coastline. Charleston and New York traders sought Spanish gold, silver, deerskins, and oranges, and the Spanish traded French muskets and ammunition for Indian furs. Desperate for supplies, officials ignored commercial restrictions and demanded bribes to share in the profits of clandestine commerce.

Slaves and free blacks, comprising a quarter of Saint Augustine's 3,000 people in 1763, worked as wage laborers, servants, farmers, ranchers, and sailors in the undermanned colony. They constructed Castillo de San Marcos outside Saint Augustine and formed a separate militia company. About 100 black men and women—under the leadership of Francisco Menéndez, a free black man—lived at Gracia Real de Santa Teresa de Mose, a fort and agricultural settlement 2 miles north of Saint Augustine. They sold surplus food to soldiers and administrators, buffered English raiders, and raided isolated Carolina plantations.

EARLY CAROLINA LOWCOUNTRY

When Henry Woodward explored the Carolina interior in the 1660s, he found "a Country soe delitious, pleasant and fruitfull, that were it cultivated doubtless it would prove a second Paradize."[10] For a few white families, Woodward's dream came true. A century later, Charles Town was the colonial South's largest city and commercial and social hub for the wealthiest men in all of British North America. Their rice and indigo plantations stretched 150 miles along the Atlantic coast from the Cape Fear River near Wilmington, North Carolina, to the Altamaha River south of Savannah and extended 20 to 30 miles inland. Their wealth, founded on grasping ambition and avarice, ruthlessly exploited human labor and nature alike. Indian men from as far away as the Gulf of Mexico and Mississippi River became full-time hunters and warriors trading deerskins and captives to Carolina merchants for guns, powder, iron tools, and other goods. By 1710, ships arrived in Charles Town laden with African slaves and departed with provisions and timber for Caribbean sugar planters and rice for European markets. More than any other place in the colonial South, the Atlantic economy shaped and transformed the work of Indian, European, and African men and women.

After planting food crops and constructing defensive works, settlers sought staple products. The colony's mixed population included great planters, small farmers, free whites, acculturated African slaves or Creoles from the Barbados, French Huguenots, indentured servants, and Indian slaves. Founders mistakenly believed Carolina's subtropical environment was well suited for Mediterranean crops of wine, cotton, silk, olive oil, citrus fruits, and ginger. Instead, provision crops of corn, hogs, and cattle and forest products of lumber, shingles, and barrel staves for sugar planters in the English West Indies became economic mainstays until the early 18th century. Labor forces comprising a mix of English indentured servants, enslaved blacks, and Indian captives (with British servants outnumbering other unfree workers 6 to 1 during the 1670s) worked in isolated fields and forests. They mixed English and African subsistence skills with local Indians' knowledge of the Lowcountry environment. Slave fishermen from the African coast built dugout canoes, cast fiber nets, and poisoned dammed streams to catch fish. Herdsmen from West African savannas became "cattle chasers," the first American cowboys. They burned underbrush to increase mast for free-ranging livestock, branded cattle to establish ownership, herded animals at night into cow pens or enclosures to protect against predators, and drove animals to Charles Town markets. After 1705, British subsidies secured ready markets for naval stores for maritime trade and the British Navy. Workers cut trees for ship masts, harvested turpentine from long-leaf pines, burned plies of pinewood covered with clay to make tar, and boiled tar to make pitch for waterproofing ropes and caulking ships.

Scarce labor, dispersed enterprises, and a mixed economy reduced class distinctions and loosened masters' control over unfree workers. Free immigrants received land warrants for every person they imported. Indentured servants comprised a third of early settlers and expected generous freedom dues—a suit of clothes, a barrel of corn, an ax, a hoe, and 100 acres of land from colonial authorities—to start farms or ply skilled trades. Little distinguished labor routines between plantations and freeholdings. Slaveholders prized jacks-of-all-trades, not specialized laborers, and self-directed individuals, not regimented gangs. Slaves worked alone or in small groups alongside whites and enjoyed a frontier "sawbuck equality." Slave herdsmen followed wandering cattle through the woods and gained knowledge of the countryside. "Slaves set the pace of work, defined standards of workmanship, and divided labor among themselves, doubtless leaving a good measure of time for their own use," historian Ira Berlin concluded.[11] Slave-owners armed blacks in self-defense against Spanish invaders and Indian warriors, and military service became a pathway to freedom. Other Africans took flight to escape abuse or overwork taking their chances with local natives or forming maroon communities in swamps or in the backcountry. To reduce labor costs, owners provided slaves planting grounds to raise food, a common practice in the West Indies sugar islands. "There are many Planters who, to free themselves from the trouble of feeding and clothing their slaves," a cleric noted in 1712, "allow them one day in the week to clear ground and plant for themselves as much as will clothe and subsist them and their families."[12] Slaves turned this to their own advantage not only provisioning themselves and their families but also producing surpluses to trade with whites, Indians, and fellow slaves. Privileges became rights as slaves insisted on working for themselves on Saturday afternoons and Sundays. Men fished, hunted, and tended their hogs and cattle, while women kept poultry and marketed garden produce. Even after the rice revolution, most slaves avoided regimented labor.

The big money first came from the Indian trade. Deerskins were prized in Europe for book covers, gloves, belts, coats, work aprons, and hats. Indian hunters eagerly traded with Carolina merchants for European iron goods like knives, axes, fish hooks, and scissors that made daily life easier; blankets, clothing, and jewelry to warm and adorn bodies; West Indian rum for social pleasure; and guns and powder to kill game and raid enemies for captives. In the race for trade goods, Indian men waged war against deer violating restraints against over hunting and upsetting spiritual balances. "They make a great Carnage among the Deers," a Carolinian observed, "kill them for the sake of their Skins, and leave their Carsasses [rotting] in the Forrests."[13] By the early 1700s, merchants exported over 50,000 skins annually and this increased to 150,000 per year by mid-century. Trade enhanced Indian men's prestige as hunters and warriors, but added to women's tedious labor of processing skins into saleable hides. The most successful hunters acquired the most trade goods, eroding reciprocity and sharing and introducing class distinctions into village societies. As local herds declined, men traveled greater distances encroaching on rivals' hunting preserves and escalating forest wars. As long as rival merchants in Virginia, Carolina, Florida, and Louisiana wooed hunters, Indians enforced gift-giving protocols and hospitality as their price for doing business and overlooked their growing economic dependency.

Enslaved women and children also became trade goods. Carolina merchants mastered intricacies of Indian politics and cynically exploited intertribal rivalries to their own ends. Rival merchant groups armed trade partners and encouraged raids against enemies with promises of higher prices for war captives. Some Indian slaves became plantation laborers, comprising 14 percent of the 1710 population, but most ended up in Barbados or in other West

Cherokee delegation visiting London. War, peacemaking, and hunting were Native men's primary responsibilities. After the Cherokee War these chiefs on a good will tour to England in 1762 sport European clothes and silver gorgets, a type of pendent received as peace medals, but retain traditional facial tattoos and hairstyles. "Man-killer" (left) carries a metal hatchet and wampum belt; the central figure, a calumet or ritual pipe; and the chief on the right is identified as "Scalpper." (Smithsonian Institution, National Anthropological Archives, BAE GN 01063 H1.)

Indies islands where merchants exchanged them for enslaved Africans. Over time, trade terms turned to Indians' disadvantage. Merchants extended generous credit but required indebted consumers to continue raiding to obtain more captives or engage in proxy wars to eliminate trade rivals. Without guns and ammunition acquired only from traders, Indian warriors could not defend their villages. Unscrupulous merchants arbitrarily set prices, forced men to serve as unpaid porters, seized Indian children, and raped Indian women. Native populations plummeted as tens of thousands of Indians died from warfare, food shortages, or disease, or were enslaved. The southeast became a charnel house of destruction and death, as merchants' divide-and-conquer strategies crushed coastal Indian resistance and dispossessed their lands.

By 1715, rice cultivation made planting ground the most valuable resource. Slaveowners experimented with seeds from Madagascar and the East Indies in the 1690s and prized Gambian and Gold Coast slaves' familiarity with rice cultivation. Dryland rice required little capital but much labor to prepare, sow, cultivate, harvest, and process the delicate plant. A few planters experimented with irrigated rice cultivation on inland swamps by storing water in reservoirs to flood fields. Clearing new land, preparing fields, and planting provisions occupied early months of the year. In April and May, gangs of male and female slaves planted seeds in holes made with their heels covering seeds with their feet as in Africa or in trenches dug with hoes. Rice fields required continual weeding with hands and hoes and guns to scare away birds. Harvesting began in mid-September. Cut plants were left to dry, then bundled and stacked or hauled to barns to be threshed with wooden flails or trodden with horses to remove the grain. Slave women used African-style flat fanning baskets made of rush and pine needles to winnow grain from chaff. Pounding grain with mortars and pestles, another African technique, was the most arduous work. The pestle's sharp end removed outer husks and flat end polished the grain. Rice planters purchased tens of thousands of African slaves directly from English traders, and blacks soon replaced white servants. By 1710, blacks outnumbered whites in Carolina, and 10 years later, the ratio was 3 to 1 in rice-growing districts. One visitor thought Carolina "looks more like a negro country than like a country settled by white people."[14] Within a generation, Carolina turned from a society with slaves to the most deeply slave society in the colonial South.

Women hulling rice. Slaves adapted African rice-processing equipment on Lowcountry plantations, including reed baskets for winnowing, or separating chaff from the grain, and mortars and pestles, shown here, for hulling, or cracking the outer husk. Locally made tools and traditional methods continued into the early 20th century as this photograph from Sapelo Island, Georgia, shows. (Vanishing Georgia Collection, sap093, Georgia Archives, Morrow, Georgia.)

LOUISIANA

The French established Louisiana to link France's Great Lakes fur traders to West Indies sugar planters and to outflank Spanish territorial claims, Carolina traders, and English settlers. Expanding from Biloxi and Mobile on the Gulf of Mexico into the interior Alabama–Tombigbee–Mobile, Mississippi, and Red rivers, by the 1720s, a handful of administrators, merchants, and soldiers established far-flung posts, and Canadian *coureurs de bois* (or fur trappers) traversed the countryside. The economy mixed subsistence with Indian trade in deerskins, corn, and slaves; forest industries, lumber, pitch, and tar; and provisioning. A thriving illicit coastal trade sent corn, beans, vegetables, guns, and ammunition from Louisiana for horses and gold from Spanish Los Adeas, Pensacola, and Saint Augustine. For even longer than in Florida, scattered male French settlers depended on imported food or provisions purchased from local natives. Indian consumers, however, preferred the more abundant, higher quality, and lower priced English goods. The French countered their disadvantages by mastering Indian languages, exchanging gifts, and promising to end the Indian slave trade. Petty traders married Indian women for sexual companionship, domestic workers to process deerskins, and kin connections into native villages. Male settlers avoided plantation work and learned horticultural, hunting, and gathering skills from natives and lived like Indians in the forests and swamps. The resulting liaisons between French men and native women produced hybrid economies and many mixed children.

Trade reoriented natives' balance between subsistence and commercial labor. Men spent more time hunting deer and women worked longer hours processing deerskins in addition to farming and gathering. European goods spread throughout Native America changing subsistence labor. Upper Creeks and Alabamans north of Mobile, Quapaws and Chickasaws on the Upper Mississippi, and Caddo at Natchitoches traded deerskins and food and raised cattle for guns, ammunition, metal goods, and rum. Spanish horses and French muskets transformed lives of the Pawnees, Wichitas, and Comanches, who became Great Plains equestrians: buffalo hunters and fierce warriors who defended their independence for over a century. Deer were sparse or overhunted in the small gulf coast societies the French called *petites nations*. Weakened by epidemic disease and needing French protection, these natives became day laborers and hunting guides for the French and sold corn, fish, game, and handicrafts in New Orleans and at trade posts.

Hoping to revive the floundering colony, the Compagnie des Indies (a private trading concern) took control of Louisiana in 1719 with ambitious plans to recruit settlers and slaves and promote agricultural development. Over the next decade, the company imported almost 6,000 enslaved Africans (mostly Senegambian men) and 2,500 *engagés* (or laborers, a mix of indentured servants, paupers, and criminals). New Orleans became the colony's political and commercial hub. Company officials deployed slaves and servants to construct levees, canals, ditches, fortifications, docks, and buildings and clear forests and swamps to plant foodstuffs, rice, indigo, and tobacco. With a large proportion of nonproducers in Louisiana's population, slaves, servants, and hired Indians workers profitably raised rice, corn, fruit trees, and vegetables, which men hauled or canoed to New Orleans markets for sale to local consumers. Some slaves were apprenticed as blacksmiths, wheelwrights, masons, and carpenters and eventually dominated urban skilled trades. A few Atlantic Creoles purchased their freedom or were manumitted for military service in suppressing Indian rebellions. Louis Congo became free as the colony's executioner, and Samba's freedom arose from serving as a translator and company plantation overseer.

Louisiana failed to become a plantation colony as neither tobacco nor indigo proved viable over the long run, and yellow fever and malaria decimated the population and demoralized settlers. Unruly servants and slaves resisted the onerous regimen of staple production and overseers' physical abuse. They sought refuge among New Orleans' black population or fled to the swamps where they established subsistence economies trading game, pelts, and stolen goods with local Indians. The final crisis came in 1729 when the Natchez, fed up with French encroachments on prime riverine planting grounds and their warriors recently augmented by runaway servants and slaves, attacked nearby plantations and killed over 200 French settlers. After a slave militia pacified the *petites nations,* the governor deployed them against the Natchez. Aided by Choctaw warriors, the mixed force crushed Natchez resistance, but in the process company control ended.

With dreams of a plantation empire on the Lower Mississippi River Valley crushed, Louisiana's polyglot 1731 population of 2,000 soldiers, convicts, vagrants, servants, and immigrants and 3,800 slaves developed a frontier exchange economy. Slave imports and free migration fell (by 1760, there were only 4,000 Europeans and 5,000 slaves in the colony) and Indian, French, and black subsistence producers traded goods, services, and knowledge. Material conditions were modest, but abundant resources and varied foodstuffs ensured collective survival and opportunities to improve one's lot. Indians, settlers, and slaves mixed subsistence labor with producing commercial goods: deerskins for overseas markets; timber, shingles, naval stores, and cattle to the West Indies; and foodstuffs sold in New Orleans, home to a quarter of the colony's nonnative population. "The forms of production practiced by settlers and slaves in colonial Louisiana resembled those long used by Lower Mississippi Valley Indians," historian Daniel Usner, Jr., concludes, "mainly because such a mixture of farming, hunting, fishing, and gathering protected them from the environmental and economic uncertainties of living in a strange land."[15]

Slaves' skills and independence increased. One planter's slave was "a black-smith, mason, cooper, roofer, strong long sawyer, mixing with these a little of the rough carpentry with the rough joinery."[16] Male slave teamsters, cattle drovers, and boatmen gained knowledge of the countryside and established contacts with local natives and with fellow blacks in New Orleans. Facing a less oppressive regime, slaves extracted rights to provision and planting grounds, keep poultry, hunt, fish, and have Sundays and sometimes Saturdays to work for themselves. The fruits of their labor improved diets and slave women marketed small surpluses of foodstuffs, poultry, eggs, baskets, and pottery in New Orleans. Men sold cotton, tobacco, game, and fish or earned money as watermen, sawyers, and farm laborers on their own time. Slaves in New Orleans had even more opportunities to earn money as women performed domestic labor and marketed goods and men hired themselves out as teamsters, dockworkers, artisans, and boatmen. By 1774, courts defended slaves' independent economic activity, citing a well-established "custom, use and style for all the Negroes . . . in the cities to work for themselves . . . without being obligated to pay anything to their masters."[17] A few slaves won the right to hire their own time by contracting independently for work and paying most of what they earned to their owners. It was but a small step toward freedom.

MATURING OF THE PLANTATION SOUTH

The plantation revolution consolidated elite planters' economic and political power. Their enormous holdings of land and African slaves greatly expanded the area of tobacco and rice cultivation, and their operations' scale cushioned temporary price declines and encouraged diversification that increased self-sufficiency and income. Large planters used their political influence to obtain huge land grants and passed laws stripping away all legal protections from slaves. Merchants imported fresh Africans, who soon replaced most whites in the fields and redefined free women's work roles. According to historian Ira Berlin, slaves "faced higher levels of discipline, harsher working conditions, and greater exploitation" and "worked longer, harder, and with less control over their own lives" than earlier generations of workers.[18] By mid-century, slaves also raised wheat in the northern Chesapeake and indigo in the Lowcountry. Some slaves, especially acculturated American-born Creoles, escaped full-time fieldwork, as women became domestic and textile workers and men artisans, carters, and watermen. With planters monopolizing the best lands and their slaves acquiring more skills, whites' economic horizons narrowed. Common planters relied on wealthy neighbors for credit, crop marketing, store goods, and occasional employment. Poor whites eked out livelihoods as day laborers or as scratch farmers on waste tracts or sought frontier land.

After 1720, tobacco cultivation spread into the Piedmont and the Southside, located below the James River, as tidewater planters with less fertile soils shifted to general farming. Planters deployed overseers, white laborers, and newly purchased Africans (mostly men and youths) to the arduous work of clearing trees and brush; planting corn, tobacco, and fruit trees; constructing roads; and building houses. While saltwater Africans possessed skills in hoe cultivation and iron tools, few were familiar with tobacco. Tutored by acculturated slaves on tidewater plantations or by white laborers in upcountry work gangs, new Africans resisted work regimens by running off in small groups or by feigning ignorance. "Let a hundred Men shew him how to hoe, or drive a Wheelbarrow," a visitor to a Maryland plantation noted, "he'll still take the one by the bottom, and the Other by the Wheel."[19]

Tobacco required closely supervised labor—careless handling ruined delicate leaves—so owners grouped slaves into gangs of four to eight workers based on gender, age, and skill. In the 1740s, half of all slaves lived in units of 10 or less, and most owners worked alongside their slaves personally overseeing their work. My tobacco was "under my own eye," one planter wrote, "and [I] may say I saw almost every plant from the planting to the prizing and striping off."[20] Planters expanded production by sending gangs to new planting grounds on plantations or to distant frontier quarters. Male slave foremen or "headmen" set work paces. Only planters with over 20 slaves hired white overseers to manage daily operations. Most were young men or aspiring small planters, who were paid in shares of tobacco and corn and in cash for extra work such as blacksmithing or their wives' midwifery and sewing. Pressed to expand production, overseers drove slaves "from daylight until the dusk of the evening and some part of the night, by moon or candlelight, during the winter."[21] Saturdays became workdays, and holidays were reduced to Christmas, New Year's Day, and Whitsunday. During evenings, slaves shelled and ground corn, stripped tobacco leaves, and chopped wood. They set out tobacco plants in the rain, stayed up all night tending fires critical for tobacco curing, and worked cold winter days clearing land, grubbing stumps and roots, and repairing fences and buildings. Children as young as 9 fetched water, fed chickens, weeded, chased off birds, and wormed tobacco. Labor gangs raised corn and other foodstuffs, reducing the importance of slaves' provision grounds.

In the 1750s, large planters in the northern Chesapeake raised wheat and corn as market crops. Small grains complemented seasonal demands of tobacco cultivation, but required fields cleared of stumps and roots and thoroughly prepared soils. After tobacco harvests, slaves sowed seeds by hand on fields raked with harrows. Wheat required little attention in the fall and spring, but ripe dry grains had to be harvested quickly between summer storms. Coordinated work teams of male cradlers with sickles or scythes cut dry wheat on hot July days, followed by several women and children gathering and stacking the sheaves. In the fall and winter, slaves threshed the grain by beating it with flails or treading it with oxen. A few large planters acquired horse-drawn plows and rakes; increased numbers of horses, oxen, and sheep; sowed oats, clover, and timothy as winter feed; collected manure; and gathered hay and corn fodder. Greater attention to animal husbandry and small grains added new chores, increased the amount of ground to cultivate, and speeded up work tempos.

Unlike tobacco, which required steady work throughout the year, general farmers needed flexible labor forces that varied with seasonal cultivation needs; carters to haul hay, manure, and wheat; millers to grind grain into flour and meal; and coopers to fabricate tight barrels. Planters initially hired whites for skilled work: men as carpenters, carters, blacksmiths, tanners, gunsmiths, shoemakers, leatherworkers, tailors, and contractors and women for spinning, weaving, sewing, and midwifery. Neighbors' sons and landless men worked alongside slaves clearing land, ditching, fencing, and during plantings and harvests. Slaveowners hired local slaves when shorthanded and hired out their surplus slaves for short periods. Planters added grist and saw mills, distilleries, tan yards, artisan and weaving shops, and stores to their operations. They hired overseers' wives to teach spinning, weaving, and sewing to slave women and artisans to train male slaves in masonry, carpentry, coopering, blacksmithing, shoemaking, and other skills. Eighteen-year-old James Madison, father of the fourth president, inherited Montpelier in 1741 and relied on skilled whites and a relative's slave to "set up hogsheads" for tobacco, build a poultry coop and brandy casks for his still, and make staves for a corn tub. Ten years later, his slaves had mastered these tasks. George and Peter, skilled slave carpenters, were hired out to neighbors, and Moses, a slave blacksmith, supervised a neighborhood shop and foundry.

Labor gangs became smaller and more specialized on mixed plantations, individualizing and making sex-specific the nature and locations of work. Some slave men on large estates escaped tedious hoe work by becoming plowman, mowers, stablemen, carters, tailors, and construction workers, developing pride in their skills and greater independence through self-directed labor. Teamsters and boatmen hauled tobacco and wheat to warehouses and market towns and returned with tales of life beyond the neighborhood and items to trade on the side. Watermen plied rivers, bays, and estuaries carrying goods, ferrying passengers, and catching fish to sell. Men hired out for a few days or weeks to their owners' neighbors and relatives deepened ties between local slaves and experienced different standards of work and of treatment. Annual hires to ironmongers and to town dwellers broadened experiences in independent labor and knowledge of a wider world. Yet, even skilled men were deployed to the fields during harvests and at other critical times.

Slave women increasingly dominated field labor. They often worked in all-female gangs, clearing brush, planting, weeding, and doing repair work. They replaced white female servants in households as domestic and textile workers, racializing class and gender identities. Only poor white women worked in the ground, while common planters' wives labored within and around their houses tending gardens, dairies, and poultry; preserving and preparing food; cleaning; making clothes; and childrearing. Wealthy planters' wives, although freed from the drudgery of housewifery, managed complex domestic operations and oversaw many slave women, typically the young and the elderly, whose labor was essential for providing lavish hospitality and entertainment necessary to advance their husbands' political ambitions and social prominence. Slave women did the work of gardening, tending cows and poultry, preserving food, making butter, cooking, baking, cleaning, and

Slave women working. In the 18th century, enslaved men performed most skilled labor, while female slaves worked fields, including arduous hoeing of new planting ground between tree stumps. A rail fence encloses the field from stray animals. The overseer's tailored jacket, long pants, and boots contrasts with enslaved women's coarse loose petticoats and bare feet. (Watercolor by Benjamin Henry Latrobe, "An Overseer Doing His Duty near Fredericksburg, Virginia," 1798 [1960.108.1.3.21]. Maryland Historical Society, Baltimore.)

waiting on guests, but plantation mistresses supervised the larder, planned menus, and organized household routines. Hired free and enslaved contractors built individual buildings for cooking, smoking meats, washing clothes, dairying, and weaving. As a result, white families' private living spaces became separate from black women's workplaces.

Full employment and close supervision curtailed slaves' independence, yet slaves exacted small concessions in exchange for laboring to enrich masters. Slaves had "an acre of ground and all Saturday to raise grain and poultry for themselves."[22] They secured the right to hunt, fish, and forage in woods and rivers; keep gardens and hogs; pass skills down to their children; keep "slaves' time" on Saturday afternoons, Sundays, and holidays; be paid for overwork and for goods produced on their own; and engage in independent trading. Slaves sold poultry, eggs, and handicrafts to owners for cash; traded surpluses with local storekeepers and itinerant peddlers for cloth, fancy goods, and rum; and swapped items with each other. Slaves prized the small fruits of their labor. Overseers who altered customary privileges were met with malingering, shoddy work, broken tools, truancy, protests to masters, or burned barns and storehouses.

The rice revolution transformed the Lowcountry with hurricane force. Slaves developed swamp and tidal rice cultivation and extended production into Georgia after the ban on slavery ended in 1749 and to East Florida, acquired by the British in 1763. Annual exports soared from 400,000 pounds in 1700 to 50 million pounds by mid-century. Planters abandoned upland rice fields where success depended on unpredictable rainfall for inland swamps, imported slaves wholesale, and deployed them to the hard work of draining marshes and constructing irrigation reservoirs to periodically flood rice fields to control weeds. Rice did not exhaust the soil, but investing in these labor-intensive improvements required at least 30 working hands. By mid-century, planters harnessed tides on coastal rivers to control the ebb and flow of irrigation and replenish fields. They also mastered the intricacies of indigo cultivation. Processing the delicate plant's leaves made a deep blue dye so valuable to British textile manufacture that the government provided a bounty for growing it. Indigo thrived on the old upland rice fields and its labor requirements complimented rice.

Rice was a demanding master, "only fit for slaves," according to one observer, "and I think the hardest work I have seen them engaged in."[23] It required not only physical stamina to endure brutal conditions but also many skills. Men and women spent numerous days barefoot in knee-deep malarial muck under broiling sun fending off insects to sow rice seeds, weed tender plants, and chase off flocks of birds. Ax-wielding men cleared swampland and swung picks and shovels to dig miles of canals, levees, dams, and ditches and controlled water flows with wooden floodgates based on African hollow-log and plug designs. Tedious threshing, winnowing, and, especially, pounding filled winter days and evenings while preparations for the next crop began. Men transported bagged rice on small boats to Charles Town. Planters' profits depended on enslaved women's endurance and men's skills in maintaining elaborate irrigation networks and sluice gates, determining when to flood and drain fields, and navigating lowcountry waterways.

Indigo's seven-month cultivation cycle introduced new miseries. Slaves sowed seed in early April on cleared fields, and plants required constant hoeing to remove weeds and insect pests. They picked leaves as they ripened and placed them into a tub (called "steeper") to ferment while constantly pumping, beating, and stirring the putrid mixture with wooden paddles. They drained the bluish liquid into a second vat ("beater") and continued stirring. At just the right moment, they poured the liquid into a third tub with limewater, which precipitated a blue sediment that slaves successively strained, dried, and cut into blocks for shipment. The continuous process was "both demanding and delicate," historian Ira Berlin notes, "requiring brute strength and a fine hand to create just the right density, texture, and brilliance of color."[24] Planters hired white artisans to train slave men in carpentry, masonry, cooperage, and mechanics to construct the vats and outbuildings and maintain pumps.

Unlike tobacco's labor gangs, tasking prevailed in rice cultivation. Under this system, slaves had a specified daily work quota; after completing their stint, their time was their own. The task system arose from the nature of rice cultivation and the Lowcountry's environment and demography. Rice plants were hardy, and slaves' labor output was easily measured eliminating need for close monitoring. Masters abandoned the sickly swamps during summers for Charles Town, turning the countryside into black enclaves. They relied on slave drivers to supervise daily work and on white overseers, usually young single men, to manage plantations. Since overseers turned over often, drivers acquired detailed knowledge about each field's fertility and each laborer's abilities and mediated disputes between masters and slaves. Some drivers were in charge of plantations. Gradually, planters and slaves negotiated a fair day's stint: a quarter of an acre per healthy adult for planting and weeding rice, so many yards of canal to clean or bushels of grain to pound, and so on, with women rated at three-fourth share and youths at one-half share. Slaves responded to new overseers' attempts to increase work quotas with truancy, slowdowns, sabotage, lodging complaints to masters—even murder, on occasion.

After finishing their daily tasks, often in the early afternoons for men, slaves worked for themselves. High profits—in excess of 20 percent in good years—focused planters' concerns solely on rice and indigo production, leaving slaves time and land to provision themselves. On afternoons and Sundays, adults and children raised corn, potatoes, peanuts, okra, melons, and other vegetables; grew rice on their own account; tended poultry and hogs; trapped, hunted, and fished; fabricated baskets and other handicrafts; and hired themselves out for wages. Slaves traded goods with one another and sold them to owners or to local peddlers for cash, clothing, or liquor. Masters acknowledged slaves' property rights. Henry Laurens, a rice planter, directed his overseer to make up shortfalls in provisions by purchasing "of our own Negroes all that you know Lawfully belongs to themselves at the lowest price they will sell it for."[25] Fisherman in African-designed dugouts used nets, hooks and lines, drugging, and weirs to establish a virtual monopoly on the Charles Town fish trade. Watermen carried slave produce to urban markets. Unlike Chesapeake slaves, who struggled to retain customary rights, the task system expanded slaves' independent labor and the slave economy, required many skills, increased knowledge of the countryside, and improved slaves' material lives.

Rice and indigo were great planters' crops, but small Chesapeake slaveowners combined tobacco with general farming and skilled trades. Common planters followed similar cultivation routines as their wealthier neighbors, but only the latter had capital to invest in wheat cultivation or animal husbandry, operate gristmills, or purchase spinning wheels and looms to make cloth. Farmers depended on them for credit, tools, grist milling, foodstuffs, blacksmithing, carting goods, tobacco marketing, and employment during winters and at harvest times. By mid-century, numerous country stores encouraged bartering tobacco and surplus farm products especially butter, eggs, poultry, corn, and meat for manufactured goods. Slaves never monopolized the most skilled crafts in the Chesapeake, and whites earned money as wheelwrights, blacksmiths, tanners, cobblers, tailors, sewers, house carpenters, joiners, and masons in addition to provisioning their families from farming. A denser free population stimulated economic development and deepened ties between white producers creating a social economy, a network of local exchanges of goods, services, and labor. Slavery's spread united whites of all ranks; three-fourths of free household heads in old areas of the Chesapeake owned at least one slave. Farmers, artisans, shopkeepers, their sons, and, occasionally, their wives and daughters worked alongside enslaved farm laborers, craft workers, and shop assistants. Once the black population grew more from natural increase than through purchasing saltwater Africans, purchasing a few slaves promised small owners that over time they would acquire a numerous labor force and join planters' ranks.

Small farmers in older coastal areas faced narrowing economic opportunities. Continued population growth and planters' large land reserves increased land prices, shrank average farm sizes to under 200 acres, and swelled ranks of the landless to one-third of white households. Leasing land became common, especially on

Maryland's Eastern Shore and Virginia's Northern Neck. Some were multiyear developmental leases requiring only nominal rents. With tenants clearing and developing land at no cost, landowners benefitted from rising land values. Tenants grew tobacco and small grains and raised livestock to pay rents, support families, and acquire money to purchase their own land, perhaps from their landlord. All family members did farmwork and most earned wages as part-time domestic workers, sewers, weavers, ditchers, harvest laborers, carters, lumber workers, and watermen or sought work in nearby towns. Rapid settlement of the Piedmont and the Southside in Virginia and the Carolina up-country after 1720 opened up abundant inexpensive land. Planters with political connections acquired huge tracts of frontier land, which they sold in small parcels on credit to raise capital for developing the rest of their property. Immigrants acquired land from headright claims, and some overseers on upcountry quarters received payment in land. By the time of the American Revolution, at least three-fourths of free householders in newly settled areas owned land and many were small slaveowners.

Unfree whites, convict laborers, and apprentices comprised a small part of rural laborers in the Chesapeake. Planters sought convicts despite their unsavory reputations as they served longer terms, 7 to 14 years compared to an average of 5 years for indentured servants, and lacking family or friends had little recourse against overwork or abusive treatment. Local officials apprenticed orphan boys and widows' sons to local artisans, joiners and house carpenters, bricklayers, and shoemakers to learn the trade until age 21 and girls to age 18 to learn the "art and mysterie of housewifery," including textile production. Youths promised obedience to masters and attentiveness to their work in return for receiving "sufficient dyet, apparell, washing, and lodging" and either wages in their final year or freedom dues of cash, corn sufficient for a year, a set of tools, or a suit of clothes. Some masters also promised to "endeaver to bring the said apprentice up in a Christian manner and to learn him to read and write" and "all other things necessary to his souls' health."[26] Ex-female servants became domestics, sewing and mending clothes, or housewives after marrying. Males found employment as general farm laborers and overseers, worked in craft shops, rented land, or sought economic opportunities in towns or in the backcountry.

With the exception of Carolina, where half of the population lived in Charles Town in 1720, few colonial Southerners were urban dwellers. No more than 5 percent of the total population lived in towns, which ranged in size in 1770 from a few hundred (New Bern) to over 10,000 (Charles Town). Except for Williamsburg and New Bern, capitals of Virginia and North Carolina, respectively, and sleepy villages until their legislatures were in session, commerce—the overseas Atlantic and West Indian and hinterland and coastal trades and retailing—was colonial towns' lifeblood. Tobacco marketing was scattered at planters' wharves, inspection warehouses, and interior stores, stunting town development; yet in the 1750s, Williamsburg still boasted a half dozen taverns and 94 artisans working in 27 different trades, mostly in construction, clothing, and luxury goods. Slaves, apprentices, and black and white free laborers worked side-by-side in artisans' shops, merchants' stores, docks and shipyards, taverns, and homes of the wealthy. Rice and wheat needed central urban places to collect and transport these bulky cargoes to the West Indies and to Europe. From the beginning, Charles Town merchants monopolized Lowcountry exports and imports of manufactured goods and slaves. (Over half of all Africans imported into the colonial South before 1770 arrived at Sullivan's Island in Charles Town harbor, making it the slave trade's Ellis Island.) After 1750, wheat and grain trade in the Upper Chesapeake spawned urban growth at Baltimore, Maryland and Alexandria, Fredricksburg, and Norfolk, Virginia, where wheat and corn were milled, packed in tight barrels, and loaded onto ships.

Expanding trade required numerous laborers to construct and maintain docks, wharves, and warehouses; carpenters, blacksmiths, caulkers, ropewalkers, riggers, and leather workers to build, outfit, and repair ships; chandlers and coopers to supply oceangoing vessels; stevedores to load and unload ships; and draymen to haul commodities to port towns and imported goods to country stores. Tavern workers provided lodging, food, and entertainment for the respectable, while the physical needs of seamen and the "lower sort" were met by grogshop keepers and by prostitutes. Rising wealth of great planters and middling folk increased demand for fine consumer goods provided by skilled master craftsmen (and their journeymen and apprentices), who fashioned wigs, furniture, guns, gold and silver objects, coaches, and watches. Shopkeepers displayed the latest imports of women's and men's fashions, books, stationary, tableware, and cutlery, and grocers supplied fancy confectionaries, tea, coffee, wines, provisions, and exotic foods to satisfy urban consumers' palates. In the fine homes of prosperous urban craftsmen, professionals, merchants, and Lowcountry planters, numerous domestic workers supported gracious dining, entertaining, and refined living. Most house lots were large enough for gardens, fruit trees, dairies, and poultry that provisioned household members.

Towns were one of the few places white women earned independent livelihoods, especially in occupations associated with women's work. Widows successfully continued family businesses after their husbands' deaths, indicating they had been business partners or "deputy husbands" all along. Women started businesses of their own. Christina Campbell and Janet Vobe ran respectable taverns in Williamsburg, where guests enjoyed lodging, food, and entertainment, and "widow Flynn" in Annapolis offered "everything necessary for the Accommodation of such gentlemen and ladies as choose private lodgings."[27] Entrepreneurs opened groceries, confectionaries, millinery, and mantua-making shops catering to female customers. Katharine Bower in Charles Town offered "a very neat assortment of millinery goods" in 1773, including "fashionable caps," several varieties of lace, sashes and ribbons, fans, gloves, handkerchiefs, shoes, pins, needles, and more, all offered on the "lowest terms."[28] In the 1760s and early 1770s, there were 36 millinery and dry goods shops owned by women in Charles Town alone. The consumer revolution raised expectations of dress and personal cleanliness and provided women employment in washing, starching, and repairing fine garments. Poor free women sought employment as shop assistants, sewers, domestic servants, and prostitutes.

Enslaved and free blacks' labor sustained urban economies. Blacks comprised about half of town populations and were ubiquitous at docks and shipyards; in streets, shops, and markets; and inside homes of the wealthy. Eliza Pinckney enumerated her domestic slaves' daily work:

> I shall keep Young Ebba to do the drudgery part, fetch wood, and water, and scour, and learn as much as she is capable of Cooking and Washing. Mary-Ann Cooks, makes my bed, and makes my punch. Daphne works and makes the bread, old Ebba boils the cow's victuals, raises and fattens the poultry. Moses is imployed from breakfast until 12 o'clock without doors, after than in the house. Pegg washes and milks.[29]

Most urban slaves worked closely alongside their owners, as urban slaveholdings were small and houses cramped. In Charles Town and Norfolk, shipwrights, rope makers, caulkers, building contractors, coopers, tailors, milliners, and other artisans owned or hired skilled slaves. Master artisans rebuffed white journeymen's demands to eliminate slave workers, claiming that "his Majesty's Ships have been repaired and refitted only by the assistance of Our Slaves, And . . . without these Slaves the worst Consequences might Ensue."[30]

Enslaved men and a few women bargained to hire their own time. Under this arrangement, slaves found their own employment, paid owners a set amount each week, and kept the remainder for themselves. Although illegal, independent working often led to independent living once slave hirers convinced masters to allow them to find their own housing. Black urban enclaves harbored runaways: skilled slaves from the countryside knew labor-short urban employers asked few questions about their status. Slave women found self-employment as cooks, seamstresses, mantua-makers, weavers, and especially as petty traders. The task system provided abundant provisions to Charles Town's urban markets. Black women at the Lower Market hired their own time as they were "seated there from morn 'til night, and buy and sell on their accounts, what they please in order to pay their wages, and get as much more for themselves as they can."[31] Like their African foremothers, slave women marketed garden produce, baked goods, dairy products, fruit, poultry, oysters, baskets, and trays, while men dominated butchering and fish mongering. Many of their customers were slaves, as black cooks made daily trips to resupply their mistress' larders.

BACKCOUNTRY

West of the plantation South were the "back settlements," the largest, most diverse, and most rapidly growing part of the colonial South. Home to land-poor English colonials from the coast and recent immigrants; Germans from the Palatine and Swiss cantons; Scotch-Irish from Ulster; Scots; French Huguenots; and others, who poured into the frontier in the 1720s just after—and sometimes before—government officials extinguished native possessors and established land titles. Recruited by colonial governors to buffer plantation districts from Indian and Spanish attacks, by eastern land speculators offering tracts on generous terms, and by religious leaders with huge land grants for group settlements, abundant cheap land promised modest economic independence. By 1770, 250,000 people lived in the backcountry, a vast region of rolling land that stretched from western Maryland through Virginia's

Shenandoah Valley and eastern Alleghenies to the vast Carolina and Georgia Piedmont. Group migration, widespread small landholdings, dispersed settlements, mixed farming, and family labor prevailed across different ethnic groups and locales. An extension of frontier settlements in southeastern Pennsylvania by German and Scotch-Irish settlers, who either had just arrived in Philadelphia or were born in the colonies, the southern backcountry also had precedents in early Virginia, South Carolina, and, especially, North Carolina. Economic connections linked backcountry settlers to the plantation South and Atlantic commerce, and settlers' woodland farming became a template for pioneer settlements in the Upper South and elsewhere after the American Revolution.

Sweat equity carved new farms from wilderness land. Adopting labor-saving clearing and planting methods—originally of Indian origin—from early settlers, migrants sought tracts of oak-hickory land near water courses, girdled trees, burned undergrowth, planted corn between stumps, pastured livestock in natural meadows, constructed log houses and barns, turned hogs into the woods, and became expert hunters and gatherers. Adding small grains, poultry, fruit trees, vegetables, flax, hemp, milk cows, cattle, and sheep increased subsistence safety nets. Without servants or slaves, every family member spent long days and many evenings on tasks that varied with the seasons but followed traditional gender conventions. Wives and daughters' labor was domestic and followed a weekly schedule. "Ordinary women [in Carolina] take care of Cows, Hogs, and other small Cattle," John Oldmixon reported in 1708, "make Butter and Cheese, spin Cotton and Flax, help to sow and reap Corn, wind Silk from the Worms, gather Fruit, and look after the House" and also plant gardens; tend poultry and dairies; grind meal; gather berries, roots, and plants; preserve vegetables and fruit; prepare food; gather wood; process flax and wool; sew and repair clothes; weave cloth and coverlets; and provide hospitality.[32] Fathers and sons' labor was seasonal. They cut timber; cleared ground; constructed cabins, out buildings, and fences; worked forest industries; planted crops; tended livestock; slaughtered animals; hunted deer; trapped small game; fished; made hand tools; carted goods; and became blacksmiths, shoemakers, and carpenters. Only poverty or dire necessity sent wives into fields on a regular basis, but family work teams helped plant, shuck, and shell corn; stack and thresh small grains; process fruit; slaughter cattle and hogs; and preserve meat and process animal by-products.

No family survived by their own labor alone. Even isolated farmers relied on neighbors, often relatives or members of their ethnic group. They swapped tools; bartered foodstuffs, butter, eggs, and poultry for grinding corn, blacksmithing, weaving, and other services; helped with harvests; carted goods for one another; and loaned out sons and daughters for short labor stints. Cabin and barn raisings became neighborhood affairs with men cutting the timber, male neighbors raising the walls, women preparing food, and everyone frolicking afterward. Women assisted with childbirths and gathered to make the tedious work of spinning, sewing, and quilting social occasions. Physical isolation and poor roads created demand for farm services, and in every settlement, individuals added specialized crafts. Men were grist millers, weavers, tanners, leatherworkers, shoemakers, blacksmiths, carpenters, coopers, and tavern keepers. Women increased household manufactures, making soap and candles, spinning, weaving linen, and sewing. Skilled labor complemented seasonal farm routines and provided "credits" for store goods, labor, foodstuffs, and services. Neighborhood exchanges, not family self-sufficiency, provided economic security.

Until recently, most historians followed contemporary observers' biases that contrasted Germans' supposedly superior farming skills, their permanent residences, cleared fields, and sturdy barns, with allegedly improvident Scotch-Irish settlers' restlessness, primitive cabins, and slovenly patches. Although members of different ethnic groups settled near one another and retained their languages, religions, foodways, and social customs into the 19th century, everyone adapted to land abundance and labor scarcity. Pioneer woodland farmers followed "slash-and-burn" or long-fallow cultivation, according to historian Maldwyn A. Jones, or "the practice of clearing temporary fields in forests by chopping and firing the natural vegetation, planting crops for a brief time, and then letting the land revert to scrub forest."[33] They cultivated only small portions of their 100 to 400-acre tracts, leaving generous reserves for future use or to pass onto children. To elite easterners, extensive farming appeared wasteful and evidence of laziness. To settlers, shifting crops to freshly cleared tracts conserved labor. Frontier diversification increased economic security with 90 percent of labor supporting the family and meeting farm and livestock needs with only "leftovers" for local trade. Newcomers learned to grow New World corn, beans, squash, and tobacco. Herding became more important in the South's mild climate, where animals ranged freely in savannas, meadows, and pine barrens instead of being penned and fed grains and grasses. Pietists like the Lutheran Salzburgers, who settled in Ebenezer, Georgia, in the 1730s, or the Moravians, who obtained a 100,000-acre tract in the North Carolina Piedmont in the 1750s, labored communally, but, like their neighbors, practiced diversified farming and opened numerous artisan shops.

The location and timing of frontier settlements created different local economies and labor routines, but even residents in the newest, most isolated areas were not cut off from Atlantic commerce. They sold surplus commodities to peddlers and local merchants for imported goods like salt, sugar, bar iron, or fine cloths unavailable locally, and for cash to pay taxes and debts to creditors. Market crops varied depending on location but favored goods that could travel over rough roads in Conestoga wagons or down rivers in flat-bottomed bateaux. By 1700, North Carolina small farmers, the first backcountry settlers, marketed tobacco or forest products (masts, barrels, tar, pitch, or turpentine), deerskins, corn, cattle and hogs, and salted meat. Access to watercourses or to ferries and improved roads—notably the Great Wagon Road stretching over 400 miles from Philadelphia to the Georgia Piedmont—encouraged market production. Subsidies encouraged hemp production, and colonial wars increased demand for foodstuffs and forage at frontier posts. Drovers moved large herds of cattle and hogs from the Shenandoah Valley and the Carolina and Georgia Piedmont to Philadelphia, Alexandria, or Charles Town, snapping their whips to control animals and giving rise to the term "cracker." Wealthier farmers built gristmills, distilleries, and tan yards; opened ordinaries and blacksmith shops; or became leatherworkers and coopers that added to farm income. Over 20 inland towns from Frederick, Maryland, to Augusta, Georgia, became market centers where farmers traded surplus products for store goods: Women earned cash and store credits by selling poultry, eggs, butter, cheese, and linen; shopkeepers and artisans offered specialized goods and services; and merchants collected processed farm products and forwarded them to urban factors. By the 1760s, a quarter of farm production was in market crops that secured household independence, provided capital for farm improvements, and purchased consumer goods to raise living standards and respectability.

By 1750 in older settled areas and 20 years later in newer places, backcountry society acquired characteristics of the seacoast. Wealthy men from established families developed plantations from choice backcountry tracts inherited from land-speculator fathers and introduced slaves, servants, and commercial outlooks. They invested in iron furnaces, mines, and commercial gristmills; developed animal husbandry; increased cultivation of staple crops; and opened stores and taverns. Successful farmers acquired a slave or two and became backcountry gentry, integrated the region into the plantation South, and prepared the Lower Shenandoah Valley and the Carolina and Georgia Piedmont for slavery's spread during the post-1790 wheat and cotton boom. Yet, the backcountry's legacy—subsistence farming, family labor, neighborhood economies, and limited market involvement—were enduring and broad. Where the cotton revolution could not reach, it persisted in Appalachia until the early 20th century. Thousands of Upper South plain folk fled the planter revolution for the Ohio River Valley and the Lower Midwest turning backcountry traditions into American pioneering.

LABOR AND INDEPENDENCE

"Who can desire more content, that hath small means; or but only his merit to advance his fortune, than to tread, and plant that ground hee hath purchased by the hazard of his life?" John Smith prophesized about the New World in 1614, "what to such a minde can bee more pleasant, than planting and building a foundation for his Posteritie, gotte from the rude earth, by Gods blessing and his owne industrie . . . ?" Private ownership of "ground . . . purchased by the hazard of his life" and abundant land made economic independence possible for settlers, but only unremitting "industry" turned promise into reality. By 1770, slave plantations, family farms, and commercial towns had replaced a landscape long shaped by natives' communal labor. Freeholders enjoyed a higher standard of living in terms of food and material comfort than most Third World peoples today. For many unfree laborers, who comprised 80 percent of immigrants to the colonial South, work brought few rewards. Thousands of indentured servants arriving in the 17th century died before they could "tread and plant" ground for themselves, and tens of thousands of enslaved African in the next century spent their working lives "planting and building a foundation" only for their owners' "posterity."[34]

Work united colonial Southerners. As people whose livelihoods depended on the land, they shared common labor routines that changed with the seasons and were marked by times of intensity (planting and harvesting) and by slack times (holidays, festivals, and celebrations). Natives and settlers were enmeshed in trade relationships, which mixed subsistence and market labor to ensure collective survival and to acquire luxuries that soon became necessities. Over time, improved technologies, economic diversification, and specialized skills facilitated adapting to new environments and changing opportunities, but added new tasks to accomplish, increased the work pace, and lengthened the workday. Everyone worked. By age 8 or 9, children did lighter tasks, such as collecting wood, picking insects off plants, scaring birds, minding younger children—before becoming adult workers around age 15.

Work created intersecting divisions of class, race, and gender peculiar to the colonial South. Plain folk spent their lives performing manual labor in homes, fields, shops, and towns; genteel women and men avoided such work. Owning property enabled male household heads to control their "own industry" by directing the work of dependents—wives, children, servants, and slaves—whose labor was essential for improving land, ensuring household sufficiency, and raising living standards. Possessing land secured liberty from dependency on others; control over your own labor marked one's freedom. Enslaved women routinely did field labor; "respectable" women performed domestic work inside their homes and around yards; and plantation mistresses directed the labor of slaves and servants. Plantation diversification upgraded some black men's skills and expanded their horizons, while confining black women to repetitive drudgery. Planters and slaves contested the hours and pace of masters' time and the privileges and uses of slaves' time. For every colonial Southerner, work was central to daily life defining who you were and where you ranked in society.

NOTES

1. This chapter examines subsistence and market labor. Food preservation and preparation, clothing, and housing are discussed in Chapters 4 and 5.

2. William Strachey, *The History of Travel into Virginia Britania* (1612), ed. by Louis B. Wright and Virginia Freund, 2nd series, Vol. 103 (Cambridge: Hakluyt Society, 1953), 80, cited in Helen Rountree, *The Powhatan Indians of Virginia: Their Traditional Culture* (Norman: University of Oklahoma Press, 1989), 44, 45.

3. Charles D. Hudson, *The Southeastern Indians* (Knoxville, TN: University of Tennessee Press, 1976), 275.

4. George Chapman, Ben Johnson, and John Marston, *Eastward Hoe* (1605), cited in Alden Vaughan, *American Genesis: Captain John Smith and the Founding of Virginia* (Boston: Little Brown and Co., 1977), 20, 21; see illustration on p. 375.

5. John Smith, *Travels and Works of Captain John Smith,* 2 vols., ed. by Edward Arber and Arthur G. Bradley (Edinburgh: John Grant, 1910), II: 407, cited in Wesley Frank Craven, *The Southern Colonies in the Seventeenth Century, 1607–1689* (Baton Rouge: Louisiana State University Press, 1949), 69.

6. Smith, *Travels and Works,* II: 202, cited in Craven, *Southern Colonies,* 100.

7. James Revel, "The Poor Unhappy Transported Felon's Sorrowful Account of His Fourteen Years Transportation at Virginia in America," in *The Old Dominion in the Seventeenth Century: A Documentary History of Virginia, 1606–1689,* ed. by Warren M. Billings (Chapel Hill: University of North Carolina Press, 1975), 138.

8. For a summary of these debates, see Alden Vaughan, "The Origins Debate: Slavery and Racism in Seventeenth-Century Virginia," *Virginia Magazine of History and Biography* 97, no. 3 (July 1989): 311–354.

9. John H. Hahn, ed. and trans., "Translation of Alonso de Leturionto's Memorial to the King of Spain," *Florida Archaeology* 2 (1986), cited in David J. Weber, *The Spanish Frontier in North America* (New Haven, CT: Yale University Press, 1992), 172.

10. Henry Woodward, cited in Verner W. Crane, *The Southern Frontier, 1670–1732* (Ann Arbor: University of Michigan Press, 1956 [1929]), 13; see illustration on p. 21.

11. Ira Berlin, *Many Thousands Gone: The First Two Centuries of Slavery in North America* (Cambridge, MA: Harvard University Press, 1998), 68.

12. Cited in Berlin, *Many Thousands Gone,* 69.

13. William De Brahm, cited in Alan Taylor, *American Colonies: The Settling of North America* (New York: Penguin, 2001), 230.

14. R.W. Kelsey, ed., "Swiss Settlers in South Carolina," *South Carolina Historical and Genealogical Magazine* 23, no. 3 (July 1922): 90, cited in Philip D. Morgan, *Slave Counterpoint: Black Culture in the Eighteenth-Century Chesapeake and Lowcountry* (Chapel Hill, NC: University of North Carolina Press, 1998), 95. Historians dispute the importance of African skills in rice cultivation's origins. Daniel Littlefield, *Rice and Slaves: Ethnicity and the Slave Trade in Colonial South Carolina* (Baton Rouge: Louisiana State University Press, 1981) and Judith Carney, *Black Rice: The African Origins of Rice Cultivation in the Americas* (Cambridge, MA: Harvard University Press, 2001) emphasize continuities in cropping, processing, and equipment between West Africa and the Lowcountry with the latter giving special emphasis to women as bearers of specialized knowledge. Philip Morgan, in contrast, argues most Lowcountry slaves came from non-rice-growing areas of Africa, men outnumbered women, and tidal rice culture was unknown in West Africa and gives more credit to planter-directed experiments. For a summary of this debate, see David Eltis, Philip Morgan, and David Richardson, "Agency and Diaspora in Atlantic History: Reassessing the African Contribution to Rice Cultiva-

tion in the Americas," *American Historical Review* 112, no. 5 (December 2007): 1329–58.

15. Daniel H. Usner, Jr., *Indians, Settlers, and Slaves in a Frontier Exchange Economy: The Lower Mississippi Valley before 1783* (Chapel Hill: University of North Carolina Press, 1992), 155.

16. Laura L. Porteus, trans., "The Documents in Loppinot's Case, 1774," *Louisiana Historical Quarterly* 12 (1929), 82, cited in Berlin, *Many Thousands Gone*, 201.

17. Gerald L. St. Martin, ed. and trans., "A Slave Trial in Colonial Natchitoches, 1774," *Louisiana History* 28 (1987), 79, cited in Berlin, *Many Thousands Gone*, 206.

18. Cited in Berlin, *Many Thousands Gone*, 106; see illustration on p. 371.

19. "Eighteenth-Century Maryland as Portrayed in the 'Itinerant Observations' of Edward Kimber," *Maryland Historical Magazine* 51, no. 4 (1956): 327, 328, cited in Berlin, *Many Thousands Gone*, 120.

20. John Custis to Robert Cary, [1729], John Custis Letterbook, typescript, Research Library, Colonial Williamsburg Foundation, Williamsburg, VA, cited in Morgan, *Slave Counterpoint*, 187.

21. William Tatham, *American Husbandry*, ed. by Harry J. Carman (New York, 1939), 275, cited in Morgan, *Slave Counterpoint*, 191.

22. Thomas Anburey, *Travels Through the Interior Parts of America in a Series of Letters*, 2 vol. (London: William Lane, 1789), 2: 333, 334.

23. [Janet Shaw], *Journal of a Lady of Quality . . .* , ed. by Evangeline Walker Andrews and Charles McLean Andrews (New Haven, CT: Yale University Press, 1923), 194, cited in Morgan, *Slave Counterpoint*, 148.

24. Cited in Berlin, *Many Thousands Gone*, 148.

25. *Laurens Papers*, cited in Berlin, *Many Thousands Gone*, 166.

26. Orange County Court, Order Books, 1760–1775, passim; *Virginia Gazette*, (Williamsburg, VA.) 1745–1746, 1756, 1773–1774, passim.

27. *Maryland Gazette* (Annapolis), April 7, 1774, cited in Julia Cherry Spruill, *Women's Life and Work in the Southern Colonies* (New York: W. W. Norton and Company, 1972 [1938]), 294.

28. *South Carolina Gazette and Country Journal* (Charles Town), February 16, 1773, cited in Spruill, *Women's Life and Work*, 281.

29. Harriott Horry Ravenel, *Elizabeth Pinckney* (New York: C. Scribner's Sons, 1896), cited in Spruill, *Women's Life and Work*, 77.

30. Cited in Berlin, *Many Thousands Gone*, 156.

31. "The Stranger," *South Carolina Gazette* (Charles Town), September 24, 1772, cited in Morgan, *Slave Counterpoint*, 250.

32. John Oldmixon, *The British Empire in America . . .* (London, 1708), cited in Spruill, *Women's Life and Work*, 83; see illustration on p. 31.

33. Maldwyn A. Jones, "The Scotch-Irish in British America," in *Strangers within the Realm: Cultural Margins of the First British Empire*, ed. by Bernard Bailyn and Philip Morgan (Chapel Hill: University of North Carolina Press, 1991), 301.

34. John Smith, "A Description of New England . . . (1616)," in *The Complete Works of Captain John Smith,* 3 vols., ed. by Philip L. Barbour (Chapel Hill: University of North Carolina Press, 1991), I: 343, cited in Stephen Innes, "Fulfilling John Smith's Vision: Work and Labor in Early America," in *Work and Labor in Early America,* ed. by Stephen Innes (Chapel Hill: University of North Carolina Press, 1988), 3. See illustrations on pp. 142, 362, and 380 for visual transformation of the landscape.

3

FAMILIES

Families were the social foundations for daily life in the colonial South as they shaped day-to-day behavior between husbands and wives, parents and children, and household heads and dependents, and linked individuals to the community. Family members provided labor, emotional support, and sexual companionship and socialized the young. Family ideals, household composition, and kin relationships established rules concerning when and whom one could marry, appropriate sexual behavior, child-reading practices, sibling relationships, residence patterns, and possibilities of divorce. Gender constructions—what it meant to be a man or a woman—limned social roles within families. Because formal institutions were often weak in the colonial South, family and kin assumed many more responsibilities than families do today including subsistence, education, vocational training, social welfare, religious instruction, and elderly care. Family life both shaped and was altered by colonialism. Agricultural systems, migration, and the African slave trade transformed family life; yet Euro-Americans' decisions over allocating labor, property, and power among individuals and Indians' and Africans' reactions to conditions forced upon them mediated their impact on family life.[1]

Reflecting the colonial South's diverse cultures, family life varied along lines of race, ethnicity, and class. European households were "nuclear," comprising a husband, a wife, and children, and headed by men; for Native Americans and for Africans, lineage (descent from a common ancestor) grounded personal identity, defined living patterns, and established primary social bonds. European patriarchs favored sons over daughters and their first-born over younger children. In matrilineal Native societies, which traced dissent through females, husbands lived with their wives' clan and maternal uncles were more important than biological fathers in rearing sons. Atlantic Creole slaves utilized intercultural skills to create new families in the colonial South, while most enslaved Africans, historian Donald Wright notes, were village people "forcibly detached from the kinship networks that had been their social, economic, and psychological underpinnings in Africa."[2] Indian women enjoyed considerable sexual freedom before marriage and divorced unwanted husbands. European men harshly penalized women who transgressed the sexual double standard. Every child born to Indian mothers in matrilineal societies belonged to her clan. English men disinherited "bastard" children stripping mothers of parental rights, denied legal protection to slaves' marriages, and ignored parent–child ties in disposing of slaves. Diversity of family life increased over time as Native American families changed from contact with Europeans and later with Africans; as slaves from different places in Africa mingled and created new African American families; as Irish, Scots, French Huguenots, Germans, Jews, and others arrived in the colonial South; and as class differences increased with development of plantation economies. By 1750, families in the colonial South varied markedly in terms of household composition, gender roles, childrearing, labor, political influence, and ceremonial participation.

Many factors affected family life including changes in the population balance between men and women and between Indians, Europeans, and Africans; or an economic shift, for example, from the Indian slave trade to rice plantations; or differences in women's legal rights; or development of the Atlantic slave trade and slave codes; or colonies' immigration patterns. Comparing Native American, Euro-American, and Afro-American families in specific regions and their alterations over time highlights the colonial South's variegated family patterns and the dynamic forces shaping their evolution. Each group of families had different cultural traditions, took different structural forms, and followed different evolutionary trajectories.

NATIVE AMERICAN FAMILIES

Traditional Family Organization

Sharply gendered work roles in Indian society structured day-to-day family life. Men were hunters and warriors; women were farmers, foragers, and food preservers and preparers. Men spent many weeks far away from villages; women labored near their homes, gardens, and fields. Women had primary responsibilities for bearing and rearing children, keeping comfortable households, and maintaining village life and lineage continuity. Because women and men spent so much time with members of their own sex, they often had difficulty forming durable relationships across the gender divide. Even after marriage, men spent spare time between hunts and warfare with other men in council houses, ate apart from women, and occupied different spaces in their homes. Women's labor provided up to 90 percent of total calories Indians consumed. Women owned access to fields and their houses and received and controlled food distribution including meals provided to guests, hospitality essential for sustaining community.

In societies that did not recognize private property but measured wealth in surplus foodstuffs, women's roles as primary food providers enhanced their autonomy over sexuality, marriage choices, pregnancy, childrearing, and divorce. Menstruation and pregnancy rituals both acknowledged and contained women's enhanced spiritual power by separating the world of women and men. Native American children grew up knowing women as well as men provided food and heard stories of a female deity's gift of corn. Native American women possessed spiritual power, joined in ceremonies, and made decisions about war and peace. This did not make Indian societies matriarchies, or ones ruled by women; men were vital for providing meat, protecting women and children from harm, and engaging in diplomacy and trade with friends. "The man's world and the women's world were separate," anthropologist Helen C. Rountree concludes, "but reciprocal and therefore intertwined." Harmony required maintaining balance between women and men, not male domination over women.[3]

Most southeastern Indians lived in matrilineal societies where blood relatives were descendents of a known female ancestor. According to anthropologist Charles Hudson, lineage defined individual identity by providing men (and women) with "a set of ready-made categories that determined who his enemies were, who his allies were, whom he could and could not marry, and to whom he could leave his property and his social prerogatives after he died."[4] A child's relatives included only individuals, both male and female, on their mothers' side traced through women. A typical household was an extended family, historian Theda Purdue observes, that

Indian man with his nephew. In matrilineal societies, uncles had special responsibilities in rearing their sisters' children. Tomochichi, a Creek chief, sports pierced ears, body markings, and a deerskin mantle while Tooanahowi, his nephew, holds an eagle, a peace symbol and gift to the English monarch. Tomochichi brokered peace between James Oglethorpe and the Lower Creeks. (Mezzotint by John Farber of a painting by Willem Verelst during Tomochichi's 1734 good will tour to London. Smithsonian Institution, National Anthropological Archives, Negative no. 1129-A.)

included "an elderly woman, her daughters and their children, the women's husbands, and any unmarried sons."[5] One's father and all his relatives, on the other hand, were *not* blood relatives. Siblings, especially brothers and sisters, were especially close; mother's brother (or maternal uncle) had primary responsibility for training his sister's sons. Except among Algonquian speakers, husbands usually lived in their wives' households, a pattern known as matrilocal residence, but they maintained close ties with their sisters, who lived in their own lineage households. Marriage, thus, did not disrupt women's social ties, and children always belonged to her lineage. Only couples from clans *other* than one's own or one's father could have sex or marry (known as exogamous marriage); individuals from the clan of one's grandfather were preferred mates. Anyone violating taboos against intraclan marriages was guilty of incest and severely punished. Women's lineage membership thus provided every child a strong social identity that extended to every other clan member beyond the village. Men, through exogamous marriages, linked different village clans that were vital to holding communities together. This mixing of personal identity and group ties extended to forming marriages and rearing children.[6]

Courtship and Marriage

Creating a family balanced individual desires and lineage obligations. A young man wooing a particular woman initiated negotiations by asking his mother's sister to speak to the mother's sister of the young woman. Consulting lineage members, who inquired into suitors' skills as providers and protectors, and obtaining their approval were vital in arranging marriages, but so, too, was women's consent. Couples, however, expressed their feelings indirectly. Among the Creek, for example, a courted woman placed a bowl of boiled hominy meal near the corncrib. As the young man stole up to her house, the woman either encouraged or prevented him from eating to indicate her desires. Powhatan men gave women presents of meat, fish, or wild plants. If she assented by offering an ear of corn, the young man's lineage members offered gifts—a house, a mortar and pestle, mats, pots, and bedding—as bridewealth in recognition of the woman's productive and reproductive value. If the woman's relatives accepted the gifts, the couple was betrothed. They were free to have discreet sex—corncribs and corn and bean fields were favorite places—but, in keeping with Indians' emotional restraint, public displays of affection were discouraged.

Semen, like menstrual blood, was polluting, and couples carefully removed all traces of their conjugal activities.

The wedding ceremony symbolized the couple's reciprocal obligations in providing for a family: the groom killed a deer or a bear to indicate he was a good hunter, while the bride provided corn or hominy to demonstrate her horticultural skills. Wrapping the couple in a blanket or exchanging poles with intertwined bean vines symbolized their sexual union, and breaking shell beads (a form of currency) denoted joining the two lineages. The wedding feast included much food, drink, and dancing to honor the couple.

Marriages lasted as long as both partners lived together in harmony. "Marriage should beget joy and happiness, instead of pain and misery," an Indian informed Indian trader James Adair, "if a couple married blindfold, and could not love one another afterwards, it was a crime to continue together, and a virtue to part and make a happier choice."[7] In some societies, the first year was a trial period when couples abstained from sex to become like brothers and sisters to each other, the most revered kin relationship, or delayed final confirmation of the marriage until the Green Corn Ceremony in late summer. In this way, incompatible couples ended marriages before they had children. Native Americans had few illusions every marriage lasted a lifetime. Women and men spent much of their daily lives apart, and Indians tolerated extramarital sex. Powhatan and Cherokee women could enter sexual liaisons with their husbands' permission. Either party could initiate divorce, and the causes were many—either party's sexual infidelity (but only if flagrant and caught in the act), abusive behavior, failing to provide sustenance, or alienation of affections. Whatever humiliation individuals suffered from their marriages' dissolution, the social fabric remained unbroken. The husband returned to his mother's household; children remained with his ex-wife's clan. Nor did the wife suffer economically: she retained ownership of her property and female lineage members provided subsistence and childcare. While many couples were deeply devoted to one another and remained together for life, the more typical marriage pattern was serial monogamy based on mutual consent.

With an important exception: wealthy and powerful men usually had multiple wives, but generally only if the first wife approved. The second wife was often the first wife's sister, a pattern known as sororal polygyny. This fostered domestic harmony as social custom restrained expressing hostility toward lineage members and husbands did not divide his time between two residences. For chiefs, multiple wives were prerogatives of power and necessities for fulfilling hospitality obligations. Tribute payments flowing into chiefly villages provided means for supporting large households, and additional women raised crops and prepared sumptuous feasts vital for entertaining their husbands' many guests. Powhatan reportedly had over 100 wives by 1610 (when he was around 70!), choosing young women he fancied from dependent villages and paying bride-wealth to their parents. Many wives only lived with him temporarily; after bearing a child, they returned to their villages where lineage members helped raise the child and support her. After several years, the child returned to Powhatan's household. Divorced ex-wives were free to marry another man, unless Powhatan gave her away as a councilor's bride. Plural wives and numerous progeny scattered throughout tribute-paying villages weakened emotional ties between Powhatan and his many wives and children, but forged familial alliances and recruited potential leaders.

Marriage rules among the Natchez elite—suns, nobles, and honored people—also diffused power through extended lineage ties. The Natchez were the most centralized of all southeastern chiefdoms, but high-status women and men were required to marry someone from a lower social rank (i.e., suns could marry nobles, honored people, or commoners; nobles, honored people and commoners, etc.). One's mother, whatever the father's rank, determined one's status, while connections to the father and his family created ties between classes. The Natchez marriage system, thus, balanced tensions arising from sharp social divisions and need to maintain political unity.

Childrearing and Rites of Passage

Pregnant women's heightened spiritual powers were seen as potentially dangerous and required separating men and women. Couples abstained from sex and refrained from participating in ceremonies and games. They bathed daily and visited shaman monthly. Women drank herbal teas to ensure safe delivery of a healthy infant. Cherokee women avoided eating squirrel, trout, and rabbit, lest the fetus acquire their undesirable physical traits. Just before childbirth, a woman retreated to a birth hut attended by a midwife and other female relatives, who administered wild cherry bark to ease labor and chanted to hurry delivery. European male observers claimed Indian women experienced painless childbirths; more likely, they witnessed women's stoic stifling of pain to acknowledge their courage. Mothers dipped newborns in creeks even during winter to make them hardy and rubbed them with bear's oil to protect against insects. Husbands buried placentas and avoided physical contact with wives for a month or more after they had given birth. Parents assisted by elders and priests named their newborns soon after birth in public ceremonies followed by feasting and dancing.

Indian parents indulged their children. They spent early years in constant contact with their mothers nursing on demand and were not weaned until four or even five years old, strengthening mother–child bonds. Prolonged nursing delayed another pregnancy, as did taboos against sex for a year or more after a child's birth, and male celibacy before, during, and after hunts and wars. Mothers carried infants swaddled in cradleboards that husbands had fashioned from wood or basketry. They could be strapped near her breasts for feeding, on her back (with the child facing backward) when working in fields, or hung on a branch or lodge pole. Natchez mothers placed cane rollers under cradleboards to rock their child. Mothers wrapped infants in skins to keep them warm, placed leather or woolen matchcoats over cradleboards to keep them dry, and tucked soft moss by the genitals to absorb excrement. Unlike modern snuggles, cradleboards were objects of parental affection painted and decorated with gender symbols (like bows and arrows for boys) and with carvings, beadwork, feathers, or porcupine quills. Cradleboards modified children's bodies to make them stronger and more beautiful by straightening spines, turning toes inward to curve the feet, and, among the Choctaw and Catawba, pressing clay to flatten the skull. Quills, feathers, or wampum decorated infants' pierced ears. At night, children rested naked between parents or in their own beds.

Children learned adult responsibilities through imitation and example, with the goal of developing autonomous individuals deeply attached to their lineages. They accompanied mothers and female relatives as they farmed, gathered wild plants, and collected firewood. Around six years of age, children joined gender-segregated work groups. Girls accompanied women in fields to learn horticultural skills and corn songs. They became proficient in preserving food, tending fires, preparing hominy and stews, weaving mats and baskets, and making pottery. Mother's brother or another male lineage member taught boys the ways of men: hunting different animals, various method of catching fish, preparations necessary for warfare, the importance of eloquent speech, and inuring bodies to physical depravation. If a parent died prematurely, another clan member reared the children.

Play rehearsed adult roles. Girls learned to make clothes by dressing dolls. Boys shot birds, small game, and targets with bows and arrows, caught fish, roamed far away from villages into forests, and joined ball games and foot races to develop strength and endurance. They competed with one another to demonstrate indifference to pain by suffering bee stings or exposure to cold without complaining. Parents used praise to reinforce desirable behavior and accomplishments, and universally condemned as barbaric the corporal punishments Europeans often inflicted on children. For especially serious misbehavior, they might scratch a child's face to leave temporary scars inviting public humiliation. In close-kin communal societies, fear of shame was an effective deterrent. Europeans frequently commented on Indian children's healthy constitutions, devotion to parents and aged lineage members, and sensitivity over their public reputations.

Rituals marked puberty's onset and initiation into adulthood. A girl's first menstruation marked her passage into womanhood. Indians thought menses, like any bodily discharges, were polluting, and believed menstruating women possessed enhanced but potentially dangerous spiritual power. Young women withdrew to small menstrual houses to avoid contact with others. They ate food from special bowls and were excused from work responsibilities. These monthly retreats avoided social conflicts arising from psychological mood changes. At the end of her period, a woman purified herself by bathing in freshwater and wearing clean clothing before rejoining the community. After her first menses, a girl was eligible for marriage and could engage in sex. Leaders might offer her as "she bedfellows" to important visitors. Adults tolerated youthful sexual exploration, and women chose partners as they pleased. Some scholars believe Natives suffered from high rates of syphilis. Couples never acknowledged these temporary liaisons publicly, and women terminated unwanted pregnancies by taking an herbal abortifacient.

Boys' transitions to manhood were more gradual. As their skills with bows and arrows improved, they joined men in winter hunts and, a bit later, on revenge raids against enemies. Triumphant returns from a first kill or a first scalp were cause for celebrations to mark entrance into the world of men. They received new names and gifts bestowed by leaders in recognition of their skills and bravery. Failing to acquire these honors kept a man a boy no matter his age.

Southern Algonquians had a special ceremony, the *huskanaw,* to mark the transition to adulthood. In chiefly societies, like the Powhatans, only young men aged 15 to 20 from wealthy families and selected as future leaders underwent the initiation, which was held only once each decade. In nonchiefly societies, all girls and boys participated. The ceremony marked symbolic erasure of childhood in preparation for adult leadership responsibilities and required prolonged separation from the community, purification of the body and spirit, and endurance tests. The Powhatan *huskanaw* began with a communal circle dance that lasted until participants were exhausted. Young men led initiates in white body paint through a series of gauntlets protecting them from blows delivered by angry men with reed bundles; women, meanwhile, gathered items for funeral preparations. After a long feast, initi-

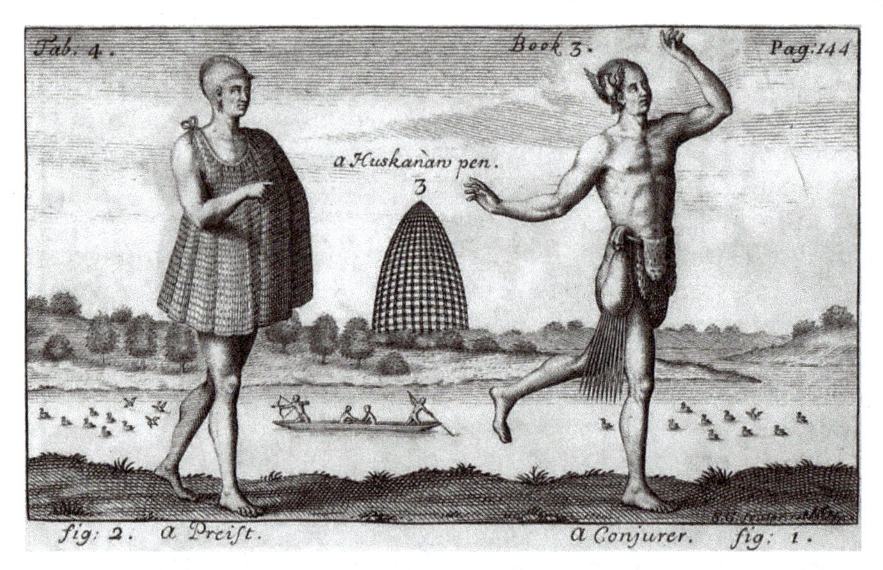

Priest, huskanaw cage, and conjurer. Algonquian huskanaws were rites of passage for young men, who were isolated in cages for ritual purification. Also shown are a priest (left) with a "Mohawk" haircut, leather earrings, and rabbit-skin cape and a conjurer or healer (right) in a sacred posture with his spirit helpers: a bird hairpiece, otter skin breechclout, and medicine bag. Engraving by Simon Gribelin after Theodor de Bry, 1590, in Robert Beverley, *The History of Virginia*, 2nd ed. [London, 1722 (1705)]. (Library of Congress.)

ates were removed to a secret place where they were confined for several weeks in cages, while male "keepers" gave them "no other sustenance but the infusion or decoction of some poisonous intoxicating roots," possibly jimsonweed, which eventually drove them "stark staring mad." Released from their cages in a zombie-like state to recover (and not everyone survived) and shorn of "remembrance of all former things, even of their parents, their treasure, and their language," keepers began their retraining so they "commence men, by forgetting that they every have been boys."[8] This shared ritual and survival of hazing forged deep bonds between the newest groups of leaders. Carolina huskanaws confined initiates for five or six weeks in distant houses where they fasted and drank intoxicating teas. The ritual included girls as well as boys with the purpose of instilling discipline and endurance among youths, and, perhaps, thinning the community of weak, infirm members.

Adapting to a New World

The pressure of European encroachment and diseases, the slave trade, and escalating warfare devastated many Indian families. Even brief contacts with Europeans unleashed invisible pathogens that destroyed Indian families before settlers arrived. Physically isolated from Europe, Asia, and Africa, Native Americans lacked immunities to European diseases, such as smallpox, influenza, measles, and typhus. Native populations began falling in the early 15th century until stabilizing and increasing briefly in the mid-18th century. The old and the young were especially vulnerable; deaths robbed lineages of memories of the past and households of continuation into the future. Most captives in the Indian slave trade were women and children, thereby rupturing households and fraying lineages. Indian slave raiders and colonial militias caused tens of thousands of deaths; destroyed fields, corn supplies, and villages; and created large refugee populations. Women had fewer marriage partners and faced greater difficulties sustaining family obligations. Perpetual conflicts increased the importance of diplomacy and war, and thus shifted the gender power balance in favor of men. Native Americans survived colonial conquest, but many families, clans, villages, and societies disappeared.

European trade altered gender roles and created new kinds of families. Women adapted useful metal objects that made work easier and added European plants and fowls to enrich subsistence. Men spent more time away from villages hunting deer for the colonial trade, which in turn required women to devote more time scraping and dressing skins for exchange at the expense of agriculture. Successful hunters and chiefs acquired considerable material wealth through trade, which enhanced their social prestige and political power and reduced women's decision-making authority. European traders formed liaisons with Indian women. Men needed entrées into Native societies, wives to provide food and process furs, and sexual companionship; women acquired powerful protectors and access to trade goods. Some unions became permanent with husbands living in native villages with their wives. Their mixed progeny, known as *metís,* belonged to their mothers' lineages, and their familiarity with both parents' cultures made them cultural brokers between Indian and European worlds.

Catholic missionaries in Maryland, Florida, and Louisiana condemned native families and hoped to instill European gender norms. They urged "lazy" men to work in fields like women, use corporal punishment to discipline children, hoard personal possessions not share with lineage members, live in family cabins not communal houses, and restrain women under male authority. They especially condemned as licentious women's premarital and extramarital sexual behavior and male polygyny. Child converts created discord within pagan families. Priests were most successful in Florida and resettled several thousand Indians into mission villages comprised of nuclear family houses. During the 16th century, some village chiefs sent their children to live in Saint Augustine to learn European ways. Governors became godparents to native children bestowing Spanish surnames and baptismal gifts.

In settler colonies of Maryland, Virginia, the Carolinas, Georgia, and Lower Louisiana, Europeans coveted Indian land, not Christianized natives. Pocahontas, daughter of paramount chief Powhatan, who married 28-year-old John Rolfe in 1614 at the age of 17 (he was her second husband; she first married in 1610), was exceptional in converting to Christianity and becoming an English gentlewoman.[9] Few natives found acceptance in settler societies. After defeating or destroying indigenous people, remnant coastal populations—deprived of economic resources and political independence, and confined to tiny reservations—slowly reoriented family lives toward European norms. Some Indians became permanently detached when they left their families to work in European households. Lineages divided into extended families. Indian women formed unions with African men and with poor white men, lived on the margins of settler society, and became petty traders or day laborers.

One can exaggerate the decline of Native Americans. In 17th-century Florida and in trading frontiers, Europeans recognized native chiefs' rule over autonomous villages, thus preserving Indian family life. External changes wrought by trade, war, and diplomacy affected men more since they were absent for long periods but, according to historian Theda Purdue, "left women in more absolute control of households and villages."[10] Continuity in women's roles as agriculturalists and as cultural conservators allowed for adaptation and survival in difficult times. To stem population losses, women married "strangers" from other tribes, adopted captives and refugee women and children into lineages, and migrated to safe havens to rebuild villages and coalesced into new people. Catawba families in South Carolina survived as an enclave within colonial society by absorbing remnant peoples, securing a reservation, renting surplus land to colonists, capturing stray horses and runaway slaves, and selling women's baskets and pottery. By becoming good neighbors yet resisting outside influences, the Catawba preserved their families to maintain their traditions and cultural identities.

EURO-AMERICAN FAMILIES

European Background

European settlers arrived with patriarchal family ideals with fathers having supreme authority over wives, children, servants, and other dependents. Proper family life modeled civil society's hierarchical organization, from king to nobles to gentry to yeomen and artisans to tenants to laborers to paupers: everyone obeyed superiors and commanded subordinates. The husband, Puritan minister William Gouge wrote in 1622, is "as a Priest unto his wife. . . . He is the highest in the family, and hath . . . authority over all . . . ; he is as a king in his owne house."[11] Men supported their families, controlled property, supervised sons' training and daughters' marriages, represented the family in politics, and defended family interests and transgressions in courts. Wives were to submit to their husbands' authority, maintain faithful sexual relations, bear children, and perform domestic labor. Married women forfeited almost all legal rights. Under English common law, a married woman could not own property (except what she brought to the marriage on her own account), sign contracts, sue or be sued, or retain earnings.

Day-to-day family life, of course, varied from these norms. Some men showered affection on family members and consulted wives before making decisions; other men treated wives and children cruelly or abandoned them altogether. Life was precarious: parents lost many infants and children, and a parent's death left behind orphans, who lived with another family or became part of blended families after their surviving parent remarried. Whether couples were happy married or miserably yoked, whether they belonged to Catholic, Anglican, or Reform churches, patriarchy governed family life and found Christian sanction. Eve, after all, first ate Satan's apple and convinced Adam to do likewise, and thus, brought original sin into the world. As sexual temptresses or as social deviants, women—it was widely believed—were ruled by passion not reason, fickle in judgment, and weak in resisting temptation making them potential threats to social order. Only firm rule by fathers and husbands aided by male-run courts and churches kept female danger at bay.

Patriarchy also created class differences within European families. Households of the wealthy were larger and included four or five children plus servants and apprentices. For the 10 percent of household heads owning substantial property, economic considerations and dynastic alliances provided surer foundations for maintaining their families' privileged positions than allowing youthful impulses or fickle emotions to determine marriage choices. Controlling female sexuality was essential for ensuring that only legitimate heirs inherited family property and name. Fathers delayed transferring property or threatened disinheritance to deter unfavorable matches, but most preferred persuasion and promises of land, livestock, and household goods to guide their children's decisions. Wealthy families planned church weddings where priests performed public marriage rites, followed by lavish banquets and balls.

Families of middling rank—small farmers and tenants, artisans, shopkeepers, and professionals—were economic partnerships where each member of the household contributed to the collective welfare. Only men able to support families could marry and establish independent households; men of modest means delayed until their late 20s. Many women and men remained single, especially in Catholic countries where religious celibacy was a holy calling. Fathers deployed their control over skills, knowledge, tools of production, or personal property to influence children's matches, but their resources were insufficient to provide for every child. They apprenticed sons or daughters into other families for education and training as artisans or in housewifery who eventually made their own way into the world. Despite church establishments' efforts to monitor marriages, humble men and women contracted private betrothals with little ceremony or religious ritual but much feasting for family and friends.

Children of laborers, cottagers, and paupers—who comprised half of the population—were freer from paternal restraints, but their freedom was a hardscrabble existence. Enclosures, which converted arable land into pastures, and periodic depressions in textile manufactures uprooted many youths who left their families and moved to towns and ports looking for work as servants or laborers. Here they heard merchants' enticing promises of new starts across the ocean. Their marriages were informal unions broken when spouses abandoned partners or died prematurely. People at the very bottom of society spent much of their short lives outside families, and respectable society saw their sexual promiscuity, abuse of spouses and children, vagabondage, vagrancy, and revelry as threats to family-based social order.

17th-Century Chesapeake

Immigrants arrived with diverse backgrounds and classes and faced harsh conditions and unhealthy environments, but shared patriarchal family ideals in creating new family forms. Saint Augustine, Jamestown, Charles Town, and New Orleans started as male garrison trading posts with few women or children. At Jamestown, this changed in 1621 when the Virginia Company sent the first shipload of "Maids for Wives" recognizing that "the Plantation can never flourish till families be planted, and the respect of wives and children fix the people on the Soil."[12] A century later, French authorities pursued the same strategy of importing women to stabilize the fledgling colony. Only families, they agreed, would encourage permanent agricultural settlement and population growth. Maryland and Carolina proprietors offered headright grants to every family member including women household heads to stimulate family migration.

Stable families appeared very slowly. Chesapeake planters intoxicated by tobacco profits imported boatloads of indentured servants to develop plantations and defend the colony from Indians and European rivals. At least three-fourths of the 75,000 migrants to the Chesapeake before 1680 arrived as indentured servants with males outnumbering females by ratios of 6 to 1 in the 1630s and 3 to 1 after mid-century. Over two-thirds of servant men and around

80 percent of servant women were between the ages of 15 and 24. Most were younger children from middling and poor families; many were orphans and had already moved several times before coming to the Chesapeake. Few lived long. Mosquito-borne malaria in coastal swamps, saltwater poisoning, dysentery from human pollution, and other epidemic diseases cut down between a quarter and a half of servants before their indentures ended. Even survivors died relatively young: in the 1630s, a 20-year-old male in the Chesapeake could expect to live until 43, about 10 years shorter than his English compatriot lived.

Female scarcity, high mortality, and prolonged servitude truncated family life, slowed natural population growth, and created complex families. Indentured women and men were not free to marry, forcing men to wait until their late 20s and women until their mid-20s. About a quarter of planters never found wives at all. Married women typically bore four or five children, but about a quarter of infants died before their first birthday and only two or three reached adulthood. Marriages lasted only seven years on average, and parents left behind orphan children. Surviving spouses needed partners to manage farm households, and most remarried within a year bringing children from earlier marriages into new families. Compared to England, there were few children and even fewer elderly in Virginia: children comprised almost 28 percent of the English population, but merely 9 percent of Virginia's in 1625; a quarter of England's population was over 40, but only 9 percent of Virginia settlers. Because families were small, marriages short, and life expectancy reduced, only continued servant migration increased Chesapeake population. This perpetuated gender imbalances and high mortality and reduced family formation and natural population growth for most of the 17th century.

Chesapeake plantations were no replacements for English families. Most European men and women lived in small villages where face-to-face relations characterized daily life; on isolated plantations, only a quarter of the population had *any* relatives outside the nuclear family. English households typically had four or five members; large plantations were factories with a dozen or more workers. Quick profits not reciprocal if unequal patriarchal relationships governed planter–servant relations, as planters controlled labor routines and local courts and servants had few family, kin, or friends to defend them.

Free immigrants paid their own and their family members' way across the Atlantic and formed the earliest families in the 17th century.

They comprised only a quarter of the population, but were older than servants with 60 percent aged 25 or above. Some men brought spouses with them, a few paid for "tobacco wives," and many more married young female servants by buying the remaining time on their contracts and acquiring another headright claim in the bargain. Before the tobacco economy stagnated after 1670, surviving male servants acquired property, married, and started families. Men needed not only sexual and emotional companions but also wives to produce children and provide domestic labor that turned quarters into households. Tobacco cultivation strengthened patriarchy. With few exceptions, only men owned land and servants; more wealth meant more choices in securing wives among the scarce female population. Husbands acquired additional land by importing family members and servants. They controlled servants' sexual activity, since servants required their owner's consent before they could marry.

For servant women, moving to the Chesapeake improved prospects for marrying property owners and escaping servitude and field labor. Lack of family relations in the Chesapeake and servant women's youthfulness—about a third were under age 20—allowed women many choices among suitors, but left them vulnerable to unscrupulous men. During the 17th century, one out of five servant women in one Maryland county was hauled before justices accused of bearing a bastard child. Premarital sex, especially between servants, was a dangerous game. It pressured some free men to marry their partners—one third of servant women were pregnant when they married—but women abandoned by men or whose owners refused permission to marry faced fines, whippings, time added to their indentures, and loss of their child. White women sexually involved with black men received even harsher punishments.

Married women faced new physical perils—and opportunities. Pregnancy and nursing made them more vulnerable to malaria and fever and cut life expectancies to just 39, about 5 years shorter than men lived. Since brides were much younger than their husbands when they married and usually outlived them, husbands came to trust wives to manage family affairs and rear their children after they died. They designated them estate executors and often provided more than the minimum dower right, which by law gave widows life interest in one-third of the real estate for their support. Propertied widows were desirable mates who needed new husbands to manage crops and livestock, and soon remarried a second or even a third time accumulating more property with each marriage.

Early parental death in the Chesapeake region during the 17th century meant most children lived in more than one family before adulthood, as two-thirds lost at least one parent and one out of three was orphaned. When surviving parents remarried, children found themselves in complex families with stepparents and half siblings. Some couples blended their earlier families successfully, but there were underlying conflicts over favoring one's natural children over stepchildren and disposing of property a "now wife" brought to the second (or even third) marriage equitably among sons and daughters-in-law. Recognizing life's unpredictability, wills of wealthy fathers included provisions for their children's care. They instructed executors and guardians (often their wives and male neighbors) to oversee their children's education and training, protect property bequests, and transfer inheritances at 18: land to sons and livestock and household goods to daughters. Parental death and material abundance facilitated early inheritance and marriage, as few parents lived long enough to guide their children's future. At age 16 or 17, Virginia-born daughters trusted their own judgment and desires in choosing husbands, usually older men. One-fifth of brides were pregnant, as most were sexually active before marriage. With few churches or ministers and scattered settlements, simple betrothals or private marriages became the norm. By living together peacefully as man and wife, neighbors recognized their marriages as legitimate. Early marriages meant larger families with 9 to 11 children, an advantage in the labor-short Chesapeake.

Orphans' courts and parish vestries, imported English institutions, protected orphan children and prevented bastard children from becoming public charges. Justices presided over orphans' courts, appointed neighbors as guardians to protect children's welfare and property, and required annual reckonings of accounts. Catholics in Maryland, Florida, and Louisiana selected godparents who promised to provide religious instruction and material support especially if children became orphans. Churchwardens apprenticed poor orphans to household heads who promised to provide shelter, food, clothing, religious instruction, and education; train boys as planters or artisans; and ensure their wives taught girls sewing and housewifery. Growing up in family settings but without the nurture of secure family ties or inherited property made an orphan apprentice's lot a hard one. Masters put children as young as three to work, and contracts bound boys until 21 and girls until 18. In theory, they could seek legal relief from abusive masters, and at the age of 14, choose their own master, but most faced years of hard labor, harsh discipline, and limited schooling. Fearing poor children and bastards would become burdens to the community, churchwardens removed them from their families and sold their labor to the highest bidders until they were 31.

Conditions of daily life in early Chesapeake society blurred lines between families and communities. With high mortality and limited family ties, historians Stephen Mintz and Susan Kellogg conclude, "Networks of kinship, friendship, and neighborhood made up for the fragility and transience of individual attachments."[13] Parents relied on neighbors as witnesses, guardians, and executors for wills and orphans' estates. Family passages—births, weddings, and funerals—became community events bringing friends and neighbors together for celebrations or remembrances. In a society of newcomers, personal reputation counted more than family name and community gossip regulated individual behavior. Planters' ability to support their families, especially keeping female members from field labor, and honesty in dealing with other men earned social standing. Planters' "good wives" received praise for housewifery skills, childbearing, and domestic economy, but scorn if they repeatedly failed to control their sexual behavior with other men.

By the 1690s, stable family life emerged in Virginia. Lowered mortality, a balanced sex ratio, and decline in the servant trade accelerated white population growth from natural increase, and native-born outnumbered immigrants for the first time. Almost all adults married and began families several years earlier than their parents had. Husbands and wives lived together longer, had more children, and named them after parents and grandparents thereby linking generations. Colonial-born children possessed greater immunities to local diseases than pioneer generations, which increased their chances of surviving to adulthood. Servant immigration declined with the shift to slave labor and reduced the proportion of unattached male youths in the population. Fathers gave sons tracts of land near their homes and encouraged marrying neighbors' daughters, establishing local networks of related kin. As life became more predictable and people lived longer, parents exerted more influence over their children's education and marriage. Denser populations and road networks facilitated visits between neighbors and extended family life beyond households. The third generation grew up surrounded by relatives and friends who attended family celebrations, childbirths, illnesses, and funerals and provided a safety net against sudden misfortunes.

Patriarchal Planter Families

Stable Anglo-American families accelerated societal change during the 18th century just as imperial recruiters shaped family life. Universal marriage, high fertility, and lower mortality created rapid growth and swarms of children. Numerous Irish, English, German, Scot, and French immigrants added to the colonial South's surging population. The 96,500 whites in 1715 just outnumbered Native Americans, but thereafter doubled every 25 years reaching 542,200 by 1775, most American-born.[14] Immigrant and settler families filled coastal areas and moved to the backcountry creating new communities and developing resources that sustained rapid economic growth. Larger families had numerous laborers who produced more crops, provided more artisan services, purchased more consumer goods, and traveled more often. Established elites supported formal institutions—churches, county courts, schools, and associations—furthering social stability and order.

In the English colonies, stronger local institutions, greater availability of consumer goods, and more frequent contacts with metropolitan society reinforced patriarchal family ideals. Wealthy tobacco and rice planters with their minions of slaves built great houses on their plantations and in Charles Town and Savannah, where they displayed the latest English fashions, cuisine, and entertainments that distinguished genteel from plain folk. Great planters imagined themselves as biblical patriarchs, heads of large households of wives, children, other kin, white laborers, and numerous slaves. Marriages between planters' children concentrated wealth and power in a handful of leading families creating networks of kin connections across each colony that assisted in securing favorable placements for sons and for resolving family crises such as marital discords or wayward children. By the mid-18th century, new English notions about personal autonomy and the rule of reason spread among the gentry. Affection complemented duty as the foundation for family ties and allowed individual members more privacy and choices.

Compared to the previous century, newborn children of the gentry enjoyed more secure lives, and historian Daniel Smith believes they became "a central emotional focus in the life of the family."[15] With slaves performing all physical labor, planter parents enjoyed much free time to devote to their children, delight in their development, and supervise childrearing. Midwives, female relatives, and servants attended childbirths, but this remained a time of great

Portrait of Dr. Joseph Montegut and family. Elite men commissioned family portraits to display in their homes. In this idealized scene of domestic harmony, the six children of Dr. Joseph Montegut, Surgeon Major in the Spanish Army in New Orleans, are performing music for his wife and her aunt. Montegut is in dress uniform, family members are accoutered in fine clothes, and a daughter sits in an imported Windsor chair. (Painting by José Francisco Xavier de Salazar y Mendoza, ca. 1794-1800. Loan of Gustave Pitot, 04944-04945. Louisiana State Museum, New Orleans.)

danger, as almost everyone knew at least one woman who had died during or shortly after giving birth. Planters' wives breast-fed infants for the first 12 to 18 months, which delayed another pregnancy and created close emotional bonds with newborns. Fathers found diversion in their young children's antics and emerging personalities, joined in their play, and when away from home, inquired for detailed reports of their activities.

Parents recognized childhood as a distinct stage of life and the importance of proper childrearing for developing their children's characters. They gave them pet names, dressed them in distinct clothing, and provided gender-specific toys such as dolls for girls and soldiers for boys. Parents nurtured their children's independence and curiosity by encouraging exploration of plantation surroundings on foot and on horseback. Accompanied by one of their siblings or a slave child, children roamed fields and forests and visited relatives for extended periods. Numerous uncles, aunts, cousins, and, especially, grandparents joined family celebrations, baptisms, christenings, birthdays, dinner parties, and picnics and provided additional nurture and emotional support. Parents' early "affectionate interest" in their children instilled "a strong sense of emotional security," Daniel Smith concludes, and most sons and daughters rewarded them with obedience and respect as they matured into adults.[16]

Around age seven or eight, children began wearing miniature adult clothing, a symbol of their entry into gender-segregated worlds of women and men. Their relations with slave children abruptly changed from playmates to servants. Girls came under tutelage of mothers, kin, and female slaves and in play rehearsed their future roles as childbearers and raisers, efficient domestic managers, and men's "agreeable" companions.[17] Young girls stuffed rags under their clothes imitating pregnancy. Girls did no physical labor, of course, for that was only for enslaved and lower-class women, but becoming a planter's wife required knowing how to manage large households where hospitality and sociability were critical for their future husbands' successful public roles. Young women learned to plan meals; oversee gardens, dairies, fowl, and kitchens; and manage household servants. This required little formal schooling beyond the rudiments of reading and writing, but accomplishments in French, music, conversation, fancy needlework, tea etiquette, and dancing instilled gentility that was becoming to women and pleasing to men. Although planters' daughters were the first American leisure class—sleeping in until late morning, reading religious tracts and elevating fiction, and engaging in seemingly endless rounds of visiting—this was serious preparation. Self-discipline—especially over personal behavior, hospitality rituals, and sexuality—was prerequisite for acquiring desired female virtues of modesty, piety, compassion, and deference. Growing up in largely female social worlds, women forged strong emotional bonds with other women. Mothers became daughters' closest companions and mentors as they experienced births, deaths, and family celebrations together. Lifelong relationships with peers continued after marriage as women friends wrote, visited, and confided in each other, reinforcing female autonomy and sense of self, yet, in the end, accepting deference to men.

Boys became their fathers' "projects." As planters' heirs, sons learned to run plantations, discipline slaves, manage households, and fulfill public obligations. Sons accompanied fathers on visits to neighboring farms, stores, county courts, and churches where they discovered political and economic realms beyond their families. At taverns, horse races, cockfights, hunts, fishing trips, and barbeques, they learned male camaraderie. Teenage boys carried messages to neighbors and relatives and supervised slaves as apprentice crop managers and slaveowners. Unlike daughters, sons required more than rudimentary education, and fathers hired tutors or sent them to neighborhood schools and when they were older to colonial colleges to learn Latin, Greek, history, logic, moral philosophy, and geography. Acquiring individual autonomy and independence necessary to command others also exposed sons to male pleasures of drinking, gambling, and whoring. Some young men learned about sex by abusing or raping young enslaved women, whose blackness, physical labor, and tattered clothing put them beyond respectability's bounds. A thriving double standard of sexual conduct allowed young men such power, while harshly condemning any scandal that undermined a young white woman's honor. Parents had good reason to emphasize self-mastery, duty, and moral character in their sons. By setting high expectations, promising generous inheritances, and adopting more emotional and less authoritarian relationships fathers hoped to secure their sons' gratitude and continuing devotion.

Children had considerable autonomy to select marriage partners, but as dutiful children, they solicited their parents and their peers' assessments of potential mates. Mothers warned daughters not to let emotion get the better of reason and the importance of couples finding "in each other a similarity of temper and good qualities enough to excite esteem and Friendship"[18] Fathers sought "suitable" sons-in-law who could advance the family's economic and political interests. Adults organized barbeques, dances, holiday celebrations, and visits to kin to ensure their children met—and fell in love with—members of their social class or even their extended family. Youths socialized without adult chaperones, but usually in company of peers as a measure of self-protection. As neighborhoods of related kin became denser and marriages between gentry families across the colony more frequent, marriages between first cousins and other relatives almost tripled during the 18th century, solidifying the gentry's class identity and their political and social power.

Navigating the gender divide was rarely easy, however, for young women and men grew up in different social worlds. They resorted to stilted courtship rituals that masked their true emotions (and save face if rejected) and maintained rigid deportment expected of each sex. Men penned florid declarations of undying love to women, often still in their teens, who coquettishly demurred cupid's arrows. Few couples persisted courting if faced with strong family opposition, but if parents approved of or, at least, acceded to the match, fathers negotiated the amount of property each side contributed commensurate with their respective wealth before making a formal announcement. Typically, the groom's family gave land and a house and the bride's family slaves, livestock, and household goods so the couple could live in a separate household. If large amounts of property were involved or a propertied woman was remarrying, prenuptial agreements provided legal protections to secure the bride's property from prodigal husbands. Marriage ceremonies were festive family affairs held in brides' homes. An Anglican minister presided over a brief ritual, followed by a day or two of eating, drinking, and dancing among numerous guests of family, kin, and close neighbors. Visiting the groom's family a week or two later initiated another round of celebrations and united newlyweds to their extended families.

As much as brides' prized esteem and mutual respect from their spouses, they knew "a Woman's happiness depends entirely on the Husband she is united to."[19] Not only did wives bear responsibility for pleasing their husbands, but they also bore the blame for any marital difficulties. As today, the quality of married life ranged from happiness to misery, but with important differences: women lacked rights under the law, slaves were part of planter households, and divorce was rare. As commanders of their domain, patriarchal husbands expected obedient wives as well as servile slaves. Men believed emotion ruled women and slaves; both required men's reason for their own self-preservation. Some wives knew little about plantation finances and debts, including property sales, despite legal requirements to obtain wives' free consent before disposing of property. Husbands had final say in childrearing decisions, and with sons living longer, planters' wills favored them over wives as executors and estate managers. Sexual tension suffused planters' households. They assumed wives would overlook husbands' (and sons') sexual exploitation of young female slaves, and men's fantasies of hypersexed black women provided pretexts for denying consideration of their wives sexual needs. Some mistresses turned to female slaves as confidents, but more often victims became perpetrators, punishing black women who were more powerless than they were. A woman might secure legal separation in cases of physical brutality, desertion, or impotency, but in doing so, she lost control over her children, could not remarry, and became dependent on support from her family of origin.

After the mid-18th century, the emotional texture of gentry family life shifted from "the 'well-ordered' patriarchal family" of the late 17th century to "a more intimate private family and kin experience." Virginia planter William Byrd's social life in the early 18th century centered as much on activities with male friends and neighbors at racecourses, courthouses, and hunts, as it did on family celebrations. He brooked few challenges to his authority over his large household. Byrd initiated sex with his wife (and with women his social inferiors), made decisions about sons' careers and daughters' marriages, and ordered slaves whipped frequently. Byrd's emotional restraint caused many "domestic gusts" over disciplining slaves and childrearing. Ideally, planters' children coming of age just before the American Revolution, in contrast, grew up in more affectionate families with nurturing not authoritarian parents. Large plantation houses separated private rooms for intimate family life, including individual sleeping chambers that recognized each member's autonomy, from public spaces for entertaining. Daughters received more schooling, and female literacy was almost universal. Concerned by reports of moral corruption in English high society, parents educated sons at home. Parents granted sons freedom to choose careers and trusted sons and daughters to select mates. They esteemed mutual affection and companionship between partners higher than familial or economic considerations, yet the value of a bride's or especially a widow's estate merited public congratulations on the groom's successful "catch." By the American Revolution, historian Daniel Smith concludes, gentry families "had turned their emotional energies inward to focus on an intimate, sentimental family unit that stood apart from the larger society as a private enclave for mutual support and sociability." This became the model for middle-class family life in the early 19th century.[20]

Variations in Patriarchy

By the mid-18th century, land cleared of Indian families allowed common planters, backcountry farmers, and their sons to establish subsistence farms in the Valley of Virginia and in the Virginia, Carolina, and Georgia Piedmont. Most Germans emigrated as families, congregations, or villages, and these ties were vital for locating land, adjusting to colonial life, and through letters home, encouraging others to make the transatlantic journey. Family members and congregants took up frontier land near one another and latecomers joined kinfolk and former villagers to form new ethnic and religious enclaves. Common folk marriages were economic partnerships. Each member contributed to the family's subsistence, and women and children did not escape field labor. Sons could expect only modest inheritances; but with abundant land, a healthy environment, and scarce labor, they were self-supporting by their early 20s. Young people courted and found spouses at dances, barbecues church services, and other social gatherings with minimal parental supervision. Ministers and churches were scarce in the backcountry, so couples married themselves in private betrothals, followed by family celebrations of kin and neighbors who feasted, danced, and offered many toasts to the young couple. Contributions from each family—grooms with land or skills and brides with livestock and household goods—assisted newlyweds in setting up their own households. Early marriages, early to mid-20s for men and late teens for women, produced many children. Many couples were already sexually active. About one-third of brides were pregnant at their wedding, and they had 9 or 10 children, on average, with two-thirds surviving to adulthood.

At five or six, childhood became a time of work with little in the way of toys, leisure time, or formal education. The parents of Devereux Jarratt, a Virginia carpenter's son, "wished us all to be brought up in some honest calling, that we might earn our bread, by the sweat of our brow, as they did."[21] Girls assisted mothers in domestic tasks like milking cows, feeding chickens, hauling firewood, food preservation and preparation, and childcare. They contributed to household production by churning butter, spinning wool and flax, weaving cloth, and sewing clothes, and assisted with plantings and harvests. Young boys helped with crops, tended livestock, hauled grain to mills and surpluses to local stores, and learned craft skills from fathers and older brothers. There were few schools in the backcountry, limited family funds to pay teachers, and scarce time spared from family labor. Literate parents taught children reading, writing, and arithmetic at home, and aspiring boys attended neighborhood schools for a few months between work stints. Apprenticeships with family members or neighbors provided vocational training. After his parents died when he was 13, Jarratt lived with his older brothers, who were carpenters and millwrights. Poor families sent sons to rural households to learn skilled trades and rudiments of reading and writing, and promising lads might get work in artisans' shops or country stores. Orphan girls were bound until 18 to learn the "art and mystery of housewifery" and orphan boys until 21 to learn farming or a craft. Prosperous members of the "middling" sort acquired a few slaves, sent sons and daughters to local schools, and sought favorable matches to move their children into the ranks of the lesser gentry.

Dissenters and Pietists provided variations to economic partnership families. As part of the God's family, they addressed one another in familial terms as "sisters" and "brothers." Members were pressured to find marriage partners within the group with threats to exclude anyone marrying a "stranger." Because backcountry settlements were patchworks of many ethnic groups, not isolated communes, enforcement became more difficult over time. Quakers shared with Anglicans a belief that nuclear families were foundations of social order, but their ideals were less patriarchal and more egalitarian. Believing everyone was equal before God, Quakers used example and persuasion to instill humility, equality, and pacifism in their children and believed threats of withholding parental affection was more effective in molding a child's behavior than corporal punishments. Divine "Inner Light" called some women as itinerant preachers to mixed congregations, even if this meant leaving families. Quaker children grew up experiencing broader women's gender roles than their Anglo-American peers.

Some radical Pietists experimented with new family forms. For Moravians (radical Pietist followers of John Hus, who established Wachovia, North Carolina, in 1753), congregations and choirs not families were primary social units. Elders divided members into 11 "choirs" based on age, gender, and marital status (Young Girls, Older Boys, Single Sisters, Married Men, etc.) to instill Moravian values. Choir members became fictive kin to each other and assumed many of the childrearing and socializing functions of nuclear families. After completing school at age 13, children moved to the Older Girls and Older Boys houses where boys learned craft skills and girls performed domestic labor. Church leaders brokered marriages between young men and women by determining if the match was advantageous for the community.

In borderland communities beyond English settlements—trade frontiers in the interior, Florida before British takeover in 1763, and

Louisiana after 1700—mixed European/Indian families provided stark alternatives to patriarchal family ideals. There were simply too few Europeans, almost all men, to recreate settler societies along European lines in these far-flung trade and military outposts. Liaisons between European men and Indian women were common. Many were only temporary: "trading girls" offered as hospitality to explorers, traders, or diplomats and "she-bedfellows" cohabiting with men for trade goods during winter camps. Traders, some already with colonial wives, lived with Indian women for physical and sexual companionship and for practical reasons. Women provided subsistence labor, dressed deerskins for trade, and provided lineage connections for their partners. Some fathers assumed patriarchal authority and raised mixed sons as colonials, sent them to schools, and set them up in trade or as planters. Daughters remained with their mothers' lineage, while sons alternated living with each parents' people as interpreters and cultural brokers or resided permanently in colonial society. Most traders eventually invested profits in land and slaves, became planters, married colonial women, and abandoned their Indian families.

Some laborers found freedom in Indian society was preferable to European servitude. Children captured in frontier wars and adopted by lineage members "went native." As adults, men formed permanent unions with Indian women, lived with her relatives, spoke her language, and assimilated into her culture. Indian matriarchal organization emancipated men from field labor and from the necessity of acquiring property to pass on to heirs, and allowed greater sexual freedom. The couple's Métis children belonged to their mother's lineage, which claimed their first loyalty; most refused to live in colonial society when given the opportunity.

Even Spanish immigrants who came to Florida and Louisiana, historian David Weber notes, "hoping to change little in their own lives except to enhance their wealth and status[,] . . . tried with only partial success to replicate the hierarchical and patriarchal social structure they had known in Spain or in its more mature American colonies."[22] Among *españoles* (men born in Spain) and their second-generation children born in the New World, Spanish women were too scarce for establishing family-based settlements. Elite and upwardly mobile men, concerned with maintaining racial purity essential for elite status, could not always arrange strategic marriages among their children. Unbalanced sex ratios weakened patriarchal authority. Under Spanish law, women retained their property after they married, which they passed onto heirs regardless of their husbands' wishes, and with women outliving men, a few elite widows became large property-owners. Husbands were obsessed with maintaining female sexual purity and family honor, yet their long absences from home allowed some women to have extramarital affairs. Catholic priests' overstretched resources and priority of converting Indians moderated their authority over marriage. They sanctioned marriages between high-ranking officials and elite Indian women as preludes for mass conversion and civilization. More often, men in authority flouted church teachings. They asserted their masculinity by raping Indian women servants or by living openly with a succession of mistresses.

Rank-and-file Spanish colonists included soldiers, convict laborers, commoners, mestizos (part Indian and part Spanish), mulattos (mixed Spanish and African), and free and enslaved blacks. Men established *barraganía* (or informal unions) with free and enslaved Indian women without priests' blessings, creating many *color quebrado* (or people of "broken color"). A former pastor at Mobile denounced settlers' preference to "maintain scandalous concubinages with young Indian women, driven by their proclivity for the extremes of licentiousness."[23] These mixed families lived in separate communities outside the central plaza or presidio (home to *españoles* families), or in Native villages. In these diffuse unstable settlements, where Natives outnumbered colonists, organizing family life along European models was impossible. Mortality remained high and women outlived men, resulting in many orphans, widows, and complex families. Children, especially girls, had few opportunities for formal schooling, but much personal freedom, including marrying across ethnic lines. In New Orleans, a governor decried, children enjoyed "great liberty and total independence, so that, from the age of ten, they are allowed to run about alone, riding from house to house, and firing off their guns."[24] The children likely did not complain.

AFRICAN AMERICAN FAMILIES

African Families and the Atlantic Slave Trade

The contexts of African American family formation were both similar to and different from Native American and Euro-American families in the colonial South. Like Native Americans, rural Africans lived in villages of extended family compounds and interconnected lineages where kin ties defined personal identity and community obligations and provided security. Most African slaves, like indentured servants, were young men who suffered new lethal environments, unremitting toil, abusive treatment, and legal impediments to marrying. Differences were even more striking, however. The slave trade stretched from Senegal south 3,500 miles to Kongo and Angola and even to Mozambique and Madagascar in East Africa, drawing captives from West and West Central African societies that were even more diverse than those of the Native southeast. African captives came from rainforests, wooded savannas, and grasslands; matrilineal and partrilineal social structures; Islamic, Christian, and Animist cultures; and village and state societies. Indentured servants, unlike Africans who became chattel property in the New World, could defend themselves in local courts. Slaves' marriages had no legal standing, and masters freely separated husbands and wives, and children from parents. Free men emigrated voluntarily with their dependents hoping to improve their social and economic standing. Africans—torn from families and lineages—were marched in chains to trading factories on the African coast, thrown into damp dungeons and cramped ships' holds, abused by crew members on the four-month "middle passage" across the Atlantic, arrived alone, disoriented, with weakened bodies, and faced uncertain futures. Only one out of every two African captives survived their first year.[25]

Enslaved Africans did not arrive with empty minds. They understood the importance of maintaining kin obligations; not marrying lineage members; praying to God, Allah, or spirits; and honoring ancestors. Carefully negotiated marriages joined two lineages with grooms' families offering bride-prices, or payments of goods and money, to compensate for loss of female members. Both women and men worked fields and tended animals, fashioned tools, participated in decision-making, and contributed to subsistence, defense, and ceremonies. Specialists created fine objects from gold, bronze, brass, and terra-cotta and carved sacred masks. Priests supervised prayers and rituals that connected the secular with the sacred world. Husbands, wives, children, aunts, uncles, and cousins lived and worked in household compounds comprised of many small buildings. Rulers, noblemen, merchants, and wealthy farmers had many wives, who produced cloth and foodstuffs, and owned numerous slaves, who cultivated fields, carried goods, provided personal service, filled armies, and staffed state bureaucracies. Slavery was "widespread and indigenous" in precolonial Africa, and slaves were traded over long distances. Because villages and states owned land collectively, historian John Thornton argues, slaves were the

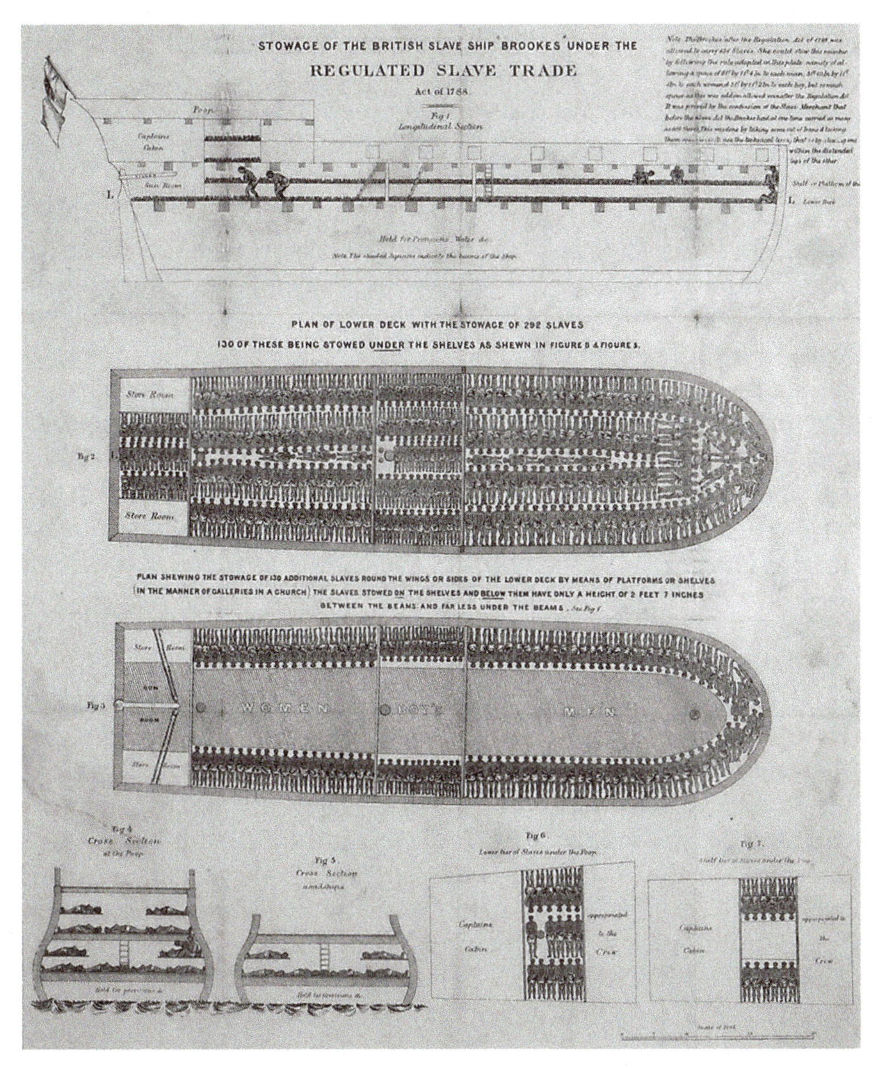

African captives stowed on a slave ship. Slaves arrived as commodities bereft of family and kin. Slavers preferred mixed cargoes assembled from different ethnic groups to deter shipboard rebellions. This antislavery image of the cross section of the Brookes, a slave ship, reveals tight packing of 482 slaves even after reforms had reduced the number of allowable slaves from over 600. Liverpool, 1884 [1808]. (Library of Congress.)

only form of "private, revenue-producing property recognized in African law," which allowed individuals to increase their wealth or extend their power.[26] Most slaves were war captives seized from the many small states of West and Central Africa, but some became enslaved through judicial decrees or sale of family members to escape debts or poverty. Slaves were nonlineage members in their owners' households, but could own property and marry, receive religious instruction, and have time to work for themselves. Nor was their servile status permanent, as masters often emancipated slaves or their children for meritorious service.

Historian Michael Gomez identifies two dimensions of black acculturation in the colonial South: "the world of the slaves, in which intra-African and African-American cultural factors were at play . . . [and] interaction with the host society—the white world—both slaveholding and nonslaveholding . . . [as] conditioned by the asymmetry of power between slave and nonslave."[27] The first process remains the most difficult to reconstruct and the most controversial. Some scholars emphasize slaves' New World experiences over African ethnicities as primary influences in creating African American cultures in the New World. No formal institutions—kingship, mosques, Yoruba priesthoods, or polygyny—survived middle passages intact. Slavers assembled cargoes through purchases from many African merchants, and during the 17th and 18th centuries, most slaves entered North America in small cargoes with blacks mixed from different places. Slaves also were disproportionately male and young, just the characteristics that made them "marketable" but less likely to be ritual specialists in their homelands. Other scholars, using studies of West African societies during the slave trade era and data compiled on over 27,000 slave trade voyages, link captives from particular African societies to specific New World destinations. Ethnic cultural practices—orientations toward time and work, spiritual beliefs, family organization, speech patterns, oral traditions, music, and aesthetics—took on new meanings under conditions not of Africans' choosing.

All scholars acknowledge the importance of Euro-American colonial societies, which were themselves evolving, in shaping slave family and cultural lives. Owners assigned slaves to work tobacco, rice, indigo, or grain, herd animals, or become artisans or domestics; organized them into labor gangs or under the task system; enforced speaking the masters' tongue (English, Spanish, or French); and set rules over slaves' nonwork time. These decisions determined the degree of slaves' physical contacts with slaveholders and with nonslaveholders and possibilities for independent family life and slave culture. Patterns in the slave trade, population, laws, economy, and religion also shaped slave life. The mechanisms of the slave trade determined the balance between recent arrivals from Africa (and which places in Africa) and acculturated American-born Creoles and between men and women. Large numbers of imports lowered prices and increased economic incentives for mistreatment to maximize production; a reduction in trade favored encouraging slave marriages to increase holdings. The possibility of manumission and self-purchase grew where slaves comprised only small portions of the population. Tobacco, rice/indigo, and nonplantation economies in Florida, Louisiana, and the backcountry had different slave densities and affected possibilities for forming families. Catholics, but not Anglicans, offered slaves religious sanction that partially protected their marriages and families.

A useful distinction in sorting out African and New World influences shaping black acculturation and family formation is to compare "societies with slaves" and "slave societies." In the former, according to historian Ira Berlin, "slaves were marginal to the central productive processes; slavery was just one form of labor among many," while in slave societies, "slavery stood at the center of economic production, and the master-slave relationship provided the model for all social relations."[28] These are not static categories but models of societal development. Virginia, Maryland, and Lowcountry Carolina began as societies with slaves in their early decades, but became slave societies by the early 18th century. Florida quickly followed suit after English control in 1763. The backcountry, always part of colonies where slaveholders ruled, was in transition. Central piedmont Virginia and North Carolina, settled in the second quarter of the 18th century, became slave societies within decades, while areas settled after mid-century were in transition. Louisiana was an exception, becoming a slave society in the mid-18th century, but with the collapse of the plantation economy turned into a society with slaves. In every area, historians T. H. Breen and Stephen Innes conclude, new cultures "developed out of an amalgam of experiences, past and present, and the end product were neither thoroughly African nor English, but uniquely Afro-American and Anglo-American."[29]

Black Family Life in Societies with Slaves

Atlantic Creoles and their children dominated the small black population in the colonial South before 1700. Drawn from the Atlantic littoral, many had lived in the Caribbean before arriving in North America. Whether these early Africans came from African, European, or West Indies ports or worked in the Atlantic maritime community, they had already separated from their homelands, understood European ways, and possessed linguistic fluency, commercial experience, geographic knowledge, and intercultural skills. Finding suitable mates among the scattered African population was difficult, as long as black numbers were small and economies undeveloped or reliant upon white laborers. Yet, some blacks exploited niches in these fluid societies' interstices to form families and even secure freedom. Numerous unions—some legal, many not—between African Creoles and whites or Native Americans created new peoples. The arrival of an American-born generation created networks of kin who assisted family members in defending their increasingly insecure position in colonial society.

The legal status of early Africans in the Chesapeake, who first arrived in Jamestown in 1619, are unclear—and a subject of much scholarly debate over the past 50 years—but they undoubtedly labored alongside white indentured servants, and, like them, became free after their terms of service expired. A fortunate few married, had children, acquired property, and became common planters. Antonio, probably a Catholic Angolan, arrived in Virginia in 1621 and worked on Richard Bennett's plantation for a dozen years. He parlayed his reputation for "hard labor and known service" to farm on his own, marry Mary (an African arriving in 1622 also working for Bennett), and baptize their four children at the local parish church.[30] Money earned from independent labor and cultivating Bennett's good will eventually gained their freedom. Renaming himself Anthony Johnson, he followed the Bennetts to Virginia's Eastern Shore, and by 1651, possessed 250 acres of land. Johnson, sons John and Richard, several servants, John Casar (a slave) tended tobacco, corn, cattle, and hogs, while Mary (now a planter's wife) cared for children and performed domestic labor, but avoided fieldwork. Their two sons and one daughter married free black and white neighbors, settled near-by, and expanded family lands by at least an additional 550 acres. Family members provided material support and emotional comfort for each other and made decisions collectively. As racial tensions rose and economic prospects fell in the mid-1660s, the Johnson clan moved north to Somerset County, Maryland, where some members merged with Nanticoke Indians.

The Johnson family was exceptional, but they illuminate broader patterns in 17th-century Chesapeake black family life. African pioneers adapted to English ways of farming, speaking, believing, and behaving, and more importantly, bargained with owners to work for themselves to purchase their freedom and emancipate their families. Until the 1660s, when laws defined blacks as slaves for life and their children after them slaves forever, many realized these aspirations. Independent labor and white patrons' assistance increased free blacks' abilities to support families, acquire property, and secure protection from hostile whites. Francisco managed the Virginia property of Jane Eltonhead, his owner, after she moved to Maryland. From 13 years of profits, he purchased his freedom, renamed himself Frank Payne, and eventually liberated his wife and children. Holding Christians as slaves was illegal before the 1660s; blacks who converted to Anglicanism and baptized their children strengthened their freedom claims.

Most blacks remained in bondage and, despite their small numbers, only 1,700 in 1668 (a mere 5 percent of the Chesapeake population) were able to form families. The Chesapeake was a marginal slave market until the end of the 17th century and unlike the male predominance among white servants imported about as many women as men. Blacks' prior acclimation to the New World meant they lived longer than did white immigrants. "This slow, irregular influx of Atlantic creoles of both sexes," historian Ira Berlin concludes, "allowed black men and women to marry and form families, or to keep established families intact."[31] Free blacks lived among white neighbors and, occasionally, black men married white women and white women took black men as husbands. Targets of community gossip, interracial unions became unlawful in 1691. More common were liaisons between unfree blacks and whites, who lived and worked together, ran off together, and spent free time carousing together. Outraged by an apparent epidemic of mulatto children—between a quarter and one-third of all illegitimate children born to white mothers had black fathers—the Maryland legislature decreed in 1664 that any freeborn white women who married a slave would hereafter serve her husband's master and their children "shall be slaves as their fathers were."[32] Existing mulatto children became servants until age 30. Although class concerns, a master's loss of a pregnant servant's labor or fears mulatto children would become public charges, probably outweighed repugnance at interracial unions, this legislation was a prelude for future governmental disruption of black family life.

Even more than in the Chesapeake, black pioneers in Lowcountry Carolina possessed the labor, linguistic, and cultural skills of Atlantic Creoles to forge family bonds. Most came with their Barbadian masters and with immunities from prior exposure to tropical diseases like malaria and yellow fever that lowered their death rates as compared to whites. Blacks took advantage of the colony's mixed herding, forest industries, and Indian slave trade economy to provision themselves and their families and sell goods or their labor in the marketplace. Although three-fourths of early black settlers were men, by 1708, blacks comprised a majority of Carolina's population, concentrated in parishes around Charles Town, with an adult sex ratio (the number of males per 100 females) of 164. Almost 30 percent of all blacks were children, most of whom lived with their parents. Carolina's mixed labor force of African and Indian slaves and Euro-American and Native servants inevitably led to much race mixing, which continued unregulated until 1717. Despite Carolina traders' efforts to keep Indians and Africans apart, the presence of large Native populations and an unsettled backcountry encouraged many slaves to seek sanctuary in Native villages or form maroon or runaway communities and create independent families.

Unlike South Carolina, where black family life developed in the context of enslavement, blacks in Spanish Florida established personal lives as free people. Most were Atlantic Creoles from Spain, Hispaniola, and Cuba. Despite their small numbers, Spanish authorities recognized their value as farmers, herders, sailors, and militiamen in undermanned Florida. In 1693, the Spanish Crown promised freedom to any fugitive who converted to Catholicism. Florida soon became a haven for fugitives, including Angolan Catholics from the Kingdom of the Kongo, whose king had converted to Christianity at the end of the 15th century. Lowcountry planters imported Angolans by the boatload during the rice revolution of the 1720s and 1730s. Fugitives eagerly joined the militia and raided Lowcountry plantations to liberate friends and family members. By 1759, three-fourths of the 70 residents of Gracia Real de Santa Teresa de Mose (located just north of Saint Augustine) lived with immediate family members with over half the households nuclear. Blacks used their knowledge of Spanish laws and institutions to file manumission petitions or purchase themselves, acquire personal property and land, defend themselves from abuse, forge patron–client ties, serve in the militia, and participate in church rituals. By 1763, about a quarter of the 3,000 blacks in Florida were free. Interracial marriages were common in this polyglot frontier and were not banned until British takeover in 1763. Black couples received Catholic marriage rites and had their infants baptized. They chose godparents to be extended kin and provide for their children's spiritual and material welfare if they died prematurely, a real possibility in Florida's lethal environment. Over time, historian Jane Landers concludes, blacks "formed intricate new kin and friendship networks with slaves, free blacks, Indians of various nations, 'new' Africans, and whites in Saint Augustine that served to stabilize their population and strengthen connection to the Spanish community."[33]

In French Louisiana, the plantation revolution went backward paving the way for free black families in a racially hybrid environment. The few blacks in early Louisiana, Atlantic Creoles familiar with French culture, sought freedom for themselves and family members. Like Frenchmen, many African men found refuge and Indian wives in Native communities along the Gulf Coast, Lower Mississippi River, and Natchez region. Attempting to turn Louisiana into a plantation colony, merchants imported some 6,000 slaves between 1719 and 1731, mostly Bambaras from Senegambia, and developed tobacco and indigo plantations on lands seized near Indian villages or worked in New Orleans. Deaths from disease and neglect outnumbered slave imports and suppressed natural population growth. With slave men outnumbering women by three or four to one, marrying Indian women or joining maroon communities comprised of Africans and Indians provided paths to making families. In theory, the *Code Noir,* French laws regarding slavery required church solemnization of blacks' marriages and their children's baptism and prohibited breaking up slaves' families. In practice, Louisiana planters simply ignored it and other laws banning interracial marriages.

The 1729 Natchez rebellion, joined by recently arrived Bambaras, unraveled the plantation regime and ended slave imports. Planters moderated their harsh regimen by encouraging slaves to marry to boost their numbers, moving them from barracks to cabins, giving slaves time off to provision themselves, and allowing Capuchin missionaries to marry slave couples and baptize their children. Slaves seized these openings to strengthen day-to-day family life. Products from garden plots, forests, and rivers improved diet and material conditions and provided surpluses for sale in New Orleans markets. In this backwater colony, where blacks outnumbered whites and Natives outnumbered both, every combination of racial mixture occurred: black men married Indian women, New Orleans slave women sold sex, and white planters took up black concubines. In the latter, known as *plaçage,* free black women's mothers negotiated agreements with planters ensuring lifetime support for their daughters and recognition of their mulatto children. When the Spanish took control in 1763 and new laws encouraged manumission, economically enterprising black families purchased their freedom, and many white men freed their black wives and mulatto children.

Black Families in Slave Societies

The consolidation of planter regimes in Virginia by the end of the 17th century and in Lowcountry Carolina two decades later degraded black family life. Planters expanded tobacco and rice cultivation by importing thousands of Africans across the Atlantic every year, who quickly overwhelmed the small Creole and free black populations. By 1720, almost all imported slaves were Africans, and blacks comprised 40 percent of Virginia's population and 70 percent of South Carolina's. African sellers valued enslaved women for their productive and reproductive labor, while European purchasers hungered after male teenagers and young men to turn raw land into profitable plantations. Males outnumbered females by two to one in Virginia and by three to one in Carolina. Sent to work on isolated plantations in small labor gangs and housed in sex-segregated barracks, they found few mates among the scattered black population. Women were scarce, fetid environments and enslavement traumas shortened lives and depressed conception rates and childbirths, kept marriages brief (if men and women married at all), and raised infant and child mortality. Black deaths exceeded births for several decades and only continued imports of new Africans sustained black population growth.

Planters desiring blacks as wealth producers but fearing their "outlandish" appearance and sullen behavior evinced contempt for slaves. As long as supplies remained plentiful, purchasing replacements was cheaper than lightening pregnant women's field labor or allowing time to nurse children. Laws upheld owners' power over black bodies. Virginia's 1705 slave code defined slaves as real estate that could be bought, sold, and inherited; made children of enslaved women slaves for life; restricted slave movement; and empowered owners to discipline slaves without fear of punishment. Planters, imbued with power and imagining themselves grand patriarchs, "granted themselves the right to enter into the slaves' most intimate affairs, demanded the complete obedience due a father, and consigned slaves to permanent childhood. This domestication of dominion," Berlin concludes, "became a central element in shaping slave life."[34] Assigning purchased slaves new names was the first sign of mastery. Diminutives (such as Betty, Sally, Jack, or Sambo) or classical monikers (such as Dido, Pompey, Cupid, or Caesar) they would never use for their own children marked the enslaved from the free. Forced dropping of surnames sought to erase lineage ties. Thus began slaves' continuing contests with owners over personal identities and family lives.

Slowly, mortality fell, plantation labor forces became larger, slave population densities greater, and a Creole, or second, generation of blacks grew to maturity. More evenly balanced sex ratios facilitated forming families. Most slaves lived in counties where blacks comprised over half of the population and on plantations with over 20 slaves. By the 1720s in Tidewater Virginia, the 1740s in the Piedmont, and 1760s in Lowcountry Carolina and Georgia, slave populations grew more from natural increase than from African imports. Encouraging slave families, planters realized, enlarged their labor forces at minimal cost and reduced black men's rebelliousness. Slaves pressed owners for concessions that recognized the importance of their families and kin ties. If owners refused, slaves took action by fleeing plantations to reunite with separated family members, claiming freedom from Spanish governors at Saint Augustine, or creating families in Indian villages or in backcountry maroon settlements. Black family formation followed different trajectories: in the Chesapeake, new Africans and acculturated Creoles forged a unified black culture, while in the Lowcountry, the rice revolution widened differences between rural and urban blacks.

Unity in Chesapeake Virginia and Maryland

Tobacco planters' dispersed slaveholdings made neighborhoods not plantations centers of black family life. Sudden influxes of Africans at the end of the 17th century disrupted black families. Tobacco was a labor-intensive, soil-exhausting crop, and planters sent new Africans to work fields (or "quarters") distant from home plantations and herded laborers back and forth between scattered tracts. Toiling in gangs of a half-dozen people, Africans were scarcely able to communicate with acculturated slaves, with their overseers, or even with each other. Intermittent additions of enslaved Africans—planters typically purchased a few slaves at a time—sustained a diverse mix of Africans from different ethnic groups alongside Virginia-born slaves. This pattern continued as tobacco cultivation spread into the Piedmont after 1720s and Southside Virginia below the James River two decades later. Living on small residential units with unbalanced sex ratios and frequently moved about, African men found few mates, as enslaved women preferred acculturated black men to saltwater arrivals and delayed childbearing.[35]

By the mid-18th century, slaves created more secure family lives. As Virginia- and Maryland-born slave children entered adulthood, by 1730 in the Tidewater and 1750 in the Piedmont, a denser population and evenly balanced sex ratios allowed for early and near universal marriages. Women began childbearing around 18 or 19, several years after becoming sexually active. Because of lower mortality, slaves' marriages lasted longer with more children surviving. Natural population growth shrank the proportion of Africans in the black population to 20 percent by mid-century, reducing tensions between different groups of "outlandish" slaves and between them and acculturated slaves. The third generation grew up surrounded by grandparents, uncles, aunts, and cousins. Their marriages deepened neighborhood bonds and attachments to place that echoed their ancestors' African villages. Slavery's uncertainties necessitated flexible marital arrangements. Half of slaves lived on holdings of over 10, most in nuclear households of husbands, wives, and children, and the latter comprised half of the enslaved plantation population. Just as West Africans found partners outside their villages, men on smallholdings preferred "broad wives," or women living on other plantations. They visited their families on nights, weekends, and holidays, but mother–child bonds became the most durable family ties.

African traditions that met needs of an ethnically diverse black population became the warp of new African American families woven by the woof of Chesapeake slavery. Rupture from Africa turned everyone into outsiders; rebuilding lineages restored identity and soothed slavery's wounds. Until well after the American Revolution, plantation neighborhoods included elderly Africans who spoke in strange accents, possessed unusual powers, sustained connections to ancestors, maintained marriage ceremonies, served as midwives, and understood the importance of lineage. Children's relatives included both their mothers' and their fathers' parents and siblings, not just one side of the family. Unlike whites, blacks did not marry cousins as they belonged to the same lineage. Slaves required owners' permission to form monogamous unions, but their ceremonies substituted an English custom for the African bride-price. "Their Marriages are generally performed amongst themselves . . ." John Brickell, a North Carolina physician, observed in 1737, "for the Man makes the Women a Present, such as a Brass Ring or some other Toy, which if she accepts of becomes his Wife."[36] Afterward, participants feasted and danced. Adults adopted enslaved children as their own, and elderly women regained responsibilities for childcare while their younger sisters worked in fields all day. Parents moved from single-sex barracks to cabins and reared children in nuclear families not in extended households. As marriages deepened ties, slave quarters became villages of interconnected lineages. Parents named children after family members, especially men, creating lineal links within and across generations. Parents preferred common English names, like James and Lucy, for their children, but at least 10 percent linked an African past to an American present with names like Let, Tamer, Tiba, Sawney, Mingo, and Muhamed. Some adults took surnames to reclaim family identities.

Slaves and owners contested black families' customary privileges. Slaves wanted the right to select marriage partners; name their children; have time to nurse infants for two or three years; live in individual cabins; supplement rations with garden crops, hunting, and fishing; visit "broad wives" and children on neighboring plantations; have Sundays and holidays to themselves; and pass down labor skills or privileged positions to their children. Tobacco planters, who lived on their estates and had personal contact with most slaves, recognized their financial interest in the annual "crop" of slave children. They boasted of their "young breeding negroes'" reproductive capacities, kept lists of mothers and their children, and assigned some tasks in family groups.[37] Owners moved their growing population of slaves away from their own families to separate slave quarters that provided physical spaces and privacy for independent black family life.

No laws protected these rights, however, and new owners or overseers might impose different rules or seek to reclaim slaves' "family time." Diversified plantations created class differences that affected black family life. Children's work gangs ran errands, swept yards and barns, and toted water and food to adults. Mother–daughter work gangs labored in fields and made cloth and clothes. Large planters selected men for training as drivers, artisans, groomsmen, boatmen, or wagoners, or hired them out, skills that slaves parlayed into better housing, living standards, and privileges for their families; knowledge of the world beyond the plantation; and opportunities for a second family. Large owners picked nannies to rear their children, black youths as their personal companions, and young girls to wait on family members. Female domestics lived in mansions away from the quarters and suffered from predatory white men's abuse. Despite owners' self-interest in encouraging slave fertility, economic considerations trumped black family stability in making most labor assignments in gifts of slaves to white family members, and in settling estates. As long as slaves were property and owners viewed mothers and children as the primary family relationship, frequent separations were inevitable.

Diversity in Lowcountry Carolina and Georgia

The rice revolution created black family lives deeply divided between Lowcountry blacks, who drew heavily on African family patterns, and urban blacks in Charles Town and Savannah, who acculturated to Anglo-American family norms. More slaves entered the colonial South through Charles Town than any other port with arrivals concentrated in the 1720s, 1730s, 1750s, and 1760s. Between a quarter and a third were Angolans from West Central Africa, and rice cultivators from Senegambia and Gold Coast comprised another quarter. Rice and indigo planters needed numerous workers, and coastal Carolina by 1710, Georgia by 1760, and West Florida by 1770 became "more like a Negro Country" than outposts of English civilization as Africans comprised 80 percent or more of the rural population and almost half of town dwellers. Only profits gratified planters; they imported adult men, who outnumbered women by three to one, and sent women to the rice fields. Blacks had partial immunity from malaria and yellow fever from prior exposure in Africa, but long hours working in standing water in mosquito-infested swamps and the brutal toil of constructing dikes and levees shortened many lives. Exhausted, demoralized African women and men found little reason to mate or bring new life into the hell of their new existence, and only massive imports sustained Carolina's black population growth before 1760.

Slave quarters, historian Ira Berlin observes, became the "heart of African American life in the countryside."[38] Blacks' concentration on large plantations along a narrow tidal coast (by midcentury, over one-third of blacks lived in units of over 50 slaves) interlaced with shallow waterways facilitated marital contacts. The task system, where owners assigned each laborer a specified work stint, a quarter-acre rice plot, for example, provided economic and personal underpinnings for independent family life. Once slaves completed their work quota, the rest of their day was their own. Slaves lived in nuclear residential units in separate plantation villages and supported their families by working family provision grounds; men fishing, hunting, and making household goods; and women sewing clothes and, like their sisters in West Africa, trading surplus items in urban markets. Artisans and watermen parlayed their skills into ready cash for their families, and slave drivers used their privileged positions in the plantation hierarchy to live in larger cabins or receive better clothing for family members. Carolina-born slave females benefited from lower mortality and balanced sex ratios; married earlier, around age 19, often to older men; and bore many children. As slaves became more numerous and population grew through natural increase, planters recognized the importance of family life for maintaining order even if it reduced their authority. At the same time, family ties kept many slaves from running away altogether. Slaves "love their families dearly," a South Carolina minister admitted, "and none runs away from the other."[39] A few slaves made alternative family arrangements. In 1765, whites discovered 40 runaways (men, women, and children) living in a maroon village in the swamps north of Savannah.

Africa left deep imprints in the Lowcountry. Isolated from Anglo-American society—overseers, owners, and their families were the sole whites in the Lowcountry and the latter there only during winter months—and absorbing many new arrivals each year, slaves drew on old traditions to organize families in a new land. They adopted African construction techniques to build individual family houses, spoke African traders' lingua franca, and honored ancestors with elaborate burial ceremonies. Parents gave their children African names or named them for their birthdays: Quaco, Juba, or Quashee were African day names and "Christmas" arrived on December 25, 1743. They created new patrilineal ties by naming sons after fathers or grandfathers to compensate for loss of sons by sale or transfer to other quarters and left behind matrilineal households. The continuing influx of Africans, presence of African grandparents, and growing numbers of Carolina-born parents, aunts, and uncles deepened Lowcountry blacks' separation from Anglo-American culture and strengthened resistance to overseers and owners' harsh demands.

Charles Town, Savannah, Wilmington, and other coastal towns, where planter grandees maintained their primary homes, presented a different black countenance. In contrast to country

Africans, city blacks were lighter, more skilled, and a few even free. Carolina planters inherited West Indian attitudes that sexual access to young enslaved women was a master's perquisite, and, unlike Virginia, these liaisons barely merited public comment much less condemnation. Planters' brown children worked as domestic servants decked in livery, in backyard shops as craftsmen and groomsmen, and as messengers and boatman. White fathers raised a few children as family members and educated though rarely emancipated them. Mulattoes' close associations with wealthy whites and extensive English acculturation separated them from larger numbers of darker slaves, who crowded into basements, garrets, or backyard barracks. Urban slaveholdings were small, and with black women outnumbering men, there were few families and fewer children. Slave men found ready employment around busy wharves, warehouses, shipyards, and shops, and women worked as weavers or sold goods in marketplaces and streets. Most prized of all was hiring one's own time. Some owners consented to allowing hired slaves to live independently. These blacks, free in all but name, lived with their families in black enclaves, the Neck in Charles Town and Under-the-Bluff in Savannah. Streets and alleys became living spaces where city and country blacks mingled, wore their best clothes, socialized, and learned the latest news, much to white's displeasure. Like an earlier generation of Atlantic Creoles, Lowcountry urban slaves used their cosmopolitan knowledge of white society and their economic skills to chart independent lives for themselves and their families. Even so, freedom's sweet rewards remained just beyond their reach.

MAKING FAMILIES SOUTHERN

Benjamin Franklin attributed Euro-Americans soaring population growth to unprecedented economic opportunities for forming families. Men married when they can support a family, he wrote in 1751, and because of abundant cheap land, "a laboring man that understands husbandry can in a short time save money enough to purchase a piece of new land sufficient for a plantation. . . . Hence, marriages in America are more general, and more generally early than in Europe . . . [where] they have but four births to a marriage . . . , we may here reckon eight, . . . [so] our people must at least be doubled every twenty years."[40]

Yet, Franklin's prescient connection between families and society overlooked considerable colonial experience. Colonization was a process of creative destruction transforming everyone and everywhere it touched. Deaths outnumbered births in the 17th-century South. Many Europeans arrived as individuals only to die before they formed new families. Staple crops created large plantation households that were more like factories than domestic families. European diseases, warfare, and dislocations destroyed many Native American families, and the Atlantic slave trade permanently severed Africans from their families and kin connections. Yet, colonial settlements survived *only* because Indian, European, and African men and women continued life by creating new kinds of families. They drew on their particular cultural traditions about organizing family life and faced radically different opportunities and constraints that shaped the array of choices individuals made. Their children inherited family lives not only marked by unprecedented diversity but also southern in the importance of kin attachments, close ties to land and place, nurturing of opportunity, and adaptability to societal change.

NOTES

1. For different approaches for studying the family historically, see Steven Mintz and Susan Kellogg, *Domestic Revolutions: A Social History of American Family Life* (New York: Free Press, 1988), 245–52. Households and families are not identical. *Households* include all individuals living together whether or not they are related; *families* include all individuals in socially recognized relationships based on marriage and parent–child ties regardless of whether they live together. Only in nuclear or conjugal families consisting of husbands, wives, and children are households and families identical. Planters often used familial language to describe their households that included slaves, white servants, employees, and kin in addition to wives and children. Native Americans and Africans, in contrast, identified themselves as members of a clan, or a lineage group descended from a common ancestor, and used familial language—"elder brother" or "sister's son"—to identify individuals with special social obligations.

2. Donald R. Wright, *African Americans in the Colonial Era: From African Origins through the American Revolution*, 2nd ed. (Wheeling, IL: Harlan Davidson, 2000), 103.

3. Helen C. Rountree, *The Powhatan Indians of Virginia: Their Traditional Culture* (Norman: University of Oklahoma Press, 1989), 89.

4. Charles Hudson, *The Southeastern Indians* (Knoxville: University of Tennessee Press, 1976), 184. Lineages tracing descent from a presumed common female ancestor are called clans, which were almost always named for an animal (deer, bear, etc.) or natural phenomenon (i.e., wind).

Clans defined a category of relatives scattered across many different villages.

5. Theda Perdue, *Cherokee Women* (Lincoln: University of Nebraska Press, 1998), 24.

6. The Powhatan lineage system is poorly documented and disputed by scholars. Helen Rountree, the foremost scholar of Powhatans believes they were matrilineal but lived in virilocal (with male relatives) settlements (Rountree, *Powhatan Indians,* 92–84).

7. James Adair, *Adair's History of the American Indians,* ed. by Samuel Cole Williams (Johnson City, TN: Wautugua Press, 1930), 480, cited in Perdue, *Cherokee Women,* 58.

8. Robert Beverley, *The History and Present State of Virginia,* ed. by David Freeman Hawke (Indianapolis, IN: The Bobbs-Merrill Company, Inc., 1971 [1705]), 107, 108. Keepers explained any initiate's death as caused by Okee, the evil spirit, who sucked blood from the initiates' left breast.

9. Pocahontas and Rolfe traveled to England in 1616; she died there the following year as they began their return voyage. Their son, Thomas Rolfe, was raised in England, but returned to Virginia in 1635 where he became a small landowner. Pocahontas was not a legend in her own time; her entry into American mythology dates from the mid-19th century.

10. Perdue, *Cherokee Women,* 63.

11. William Gouge, *Of Domesticall Duties* (London, 1622), cited in James Horn, *Adapting to a New World: English Society in the Seventeenth-Century Chesapeake* (Chapel Hill: University of North Carolina Press, 1994), 205.

12. "Letter to the Governor and Council in Virginia, August 12, 1621," *The Records of the Virginia Company of London,* 3 vols., ed. by Susan M. Kingsbury (Washington, D.C.: Government Printing Office, 1906), 3: 493.

13. Mintz and Kellogg, *Domestic Revolutions,* 39.

14. Table 1.2; Peter Wood, "The Changing Population of the Colonial South: An Overview by Race and Region, 1685–1790," in *Powhatan's Mantle: Indians in the Colonial Southeast,* rev. ed., ed. by Gregory A. Waselkov, Peter H. Wood, and Tom Hatley (Lincoln: University of Nebraska Press, 2006 [1989]), 61.

15. Daniel Blake Smith, *Inside the Great House: Planter Family Life in Eighteenth-Century Chesapeake Society* (Ithaca, NY: Cornell University Press, 1980), 26.

16. Ibid., 53.

17. See illustration on p. 171.

18. Letter from Anne Randolph to St. George Tucker, September 23, 1788, "Randolph and Tucker Letters," *Virginia Magazine of History and Biography,* 42, no. 2 (April 1934): 49, 50, cited in Smith, *Inside the Great House,* 142.

19. Ibid.

20. Smith, *Inside the Great House,* 21, 22.

21. Devereux Jarratt, "The Autobiography of the Reverend Devereux Jarratt, 1732–1762," Introduction and Notes by Douglass Adair, *William and Mary Quarterly*, 3rd ser., vol. 9, no. 3 (July 1952): 361.

22. David J. Weber, *The Spanish Frontier in North America* (New Haven, CT: Yale University Press, 1992), 313, 326.

23. Daniel H. Usner, Jr., *Indians, Settlers, and Slaves in a Frontier Exchange Economy: The Lower Mississippi Valley before 1763* (Chapel Hill: University of North Carolina Press, 1992), 57, 58.

24. Weber, *Spanish Frontier*, 332.

25. West African societies were generally patrilineal, while West-Central and Central African societies were matrilineal. Less than 5 percent of the estimated 11.5 million Africans carried across the Atlantic ended up in the colonial South. Most slaves arrived between 1700 and 1760 with some 80 percent imported directly from Africa.

26. John Thornton, *African and Africans in the Making of the Atlantic World, 1400–1800*, 2nd ed. (Cambridge: Cambridge University Press, 1998), 73, 74. In Europe, investing in land was the means for becoming wealthy and powerful. African slaves were more like European peasants or serfs than New World chattel slaves.

27. Michael A. Gomez, *Exchanging Country Marks: The Transformation of African Identities in the Colonial and Antebellum South* (Chapel Hill: University of North Carolina Press, 1998), 8.

28. Ira Berlin, *Many Thousands Gone: The First Two Centuries of Slavery in North America* (Cambridge, MA: Harvard University Press, 1998), 8.

29. T.H. Breen and Stephen Innes, *"Myne Owne Ground": Race and Freedom on Virginia's Eastern Shore, 1640–1676* (New York: Oxford University Press, 1980), 69. The reference is to Virginia's Eastern Shore, but applies to all areas of the colonial South, if one includes Native Americans, Spanish Florida, and French Louisiana.

30. Ibid, 10.

31. Berlin, *Many Thousands Gone*, 40, 41.

32. "An Act Concerning Negroes & Other Slaves," *Archives of Maryland: Proceedings and Acts of the General Assembly of Maryland, January 1637/8–September 1664*, ed. by William Hand Browne (Baltimore: Maryland Historical Society, 1883), 533, 534.

33. Jane Landers, *Black Society in Spanish Florida* (Urbana: University of Illinois Press, 1999), 25.

34. Berlin, *Many Thousands Gone*, 99.

35. Between 1695 and 1770, almost 95,000 slaves disembarked in Virginia and Maryland: about one-third were from the Bight of Biafra, 15 percent from Senegambia, and 10 percent from West-Central Africa. These proportions shifted over time and between different markets, and planters had little influence on the ethnicities of arriving slaves, making difficult tracing influences of particular ethnic groups in the Chesapeake.

36. John Brickell, *The Natural History of North Carolina* (1737), cited in Betty Wood, *Slavery in Colonial America, 1619–1776* (Lanham, MD: Rowman & Littlefield Publisher, 2005), 102; see illustration on p. 220.

37. Cited in Berlin, *Many Thousands Gone*, 127.

38. Ibid., 162.

39. Klaus G. Loewald, Beverly Starika, and Paul S. Taylor, trans. and eds., "Johann Martin Bolzius Answers a Questionnaire on Carolina and Georgia," *William and Mary Quarterly*, 3rd ser. 14, no. 3 (July 1957): 236.

40. Benjamin Franklin, "Observations Concerning the Increase of Mankind and the Peopling of Countries (1751)," *The Autobiography and Other Writings by Benjamin Franklin*, ed. by Peter Shaw (New York: Bantam Books, 1982), 221.

4

POSSESSIONS

Material culture—housing, furnishings, and clothing—met colonial Southerners' physical needs, but "human-made things are far more than mere tools," Ann Smart Martin observes, "they are complex bundles of individual, social, and cultural meanings grafted onto something that can be seen, touched, and owned." Objects exhibit personal and collective identities that "mediate social relations and cultural behavior."[1] In the 17th century, chests stored prized possessions, fine linen, and silver plate but became benches at mealtimes. European-made cabinets reminded people of places left behind, and ones with stenciled decorations expressed German artistic traditions. By mid-18th century upright chests of drawers organized suits of imported satin clothes, and genteel diners sat in matched sets of individual chairs at mealtimes. Indian and African American material culture was spartan and much less survives than from acquisitive colonials, but archeologists provide clues on their material lives that are missing from written records. Since everyone creates and uses artifacts, it is "in the seemingly little and insignificant things that accumulate to create a lifetime," James Deetz argues, where "the essence of our existence is captured."[2]

Surviving artifacts are neither representative nor unambiguous records of past material life. Garments were used until the clothes wore out, and only the most expensive and least used specimens (e.g., ball gowns) ended up in museum collections. Discarded objects remained buried in the ground until modern researchers chanced to uncover them. Houses, furnishings, and clothing owned by wealthy families survive in much greater abundance than possessions of the poor, the dependent, and the enslaved. Durable metal and ceramic objects outnumber baskets and textiles made of quickly decomposing plant fibers and animal matter. Artifacts itemized in probate inventories or found in museum collections do not always reveal how or why objects were used. Women and men understood and used tools in ways particular to gendered work processes and possessed technological skills now lost. Meanings change. A "looking glass" in the 17th century was a chamber pot, not a mirror. Sieves perform the same function in food preparation today as they did 400 years ago, but conjurers also utilized them to tell fortunes. Native American women's subsistence tools possessed spiritual power and were also used in sacred rituals. Uses shifted depending on owners' desires and cultural contexts. Indians turned European metal objects (labeled "trinkets" by Europeans) into items of personal adornment, while slaves used English consumer goods in West African spiritual rituals.[3]

Although housing, furnishings, and clothing reveal different aspects of daily life in the colonial South, they share common themes. Material culture reveals physical textures of daily life. Early humans fashioned tools first to survive and then to improve living standards. Europeans, Native Americans, and Africans each devised different ways of meeting physical needs mediated by particular environments, subsistence systems, beliefs, and social organizations. Material culture is never static but changes through migration, trade, and contacts with others. The arrival of Europeans and Africans in the colonial South dramatically altered existing material cultures of Natives and newcomers alike, but initially they incorporated new objects into existing practices and meanings. Englishmen brought everyday necessities with them to Jamestown to recreate English culture, but needed Indian foods and local building materials to survive. Powhatans eagerly traded corn for metal implements that made everyday tasks lighter. Neither anticipated a revolution in their material culture or ways of life.

Material culture richly documents how daily life changed through cultural interactions between Natives, Europeans, and Africans in the colonial South. Disparities of power and regional variations created many different Creole cultures, but all mixed old and new. Plantations never recreated English villages or 17th-century landed estates. Indian corn became a staple of southern diet, and Indian tobacco measured planters' self-worth. In the backcountry and in Louisiana, settlers brought European guns and books but wore indigenous dress, ate local fare, and adopted Native construction methods. European guns, hatchets, and cooking pots made native subsistence easier; textiles added comfort to bodies and beds; and mirrors and beads adorned bodies. At first, using these objects required no changes in values or social organization, but once material luxuries became cultural necessities, Europeans became an indispensable presence in Natives' lives. Africans arrived in chains almost naked, but brought material cultural knowledge to the colonial South. They made "bangars" (or banjos) out of stringed gourds, wove grass baskets to fan rice, incorporated African designs onto European objects, and used African ingredients to prepare owners' meals.

Colonial Southerners' material culture was part of the Atlantic world of commerce and ideas. Indian corn and deerskins traded for English guns, and Venetian glass beads linked natives and colonial merchants to international production and exchange networks. Early settlers depended on regular shipments of powder, shot, manufactured goods, textiles, and communion plate from Europe for physical and spiritual survival. African Creoles created new cultural forms from forced migrations across the Atlantic. Free blacks from Haiti brought "shotgun" houses to New Orleans in the early 19th century: a mix of Yoruba floor plans, Arawak Indian porches, and French construction techniques. Metropolitan standards of material culture measured provincial identities. Seventeenth-century Chesapeake tobacco planters prioritized quick riches over permanent communities and lived in flimsy dwelling houses. After 1720, inexpensive English consumer goods (ceramic wares, tea, furniture, furnishings, and clothing) allowed colonials to upgrade necessities and purchase luxuries. Members of elite families followed the latest English fashions and adopted new ways of eating, dressing, socializing, and behaving. Their social inferiors soon followed suit. A century earlier, Indians had participated in a consumer revolution trading deerskins for metal and textile goods.

Finally, material objects created or reinforced class and ethnic boundaries and revealed patterns of domination and resistance. Royal governors and Native chiefs donned embroidered silk suits and deerskin mantels, respectively, to denote elite status. Europeans perceived scantily clad Indians as savages. Solid barns marked German farmers' industriousness, while indifferent English ones their owners' apparent improvidence. Fine dining, expensive furniture, silk clothes, and correct deportment separated gentlefolk from commoners. Tea sets possessed cultural capital, as proper use required privileged knowledge and special entertainment spaces. Yet, families of middling rank and even the poor acquired cheap versions to purchase gentility and imbibed colonials' favorite hot beverage. Planters supervised construction of impressive Georgian mansions that followed English models with exteriors denoting their owners' social status to passersby and interiors separating private and public life. Planters imposed their wills on plantation landscapes by spatially segregating work spaces, slaves' housing, and whites' leisure. Clothes made of coarse cloth and meals of cheap cuts of meat reminded slaves of their inferior status, even as they contested masters' authority by creating their own paths in the landscape or acquired goods to improve personal appearance.

HOUSING

Houses—the largest and most costly material objects—provided shelter from physical elements, workspaces for daily subsistence, and areas for family living and social life. In their construction methods, exterior presentations, and interior spatial arrangements, houses contained and expressed material life. At a glance, houses revealed their dwellers' family structure (nuclear or clan), livelihood (farming, craft, or trade), status (elite or commoner), caste (slave or free), ethnicity (English, German, or Cherokee), and values (materialistic or communal). Evidence from surviving colonial structures and from historical archaeology reveals a bewildering variety of housing types reflecting the colonial South's social diversity and societal transformations between the 16th and the 18th centuries.

Native Americans

Many Native American dwellings were quite large by European standards, typically housing between 6 and 20 linage members, and some were 60 or more feet long and 2 stories high. Indians living in temperate climates did not require durable houses and never developed the technology to build permanent structures. Since ordinary families in woodland cultures resided in dispersed hamlets near planting grounds and moved every 10 years or so as declining soil fertility reduced crop yields, practical, easily constructed houses perfectly suited their needs. Dwelling houses consisted of rectangular, circular, or oval frameworks of rot-resistant pine or black locust saplings set into the earth about a foot apart and lashed together to form barrel-shaped or circular roofs that were reinforced with horizontal cane, white oak, or hickory splints. These one-room houses had packed dirt floors and central smoke holes that partially vented perpetually burning fires.

Wall coverings and roofs varied depending on local materials and climate. The Powhatan's 25 to 50-foot long barrel-shaped houses were covered with bark or reed mats with small mat-covered doors at one end. Women carried house coverings to hunting quarters in the fall and winter and in a few hours built new house frames. Shingles or clapboard siding made of cypress or pine and thatched roofs of palmetto leaf were also common coverings. Naturalist William Bartram described Yuchi houses in Georgia as being "large and neatly built; the walls of the houses are constructed of a wooden frame, then lathed and plastered inside and out with a reddish well-tempered clay or mortar, which gives them the appearance of red brick walls, and these houses are neatly covered or roofed with cypress bark or shingles of that tree."[4] The Cherokees, Choctaws, Creeks, and Chickasaws constructed framed houses with gabled roofs that were left open for ventilation and supported by upright pine posts and horizontal wattles of small saplings and splints lashed to uprights with leather. Daub walls from a wet clay–grass mixture were allowed to dry and then whitewashed with "tabby," a concrete mixture of burnt lime, sand or clay, and shells. Timicua houses, known as "chickees," dispensed entirely with walls and had only posts and palmetto-leaf roofs.

In addition to large rectangular summerhouses, Appalachian Indians built smaller winter dwellings. These small, circular structures were dug several feet into the ground with cylindrical walls and conical roofs insulated with six inches of clay stucco and shingled with pine bark or grass thatch. Small doors made of mats and entered along L-shaped passageways blocked cold drafts. With fires perpetually burning in centers and central small holes in roofs for ventilation, the natives' snug houses struck English visitors as "warme as stooves, but very smoaky."[5] Small storage buildings completed these household complexes.

Chiefly dwelling houses were of similar construction but much larger or multibuilding compounds as befitting their occupants' high status, large households, and hospitality responsibilities.

Powhatan's seat was reportedly 40 yards long with mat partitions creating separate rooms. Visitors passed through guards and "many darke windings and turninges" to Powhatan's chamber where he greeted them surrounded by numerous wives, councilors, and bodyguards, all of which impressed visitors.[6]

By the late colonial period, European influences introduced more diverse housing in many villages. Treaty Indians near colonial settlements replaced bent saplings with European rectangular framing of squared logs and rafters but retained traditional bark siding. Children of English traders and Indian mothers lived in English-style two-story buildings of framed timber and clapboard. Creeks, Cherokees, Chickasaws, and Choctaws increasingly abandoned communal long houses for family log cabins and chimneys.[7]

17th-Century Chesapeake

English emigrants brought various regional housing traditions and construction methods to the Chesapeake, and through trial-and-error devised new house forms to meet novel social and environmental conditions. Durability, flexibility, and variety characterized English housing. Yeomen's houses in England were one- or two-story structures either framed with seasoned timber or made of stone-and-rubble with wooden plank floors, glazed windows, and roofs of stone, tile, or thatch. Multiple rooms partially separated work and living spaces, and ladders or stairs led to storage lofts and additional sleeping chambers. In northern England, one-story houses were divided into several rooms with detached food preparation areas forming loose courtyards. In all but the largest houses, halls with central fireplaces were the principal rooms for cooking, seating, eating, and entertaining with smaller inner parlors or sleeping rooms. Additions and second stories were added as households grew in wealth and size. Even landless farm laborers lived in sturdy small 2- or 3-room cottages of about 600 square feet, while homes of the wealthy had 8 or more rooms, multiple fireplaces, and specialized areas for cooking, eating, socializing, and sleeping.

Chesapeake houses, in contrast, were primitive, impermanent, and untidy. Archaeological evidence on early Jamestown houses reveal lightweight frame construction with posts set directly into the ground (known as "earthfast" or "posthole"), walls of packed clay between upright poles, and reed thatch roofs. These wattle-and-daub structures suited the Virginia Company's need for quick, cheap, and easily repaired barracks with multiple small rooms for sleeping and working. After the Virginia Company shifted to private landholdings in the 1620s, planters experimented with a variety of earthfast structures. By mid-century, dwellings utilizing box framing with heavy cedar or cypress upright posts set into the ground; sills, plates, and tie beams for stability; walls of riven (not sawn) overlapping clapboard; window shutters; and shingle roofs were so common, they were called "Virginia houses." "Welsh chimneys" of clay and timber placed outside on gable ends and tilted away from houses reduced danger from fires. Interior walls were usually covered with burned oyster shell plaster.

Visitors viewed Virginia houses' rough unpainted exteriors and clapboard siding, which warped as green wood dried, as mean hovels suitable for cottagers but beneath proper yeoman. Planters, however, preferred these flimsy unadorned dwellings as they freed capital to purchase indentured servants and develop their plantations. Skilled carpenters could construct earthfast box-framed structures from local timber (preferably oak) in a few weeks; but

Reconstructed houses in Jamestown, Virginia. English settlers adapted familiar building techniques in the colonial South. These reconstructions of the first houses inside Jamestown Fort are of wattle-and-daub construction with thatched roofs and small open windows. Common planters and their indentured servants lived in impermanent earthfast dwellings for most of the 17th century. (Photograph courtesy of Jamestown National Historic Park, National Park Service.)

after a decade or so, sagging and rotting posts required major repairs, conversion to animal barns or storage shelters, or abandonment as planters relocated to new tobacco ground. Virginia houses were up to 20 feet wide with about half subdivided into 2 or 3 rooms with larger halls for eating, entertaining, and sleeping, and smaller "inner" rooms or chambers where owners and wives slept. One or two small shuttered windows made interior lighting dim. Lofts reached by ladders provided additional sleeping and storage space.

In the late 17th century, winners in the race for servants diverted some new wealth into additional buildings and finer dwellings. They paid workmen to construct earthfast kitchens, workshops, and storage sheds to accommodate growing households and provide workspaces for diversified plantation economies. Some planters enlarged dwelling houses with additional rooms to form T- or L-shaped floor plans or built second stories reached by staircases and added bricked cellars, more windows, plastered ceilings, paneled walls, planked floors, and brick fireplaces and chimneys. Small rooms provided private spaces for planters and their wives, while other rooms were flexible and unspecialized for daily social and work needs. Servants slept in unheated lofts, rooms, passageways, cellars, or work buildings.

The wealthiest men created new plantation complexes comprised of large brick dwelling houses surrounded by numerous small "dependencies": overseers' houses, servant housing, workshops, animal shelters, and storage buildings. Brick masons, in short supply before 1650, followed English styles and constructed two-story houses with full cellars, multiple chimneys, and leaded casement windows. Bacon's Castle in Surry County, built in 1665, is the oldest surviving brick house in Virginia. Two stories tall and set on a raised cellar with a full attic, the 8-room house seemed much larger than its modest 25 by 45-foot footprint. English bond brickwork with alternating courses of headers and stretchers and projecting Flemish gables and triple chimneystacks indicate fine craftsmanship. A formal garden, dating from about 1680 and likely the first in Virginia, denoted owner Arthur Allen's gentility. As planters shifted some work areas into separate structures and replaced indentured servants with African slaves, they relocated workers from attics and cellars to barracks or duplexes. Space inside dwelling houses was reorganized; additional rooms allowed separating private from public activities and created specialized areas for dining and entertaining.

18th-Century Chesapeake

After 1700, wealthy planters supervised construction of great houses on river bluffs near landing places that commanded fine views and displayed their eminence to passersby. Robert Beverley applauded gentlemen's new "large brick houses of many rooms on a floor and several stories high. . . . They always contrive to have large rooms that they may be cool in summer." An English visitor traveling up the York River in the 1730s noted many "pleasant Seats on the Bank, which Shew Like little villages, for having Kitchins, Dayry houses, Barns, Stables, Store houses, and some of the 2 or 3 Negro Quarters all Separate from Each other but near the mansion houses."[8] The Governor's Mansion, constructed between 1706 and 1722 in the new capital at Williamsburg, was the prototypic great house. The mansion's position at the end of a broad green and framed by two office buildings enhanced its visibility, imposing size, symmetry, and formal design. A balustrade roof and cupola and luxurious interiors expressed royal governors' power and prestige. Multiple rooms with rich paneling, elaborate fireplace mantels, and decorated ceilings created specialized areas for receptions, formal dinners, male socializing, dances, and musical entertainments. The enclosed formal garden enchanted visitors and provided vistas for admiring the palace as a place of genteel refinement as well as a seat of royal authority.

Wealthy planters and merchants purchased elegance through design, replacing wooden dwellings with multistoried brick structures, the plantation and town houses that still attract modern visitors to Virginia and Maryland. They adopted the latest Georgian styles from English architectural design books with geometric designs, symmetrical facades and floor plans, raised half basements, fine brickwork, classical decorative details, flanking dependencies, and richly paneled interiors that proclaimed patriarchal order and gentility. Visitors entered through elevated portico doorways into central halls that ran through the house to a rear door with two rooms on either side entered directly from the hall. A staircase led to four upper rooms, the family's private living areas. Corner rooms had high ceilings, large double-hung sash windows with multiple glass panes, wainscoted walls, and individual fireplaces that brought comfort: breezes to cool humid summer afternoons and warmth to brighten dark winter days.

Great houses revolutionized domestic life. Halls, no longer work centers, became reception areas for receiving visitors and determining

Virginia plantation landscape. Wealthy planters fashioned landscapes as expressions of social power and English taste. Numerous dependencies—stable (front); kitchen, work buildings, and coach house (right); and schoolhouse (left)—magnify the two-story white-plastered brick mansion house at Nomini Hall (circa 1730; altered, 1771), Westmoreland County, Virginia. Philip Fithian, the tutor, thought the double row of poplars on the left "form an extremely pleasant avenue, & . . . through them, the House appears most romantic . . . [and] truly elegant." Philip Fithian, *Journal and Letters of Philip Vickers Fithian, 1774–1774: A Plantation Tutor of the Old Dominion* [Charlottesville: University Press of Virginia, 1957], entry for March 18, 1774, p. 81. (Library of Congress.)

who was admitted into formal entertaining spaces—parlors, dining rooms, and ballrooms—or to private living quarters upstairs. Lavishly appointed public rooms with exotic paneling, carved mantelpieces, detailed molding, decorated ceilings, fine furniture, and family portraits staged genteel living. Staircases descending into central halls provided grand entrances for welcoming guests. Rooms opening directly into central halls and back stairways allowed slaves to move between rooms without passing through them, to serve without been seen. Domestic slaves labored in raised basements and dependencies convenient to but separated from their owners' private living areas.[9]

Aspiring common planters replaced earthfast dwellings with diminutive clapboard or brick versions of great houses. Bloomsbury, built in the 1730s in frontier Orange County, was a one-and-a-half-story frame structure over a brick basement with two brick end chimneys and a back porch framed into the house. A dining room and central hall downstairs and a large upper chamber and two small rooms reached by a stairway separated family living from public entertaining. Reuben Daniel's 250-acre plantation in Orange County included a 20 by 28-foot frame dwelling house with a brick chimney, kitchen, barn (24 feet square), and tobacco houses (20 by 32 feet). James Madison, Sr., replaced his father's earthfast dwelling at Mount Pleasant with a handsome two-story brick house constructed in the fashionable Georgian style with two rooms on either side of a central hallway, the nucleus of the present-day Montpelier mansion house.

Most small planters, tenants, and indentured servants in the Chesapeake lived in two- or three-room unadorned framed houses one-room deep with clapboard siding, pine or cypress shingle roofs, small windows with shutters, and end chimneys. "Houses here are almost all of wood, covered with the same," an English visitor wrote in the 1780s, "the roof with shingles, the sides and ends with thin boards, and not always lathed and plastered within; only those of the better sort are finished in that manner, and painted on the outside."[10] Owners added new rooms oblivious to formal rules of symmetry expected of genteel houses. Expansion into the backcountry in the 18th century perpetuated impermanent building traditions. "Patent" houses, hastily constructed to confirm land grants, were one-and-a-half-story earthfast structures about 16 or 20 feet square with one or two rooms heated by single chimneys with unheated lofts reached by ladders.

Lowcountry

The Lowcountry's heterogeneous population, semitropical environment, and Caribbean connections created regional housing styles, which by mid-18th century increasingly modeled the new Georgian architecture. Twentieth-century preservationists, who restored old Charles Town and Savannah houses with bright pastel-shaded stucco exteriors to recreate an imagined colonial appearance, masked Lowcountry housing's rude beginnings and diversity. As in the Chesapeake, early homes were earthfast frame dwellings of two or three rooms, a sleeping loft, clapboard siding, shingle roofs, and end chimneys. Georgia Trustees ordered construction of uniform 16 by 24-foot earthfast houses in Savannah of three rooms (large halls and two small chambers), garrets reached by ladders, and back lots for gardens and livestock. Most cooking, eating, and work activities took place in halls with other rooms for private entertaining and sleeping. Although termites ravaged these impermanent frame structures within a decade, settlers continued to build them. Even Charles Town boasted but one brick house in 1680, and Savannah had just three in 1762. Sixty years later, wealthy Charles Town merchants and planters lived in brick dwellings built in a mélange of styles: Dutch Huguenots' Flemish-gabled houses, homes with shops in front rooms, and two- and three-story dwellings with shallow upper balconies and various roof designs. Colonel William Rhett, a merchant slaveowner, lived in a handsome two-story house facing the Cooper River set on a raised, or "English," basement with dormer attic windows and a cupola. A central passage provided access to two small front rooms and two large back rooms.

Planters located early country homes by unhealthy swamps to supervise slaves in rice cultivation. These modest wood or brick dwellings one or two stories high had two to four unequally sized rooms on each floor and kitchens and workspaces in raised basements. After 1700, profits from slave-produced rice purchased grand brick houses one-and-a-half or two stories in different styles and varied floor plans and room sizes. Mulberry (1714), Thomas Broughton's plantation, featured four symmetrical flanking pavilions with interrupted double-hipped roofs reflecting his Huguenot French Renaissance tastes, while Fairfield (1730) was an unadorned two-story frame dwelling set on a half basement that opened onto a large hall and three smaller rooms.

Like the Chesapeake, Lowcountry plantations became manor villages with slaves living and working in nearby dependences that sometimes mimicked styles of mansion houses. Planters gazed through large multipaned glass windows from houses set on high grounds to view riverscapes, formal gardens, and rice fields. Their slaves planted long rows of oaks to create tree-lined approaches opening onto broad greens framing mansion houses, physical expressions of their owners' wealth and gentility. Drayton Hall (1738–1742) followed the latest Palladian designs from English architectural books and impressed visitors, who entered the 52 by 72-foot mansion, set on a half-basement pedestal, by a double-staircased, two-story portico. Two rooms flanked each side of the grand entry hall, and two sets of double staircases led up to the second floor and descended to the formal gardens. The gardens at

William Middleton's Crowfield (ca. 1730s) impressed young Eliza Lucas. "From the back door is a spacious walk a thousand feet long . . . " with serpentine flower beds, "a large boleing (bowling) green, . . . a double row of fine large flowering Laurel and Catalpas . . . a large fish pond with a mount rising out of the middle—the top of which is level with the dwelling house and upon it is a Roman temple."[11] Yet, for every Drayton Hall or Crowfield, there were dozens of plain two-room frame dwellings with sleeping lofts, homes of small planters and tenants.

After a 1740 fire consumed much of Charles Town, planter grandees' new town houses became lavish showcases for genteel living. Population growth limited building sites and increased land prices resulting in long narrow house lots. English architects and local craftsmen adapted classical design elements from architectural handbooks to construct two- and three-story brick houses on half or full basements to reduce danger from fires. They followed the latest Georgian styles but turned gabled roof ends toward streets, covered brick with stucco to imitate prestigious stonework, and added walled enclosures for privacy and to supervise slaves. Entry gates provided access to covered side porches or piazzas. Entry doors set halfway down opened into basements and stairs leading to main floors with a single set or double sets of flanking symmetrical rooms on either side. The floor plan repeated on the second floor; by the late eighteenth century, these rooms opened onto upper porches. High ceilings improved air circulation, and multipaned double sash windows brightened interiors. One-story service wings or separate structures housed kitchens, laundries, stables, and slave quarters with the rest of the lot planted in kitchen and pleasure gardens and orchards. Single houses often used front rooms as shops or offices opening off streets with living quarters in rears and upper stories.

Scholars debate the origins of Charles Town's distinctive narrow front houses with multistory piazzas. Early Carolina settlers' Barbadian origins and frequent Caribbean contacts brought familiarity with verandas found on some West Indian plantation houses and military structures. By mid-century, they were a distinct feature of gentlemen's homes. The "inhabitants of both Carolinas and Georgia generally build piazzas or one or more sides of their houses which is very commodious in these hot climates," noted naturalist John Bartram, as "they screen of[f] the violent scorching sunshine & draws the breeze finely, & it must be extremely hot indeed if one cant sit or walk very comfortably." Not only did piazzas provide healthy ventilation and "refreshing breezes from the sea" that relieved long humid summers and reduced pesky insects, but they also served as outdoor parlors for conversation and entertaining, places to see passersby, and to be seen from streets simultaneously hiding and disclosing residents' lives.[12] Verandas became physical metaphors of Charles Town's competitive social life.

Florida

European architectural traditions, West Indian connections, and semitropical environment shaped housing styles in the garrison outposts of Spanish Saint Augustine, Pensacola, and San Antonio and French Biloxi, New Orleans, and Natchitoches. Marginal settlements on colonial peripheries, imperial urban ideals, and military engineers shaped initial designs. Massive fortifications with barracks, chapels, and officers' housing dominated these towns—Castillo de San Marcos (1672–1696) alone survives—and Saint Augustine, New Orleans, and San Antonio still retain their original central plazas and grid plans. With skilled artisans scarce and poverty widespread, settlers adopted local materials to European building traditions and relied on native knowledge to construct palmetto thatch and bark huts on the Atlantic and Gulf coasts and adobe structures in Texas. As in Charles Town, West Indian influences added verandas and balconies to wealthy men's homes. Few wood and masonry houses survived damp coastal climates, and others succumbed to fires, floods, and hurricanes. Archaeology, particularly in Saint Augustine, provides insights on domestic housing to supplement the few surviving pre-1750 domestic structures.

Saint Augustine's earliest houses—military barracks and homes of civilians, government officials, and soldiers—were flimsy one- or two-room single-story posthole dwellings constructed from timber frames, thatched roofs, and either wattle-and-daub or vertical board walls. Threats from English marauders and Carolina settlers, however, required durable defenses, and in the 1670s, locally quarried shell-stone or "coquina" was used for Castillo de San Marcos's exterior walls.[13] After Carolinians burned the town in 1702, this became the preferred building material for anyone who could afford it.

The Governor's House (1706–1713) became the prototype. Located on the plaza, the two-and-a-half-story shell-stone house was plastered smooth with lime with a projecting second-story balcony supported by heavy wood brackets and wooden columns holding up a roof. A Tuscan Doric entryway on the asymmetrical façade's left side led to a shaded piazza running the depth of the house and overlooking an enclosed formal garden. Elite men's homes, according to naturalist John Bartram, were built "after the Spanish fashion, all or most with pleasant covered balconies . . . [and] on the back side of the house or yard where the chief entrance is . . . there is generally A terraced [tabby] walk with seats . . . next [to] the house wall," adding, "it must be very pleasant walking here in a hot summers evening."[14] Shingled gabled roofs were common, but a few were flat with terraces that provided views of the town and gardens. Large windows projecting out a foot or more and covered with wooden grates (*rejas*) and second-story five-foot wide balconies fronting streets allowed one to observe street life, while covered side porches, loggias enclosed on two sides, or interior arcades around walled courtyards were private open-air rooms. Houses faced south to catch warm winter sunshine and cooling summer breezes. Kitchens were detached (central fireplaces were rare), and the largest houses had single-story wings for servants and slaves. Yet, even these large homes were relatively small, four or so irregularly arranged rooms, to fit the small 44 by 88-foot town lots. After Britain acquired Florida in 1763, English settlers added framed second stories, glazed windows, and fireplaces.

Ordinary settlers, Creoles, common soldiers, and mestizos lived in plain one- and two-room timber-framed houses covered with weatherboarding or in-filled with "tabby," with unglazed shuttered or latticed windows and thatch or shingled roofs. Visitors entered from streets into unspecialized rooms for cooking, eating, socializing, working, and sleeping filled with smoke from cooking fires lazily escaping through roof holes. Simple to build but requiring constant maintenance, tabby houses provided flexible living spaces that could be enlarged with additional rooms or wood-framed second stories. Like homes of wealthier neighbors, their asymmetrical facades and unadorned exteriors contrasted with the British Georgian ideal.

Louisiana

French housing on the Gulf Coast shared many features of Spanish designs. Military engineers designed barracks inside wooden forts mixing European and native construction techniques. Utilizing abundant forests, half-timbered (*colombage*) posthole (*poteaux-en-terre*) structures with diagonal struts, mansard roofs, dormer windows, and ground-level galleries housed soldiers and workers. A mixture of mud and Spanish moss (*bousillage*) or tabby rather than brick filled spaces between frame timbers. Government officials, merchants, officers, and professionals lived in brick houses whitewashed with oyster lime, some of which had second stories and bay windows with front and rear galleries and single-story wings for servants and slaves. Ordinary settlers constructed single-room posthole houses or bark or palmetto huts.

New Orleans's founding in 1718 and private land grants or concessions for plantations created urban and rural versions of distinctive Louisiana housing styles that featured large roofs and either full galleries or balconies. By mid-century, brick and masonry had replaced wood in civic buildings, churches, and homes of the wealthy despite rapid deterioration from dampness. The few domestic structures to survive the fires in 1788 and 1794 that destroyed most of New Orleans are three- and four-room one-and-a half to two stories made of stucco-covered brick or of brick-filled *colombage*. Other features included tall French doors, bay windows, shingle roofs, and full street-side balconies either on the second floor or on the main floor or a "raised cottage" set on elevated basement stories.

Early plantation houses replicated diminutive French château; but by mid-18th century, planters created a Louisiana Creole style that became models for Mississippi Valley plantation mansions in the next century. Traveling upriver from New Orleans, visitors approached Jean Baptiste Le Moyne's Bienville Plantation (1718) through an avenue of trees to behold an impressive symmetrical brick mansion three stories high with seven windows, a full-length second-story balcony, and two adjoining dependencies. Behind the house was a formal garden and row of slave huts. La Pointe Concession in Mississippi marked the transition from country French Renaissance to Louisiana Creole styles. The original 1718 brick house was two stories set on an elevated platform with doors opening onto each level of a two-story gallery. The landscape mirrored the mansion's symmetry with arranged dependencies: a warehouse, slaves' housing, milk house, kitchen, a forge, sawmill, dovecotes, and chapel. Destroyed by a hurricane, the house was rebuilt in the 1770s as a smaller story-and-a half Creole house, which mixed timber-frame, tabby, and *bousillage* construction with ground-level galleries on three sides.

Similar two- to four-room houses often set on high basements housed freeholders and small slaveholders. Other homes of *bousillage* construction were set on wooden platforms with steep hip

Louisiana Plantation House. An excellent example of Creole style reflecting French and New World influences. Parlange (1757), Pointe Coupee Parish, Louisiana, is set on a ground-story working basement, with living quarters on the second floor. Visitors entered by a grand exterior staircase to the surrounding gallery from which owners observed their slaves and sugarcane fields. (Library of Congress)

roofs that projected beyond the house frame to form verandas on all four sides, a design of Afro-Caribbean origins. Parlange in Pointe Coupée Parish (1757) exemplifies wealthy planters' mansions. Set on a ground-story brick basement used for workspace and storage, the second story was framed with galleries on all four sides. An enlarged hip roof covered the galleries and a staircase from the lawn to the second floor magnified the house's appearance. An exterior staircase and rooms with shuttered French doors opened onto the veranda, eliminated interior passageways, and allowed for functional asymmetrical room arrangements with specialized entertaining, dining, and sleeping areas. Elevated mansions matched masters' egos: to be viewed by river travelers and to survey their slaves and cane fields.

African American

Waking to cock's crows in the predawn darkness on a tidewater Virginia plantation in the mid-18th century, slave inhabitants treaded carefully to avoid stepping on the half-dozen family members in the 12-foot square room. Their cabin, a duplex shared with another family divided by a partition, was better than most. Several years earlier, slave carpenters following their owner's directions used simplified framing techniques to build a half-dozen log huts arrayed in a cluster several hundred yards away from the mansion house and screened by a row of trees. Setting the cottages on piers of handmade brick, they added plank wooden floors, clapboard siding, a doorway and lock, one small shuttered window, an upper loft for storage, whitewashed walls, and a central brick fireplace with individual family hearths. Slaves on other plantations, in contrast, might live in flimsy one-room earthfast cabins with packed dirt floors, poorly chinked drafty walls, and log chimneys daubed with clay where four people cramped into an 8 by 12-foot space.

A century earlier, the scant population of slaves lived with white indentured servants in 20 by 16-foot earthfast barracks with end chimneys each holding a dozen or more laborers. As slaves replaced servants in the late 17th century, owners herded newly purchased African males into old dormitories where poor ventilation added to the high mortality from "seasoning" in unhealthy Chesapeake and Lowcountry swamps. As slaves gradually formed families in the 18th century, planters rewarded married couples with separate living spaces, and by mid-century, family cabins became customary with fenced garden plots, poultry yards, and hog pens. The quality of slave housing reflected not only individual planters' dispositions but also regional differences.

Blacks on home plantations in the Chesapeake generally had better houses than field slaves on outlaying tobacco quarters. Plantation landscapes magnified planters' mansion houses by creating ensembles of numerous diminutive outbuildings: dependencies for domestic slaves, sex-segregated barracks for single slaves, cabins for couples, and sleeping rooms in kitchens, laundries, and artisan shops. The reconstructed mid-18th-century slave quarter at Carter's Grove near Williamsburg, located just below the mansion house, created hierarchies within the enslaved population. It included a one-room log home for the slave foreman and his family with an enclosed rectilinear yard, a symmetrical log duplex aligned with the mansion house with adjoining doors and Welsh end chimneys, and a clapboard structure with a central brick chimney to house male carpenters. The "quarter for families" at Mount Vernon housed over 50 slaves in a 20 by 60-foot barrack. House slaves on call 24/7 slept in cellars, garrets, and hallways in great houses. Some planters placed slave houses nearby; others, distant and out of sight.[15] Frontier living conditions were primitive. Orange County planter James Madison, Sr., spent 40 shillings to build a 16-foot square overseer' house at Black Level Quarter in the 1750s, but a mere 3 shillings each for slave cabins, flimsy earthfast log cabins with listing wooden clay-daubed chimneys. No wonder yards, swept the dirt spaces between cabins and surrounding work buildings, became outdoor living areas. On warm days, women and girls preserved food, mended worn clothes, and prepared meals over open fires, while men and boys cleaned game and livestock, repaired tools, and fabricated handicrafts.

Slave housing in the Lowcountry and in Louisiana was even more diverse. Charles Town slaves lived near their owners in crowded 10 by 15-foot lofts above dependencies and kitchens or in small structures in the rear. As in the Chesapeake, planters arrayed slave housing to order plantation landscapes. Slave houses at Mulberry not only framed the mansion house but their steep hipped thatched

Slave quarters and mansion house. By mid-18th century, more slaves survived and formed families. Families of skilled artisans, domestics, and drivers likely lived in this double-row of symmetrical brick slave houses. Mulberry (1714) is set on a raised half basement with four corner pavilions whose double-hipped roofs mirror the African-influenced thatched roofs of the slave houses. ("View of Mulberry, House and Street," 1805, by Thomas Coram [American, 1756–1811], oil on paper, © Image Gibbes Museum of Art/Carolina Art Association, 1968.018.0001.)

roofs also echoed the French corner pavilions. Other planters placed houses in linear rows along roads or near rice fields or in blocks adjacent to work sites. Rice and indigo workers, most were African-born before the American Revolution, lived away from their owners and adopted indigenous construction techniques and spatial arrangements for rice and indigo cultivation's labor demands. They built windowless wattle-and-daub circular houses with mud or tabby walls, dirt floors, and flat palmetto thatch roofs and grouped houses into compounds with central yards of swept packed earth and outlaying gardens. Away from masters' gazes, enslaved people partially recreated the physical appearance of ancestors' villages.[16] Even more unusual are two structures at Melrose Plantation in Natchitoches Parish, Louisiana. Yucca—home of Marie Thereze Coincoin Metoyer, a free black female—combined a Creole single-story frame and *bousillage* structure with a recessed loggia and an African steep hip roof. Even more striking is a two-story storehouse with a wide projecting roof without columns that created outdoor workspace.

Backcountry

Log cabins housed backcountry people. Fifty years after the Lower Shenandoah Valley was settled, a survey listed but one frame and one stone dwelling out of 140 houses. Historians dispute whether 17th-century Swedish and Finnish settlers in the Lower Delaware Valley first introduced log cabins or if German emigrants made the earliest log cabins in Pennsylvania and introduced them into the Valley of Virginia. James Patton described numerous "round log buildings" in the 1750s with clapboard roofs, dirt floors, log and mud chimneys on either end, and chinks between logs "all funked and daubed both inside and out."[17] The Scots-Irish, without wooden building traditions, and Anglo-Americans adopted log construction from German neighbors. Log cabins spread as settlers moved south into the Carolina and Georgia backcountry and Appalachia, and by late 1800, they housed pioneers and poor whites.

One-room log cabins were also frontier versions of impermanent earthfast structures of the tidewater South and adaptations of new building materials to old house plans. With abundant forests, early setters built "huts of logs," Thomas Jefferson noted, which were "laid horizontally in pens, [and] stopping the interstices with mud," which made them "warmer in winter, and cooler in summer, than the more expensive constructions of scantling and

Creek log cabin. Most backcountry settlers lived in one or two-room log cabins with mud and straw chinking. Improvements included plank flooring, clapboard siding, glass-pane windows, and room additions with open breezeways in between. Many acculturated Natives shifted from communal lodges to family dwellings, yet retained some traditional construction methods like the bark roof shown here. Drawing by J.C. Tidball in Henry R. Schoolcraft, *Information Respecting the History, Condition, and Prospects of Indian Tribes of the United States* (Philadelphia: J.B. Lippincott & Co., 1855). (Courtesy of DePauw University, Greencastle, Indiana.)

plank."[18] Two or three men could construct a single log cabin or "pen" in a few days from local timber using saws, axes, and adzes. Square notches on hewn logs produced tight-fitting walls needing only narrow clapboard chinking, while V-notched round logs required mud and straw to fill large gaps. Setting frames on stone posts allowed for wooden plank flooring. Square or rectangular pens between 16 and 22 feet per side formed modular units for larger dwellings. Two pens joined by open porches between them and covered with continuous roofs created "dogtrot" cabins with central breezeways that were outdoor halls for everyday activities and for sleeping dogs. "Saddleback" cabins comprised two separate pens that shared a large central chimney; "double-pen" houses each had separate doors and end chimneys. Owners enlarged and improved log cabins as means allowed by underpinning flooring with stone cellars, constructing additional pens, covering logs with weatherboarding or shingles, adding front porches, enclosing dog-trot breezeways to create central passages, plastering interior walls, and replacing window shutters with glass panes.[19]

Floor plans and building materials reflected Old World cultural traditions and New World adaptations. Central hearth fireplaces in mud and stone Scots-Irish houses moved to end walls of log cabins. Scots-Irish and Anglo-American cabins were usually rectangular with front and rear doors opening into large halls with fireplaces for cooking, eating, sleeping, and daily activities. Partitions created smaller chambers, often unheated, where husbands and wives entertained and slept. Ladders led to upper lofts for additional sleeping and storage. German *flurküchenhauser* (story-and-a-half or two-story hall–kitchen houses), often made of thick limestone with small windows, had three or four rooms clustered asymmetrically around a central chimney each with its own fireplace. Interiors were divided into large workrooms entered from the front door that centered on fireplaces with elevated hearths and bake ovens for cooking and eating, coal-fed stove rooms that provided smoke-free eating and living spaces, and unheated sleeping chambers on the second floor. Vertical boards covered interior walls and stone cellars provided storage. The Moravians (German Pietists who settled Wachovia, North Carolina, in the 1750s) soon replaced log cabins with German half-timbered houses of wattle-and-daub or brick noggin. By late 18th century, affluent German American farmers adopted English styles building two-story frame and stone houses with symmetrical facades, three-room floor plans, central passages, end chimneys, large glass-paned windows, and detached kitchens.

FURNISHINGS

Household furnishings were props for food preservation and preparation, eating, sleeping, and socializing.[20] Objects' physical appearance and frequency revealed their origins from native fabricators or as imported luxuries, their provincial rudeness or metropolitan refinement, and their value as utilitarian equipment or as fashionable possessions. Furnishings linked producers and consumers in networks of local and long-distance trade, even as they expressed their owner's gender, class, and caste status and personal identity. In the 18th century, household furnishings acquired new purposes in making daily life more comfortable and convenient and as markers distinguishing the genteel from the unrefined.

Native Americans

Although Native American's subsistence economy limited accumulating acquisitions, furnishings had utilitarian, ideological, and economic value and expressed gender roles and connectedness to the natural world. Objects' quality varied according to their makers' skills and decorative additions, but Indians expressed individuality less by acquiring material objects and more through clothing, accessories, and body decoration. High-status peoples' control over indigenous trade provided access to exotic items: copper gorgets and headdresses and shell and pearl bracelets and necklaces. Their large households included craft workers who made high-quality furnishings and personal adornment items. Visitors encountered Powhatan-in-state sitting on a dozen mats beside feather pillows embroidered with pearls and shell beads.

Most furnishings served practical needs. Women and men slept on four-foot wide raised platforms attached to house walls about two or three feet above floors to reduce contact with vermin and to store personal belongings such as clothing, storage containers, and tools. Bedsteads were sapling frames and splints covered with cane or reed mats for bedding and animal skin blankets. Beds were folded up when not in use to provide additional working and living space. In large communal houses, mat partitions created specialized work areas and some privacy. Women wove reed mats of various sizes for sitting, working, and eating, and wooden bowls and trays and leather storage bags met food and storage needs.[21]

Basketry and pottery were women's special crafts. Cherokee women made baskets from splints of river cane; the best were double woven with geometric patterns on the inside and the outside from brown, black, and red plant and bark dyes. Women burned canebrakes during winters to ensure healthy regeneration and passed down to daughters and female relatives family weaving patterns and knowledge about which plants made the best dyes. Everyday baskets were single-weave and made in a variety of sizes and shapes: pack baskets three feet high for harvesting crops; small square baskets for gathering mushrooms, nuts, and berries; winnowing and sieves for food processing; and lidded hampers for storing. Women wove ritual mats for New Green Corn Festivals and seat covers for priests during other rites. Food baskets held sacred fruits, which were blessed and distributed to the people, and special baskets stored ritual objects. Ceremonial baskets symbolized women's importance as life-sustaining vessels.

Pottery also had practical and ideological purposes. An ancient women's craft—some recovered potsherds are over 4,000 years old—pots came in many sizes, colors, and shapes depending on clay and traditional construction, firing, decorative, and polishing techniques. Most were for food preparation and storage, but fine-crafted ceremonial vessels and bottles were part of rituals, and pottery effigies were buried with high-status people. Choctaw women made round-bottom cooking pots from coiled clay, tempered with crushed shells or fine sand for firing, decorated with incised lines and indentations made with small tools or impressed fabric, polished with smooth stones, and fired in hot pitch pine coals. Some bowls and jars were stamped with bird or serpent motifs using wooden paddles or painted.

The oldest artifacts—projectile points for javelins and arrows—were men's craft and required knowing where to find the best flint and patient chipping with stone or sharpened bone to form the right sizes and shapes. Points were notched or flared to ease attachment to wooden shafts. Essential for hunting and warfare, spears and arrows became sacred objects in preparatory rituals and were part of male identities. Men stacked "their whole happiness upon the beauty and polish of their weapons," a Spanish observer recorded, "Those that they make for ornament and daily use, they fashion with all the skill they possess, each striving to outdo the other with some new invention or a finer polish."[22] Men also fabricated practical stone objects: chipped scrapers, choppers, knives, and hoes and polished stones to grind seeds, adzes, axes, and finely polished weights for spear throwers and carved stone effigy pipes. They crafted animal bone into pendants, beads, fishhooks, awls, and needles.

Through trade with Europeans or living in mission communities, Indians acquired new metal goods and textiles, which they initially incorporated alongside existing handmade artifacts of skin, stone, shell, bone, leather, and wood. Many European objects lightened labor but did not immediately replace traditional objects. Metal hooks and guns made fishing and hunting more efficient; hatchets and axes cleared land more quickly; and iron hoes, copper kettles, knives, and needles eased women's horticultural, food preparation, and clothing production. Chiefs controlled early trade with Europeans and first acquired prestigious clothes and exotic goods, which they distributed to family members and local leaders. Over time, taste for new things spread to commoners. After male hunters dealt directly with colonial traders, a Virginia visitor noted, "many Things which they wanted not before because they never had them . . .

[have] become necessity both for their use and ornament."[23] Skills needed for fabricating traditional objects declined as natives came to depend on European material culture for hunting, warfare, farming, and cooking.

European's indispensable presence also created new markets for traditional native crafts. Women made dyed fiber baskets and mats, clay cook pots, wooden trays and bowls, and leather clothing for sale to European neighbors. Cherokee women fashioned sets of nested baskets for trade, "masterpieces in mechanicks," wrote a contemporary observer, "[and] . . . beautifully dyed in black and red with various figures."[24] Colono-Indian pottery, a melding of native fabrication methods and European designs, became popular trade goods. Settlers prized Catawba cooking pots for their durability and low cost. Men carved wooden canoes and fashioned stone and clay pipes for sale. Indian markets with objects made to satisfy non-Indian consumers' tastes were well established long before the American Revolution.

Euro-Americans in the 17th Century

Sparse furnishings matched early settlers' rude houses. "If the untidy, unplanned, and unsymmetrical layout of the typical plantation is dismaying," historian Gloria Main observes about Maryland houses, "the interiors of the homes prove even bleaker. There we find few comforts and no conveniences. Most colonial furniture consists of homemade pieces from local soft woods, roughly dressed and nailed together. Dirt or plan floors bear no coverings, nor do curtains hang at the glassless windows."[25] Planters invested in expanded tobacco cultivation over home manufactures and improved physical comfort. With skilled craftsmen scarce, they imported furniture, clothing, cookware, textiles, leather goods, and guns; made simple furniture; and repaired rather than replaced worn items. Planters made do with basic necessities: cooking pots and utensils, spoons, ceramic and pewter plates, shared drinking vessels, one or two chairs, a table, bench, storage chest and cupboard, mattresses, shared bedsteads, sheets, and blankets. In poor households (over half were in this category), people did without and slept on straw or cattail-filled ticking on dirt floors; stood, squatted, or sat on upturned chests for meals; and ate off shared wooden trenchers.

Even by 1720, only the wealthiest third of Maryland households owned possessions that approached living standards common in

England: course earthen or stoneware ceramics to keep milk and beer; bedsteads, bed, and table linen; chamber pots and warming pans; books; and candles and candlesticks for artificial lighting. Robert Beverley, a wealthy Virginia planter, "lives well," a foreign visitor observed in 1715, "but though rich, he has nothing in or about his house but what is necessary. He hath good beds in his house, but no curtains; and instead of cane chairs, he hath stools made of wood."[26] Few ornaments, carpets, or curtains softened wooden, plain interiors. Wealthy planters and their wives slept in comfortable beds (down-filled mattresses were especially prized) on bed frames off floors; sat in chairs at tables during meals, which were prepared with more varied cooking equipment and served on ceramic ware; ate with knives not just spoons; owned blankets, table linen, and curtains; and stored or displayed valuables like silver, jewelry, and books (even if they could not read them) in cupboards. While they owned more and better quality of the same things as their lesser neighbors, as long as houses remained small with unspecialized working and living areas, rich and poor shared similar lifestyles.

By late 17th century, in the Chesapeake, well-connected men—elite planters, officials, and merchants—began filling their enlarged dwellings with English furnishings. More rooms allowed for separating public and private social spaces and for specialized uses. Visitors waited on benches or chairs in central passageways before being dismissed, were ushered into adjoining parlors, or admitted into family rooms upstairs. Former multipurpose halls became formal parlors with finely crafted tables, matched sets of cane or upholstered chairs, and gilded mirrors. Separate dining rooms featured large tables and chairs with matching individual place settings of decorated porcelain dishes, etched water and wine glasses, and sets of silver knife, fork, and spoon utensils; sideboards to store imported table linens; and cupboards to display plate, glassware, punch bowls, tea dishes, and other specialized dining ware. Fine objects possessed social capital. "I esteem it as well politic as reputable," mused William Fitzhugh, a planter-merchant in 1688, "to furnish my self with a handsom[e] Cupboard of plate which gives my self the present use and Credit, [and] is a sure friend at a dead lift."[27]

Euro-Americans in the 18th Century

By the early 18th century, matched sets of *en suite* possessions bespoke an emerging style of elegant living that distinguished genteel folk from rude neighbors. Germanna (1730), Governor Alexander Spotswood's frontier home, impressed the urbane William Byrd with its elegant furnishings—mahogany tables, japanned chest of drawers, mounted arms, window curtains, framed prints, and pet deer (one smashed mirrored glass in the drawing room)—and formal gardens that included an avenue of cherry trees, terraces, and a marble fountain. Lowcountry rice and indigo grandees imported English furnishings wholesale, making their new town houses showplaces for genteel living. Elaborately carved woodwork, coffered ceilings, matching mahogany furniture, marble chimneypieces, Delft hearth tiles, and plastered walls covered in Chinese wallpaper impressed visitors. One thought Miles Brewton's Charles Town house had "the grandest hall I ever beheld, azure blue satin window curtains, rich blue paper, with gilt, mashee (cut?) borders, most elegant pictures, excessive grand and costly looking glasses."[28]

By mid-century, the number of desirable objects exploded, filling gentry homes with props for practicing the art of fashionable living: refined manners, luxurious dress, and elegant dining. Bedrooms included chamber tables, looking glasses, and dressing boxes to prepare bodies for public display and chests of drawers and wardrobes to hold soft delicate clothes. Serving tea became a genteel ritual requiring extensive equipage—silver or Chinese porcelain teapots, milk pitchers, slop bowls, matched sets of tea cups and saucers, sugar bowls and tongs, teaspoons, and tea trays and tables—and proper etiquette of serving and drinking tea and mastering polite conversation. Proper use of these material objects measured one's social status.

Keeping up with quickly changing fashion required new rounds of conspicuous consumption. Homes were refurbished to create a modern look: Chippendale chairs with shaped curved legs and backs and upholstered cushions; cabinets of fine walnut and mahogany with detailed ornamentation; rugs on parlor and dining room floors; Chinese-designed paper and bright colored paints covering walls; clocks, prints, and family portraits on walls; and coaches and carriages sporting family coats of arms. Newly married Robert Beverley wrote his London factor in 1762 about needing china "of the most fashionable sort . . . sufficient for 2 Genteel Courses of Victuals." Less than a decade later, he despaired that his furnishings were already out of date requiring him to "consult the present Fashion for you know that foolish Passion has made its bray, even into this remote region."[29]

Conveniences of the rich inevitably became necessities for common folk. After 1740, acquiring the latest consumer goods purchased respectability: specialized cooking equipment, better tables, matched chairs, fine earthenware, glassware, ceramic dish sets, table knives,

A wealthy planter's parlor. Large gentry houses separated private family living areas from reception and entertainment rooms. Miles Brewton, a Charles Town merchant and slave trader, and his wife hosted intimate gatherings in their parlor (circa 1769) with its impressive coffered ceiling, crystal chandelier, elaborate paneled walls and doorways, imported mahogany furniture, paintings, and matched sets of chairs. (Library of Congress.)

display cupboards, raised bedsteads, down mattresses, mirrors, candles and candlesticks, and, most symbolically, ceramic tea equipment. If their houses' exterior appearances remained modest, acquiring less expensive versions of new consumer goods provided measures of "elegance as well as comfort . . . in very many of the habitations" even in the countryside, an English visitor noted. An Englishwomen found it "droll enough to eat out of China and be served in plate" at the home of a sawmill operation in frontier North Carolina in 1775, as the "house [was] no house" yet "the master and the furniture made you ample amends."[30] By mid-century, colonial craftsmen produced high-quality furniture with carved legs, decorations, and inlaid wood for elite families and simpler and less expensive styles for the less affluent. Country storekeepers pleaded with factors to supply them with quality goods at attractive prices to meet rural customers' discerning tastes. Women made many store purchases and their preferences shaped the emerging consumer culture. Unsurprisingly, clothing and textiles, which lightened women's labor, accounted for half of all purchases at one Virginia country store.

Historians give different explanations for the consumer revolution's origins and spread across England and British North America long before the better-known industrial revolution of the late 18th century. Mass-produced consumer goods especially ceramics, glasswares, utensils, and textiles; declining shipping costs; a network of country stores; and entrepreneurs, like Josiah Wedgewood, who marketed creamware in the 1760s, an ivory-covered earthenware substitute for expensive porcelain; all made goods plentiful and affordable for most householders. Declining mortality increased population densities and the number of consumers. Diversified farming in the Chesapeake stabilized income fluctuations from tobacco cultivation and provided more disposable income.

Greater availability does not explain why colonials eagerly purchased consumer goods. In a society of immigrants, high internal migration, and uncertain social status, acquiring the right possessions provided newcomers with badges of gentility. For middling planters, material goods measured economic success and social respectability. Aspiring men purchased the accoutrements that made them gentlemen. Provincials found material goods tangible proofs of their English identity and connections to metropolitan society.

While the consumer revolution increased the availability, variety, quantity, and quality of furnishings and marked a general rise in free people's living standards, it did not create a uniform material culture in the colonial South. Class, residence, and ethnicity influenced individual choices in acquiring goods. Homes of backcountry farmers were furnished more simply than their economic counterparts in settled areas where families of even modest wealth had tables, chairs, feather beds, bedsteads, bed and table linen, pewter plates, tinware, and individual knives and forks. Backcountry consumers avoided breakable ceramics, glassware, and tea sets for goods that made eating more refined and sleeping more comfortable. Farmers only gradually replaced plain tables and chests with case furniture and purchased ceramics and tea equipment. Town shopkeepers and artisans placed newspaper advertisements promoting the "latest English goods" and acquired items for social activities: tea tables and tea sets; dining tables with matched sets of chairs, plates, and glassware; and artificial lighting. German emigrants sought familiar goods and styles preferring red, yellow, and green colors for stoneware and porcelain, and painted wooden furniture with stenciled designs. They purchased pewter not tinware and iron-stove plates as substitutes for German painted tiles. They hung *Haussegen* (house blessings) in *fraktur* lettering to record marriages, births, and deaths, and hired painters to make stylized hex signs and *distelfink* (bird of

Blanket chest. Lacking closets settlers stored clothes and bedding in chests. Elite family members imported fine furnishings in the latest English styles, but local craftsmen supplied ordinary families. This chest's bright folk painting is a fine example of German American vernacular style. (Attributed to Johannes Spitler, 1795–1800. Shenandoah [now Page] County, Virginia. Museum of Early Southern Decorative Arts, Winston-Salem, North Carolina, Anne Bahnson Gray Purchase Funds [acc. 3806].)

good fortune) outside their houses. Craftsmen made brightly decorated German-styled furniture and objects well into the 19th century.

Florida and Louisiana

Material culture in Florida and Louisiana followed strikingly different patterns from British settlements. Scant surviving colonial furniture and objects, most of which were imported from the West Indies, and the abundance of ceramics from archaeological sites make generalizations tentative. Objects of European manufacture or, at least, design were highly prized, yet incorporation of some Native American objects created a hybrid material culture. Imported Spanish or French chests, gilded mirrors, chairs, and tables were important status symbols and emblems of authority in remote outposts.[31] Some of the oldest surviving furniture is from the Ursuline Convent in New Orleans, founded in 1727, and was fabricated in high Louis XV style but made of local walnut and cypress with fewer elaborate carvings and decorative paintings expected of French-made pieces. Ordinary settlers made do with spartan furnishings of local manufacture, yet even these followed Old World craft guild designs. In Florida, native women who married Spanish men continued to make Indian ceramics for food storage and preparation. The quality of artifacts uncovered from several Florida sites reveals a close relationship with social status. Spanish pottery—coarse earthenware, olive jars, and fine hand-painted tin-glazed ceramics from Majolica—prevailed in high-status households, while Indian pottery dominated mestizo families. After Britain acquired East Florida in 1763, English planters quickly introduced British ceramics, glassware, and other artifacts.

African Americans

Sympathetic observers of slaves' material possessions judged them as spartan as their mean cabins. A French traveler in Virginia inventoried one slave family's household goods: "A box-like [bed] frame made of boards hardly roughed down, upheld by stakes. . . . Some wheat straw and corn-stalks, on which was spread a very short-napped woolen blanket that was burned in several places. . . . An old pot . . . [and] A few rags soaked in water were hanging in one of the corners of the fireplace. An old pipe, very short, and a knife blade, which were sticking in the wall."[32] If left only to masters, slaves' material world was confined to objects for work and subsistence. Slaves received tools (hoes, plows, axes, saws, grindstone, hammers, knives, rakes, and iron), cook pots, coarse blankets every other year, two suits of clothing, and food rations. Favored slaves received their owners' worn clothes, old furniture, out-of-style porcelain, and household castoffs.

Yet, slaves did what they could to improve living standards. Slave carpenters made bedsteads to sleep off damp dirt floors, stools and benches for sitting, and shelves and hooks for storing possessions. Women carved spoons, ladles, cups, and bowels from gourds and sowed mattress ticking and filled them with straw. Masters conceded what laws unrecognized: slaves' personal property was their own. Slaves used income from their personal labor (garden produce, poultry, fish, overwork payments, baskets, wooden objects, and tips for personal service) to purchase pewter plates, ceramic ware, knives, iron pots, alcohol, fabric, textiles, clothing, mirrors, and violins from country stores and from fellow slaves. In their own small way, slaves, too, participated in the consumer revolution.

African skills and designs, New World materials, and, perhaps, Native American influences created new objects. Chesapeake slaves dug three-foot deep root cellars, or "hidey-holes," in earth floors near hearths lining them with boards and into separate compartments for storing treasured possessions, root vegetables, and, likely, stolen goods. Archeologists have recovered coins, buttons, beads, ceramics, West African cowrie shells, cutlery, wine bottles, and musical instruments—objects that were often modified based on African designs and took on new uses and meanings. Men made cedar drums covered in deerskins, stringed "bangars" (banjos) from gourds, and carved wooden mortars and pestles. Lowcountry women used African designs to weave coiled baskets from sweetgrass and long pine needles. Indian and African skills mixed in decorating clay smoking pipes in the Chesapeake with incised and punched geometric designs, fashioning dugout canoes to navigate coastal Carolina waterways, and fabricating flat-bottomed ceramic pots (called "colonoware") from low-fired unglazed coiled clay for cooking and eating stews. The scarcity of recovered slave artifacts from the colonial period does not diminish their significance for understanding slave culture. Material objects improved slaves' lives and through new forms of cultural expression created new identities that existed outside enslavement's harsh realities.[33]

CLOTHING

Clothes not only protected bodies from harsh climate or inclement weather but also presented the self to society.[34] A mere glance revealed your social identity: a wealthy planter, a female servant, an enslaved African, or a Powhatan warrior. By concealing and revealing the body or by flaunting or fulfilling social conventions, clothes marked individuals as civilized or savage, as genteel or mere "upstarts," and as free or enslaved. Modifying existing clothes or acquiring new ones expressed individuality and the possibilities of assuming a new status. The right costume turned common planters into gentlemen, field hands into liverid servants, female English captives into Indian wives. Colonial encounters and the consumer revolution unsettled existing linkages between clothing and social status, provided individuals more choices over what to wear, and sparked debates over the meaning of these changes. Finally, as objects of production and of consumption, clothes linked poor women and female slaves to plantation mistresses and European manufacturers to Native hunters.

Native Americans

Native Americans' skimpy attire maximized ease of work and travel, but required physical stamina for enduring rain and cold. As in other aspects of native life, dress reinforced gender identities and reflected particular environmental resources. Men universally wore breechclouts made of animal belts, leather, woven fiber of grass or bark, or braided palmetto leaves, which were about 5 feet long and 18 inches wide, placed between the legs with the ends or flaps hanging over a belt in the front and the back. Women wore a knee-length aprons or skirts made from deerskin, bark or grass fiber, or Spanish moss, which were tied at the waists with upper bodies uncovered. During winter, women and men donned fur cloaks or "matchcoats" made from bison, deer, or cougar draped and tied over left shoulders dropping to the knees leaving right breasts exposed. Deerskin moccasins tied at ankles protected against the cold and travel; otherwise, Indians went barefoot. To prevent scratches when going into forests, women and men donned deerskin leggings, which they suspended from belts, tied below knees with garters, and tucked into moccasins, leaving exposed—Europeans frequently eyed—muscular thighs. Men tied bird-shaped leather pouches from belts where they put tobacco, pipes, flint, and other useful items. Until puberty, children went unclothed in warm weather. Girls began wearing aprons around 8 or 9, and boys breechclouts about age 12. Pocahontas, 11-year-old daughter of Powhatan paramount chief Wahunsenacawh, was "naked" when she first visited Jamestown in 1608.[35]

High-status men and women wore similar items as commoners, but their clothes were highly decorated, made from exotic materials, and included mantles worn over their left shoulders year round. Women's aprons and dresses, men's breechclouts, and skin or feather mantles had fringed edges, painted geometric or animal designs, and shell bead or animal teeth decorations. An early account of the Powhatans noted: "The better sort of women cover them . . . all over with skyn mantells, fynely drest, shagged and fringed at the skirt, carved and coulored with some pretty worke or the proportion of beasts, fowle, tortoyses, or other such like Imagery as shall best please or expresse the fancy of the wearer." Feather mantels, another writer added, were "prettily wrought and woven with [mulberry] threeds that nothing could be discerned but the feathers, which were exceeding warme and very handsome."[36] Accessories included elaborate purses made of buckskin with small shells interwoven into the leather. Chiefly family members donned fancy clothes only for ceremonial or diplomatic occasions such as presiding over religious rituals, where all participants wore special costumes or headgear made of animal skins and feathers, or when hosting important guests. Fine garments also made prestigious gifts: Powhatan offered John Smith his personal mantle to cement an alliance.

Women performed the laborious work of making clothes. Men did preliminary dressing of animal skins, but women spent laborious hours removing flesh; drying, soaking, and scraping to eliminate hair; and pounding, smoking, and stretching on frames to make supple leather. After cutting the leather with bone or shell knives, they sowed pieces together with bone needles and sinew thread to makes clothes, pouches, containers, and other items. Women added individual touches with natural dyes, fringe edging, painting, and porcupine quills.

Little wonder European cloth and sewing tools became desired trade goods. Compared to leather, textiles were lighter and softer, dried faster, remained warmer when wet, came in many bright colors, and were easier to fashion with iron scissors, knives, awls, and needles. Chiefs received military coats as signs of rank, and by controlling trade, they were the first to don European textiles and clothes. Ordinary women and men developed a taste for European clothes, and men increased deer hunting and slave raiding to acquire them. Indians were highly selective consumers passing up tight-fitting breeches or dresses that restricted movement but prizing brightly colored cloth, scarves, blankets, and ready-to-wear ruffled calico shirts, which they wore unbuttoned with shirttails out. Even more common was simply substituting textiles for skin and grass aprons, breechclouts, and mantles. By 1760, Indians exhibited a wide range of clothing styles from retention of traditional garb, to mix-and-match of English and native items depending on availability of trade goods and personal tastes, to adopting European dress, shirts, breeches, and coats for men and shifts, petticoats, and jackets for women by Indians who worked for or lived near whites.

Elite European Settlers

Europeans wore multiple layers of richly colored clothes that must have seemed strange to natives and uncomfortable during hot humid summers. Heavy clothes were practical in northern Europe's cool damp climate, but even the Spanish, who moved from the semiarid Iberian Peninsula to the semitropical Gulf of Mexico, maintained traditional dress as long as possible. To Europeans, clothes covered Adam and Eve's shameful nakedness after eating forbidden fruit in the Garden of Eden. Extensive wardrobes separated civilized, Christian Europeans from "unclothed" savage, heathen Africans and Indians. Differences in fabric, cut, or decoration of apparel or accessories encoded a divinely sanctioned hierarchy: women from men, leisured elites from ordinary laborers, officials from common folk, professionals from illiterates, and town dwellers from country people. Extensive vocabularies described the cut, style, and fabric of clothes; assessed the wearers' social status; and determined appropriate interpersonal behavior. Devereux Jarratt, a carpenter's son who grew up in Virginia during the 1730s, recalled:

> We were accustomed to look upon, what were called *gentle folks,* as beings of a superior order. For my part, I was quite shy of *them,* and kept off at a humble distance. A *periwig,* in those days, was a distinguishing badge of *gentle folk*—and when I saw a man riding the road, near our house, with a wig on, it would so alarm my fears, and give me such a disagreeable feeling, that, I dare say, I would run off, as for my life. Such ideas of the difference between *gentle* and *simple*[folk], were, I believe, universal among all of my rank and age.[37]

Colonials adopted European attire: shirts, breeches, waistcoats, and long coats for men and shifts, corsets, petticoats, gowns, and short jackets for women with everyone but the very poor wearing stockings and shoes. (Modern underwear was unknown.) The Virginia Company advised male emigrants to bring a Monmouth cap, three shirts, three suits of a doublet and breeches, a waistcoat, three pairs of silk stockings, and four pairs of shoes. Costly in the time and labor needed to produce cloth and requiring great proficiency to make all but the simplest apparel, clothes were among the most frequently imported items and prized personal possessions. Planters hired male tailors and female seamstresses to alter and mend apparel, and they passed down fine garments to family members. Even in the early 18th century, Robert Beverley, a planter, observed that Virginians "have their clothing of all sorts from England, as linen, woolen, silk, hats, and leather."[38] By mid-century, textiles comprised over one-third of British exports to colonial North America. Common planters and backwoods farmers purchased imported cloth from country merchants and made and mended plainer versions of elite garments. Quakers and German Pietists wore unornamented "plain style" garb of their European coreligionists.

Elite provincials strove to keep pace with European fashion. "So much does their Taste run after dress," the Rev. Jonathan Boucher quipped, "that they tell me I may see in Virginia more brilliant Assemblies than I ever c'd [saw] in the North of Engl'd."[39] Wealthy planters, merchants, and government officials ordered Chinese silk gowns, Dutch linen underwear, silk English footwear, India printed calicos, and custom-made suits from measurements sent to skilled tailors in Europe. Their close-fitting clothes were made from expensive fabrics like brocaded silks, satins, velvets, superfine woolens, and cotton chintz, which had smooth textures, bright colors, and vivid patterns. They required yards of expensive cloth and included elaborate trimmings of ruffled collars, lace cuffs along sleeves, patterned brocades, hand-stitched gold and silver embroidery, decorative sequins, silk buttons, and gold and silver shoe buckles. In 1774, Philip Fithian—tutor to wealthy Virginia planter Robert Carter's children—eyed 26-year-old Elizabeth Lee, who wore "a light Chintz Gown, very fine, with a blue stamp; elegantly made, and which set well upon her. She wore a blue silk Quilt. In one word Her Dress was rich & fashionable."[40] By mid-century, merchants provided fashion dolls wearing the latest gowns and pattern books of gentlemen's garments. Local tailors, seamstresses, and mantua-makers advertised to customers their skills in fashioning stylish clothes from the finest fabrics and garment pieces. Each morning, as free colonials put on their European-made clothes or locally sown apparel made from imported cloth, they visually expressed their European identities and replicated hierarchies essential for maintaining social order.

Or, so it seemed. Some found opportunities in the colonial South's fluid, diverse society for assuming new identities by adopting new clothing styles. "We are not the veriest beggers in the worlde," boasted John Pory, Virginia colony secretary, in 1619, during the tobacco boom, as "our cowekeeper here of James citty on Sundays goes accowtered all in freshe flaming silke; and a wife of one that in England had professed the black arte, not of a scholler, but of a collier [a charcoal maker] of Croydon, weares her rough bever hatt with a faire perle hatband, and a silken suit thereto correspondent."[41] Men on the make ignored sumptuary laws that forbade wearing clothes or using fabrics "above" one's station, and urban consumers unheeded moralists' condemnations of chasing after fashion. In the South's humid climate, the wealthy abandoned formal wear for loose-fitting garments of cooler thinner fabrics. "In Summertime even the gentry goe Many in White Holland [linen] Wa[i]st Coat and drawers and a thin Cap on their heads and Thread stockings [knitted linen]," reported William Grove from Virginia in 1732, and a 1775 Wilmington visitor confessed it was so hot she "dressed in a single muslin petticoat and a short gown." A friend advised a new College of William and Mary student to bring many large thin shirts so they "mayn't stick to your hide when you perspire."[42] Baptist converts condemned stylish gentry fashion as mere vanity and favored working people's looser fitting plain clothes. As in other areas of colonial life, clothes became front lines of cultural change.

A planter's wife awoke in a loose-fitting white linen or cotton shift that covered her body from the elbows to just below the knees. As her only underwear (panties and brassieres are 19th- and 20th-century additions, respectively), she put on a clean shift every morning. A servant or slave assisted with tying the bodice, or corset, stiffened with whalebone, wooden or metal "stays," which were laced loosely at home but tight for formal occasions. Bodices gave women pleasing figures: cone shaped, shoulders pulled back and down, breasts pushed high and rounded, and posture erect. She selected one of her many petticoats, or full skirts, an heirloom handed down from female relatives and altered to remain fashionable, perhaps, or one newly acquired. Some were simple skirts and a few had hoops requiring yards of fabric for formal occasions. Pockets were separate accessories tied to petticoat strings. If visiting or receiving company, she donned a long gown that covered the upper body to the floor that might include a "stomacher" insert over the bodice. Gowns usually opened to reveal matching or contrasting petticoats. Stockings, sown not knitted and held up with garters, and silk or worsted fitted shoes completed her ensemble. When going outside, she put on a hooded cloak or cape and in cold or inclement weather added headscarves, leather gloves, and muffs. Women's fashion changed slowly. Farthingale hoop skirts disappeared in early 17th century only to reemerge larger than ever early in the next. Exquisite lace-trimmed gowns with plunging necklines replaced high collar ruffs that, much to men's delight, bared necks and shoulders and exposed breasts.

Her planter husband arose in a loose, long-sleeved shirt if he wore anything at all. For informal breakfasts, he might simply don a loose gown, or "banyan," but if he expected company or attended to business before eating, he would first put on a clean, white linen or cotton dress shirt with ruffles of fine linen or lace at the neck and cuffs. Next came a three-piece suit: a waistcoat or vest, knee-length breeches (the best included cotton or linen liners) buttoned at center front, and long outer coat. He chose from several suits: looser fitting, plain garments for every day, elaborately embroidered tailored ones for formal occasions, coordinated outfits of similar fabric and cut, or mix-and-match sets of contrasting colors. Wool, linen, cotton, or silk sown stockings covered the legs, and leather shoes, sized but not distinguished between left and right, protected the feet. He took special pleasure in wearing fashionable silver shoe buckles. If stepping out into rain or cold, he would put on a greatcoat or long cape of wool over a heavier sleeved waistcoat, a second pair of stockings, a hat, and gloves.

Men's high fashion changed during the colonial period. In the early 17th century, padded Spanish styles were hauteur: stiff tapered doublets worn over linen shirts with attached close-fitting sleeves, lace wrist cuffs, and flowering pleated neck ruffs. Padded trunk hose with attached tailored stockings covered the legs and heavy boots protected feet. After mid-century, coats, breeches, and shoes replaced doublets, trunk hose, and boots. Fine linen shirts with elaborate collars, cuffs, and ruffled sleeves and worn under vests were all the rage. By 1700, fashionable men sought a long, loose look with waistcoats covering most of the breeches and jackets with full sleeves and wide skirts that fell below the knees and became short gowns. By mid-century, lean and trim was in: waistcoats became shorter, cuffs smaller, and coats narrower.

Children's attire changed slowly from constricting garments styled after adult clothing in the 17th century to special children's clothes a century later. Very young children of both sexes wore close-fitting bodices to encourage upright posture and long petticoats with lead strings for warmth and aid in early walking. Toddlers wore padded "pudding caps" or crash helmets. Children of humbler parents made do with simple gowns or long shirts that

Gentry children dressed as miniature adults. Clothes not only marked children's passage from infancy to adult gender roles but also expressed class position. Mann Page, age eight, and Elizabeth Page, age six, are dressed as miniature gentleman and lady wearing smooth fabrics, full cuffs and trim, décolleté gown, silver buttons, silk stockings, and shoe buckles. Mann holds a pet cardinal, while Page shows off her similarly clothed doll. (John Wollaston, "Mann and Elizabeth Page," circa 1757. Courtesy of the Virginia Historical Society, Richmond, [acc. No. 1973.16].)

covered infants' feet and toddlers' ankles. In an important rite of passage around age six or seven, children were dressed as small replicas of adults: shirts and breeches with vents in the crotch and rear for boys and shifts, corsets, petticoats, and gowns and aprons for girls. Basic attire continued past puberty. Harry Willis and Robert Balden Carter, wealthy planters' sons and both in their teens, wore only shirts and breeches about the plantation in the summer. By mid-18th century, following changes in childrearing practices, young children wore less restrictive white dresses or "frocks" with sashes. Wealthy parents provided children special clothes of fine fabrics: skeleton suits with trousers, not knee breeches, for boys and muslin frocks for girls.

Lower Classes

Working people wore practical ready-made clothes suitable for labor made of durable inexpensive fabrics, like unbleached linen osnaburg, coarse cottons, cotton–linen mixes, linsey-woolsey, a wool–flax blend, and leather. Women slept in the same shifts worn during the day and put on petticoats or full-sleeved "short gowns" that left the feet exposed; loose-fitting "jumps," or corsets; short-sleeved jackets laced with buttons; and full aprons to protect petticoats. Men donned loose-fitting long-sleeved jersey shirts that covered the waist and either leather breeches cut at mid-thigh or loose mid-calf trousers made from canvas, and roomy, short-frocked jackets. Sewn stockings, locally made leather shoes with brass buckles or wooden clogs, and a heavy coat or cloak gave protection in cold or wet weather. Devereux Jarratt recalled his entire young adult raiment consisted of homemade "pair of course breeches, one or two oznaburgs shirts, a pair of shoes and stockings, an old felt hat, [and] a bear skin *coat*."[43] Common planters had at least one set of good clothes for church, weddings, and other special occasions that were plainer, cheaper versions of fashionable clothes and made by sewing pieces of store-bought cloth. Only the very poor went sockless and barefoot and wore the same outfits every day.

There was much variety in plain folk's attire. As in Europe, many occupations had distinctive garb: drovers' long smocks or roomy shirts, blacksmiths' leather aprons, watermen's loose canvas trousers and pea jackets, and serving girls' calico dresses and checked aprons. Garments included ready-made, homemade from store-bought cloth, homespun, and old clothes repaired with cloth patches. By mid-18th century, country merchants offered an array of cheap European cloth in new colors and designs for wives and daughters to sow into loose-fitting, plain garments for family members and for sale. Spinning linen and cotton into thread and wool into yarn, weaving cloth, and knitting garments supplemented incomes of poor farmers, laborers, and widows. Backwoodsmen adopted postcontact Indian attire with young men in homespun hunting shirts that reached to mid-thigh and were tied in back with a sash, leather leggings, moccasins, and deerskin jackets functional in the forests but scandalous to genteel society. Charles Woodmason, an itinerant Anglican cleric in Carolina, thought it deficient: the "Men with only a thin shirt and a pair of Breeches or Trousers on—barelegged, and barefooted," and "The Women bareheaded and barelegged, and barefoot with only a thin shift and under Petticoat." Sweating under the weight of a heavy black gown, starched collar, and powdered wig, Woodmason likely seemed inappropriately attired to his would-be parishioners.[44]

Indentured servants wore the plain clothes of England's working poor. James Revel, a Virginia servant, recalled in verse donning fresh clothes before his sale, but afterward receiving ill-fitting ready-made clothes made of durable coarse fabrics that marked servants' garb:

Our things were gave to each they did belong,
And they that had clean linen put it on.
Our faces shav'd, cob'd out our wigs and hair,
That we in decent order might appear. . . .

A canvas shirt and trowsers then they gave,
With a hop-sack frock [smock] in which I was to slave:
No shoes nor stockings had I for to wear,
No hat, nor cap, both head and feet were bare.

Thus dress'd into the Field I nex[t] must go,
Amongst tobacco plants all day to hoe.[45]

Women received plain dresses and short jackets. Most owners provided a second suit of winter clothes: a heavy jacket, a hat, stockings, shoes, and a blanket along with another suit of trousers, waistcoat, and shirt or shift, petticoat, and jacket. They were made from cheap rough-textured cotton, woolen, and linen fabrics that were colored in dull browns, greens, blues, and off-whites, or simple striped or checked patterns. Wearing the same clothes day after day, washing them infrequently, and patching tears in sleeves and knees, servants presented a ragged countenance.

Most servants aspired to appear better. They sued owners who clothed them inadequately and rejected clothes made of "negro cloth." Runaways absconded with the fashionable, colorful garments of free men and women hoping to mask their servility. By law, new suits of clothes were part of servants' freedom dues, emblems of their passage from servitude to freedom. A 1717 South Carolina law allowed men "One new hat, a good coat and breeches either of kersey or broadcloth, one new shirt of white linen, one new pair of shoes and stockings" and women a "Wa[i]st coat and Petticoat of new Half-thicks or Pennistone, a new Shift of white Linnen, a new Pair of shoes and stockings, a blue Apron and two Caps of white Linnen."[46]

Africans and African Americans

As with Native Americans, Europeans emphasized Africans' skimpy attire. Olaudah Equiano, an Igbo captured as a boy in the 1750s, recalled men and women in his West African village wearing "a long piece of calico, or muslin, wrapped loosely round the body . . . usually dyed blue, which is our favorite color" with the upper body and feet bare.[47] Women added headscarves and metal ornaments around the neck, arms, and legs, embellishments for tedious hours spent spinning and weaving cotton cloth, dyed textiles with vegetable extracts, and fashioned garments. Except for charms worn around the neck, children were unclothed until puberty. Elite men wore long shirts, baggy drawers, cloth caps, and leather sandals. African merchants and high-status individuals were the first to incorporate brightly colored European and Asian fabrics into traditional dress and don European clothes. Creoles from African slave ports brought a mix of clothing styles to the New World, and contrary to popular images of naked Africans on slave ships, most were dressed in native attire with uncovered upper bodies.

Owners clothed slaves in cheap ready-made imported garments. Annual allotments for women typically included two shifts, a short petticoat or gown, a jacket or coat, and several caps and aprons, and for men, two shirts, a pair of trousers or breeches, a jacket or waistcoat, and a felt hat. Made from coarse durable fabrics, like linen osnaburg, inexpensive woolens, heavy canvas, and linsey-woolsey, slaves' drab, poorly tailored clothes visibly marked their lowly status. Without stays to ensure proper erect posture, enslaved women's backbreaking labor gave them a stooped appearance. Chesapeake slaves received a second suit of winter clothes and a pair of sewn stockings and shoes that were sized by age not foot size, and, like the rest of their clothing, were ill fitting and uncomfortable. On cold nights, slaves slept in their winter clothing adding to their shabby appearance. Rural slaves in the warmer Lowcountry wore less: African-style waist ties and loincloths for men and women in wraparound skirts or petticoats and bare upper bodies. Everywhere slave infants went naked, and young children made do with thin frocks or long shirts in the summer until puberty or even older. Even town slaves, "Boys of 10 & 12 Years of Age," observed a Virginia visitor, are seen "going through the Streets quite naked, and others with only Part of a Shirt hanging Part of the Way down their Backs."[48]

Readily available imported clothes, generally dull blues in striped, checked, or calico patterns, reduced planters' costs and standardized slave garments' cut, color, and size. Parsimonious owners expected summer clothes to last an entire season of hard labor; delayed fall shipments meant Chesapeake slaves in tattered clothes suffered from the cold until winter allotments arrived. Five yards was deemed sufficient to clothe a Carolina slave for a year, about a quarter of the cost of an indentured servant's freedom suit, and James Madison, Sr., shoed his adult slaves for seven years for less than half of what he paid for one-year's dancing lessons. William Byrd, a wealthy Virginia planter, justified slaves' ragged attire by insisting they were inured to outdoor labor and remained in "perfect health" disclaiming: "Negroes which are kept the barest of clothes and bedding are commonly freest from sickness."[49]

By mid-18th century, slave clothing became more varied. Planters accoutered favored house slaves in livery, wool suits with contrasting colors and elaborate edgings, stockings, and shoes when entertaining guests. Slave blacksmiths wore leather aprons and watermen sailors' trousers, and owners rewarded domestic workers, drivers, and artisans with better quality and more colorful clothing. Diversified Chesapeake planters trained slave men to be weavers, assigned older slave women to fashion coarse store-bought "Negro cloth" into rough garments for women and children, and hired local white tailors to sew the more complicated shirts, breeches, coats, and petticoats. Slave women used vegetable dyes to color neutral fabrics (indigo blues and red oak bark were especially popular), repaired tears with colorful patches, and added embellishments like buttons, cuffs, and trimmings.

Slaves seized opportunities to personalize wardrobes from the monotonous uniformity of field garb. Spanish law in Florida and social custom in Louisiana protected slaves' personal property rights, and English colonial laws banning wearing clothes of fine white linen instead of the usual cheap blue and checkered pattern went unenforced. Slaves spent cash earned from independent labor for brightly colored and patterned felt caps, headscarves, silk hats, ribbons, shirts, breeches, and accessories and for tailored waistcoats, petticoats, and chintz gowns. Black women in Charles

Town paraded about "in Apparel quite gay and beyond their Condition" on Sundays and holidays in the 1740s offending whites who were powerless to curb slaves' behavior. Adults acquired at least one set of good apparel worn on Sundays, holidays, and other special occasions through the used clothing trade, by receiving cast-off items from owners, or from stealing garments from whites. Bacchus, a fashion-conscious Virginia slave, ran off in 1774 with "two white Russia Drill Coats, one turned up with blue, the other quite plain and new with white figured Metal Buttons, blue Plush Breeches, a fine cloth Pompadour Waistcoat, . . . a fine Hat cut and cocked in the Macaroni Figure," among other items.[50] Francisque, a runaway slave in New Orleans, reportedly attended blacks' Saturday evening festivities sporting a silver-accented snuffbox and accoutered as a gentlemen with a "ruffled shirt, blue waistcoat, white hat, and wearing three or four handkerchiefs around his neck, elsewhere about him."[51] The garments might be English, but by embellishing with colorful contrasting patterns and creative matching of individual articles, slaves created sartorial styles of their own.

A WORLD OF GOODS

In 1771, William Eddis, an Englishman living in Maryland, found the colonial South's rapidly changing material culture surprising. "The quick importation of fashions from the mother country is really astonishing. I am almost included to believe," he added, "that a new fashion is adopted earlier by the polished and affluent American than by many opulent persons in the great metropolis."[52] Provincials' seemingly uncritical acceptance of English fashion was one of many paradoxes in the importance of material possessions in daily life. The consumer revolution affected all ranks of colonial society raising living standards for rich and poor alike, yet increased material and social distances between the wealthy and everyone else. The necessity of money for purchasing comfort and conveniences created a common ethic of materialism, yet aspirations of society's lower ranks required elites to engage in ever more competitive bouts of conspicuous consumption. Wholesale adoption of European, especially English, consumer culture strengthened ties between colonial Southerners and mother countries, yet pursuit of acquisitions bespoke a culture of change whose sources also originated from indigenous and from West African peoples. Goods were physical embodiments of new societies in the postcontact South even as they created individual appearances. Finally, imported goods, historian

T.H. Breen argues, created a "shared language of consumption . . . [and] a shared framework of consumer experience" that forged a common provincial identity, a forerunner of a postrevolutionary American identity.[53] It should come as no surprise that possessions were at the center of early conflicts between new British colonial policies and colonials' aspirations after 1763. What we own and, even more, what goods we desire to possess both reflects and affects daily living and collective and personal identities.

NOTES

1. Ann Smart Martin, "Material Things and Cultural Meanings: Notes on the Study of Early American Material Culture," *William and Mary Quarterly, 3rd ser.*, 53, no. 1 (January 1996): 5, 6.

2. James Deetz, *In Small Things Forgotten: An Archaeology of Early American Life,* rev. and expanded ed. (New York: Doubleday, 1996), 259.

3. Written evidence remains essential for interpreting what archaeologists dig from the ground and for contextualizing artifacts. See Deetz, *Small Things Forgotten,* Chapter 1, for challenges in interpreting excavated materials in context of historical documents.

4. William Bartram, cited by Colin G. Calloway, *New Worlds for All: Indians, Europeans, and the Remaking of Early America* (Baltimore: Johns Hopkins University Press, 1997), 60; illustrations on pp. 7 and 44 show Timucuan and Algonquian houses, respectively.

5. John Smith, "A Map of Virginia," in *The Complete Works of Captain John Smith,* 3 vols., ed. by Philip L. Barbour (Chapel Hill: University of North Carolina Press, 1986), 1: 161, cited in Helen C. Rountree, *The Powhatan Indians of Virginia: Their Traditional Culture* (Norman: University of Oklahoma Press, 1989), 61.

6. Henry Spelman, "Relation of Virginia," in *The Travel and Works of Captain John Smith,* ed. by Edward Arber and A.G. Bradley (Edinburgh: John Grant, 1910), cvi, cited in Rountree, *Powhatan Indians,* 106.

7. See illustration on p. 153.

8. Robert Beverley, *The History and Present State of Virginia,* ed. by David Freeman Hawke (Indianapolis: The Bobbs-Merrill Company, Inc., 1971), 152; Gregory A. Stiverson and Patrick H. Butler, III, eds., "Virginia in 1732: The Travel Journal of William Hugh Grove," *Virginia Magazine of History and Biography* 85, no. 1 (1977): 26–28, cited in Rhys Isaac, *The Transformation of Virginia, 1740–1790* (Chapel Hill: University of North Carolina Press, 1986), 35; see illustrations on pp. 142 and 220.

9. See illustrations on pp. 160 and 193.

10. John Ferdinand Dalziel Smyth, *A Tour in the United States of America . . .* (London, 1784; facsimile reprint, New York, 1968), 49, cited in Isaac, *Transformation of Virginia,* 33; see illustrations on pp. 153, 313, and 361.

11. Eliza Lucas, *The Letterbook of Eliza Lucas Pinckney* (Chapel Hill: University of North Carolina Press, 1972), 61, cited in James D. Kornwolf, *Architecture and Town Planning on Colonial North America*, 3 vols. (Baltimore: Johns Hopkins University Press), 2: 914, 915; see illustration on p. 220.

12. John Bartram and Francis Harper, "Diary of a Journey through the Carolinas, Georgia, and Florida from July 1, 1765, to April 10, 1766," entry for September 26, 1765, *Transactions of the American Philosophical Society* 33, no. 1 (December 1942): 30.

13. See illustration on p. 10.

14. Bartram and Harper, "Diary," 52.

15. See illustration on p. 142.

16. See illustration on p. 220. Scholars debate the extent of African influence on slave housing. Citing stylistic similarities between some African and slave houses, Steven L. Jones concludes: "The persistent presence of traditional Central and West African elements in terms of plan, spatial distribution, materials, and form in New World architectures patterns from the seventeenth to the nineteen centuries suggests indeed that the origin of these patterns is African" ("The African-American Tradition in Vernacular Architecture," in *The Archaeology of Slavery and Plantation Life*, ed. by Theresa Singleton (Orlando, FL: Academic Press, 1985), 195). This perspective overlooks possibilities of Native American influences on housing materials and construction and ignores the Creole nature of African American culture. Kornwolf is closer to the mark: "Although there may appear to be superficial similarities between these and other African dwellings and communities, on the one hand, and the settlement traditions developed for slaves in North America, on the other, there is little evidence that African traditions of building, whether in terms of form, function, or structure, were truly expressed in North America" (*Architecture and Town Planning*, 1: 470).

17. Cited by David Hackett Fisher, *Albion's Seed: Four British Folkways in America* (New York: Oxford University Press, 1989), 658.

18. Thomas Jefferson, *Notes on the State of Virginia*, ed. by William Peden (Chapel Hill: University of North Carolina Press, 1955), 152.

19. See illustration on p. 313.

20. Ritual objects are discussed in Chapter 8 and items of personal adornment in Chapter 7.

21. See illustration on p. 186.

22. Garcilaso de la Vega, *The Florida of the Inca: A History of the Adelantado, Hernando de Soto, . . .*, trans. and ed. by John Grier Varner and Jeannette Johnson Varner (Austin: University of Texas Press, 1951), 306, cited in James H. Merrill, *The Indians' New World: Catawbas and Their Neighbors from European Contact through the Era of Removal* (New York: W.W. Norton and Co., 1991 [1989]), 39.

23. John Banister, *John Banister and His Natural History of Virginia, 1678–1692*, ed. by Joseph and Nesta Ewan (Urbana: University of Illinois

Press, 1970), 42, cited in James Axtell, "The First Consumer Revolution," in *Beyond 1492: Encounters in Colonial North America* (New York: Oxford University Press, 1992), 132.

24. Mark Catesby, *The Natural History of Carolina, Florida, and the Bahama Islands* (Savannah, GA: Beehive Press, 1974 [1731]), 21, cited in Sarah Hill, "Weaving History: Cherokee Baskets from the Springplace Mission," *William and Mary Quarterly*, 3rd ser., 53, no. 1 (January 1996): 126. Vine baskets appeared only in the 19th century after whites turned canebrakes into plantations and were produced mostly for trade to white missionaries.

25. Gloria L. Main, *Tobacco Colony: Life in Early Maryland, 1650–1720* (Princeton, NJ: Princeton University Press, 1982), 140.

26. John Fontaine, quoted in W.G. Standard, "Major Robert Beverley and His Descendants," *Virginia Magazine of History and Biography* 3, no. 2 (1895): 171, cited in Kevin M. Sweeny, "High-Style Vernacular: Lifestyles of the Colonial Elite," in *Of Consuming Interests: The Style of Life in the Eighteenth Century*, ed. by Cary Carson, Ronald Hoffman, and Peter J. Albert (Charlottesville: University Press of Virginia, 1994), 4.

27. Letter from William Fitzhugh to Nicholas Hayward, June 1, 1688, in *William Fitzhugh and His Chesapeake World, 1676–1701: The Fitzhugh Letters and Other Documents*, ed. by Richard Beale Davis (Chapel Hill: University of North Carolina Press, 1963), 246; See illustration on p. 193.

28. Josiah Quincy, Jr., "Journal of Josiah Quincy, Junior, 1773," entry for March 7, 1773, *Massachusetts Historical Society Proceedings* 49 (1916): 444, 445.

29. *Robert Beverley Letterbook, 1761–1793*, cited by Lois Green Carr and Lorena S. Walsh, "Changing Lifestyles and Consumer Behavior in the Colonial Chesapeake," in Carson et al., *Of Consuming Interests*, 68.

30. William Eddis, *Letters from America*, ed. by Aubrey C. Land (Cambridge, MA: Harvard University Press, 1969), 57, 58; Janet Schaw, *Journal of a Lady of Quality*, ed. by Evangeline Walker Andrews and Charles M. Andrews (New Haven, CT: Yale University Press, 1921), 185, cited in Cary Carson, "The Consumer Revolution in Colonial British America: Why Demand?" in Carson, et al., *Of Consuming Interests*, 504, 546.

31. See illustration on p. 105.

32. Ferdinand-Marie Bayard, *Travels of a Frenchman in Maryland and Virginia with a Description of Baltimore and Philadelphia*, trans. and ed. by Ben C. McCary (Williamsburg, VA: Ben C. McCary, 1950), 13, cited in Martha B. Katz-Hyman, "'In the Middle of this Poverty Some Cups and a Teapot': The Furnishing of Slave Quarters at Colonial Williamsburg," in *American Home: Material Culture, Domestic Space, and Family Life*, ed. by Eleanor Thompson (Hanover, NH: University Press of New England, 1988), 202.

33. See illustration on p. 199.

34. For jewelry, cosmetics, piercing, hairpieces, and tattoos, see Chapter 7.

35. See illustrations on pp. 3, 88, 94, and 186.

36. William Strachey, *The Historie of Travell into Virginia Britania,* 2nd series, Vol. 103, ed. by Louis B. Wright and Virginia Freund (Cambridge: Hakluyt Society, 1953), 71, 72 and Smith, *Works,* 1: 160, 161, cited in Rountree, *Powhatan Indians,* 102.

37. Devereux Jarratt, "The Autobiography of the Reverend Devereux Jarratt, 1732–1763," ed. by Douglass Adair, *William and Mary Quarterly,* 3rd ser., 9, no. 3 (July 1952): 361.

38. Robert Beverley, *History and Present State of Virginia,* 155.

39. "Letters of Rev. Jonathan Boucher," *Maryland Historical Magazine* 7 (1912), 5, cited by Linda Baumgarten, *Eighteenth-Century Clothing at Williamsburg* (Williamsburg, VA: Colonial Williamsburg Foundation, 1986), 11.

40. Philip Fithian, *Journal and Letters of Philip Vickers Fithian, 1774–1774: A Plantation Tutor of the Old Dominion,* entry for July 4, 1774 (Charlottesville, VA: University Press of Virginia, 1957), 130, 131.

41. Letter from John Pory to Sir Dudley Carleton, September 30, 1619, in *The Old Dominion in the Seventeenth Century: A Documentary History of Virginia, 1606–1689,* ed. by Warren M. Billings (Chapel Hill: University of North Carolina Press, 1975), 305.

42. Gregory A. Stiverson and Patrick H. Butler, III, eds., "Virginia in 1732: The Travel Journal of William Hugh Grove," *Virginia Magazine of History and Biography* 85, no. 1 (1977): 29, cited by Baumgarten, *Eighteenth-Century Clothing,* 12; *Journal of a Lady of Quality,* cited by Anna C. Eberly, "What Our Southern Frontier Women Wore," in *Eighteenth-century Florida: The Impact of the American Revolution,* ed. by Samuel Proctor (Gainesville: University Press of Florida, 1978), 145; and Letter from Stephen Hawtrey to Edward Hawtrey, March 26, 1765, Alumni File, College Archives, Earl Gregg Swem Library, College of William and Mary, Williamsburg, VA, cited by Baumgarten, *Eighteenth-Century Clothing,* 13.

43. Jarratt, "Autobiography," 367.

44. Charles Woodmason, *The Carolina Backcountry on the Eve of the Revolution: The Journal and Other Writings of Charles Woodmason, Anglican Itinerant,* ed. by Richard Hooker (Chapel Hill: University of North Carolina Press, 1953), 61.

45. James Revel, "The Poor Unhappy Transported Felon's Sorrowful Account of His Fourteen Years Transportation at Virginia in America," in Billings, ed., *The Old Dominion in the Seventeenth Century,* 138.

46. Abbot Emerson Smith, *Colonists in Bondage: White Servitude and Convict Labor in America, 1607–1776* (New York: W.W. Norton and Co., 1971 [1947]), 239.

47. Olaudah Equiano, *The Interesting Narrative of the Life of Olaudah Equiano, Written by Himself,* 2nd ed., ed. by Robert J. Allison (Boston: Bedford Books, 2007 [London, 1789]), 46.

48. Fred Shelly, ed., "The Journal of Ebenezer Hazard in Virginia, 1777," *Virginia Magazine of History and Biography* 62, no. 4 (1954): 409, 410, cited

by Linda Baumgarten, "'Clothes for the People': Slave Clothing in Early Virginia," *Journal of Early Southern Decorative Arts* 14 (1988): 27.

49. William Byrd, "A Progress to the Mines," *The London Diary, 1717–1721, and Other Writings*, ed. by Louis B. Wright and Marion Tinling (New York: Oxford University Press, 1958), 350; see illustrations on pp. 69 and 371.

50. *South Carolina Gazette*, November 5, 1744, cited by Shane White and Graham White, "Slave Clothing and African-American Culture in the Eighteenth and Nineteenth Centuries," *Past and Present*, no. 148 (1995), 161; *Virginia Gazette* (Purdie and Dixon), ibid., 155; see illustration on p. 220.

51. Trial of Francisque, 1766, Records of the Superior Council of Louisiana, cited by Sophie White, "'Wearing Three or Four Handkerchiefs Around His Collar, and Elsewhere About Him': Slaves Constructions of Masculinity and Ethnicity in French Colonial New Orleans," *Gender & History* 15, no. 3 (2003): 536.

52. Eddis, *Letters from America*, 19, cited by Louis Green Carr and Lorena S. Walsh, "Changing Lifestyles and Consumer Behavior in the Colonial Chesapeake," in Carson, et al., *Of Consuming Interest*, 131.

53. T.H. Breen, "'Baubles of Britain': The American and Consumer Revolution of the Eighteenth Century," in Carson, et al., *Of Consuming Interest*, 448.

5

FOOD

Food is the most enduring aspect of material culture yet one most open to absorbing new ingredients, technologies, and methods. Unlike houses, furnishings, and clothes, only Europeans' accounts of eating and archaeologists' recovery of buried remains of meals survive. But, alas, no food. Foodways result from interactions between the environment (what foods are available), culture (what is good to eat), cooking (how foods are prepared), and eating (social protocols of meals).[1] Native Americans, the English, Europeans, and Africans ate in different ways but selectively borrowed and adapted new foods, new equipment, and new cooking methods from one another, modifying traditional cuisines in the process. During the 18th century, colonial elites created new table manners, new eating rituals, and new foods in emulation of English genteel styles, which, in turn, were embraced by common folk. By 1770, there were distinct but overlapping foodways among Native Americans, the English, Europeans, and Africans in the colonial South. Three different southern cuisines—formal dining, down home cooking, and backwoods subsistence—had also emerged through two centuries of cultural exchange.[2]

NATIVE AMERICANS

The colonial South's diverse environments made for extremely varied seasonal and regional diets. Native Americans consumed over 100 different foods each year. Corn (maize), beans, and venison were staple foods for woodland peoples. Depending on local resources, these were supplemented by many kinds of fish, shellfish, pumpkins, squashes, small game, birds, fowl, bear, nuts, berries, roots, and wild fruits and plants. Women preserved and stored food for the winter as security against future harvest failures, for community ceremonies, for chiefly entertainments vital for diplomacy, and for travel. Berries, small fruits, and mature corn were sun-dried, but fire was used to cure fish, small game, fruit, unripened corn, and pumpkins on hurdles or horizontal wooden frames. They cut animal carcasses into meat strips and placed them on spits over low fires. Dry meat lasted six months, and shelled dried corn could store indefinitely. Both were common travel fare. Women extracted oil by heating bear fat, which they used for cooking and as condiment with dried meat, as body lubricant and as cosmetics. Wild roots required baking, pounding with mortars into meal before baking, or were cut up, pulverized, boiled, and dried into a powder as emergency winter food. Women broke nuts, dried the meats, beat them into powder, then boiled them to skim off the oil or until it turned into thick pudding. Hickory and walnut milk were favorite seasonings; acorns produced oil for cooking and for medicine.

Indian women raised several varieties of corn and prepared them in many different ways. A Frenchman reported Indians in Louisiana had over 40 named corn dishes. In spring, women roasted fresh green corn in coals, welcome fare after lean winters. Corn hominy, a meal made from slowly boiling kernels for 10 or 12 hours with heated stones dropped into water, was the staff of life. Dried corn kernels were soaked in water and wood-ash lye, lightly pounded with mortars (made from logs with eight-inch holes burned into them) and pestles (thick, five-foot trimmed hickory sticks) to crack the grain. Using flat fanner baskets, women separated grains from hulls. Cooking cracked hominy for several hours with a little wood-ash lye made a fine base for soups and stews or was stored in jars and allowed to ferment slightly as a refreshing drink. Women also made cold meal by parching firm kernels in the fire until brown, pounding with mortars and pestles into a fine meal, and fanning to remove hulls. When dried over a smoky fire, parched meal was ideal for travelers who ate it dry or mixed it with cold water into thin gruel. Wood-ash lye, made by pouring cold water on containers of hardwood ashes, added flavor and enhanced corn's nutritional value by increasing the amount of amino acid lysine and niacin, which reduced incidence of pellagra.

Fine hominy meal, made by thoroughly beating corn kernels with mortars and pestles and sifting with basket sieves, when mixed with boiling water made bread batter. Thin batter cooked in bear grease in flat-bottom pots became unleavened fry bread or corn fritters. Thick batter wrapped in corn shucks and simmered in boiling water for an hour made rolls. Dough dropped into boiling water formed dumpling balls. These were dried for travel. Women baked bread by shaping loaves or flat cakes and placing them on heated baking rocks or in flat-bottom, ceramic pots either covered with wrapped corn shucks or buried under coals. Pumpkin, boiled beans, sunflower seeds, berries, and nuts (especially chestnuts) made corn bread even more flavorful.

Indians preferred slow cooking and ate only raw oysters, ripe berries and fruits, and wild greens in early spring. Women broiled, boiled, or smoked fish and meat. Smoked oysters and fish were prized delicacies. They put fish, shellfish, cut pieces of meat, and skinned small animals on hurdles or spits for roasting. "Venison *barbecuted,* that is wrapped up in leaves and roasted in the Embers," an Englishman explained, was a favorite Powhatan dish.[3] Fish, small animals, and small cuts of meat were also slowly barbecued and smoked on sticks placed into the ground to lean over the fire. They boiled or roasted beans, pumpkins, and squashes. Succotash, a mixture of hominy and beans or pumpkins with nuts and berries added for flavor, made a fine meal. Women baked or boiled processed roots, like tuckahoe or wild potatoes, before green corn ripened in the spring.

Cooking utensils made from local materials comprised most Indians' material goods. Women fashioned different kinds of ceramic pots, pitchers, bowls, dishes, basins, and platters from coiled clay that they smoothed, decorated, and glazed by placing "them over a large fire of smoky pitch pine, which makes them smooth, black and firm," James Adair, a British Indian agent, observed. Sturdy baskets of different sizes woven from dyed river cane made containers to collect and store food and sieves and fanners for processing. Cherokee basket-makers "manage the workmanship so well," he continued, "that both the inside and outside are covered with a beautiful variety of pleasing figures."[4] Women hollowed out large gourds as water containers and scraped small ones into eating dishes, spoons, ladles, funnels, and cups. They sowed animal skins for oil and honey containers and carved wood into plates and spoons. Coastal women used shells as spoons and bent turtle shells into cups.

Ordinary Indians had no set times for meals, but ate whenever they were hungry. Menus varied seasonally and regionally but usually included a cool drink of hominy gruel, corn bread, and hominy soups or stews simmering over a low fire with whatever was in season added to the pot. Depending on the time of year and location, one could enjoy barbecued meat or fish with hominy; boiled meats, fish, corn, and other vegetables; kidney beans, meat, and bear oil seasoning; or boiled shellfish and hominy bisque. One Cherokee meal consisted of honey-locust pod soup, sour corn-broth, and corn-bean bread. A carpenter in Louisiana enjoyed a repast of smoked buffalo, bear, and deer meats at a Pascagoula village along with several kinds of melons, wild fruits, and sagamité, "which is a kind of pap made from maize and green beans that are like those

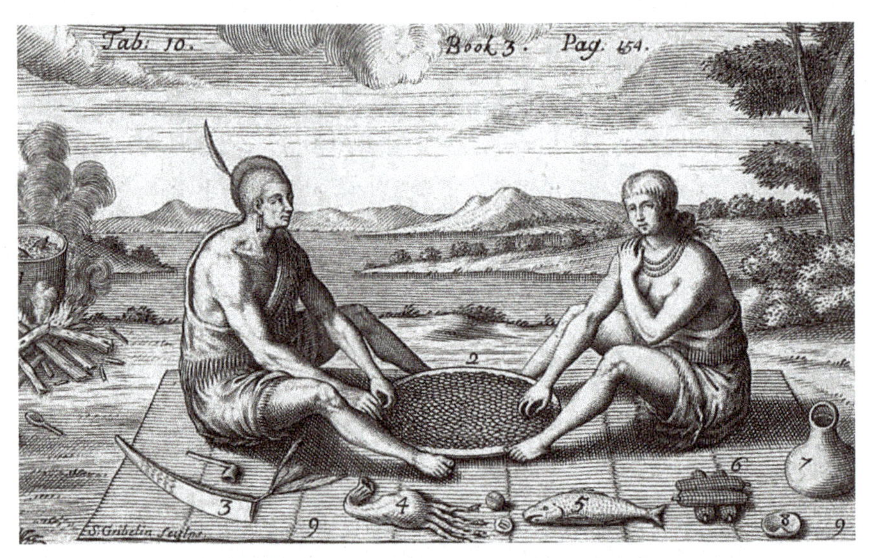

Algonquian husband and wife enjoying a meal. This European rending of an archetypal Native meal of corn, fish, and water included cooking methods, one-pot meals of simmered hominy and fish (1) and roasted fish and corn (5 and 6); serving utensils, a gourd drinking jug and seashell utensil; squatting on a grass mat (9); and finger dipping from a basket (2). Engraving by Simon Gribelin after Theodor de Bry, 1590, in Robert Beverley, *The History of Virginia,* 2nd ed. [London, 1722 (1705)]. (Library of Congress.)

in France."[5] Birds and animals were never in the same pot: even as food, beings of the air were kept separate from those of the ground. Salads were nonexistent except during late winter when little else was available. Sassafras tea and water sufficed for beverages.

Before eating, women and men washed their hands and said prayers, but ate separately even at formal banquets. Individuals sat on mats with legs spread apart and ate from common vessels or shallow wooden boards, and sometimes shared spoons and cups. During times of plenty, common people gorged themselves but were "patient of hunger" during the late winter and early spring months. Elite families enjoyed regular meals throughout the year and had more refined table manners. Servant women brought food in individual dishes. Chiefs entertained visitors lavishly with delicacies like walnut milk, fish, shellfish, and meat to impress them with their abundance and prestige. One Powhatan feast in 1607 included mulberries, boiled corn and beans, corncakes, and venison. Guests received prodigious amounts of food they were expected to consume or share with their retinue.

Europeans revolutionized Native American diet and cooking. They introduced new foods: wheat and small grains; cabbage, onions, and garlic; beef, pork, and barnyard poultry; honey; peaches, oranges, and apples; rice, okra, sorghum, and watermelons from Africa; and sweet potatoes from the Caribbean. High-status individuals were the first to adopt them as exotic trade goods. Plants and animals traveled faster than European settlers. Louisiana frontiersmen were surprised to encounter the Natchez enjoying "wild" peaches and pork from penned hogs. As long as natives had access to their gardens, fields, and hunting preserves, they incorporated European foods selectively into traditional cuisine. Choctaws readily added sweet potatoes, watermelon, peaches, and African guinea corn to traditional recipes but shunned wheat, beef, and dairy products and raised poultry and hogs mostly to sell to Louisiana settlers. Native women marrying European traders introduced domestic animals, dairy products, sugar, coffee, tea, and European dishes into their communities. Male Powhatans became commercial fishermen and hunting guides. Creek and Cherokee women sold surplus corn and other foods at military posts and frontier settlements. Members of the petites nations, who lived along the coastal Gulf of Mexico and Lower Mississippi River, relocated their villages to be closer to New Orleans markets. Cooking technology changed quickly. European brass kettles and metal knife blades made food preparation easier, iron flat pans and leavenings created modern fry bread and increased fried foods, and forks changed eating habits.

For most Indians of the colonial South, Europeans' presence marked an irrevocable change from abundance to scarcity. Without natural predators, European domestic animals quickly spread beyond colonial settlements. Hogs ran wild in forests uprooting forage crops and driving away wildlife. Cattle trampled unfenced cornfields. Animal droppings spread weeds that crowded out native plants. Settlers encroached on Indians' land, and colonial militias destroyed fields and stored food supplies. As European goods replaced traditional objects, women abandoned subsistence skills. James Adair observed that Cherokee women whose baskets were once "so highly esteemed . . . for their domestic usefulness, beauty, and skilful variety . . . by reason of our supplying them so cheap with every sort of goods, have forgotten the chief part of their ancient mechanical skill."[6] Cherokee and Choctaw women continued to make baskets to sell to settlers, but pottery traditions disappeared until their revival in the 19th century.

Traders introduced English rum and French brandy to natives with uniformly pernicious results. Natives' prior experience with alcoholic beverages was limited to sacred rituals. Many men and women drank to excess and succumbed to alcoholism, sometimes even dying from alcohol poisoning. The Cherokee, Indian agent Adair observed, were "excessively immoderate in drinking. They often transform themselves by liquor into the likeness of mad foaming bears."[7] Their inebriated states loosened social restraints and unleashed interpersonal hostilities. Drunken Indians shouted profanities to the English with impunity, some historians have suggested, as release from psychological stresses of living in a world of diminished autonomy and declining prosperity. Aggression turned inward led to social mayhem of fights, murders, licentiousness, and revenge killings. Alcohol weakened the vulnerable social fabric holding Indian societies together, encouraged over hunting and depletion of deer, and increased indebtedness to traders. Leaders were helpless in stopping alcohol's deleterious effects. "When the Clattering of the Packhorse Bells are heard," a Choctaw chief complained in 1772, "our Town is Immediately deserted young and old run out to meet them Joyfully crying Rum Rum; they get Drunk, Distraction Mischief Confusion and disorder are the Consequences and this is the Ruin of our Nation."[8] Colonial officials had no more success in regulating the rum trade. Indians' needs for durable goods was limited and threatened to end a lucrative trade. Only their unquenchable thirst for alcohol sustained traders' profits.

Native American crops transformed Western diet and formed one foundation for southern cuisine. Corn, beans, and squash quickly spread to Europe, Africa, and Asia providing additional nutrition that allowed their populations to grow, and, in turn, resettle the New World as Native populations plummeted. Without Indian crops and trade, without Indian knowledge of what was edible and what was not, and without Indian expertise in hunting, fishing, and foraging, Europeans likely would have abandoned early settlements from starvation. Powhatan's refusal to continue supplying corn to his rude guests over the winter almost eliminated Jamestown by spring 1610. Hunting changed from an upper-class leisure pursuit in Europe to common men's subsistence in the New World. Ex-poachers became colonial frontiersmen by adopting Indian hunting techniques and learning to eat bear, deer, raccoons, squirrel, turkey, and opossum. Survival required owning a gun but encouraged settling far from government authority. Indian foods—especially corn, beans, squash, and pumpkins, but also many varieties of fish, shellfish, and game—and Indian barbecuing became the foundation for southern staples of grits, hoecake or johnnycake, corn pone or corn bread, and hush puppies. Boiled beans and peas, succotash of mixed corn and beans, and cooked greens filled many southern tables and became staples of "American" cuisine. Who has not enjoyed slow-cooked smoked or barbecued meat and roasted corn "on the cob"?

EURO-AMERICANS

European accounts of the colonial South marveled at its rich food resources, but early settlers intended to transplant familiar foodways by importing cattle, hogs, sheep, goats, chickens, and other poultry; seed stocks of wheat, cereal grains, and vegetables; and cuttings for vineyards and fruit trees. The English brought preferences for roasted meats, boiled porridges and puddings, dairy products, wheat breads, and alcoholic beverages along with metal cooking technology. Adding European plants and animals to the New World's abundant subsistence promised a culinary cornucopia. Instead, malnutrition, disease, even starvation met the earliest settlers who lacked farming, hunting, and fishing skills; misjudged environmental challenges; unwittingly selected unhealthy building sites; and alienated Indians with surplus food to trade. Europeans arrived near the end of the Little Ice Age, a period of an unusually wet cold climate that shortened growing seasons, lowered crop yields, and created food shortages by early spring.

Early colonial diet fused new and old. Indians traded surplus food and taught settlers how to grow corn, beans, squash, pumpkins, and chili peppers; drink caffeinated black tea; hunt deer, bear, and small game; forage for wild plants; and gather fish, turtles, and shellfish. English and Spanish settlers abandoned wheat, wine grapes, olive trees, silk cultivation, and sheep as unsuited for the subtropical southeast. Most European animals and grains eventually thrived, but it took time to build stocks of cattle, hogs, and poultry and for fruit trees to mature; clear ground for small grains and vegetables; and introduce honeybees for pollination. In the early Chesapeake, wild foods—deer, turkeys, raccoons, opossums, turtles, shellfish, and seafood—provided settlers about one-third of their meat, and, like the Powhatans, their diet varied with seasonal availability of domestic and wild foods. Rich forest, river, and estuary resources, not European domestic animals or European grain crops, sustained early settlers in Florida, Carolina, and Louisiana.

Southern colonial cuisine emerged in the Chesapeake by mid-17th century based on Europeanized corn dishes, Indian preparation and cooking methods, and meat from domestic animals. While poor householders had only iron kettles, pots, hooks, and racks for cooking, common planters possessed frying pans and roasting spits and pans, raised corn and root crops, and owned cattle and hogs. Using native methods of corn preparation learned from Indian female servants, women soaked hard kernels, beat them with wooden pestles in hollowed mortars, and sifted to separate fine meal from coarse hominy. "Pottage" was standard fare, a stew of fresh or salted meat braised and slowly boiled in iron pots or kettles hung from iron or green wood lug poles over open fires, with cornmeal thickener and various vegetables such as peas, beans, greens, sweet potatoes, cabbages, and apples added for flavor. Slow cooking required little tending and allowed women to perform other household and farm chores. Replenishing pots with whatever foods were available varied the daily fare. Hot unleavened coarse corn bread baked on hearths or in kettles buried under coals and water or hard cider completed most meals.

By mid-century, beef provided over two-thirds of all meat, swine about a quarter, and wild game less than 10 percent. A Frenchman living in Virginia noted in the 1680s, "there is not a house so poor that they do not salt an ox, a cow and five or six large hogs."[9] Men slaughtered old steers and hogs during cold fall and winter months. Women roasted fresh beef and poultry on spits over open fires. Because beef and poultry spoiled quickly, women rubbed salt into cuts of swine or soaked them in salt brine followed by smoking them over low fires, thereby preserving pork for several months. Virginia planters prided themselves on the quality of their smoked hams. As in Europe, little was wasted. Beef tongue was a prized delicacy; hoofs made gelatin; and ears, heads, intestines, internal organs, utters, snouts, and even blood became "sweetmeats" for meat pies or blood puddings. Cattle were sound investments against uncertain tobacco prices and provided milk, daily products, and meat. A pair of cattle given as a wedding present gave milk the following year and within five years half a pound of meat per day. A warmer climate after 1700 lengthened growing seasons, encouraged planting vegetables and fruit trees, and provided more fodder for cattle. Preserved meat and stored corn and root crops like potatoes, turnips, carrots, and parsnips eliminated early spring famines and provided ample plain fare for rich and poor alike, even if the former complained they ate like peasants not as gentlemen or hidalgos.

The plantation economy or its absence created class and regional differences in southern cuisine by 1700. As common planters became wealthier and acquired slaves, they purchased specialized cooking utensils, ceramic dairy equipment, hand mills, and food storage containers and constructed bake ovens. Their meals included whole poultry and better cuts of meat roasted on spits over fires and served with special sauces and condiments; corn breads baked in covered kettles and beaten biscuits baked in ovens; a variety of cooked vegetables; regular supplies of milk and butter; seasonal game, fish, or seafood; baked pastries and cakes; and hard cider, fruit brandies, and rum. They acquired tables covered with cloth, several chairs for sitting at meals, ate off pewter or earthenware plates with sets of knives and spoons, drank from individual cups, and, perhaps, enjoyed candlelit meals in the evenings. Planters ate at set times, with light breakfasts around eight of tea or milk, hot breads, and porridge with fruit or cold meat; dinner, the main meal, in the early afternoon, consisting of meat, vegetables, seasonal fruits, starch, desserts, and beverages; and light suppers in the evening of meats or seafood, fruit, and drink. Indians and slaves in Carolina and in Louisiana provisioned settlers with corn and other cultivated crops, wild game, fish, and shellfish, and the spread of rice cultivation after 1700 provided a new cooking staple. Mission Indians in Florida raised oranges, apricots, peaches, beef, pork, poultry, garlic, and European vegetables for Spanish settlers. Germans in the backcountry prepared boiled vegetable and fruit dishes like sauerkraut and apple butter, stuffed sausages, pickled vegetables, dumplings, and rye bread that their English neighbors also came to enjoy.

Servants and small planters scarcely shared in this rising culinary bounty and developed traditional southern fare of "hog meat and hoecake." In early decades, servants subsisted on corn porridge not game. A Virginia servant complained in 1623 that they were fed only "a messe of water gruel, and a mouthfull of bread and biefe (beef)," and not allowed to hunt deer or wild fowl. Over 50 years later, a visitor reported that Maryland servants received only "maize bread to eat, and water to drink, which sometimes is not very good and scarcely enough for life, yet they are compelled to work hard."[10] Despite planters' increasing stocks of cattle, they provided servants only salt pork, poor cuts of meat, and boiling pots and frying pans for cooking. This corn-hog diet became slaves' and poor whites' staple foods. Where possible, they supplemented their plain fare with small game, fish, shellfish, nuts, berries, wild plants, deer, wild birds, hard cider, peach brandy, rum, and molasses. Frontier settlers combined Indians' mixed economy of hunting wild animals and birds, gathering wild foods, and planting corn with English livestock husbandry.

Ordinary folk ate plain meals. Everyone crowded around the open hearth as women broke off pieces of corn bread and ladled porridge or stew flavored with salt pork or game into wooden porringers or trenchers often shared by two people. Few households had chairs, so adults pulled up benches and trunks around the single table, if there was one, while children stood and servants leaned against walls, sat on dirt floors, or went outside. Wooden spoons, oyster shells, and fingers served as eating utensils. Water or cider passed from a common mug washed down the meal, and hot corn bread mopped up any remnants. The main meal was at midday with lighter versions of the same fare in mornings and evenings. Something was always cooking in the hearth, encouraging grazing all day. Devereux Jarratt, son of a Virginia carpenter, recalled as a child in the 1730s, "Meat, bread, and milk was the ordinary food of all my acquaintance," all "produce of the farm." They "made no use of *tea* or *coffee* for breakfast" and sugar was "rarely used." The meal of a Maryland ferry keeper's family in 1744 consisted of "a homely dish of fish without any kind of sauce . . . no cloth upon the table, and their mess was in a dirty, deep wooden dish which they evacuated with their hands, cramming down skins, scales and all. They used neither knife, fork, spoon, plate, or napkin, because, I suppose, they had none to use."[11]

Great planter's dining room. Thomas Lee of Stratford Hall (circa 1738), Westmoreland County, Virginia, entertained friends with sumptuous multicourse meals served in this well-appointed dining room with matched sets of furniture, dishes, tableware, and glassware. Candles for artificial illumination, high ceilings, large windows, floor-length draperies, and an arched entryway into the parlor for after-meal entertainment enhanced the room's spaciousness. (Library of Congress.)

The same year the ferryman's family subsisted on plain fish, William Black, a gentleman, dined with Maryland governor Thomas Bladen where he enjoyed a "Great Variety of Dishes, all serv'd up in the most Elegant Way, after which came a Dessert no less Curious; Among the Rarities of which it was Compos'd, was some fine Ice Cream."[12] Southern high cuisine featured meals with many different dishes using complicated preparations and exotic ingredients. Large planters' dwelling houses included formal dining rooms filled with lavish appointments, stylish tables, matching chairs; sets of fine china, spoons, blunt-end knives, and forks, the latter a recent English innovation. Their plantations had special spaces for food preservation and storage: smokehouses, corncribs, dairies, and icehouses. Separate brick kitchens contained distinct areas for food preparation, cooking, and storage and living quarters for the head cook. They were filled with specialized equipment to boil, braise, poach, steam, fry, sauté, roast, grill, bake, pickle, and store food.

From their growing numbers of slaves, owners selected hunters and watermen to collect local foods from forests, rivers, and estuaries; herders to care for livestock; kitchen workers and cooks to prepare elaborate dishes; and house servants, some accoutered in livery, to serve family members and guests and clean up afterward. Slaves on diversified plantations raised small grains of wheat and rye, tended sheep, maintained fruit orchards, and planted extensive kitchen gardens filled with herbs, vegetables, and berries: lettuce, spinach, cucumbers, cabbages, beets, turnips, carrots, onions, broccoli strawberries, blackberries, and much more. Growing Atlantic and coastal trade brought new foods: sugar, molasses, citrus fruits, and rum from the West Indies; tea, coffee, cinnamon, cloves, and pepper from Asia; almonds, raisons, wines, salt, and olive oil from the Mediterranean; and apples, white potatoes, wheat, butter, and cheeses from northern colonies.

Planters' wives supervised planning meals, preparing dishes, and hosting dinners. They purchased English cookbooks with the latest recipes and table settings. *The Art of Cookery Made Plain and Easy . . . by a Lady,* first published in London in 1747, was a bestseller in Virginia and promised to make "every servant who can but read . . . a tolerable good cook" and to avoid popular but extravagant French cuisine.[13] Women kept personal cooking journals, compilations of British and French recipes from printed books and personal dishes using local foods. They instructed slave cooks in the latest continental preparation methods and read complicated recipes to them. Unlike stews, roasting, broiling, and frying required constant attention to avoid overcooking meat and fish. Mothers passed culinary expertise to their daughters. When 20-year-old Harriott Pinckney married Daniel Horry in 1768, she was already an expert dairy manager and knew how to prepare complex English and French–style dishes.

Planters' formal dinners included a mix of traditional British foods like roast beef, stuffed birds, meat pies, puddings, stuffing, and sweetbreads; French-influenced dishes like fricasseed chicken, beef "alamode," and ragouts; and local foods, dishes using corn, rice, squash, pumpkins, turkeys, venison, wild game, fish, and turtles. Dinner included two settings with almost as many different dishes as there were guests. The first course was large cuts of boiled or baked meat, fish, or fowl, prominently displayed at the top, center, and bottom of the table, and a second course of smaller cuts of meat, roasted game, wild birds, or seafood. Both courses included many side dishes of seasoned boiled vegetables, baked or stewed fruit, green salads, puddings, pastries, jellies, and sweetmeats, most accompanied with special sauces or garnishes. During and after meals, slaves offered guests Madeira wine, teas, coffee, water, chocolate, or a variety of mixed drinks or "punches." Fresh fruit and sugar-laced desserts, like pies, tarts, fruit puddings, cakes, or ice cream, completed meals. Following French fashion, hostesses served the top dish, hosts the bottom one, and guests passed around other platters and plates in "family style" with everyone serving himself or herself.

Quality, variety, delicacy, and presentation of dishes established hostesses' reputations. Unlike common people, the wealthy feasted on meat from young animals (lamb, veal, shoats, and heads) and on "choice" cuts of meat like hams, chops, tenderloin, and shoulders. Wild foods like roasted venison, turkeys, marine turtles, and ducks; fried oysters; fish chowder; baked shad; stewed crabs; boiled rabbits; vegetable dishes; and cold salads were markers of elite status and provincial abundance. Mary Randoph had seven different recipes for white potatoes and served sweet potatoes boiled, stewed, broiled, in puddings, and as buns. Preparation methods became more complex with meat pieces parboiled or fried before stewing in highly seasoned gravies or whole game filled with seasoned bread stuffing and roasted. Individual sauces and condiments accompanied meat and vegetable dishes, and even cold salads were "dressed" with toppings of egg yokes, oil, sugar, salt, mustard, and vinegar. Liberal use of imported spices, milk and butter (which are hard to preserve in the colonial South's hot climate) and, most of all, West Indian sugar displayed planters' wealth. Planters' tables groaned with sugar-sweetened sauces, breads, pastries, puddings, fruit pies, tarts, jellies, and marmalades and with delicacies like "macaroons" and "coconut puffs." As sugar prices dropped over the 18th century, sweets became essential staples of southern cuisine. Southern fine dining and hospitality had arrived.

AFRICANS AND AFRICAN AMERICANS

West Africans shared many foods and cooking methods with Native Americans and Europeans that facilitated African contributions to southern cuisine. Traditional foods varied across West Africa and included starchy staples: yams, cereals (millet and sorghum, also called "guinea corn"), and rice; cultivated vegetables (legumes including cowpeas or black-eyed peas and groundnuts, greens, okra, ackee or breadfruit, watermelon, and others); strong seasonings like melegueta peppers; oil palms, nuts, and seeds (kola nuts and benne or sesame); and sparing use of fruits, honey, fish, shellfish, wild game, or domestic animals (cattle, sheep, goats, pigs, poultry, and guinea hens). Trade brought new foods, which were adopted into African meals. Arab merchants introduced Asian plantains, eggplant, and bananas. Portuguese traders brought European vegetables and Mediterranean citrus fruits; North American corn, beans, pumpkins, squashes, and tobacco; and South American cassava, chili peppers, peanuts, sweet potatoes, papayas, and pineapples to African ports. Some food plants originally from the New World arrived in the colonial South by way of Africa. By the slave trade era, African women created meals from a mix of African, European, and American foods by selectively incorporating new plants and seasonings into traditional dishes and substituting iron pots and pestles for earthen and wooden cooking vessels. Olaudah Equiano, a captive slave from an interior Igbo village, recalled eating stews of "mostly plantains, eadas [cocoa yams], yams, beans, and Indian corn" slowly cooked in iron pots and seasoned with pepper, spices, and wood-ash salt.[14] It was truly an international meal.

African women prepared two-dish meals consisting of starchy carbohydrates made from yams, plantains, millet, or rice and served with side dishes of thick spicy vegetables. Women first pulverized corn on grating stones or pounded rice, yams, millet, cassavas, seeds, and nuts with wooden pestles and mortars to make coarse meals, which they slowly boiled in large ceramic pots until becoming thick porridges, such as couscous and fufu. They also sifted meal into flour for baking or frying breads. Women made savory vegetable sauces in small pots from chopped leaves with bits of meats or dried fish added on occasion. They slowly cooked the mixture in iron or ceramic pots over small open fires or steamed them in ceramic double boilers with an okra thickening agent and flavorful spices of melegueta, cayenne or chili peppers, palm oil, sesame seeds, citrus juices, or herb sauces. Batter wrapped in banana leaves and placed under hot coals or boiled made coarse breads that complemented seasoned stews. She tenderized meat by boiling it in papaya leaves or by barbecuing and basting it with flavorful sauces and peppers, dried fish in the sun or by smoking, and extracted cooking oils for deep-frying from palm nuts and benne, or sesame seeds. Calabash gourds of different sizes served as mixing bowls, water jugs, storage containers, bowls, cups, and spoons.

Meals began by thoroughly washing oneself and offering small amounts of food and drink to ancestors. Women served men, women, and slaves separately ladling the starch base into clay, gourd, wooden, or wicker bowls or saucers or on banana leaves. Everyone added seasoned vegetable relishes on top of the starch base or dipped them into the bowls and ate with spoons or with their fingers. Water or palm or honey wine washed down meals.

African-European fusion cuisine that slaves brought to the colonial South first developed around West African slave trade ports, where African workers provisioned merchants and sailors with new dishes made from American corn, European small grains, and local crops, fish, and spices. Atlantic Creoles, especially those who arrived in the colonial South via the Caribbean, carried this cuisine of highly seasoned corn and rice dishes to the colonial South in the 17th century. Slavers provided another food link between Africa, West Indies, and the colonial South by importing guinea hens and by provisioning captives with native foods: yams to Ashanti, Yoruba, and Ibo from interior West Africa; cassava or plantains to slaves from West Central Africa; and rice, millet, or corn to Senegambian coastal peoples. Many African plants thrived along the subtropical Atlantic and Gulf coasts. Slaves cultivated Madagascar rice as a staple and a subsistence crop and raised sorghum, yams, millet, greens or kale, spinach, peppers, sesame seed, black-eyed peas, okra, watermelons, eggplants, plantains, and oil palm to feed themselves and various gourds to prepare foods. Guinea hens took up residence in woods near plantations. Creoles and fugitive slaves settled among Native Americans in Carolina before 1700 and in 18th-century Florida and Louisiana where they learned to cultivate corn, beans, and squash and substitute deer, raccoons, squirrels, opossums, fish, shellfish, and edible plants for lost African foods. Before planter regimes were established, slaves kept barnyard fowls and owned hogs and cattle that foraged in woods and meadows adding poultry and meat into their diet.

As the Chesapeake and Lowcountry Carolina became slave societies after 1700, planters sought to regiment slaves' time and material conditions through weekly food rations, bans on owning cattle and hogs, and central meal preparation. Owners stinted weekly rations of slave-grown corn, typically a peck for each working adult and less for children and the elderly, and eight ounces of salted herring or meat. They doled out tough meat from old steers and only the fattier and less desirable cuts: salted "fat Backs, Necks, and other Coarse pieces" of hogs, chitterlings or hog intestines, calves' "pluck" (heart, liver, lungs, and neck), and chicken feet, neck, and gizzards.[15] Older women cooked some meals for single laborers and children. Owners allowed couples to live and eat together as families, but provided only basic cooking utensils, an iron kettle or cooking pot and a frying pan.

Diversified plantations in the mid-18th century Chesapeake expanded the range of food crops, especially wheat, and created more variation in slaves' eating habits. Owners distributed extra beef, pork, and rum during holidays and wheat harvests and provided slave foremen, domestics, and artisans more and better quality pork and beef. Cooks took leftover food from masters' meals to quarters for distribution. Slaves stole food to make up short rations or to sell for liquor or clothes.

Slaves supplemented owners' parsimony with garden provisions and wild foods that provided a healthier and more varied diet. Chesapeake slaves won privileges to forage and hunt in woods, rivers, and estuaries and use "slaves' time" during evenings, Saturday afternoons, Sundays, and holidays. Men and women worked their own corn plots. Women tended gardens with sweet potatoes, black-eyed peas, watermelons, squashes, snaps, collards, and sesame. Men hunted squirrel, raccoons, and opossums and caught catfish. At a typical Virginia plantation in the 1770s, slaves had "an acre of ground, and all Saturday to raise grain and poultry for themselves." Slaves sold surplus poultry, eggs, and garden produce to whites and used the cash to improve their diet or expand their wardrobe.[16]

Under the task system in the Lowcountry, slaves relied even less on rations. A cleric in Carolina observed in 1712 that "many Planters who, to free themselves from the trouble of feeding and clothing their slaves allow them one day in the week to clear ground and plant for themselves as much as will clothe and subsist them and their families." On their provision grounds, or "little plantations," slaves raised rice, sweet potatoes, corn, beans, eggplants, and other garden vegetables, including many African crops like yams, tania, chickpeas, millet, sorghum, okra, and sesame. Women kept barnyard fowls and hogs, and men trapped and fished in the Lowcountry's rich maritime forests and estuaries. Almost half of rural Lowcountry slaves' diet came from wild species.[17]

Slave self-provisioning went even further in Louisiana and Florida where Indians outnumbered Europeans and Africans, and the plantation system only took root in the 1760s. Slaves fed themselves by growing Indian corn, European grains, and African plants, keeping barnyard fowl, and by hunting, trapping, and fishing in local forests, swamps, and rivers. A visitor to 18th-century Louisiana noted that "slaves clear the grounds and cultivate them on their own account, raising cotton, tobacco, etc., which they sell."[18]

Slaves utilized African fishing, hunting, and farming skills to process African plants introduced to the colonial South and to find plant and animal substitutes from the region's rich resources. Slaves probably ate more meat than their African ancestors did. Men from coastal Africa used nets, lines, and hooks to gather shellfish, marine turtles, and fish from estuaries and rivers. Herders from the African savannas tended cattle and hogs on colonial frontiers. Black men with their hunting dogs and accompanied by Indian hunters in Carolina and Louisiana trapped small game, shot deer, and caught birds and wild fowl. Women made African-style unglazed round-shaped ceramic pots or "colonoware," for storing, cooking, and eating. They coiled strands of clay, smoothed interior and exterior surfaces, and fired the pots at low temperatures in open-air kilns. Colonoware pots were ideal for slow cooking and simmering. Slave women in the Lowcountry fashioned broad "fanner" baskets from local sweetgrass and needles to "fan" rice or separate grains from hulls and

Colonoware bowl, 1750–1800, South Carolina. Like their forbearers, enslaved Africans in the Lowcountry made slow-cooked, one-dish meals in low-fired pots of local clay. They mixed a starchy rice base with seasonal vegetables, game, fish, or shellfish, thickened with okra, and seasoned with peppers. (Museum of Early Southern Decorative Arts, Winston-Salem, North Carolina, gift of Frank L. Horton [acc. 41830].)

prepared African rice dishes. Men made wooden and gourd storage vessels, serving bowls, eating utensils, and drinking cups.

Africans, Native Americans, and Europeans all made slow-cooked one-pot meals using similar cooking utensils and methods, the basis for fusion African American foods and their incorporation into regional southern cuisines. By the 1720s, a Virginia cleric noted that corn "made good bread, cakes, mush, and hommony [hominy] for the Negroes, which with good pork and potatoes (red and white, very nice and different from ours) with other roots and pulse, are their general food."[19] Male and females slaves in the Chesapeake used hand mills to grind corn that women turned into corn hominy and coarse corn breads baked in ashes (ashcake) or on hoe blades (hoecake). Women slowly cooked leafy greens like kale, collards, and turnip tops to leech out the bitterness and beans and chopped pieces of tough meat to tenderize them. Women threw into the pot whatever was at hand: black-eyed peas, okra, squashes, beans, cabbages, pumpkins, yams, or sweet potatoes seasoned with bits of salty fatback, beef body parts and bones, peppers, sesame, and herbs. The task system gave Carolina slave women more time and more ingredients for meals. Women jointly pounded rice with mortars and pestles and made slow-cooked rice puddings, parched brown rice cakes, and rice breads. They added crabs, fish, turtles, or oysters to pots of rice, okra, and vegetables to make a fine gumbo. Men caught squirrels, rabbits, raccoons, or opossum that women skinned and roasted with sweet potatoes and served with gravy or turned into thick stews, known as "burgoo." Sorghum was a corn substitute and boiled into mush or baked into bread. Slaves prized "pot liquor," the liquid remaining from boiling vegetables that they flavored with breadcrumbs, pepper, and sesame. Fat pork provided ample stores of lard for frying small pieces of poultry, shellfish, fish, and wild games served with rice or corn for a quick meal.

Eating occurred around the demands of long workdays forcing slaves to simplify food preparation and shorten meal times. Unlike Africa, where starch and seasoned vegetable dishes were prepared separately, slaves used corn or rice meal as thickenings for one-dish vegetable and meat stews eaten with coarse bread. Breakfast was a hurried affair of cold hoecake or ashcake or hominy and molasses prepared the night before and washed down with water or cider as adults prepared for their daily toil. Children "toted" midday meals, consisting of corn bread and stew either reheated from the previous night or prepared in communal kitchens, carried out to the fields in baskets balanced on their heads, as in Africa. Later, children ate cornmeal mush from communal troughs. Family members ate their main meal, the only one with meat, in the evening, but it was much the same fare: fresh corn or rice bread and stews using leftovers as a base with fresh potatoes, peas, turnips, or other vegetables and maybe bits of salt pork, meat, game, or fish. Sitting on the cabin's dirt floor or outside, everyone ate out of the skillet or from small ceramic bowls using hands, spoons, or shells. By the mid-18th century, slaves acquired coarse earthenware plates, spoons, and knives for eating, either cast off from owners or purchased from independent labor. Before dropping off to sleep, women prepared the next day's meal.

Modern studies of colonial slave foodways conclude that planters' rations, while providing sufficient amount of calories, were monotonous, unbalanced in quality, and insufficient to sustain health, especially for hard labor. Rations were high in starchy carbohydrates but low in protein, vitamins, and minerals. Not only did slaves receive small amounts of meat, and only salted, fatty pieces at that, but many adult slaves were also lactose intolerant and avoided dairy products that provided additional protein for indentured servants and poor whites. Slave gardens, provisioning activities, and occasionally taking food from owners were essential if slaves were to sustain themselves.

During the 18th century, slave women introduced African foods to whites by selling foodstuffs to urban consumers in Annapolis, Williamsburg, Charles Town, Savannah, and New Orleans. As in Africa, men butchered animals and caught fish and shellfish that enslaved women marketed along with fresh vegetables, poultry, and eggs from slaves' provision grounds or stolen from owners. Working in market stalls, Charles Town's market opened in 1722, hawking goods from pushcarts, or trading at the edge of towns, women became purveyors of a broad range of country produce, including African crops. By 1734, Charles Town blacks were "hucksters of corn, pease, fowls" and other goods to poor whites and to slave cooks filling their masters' larders.[20] Black women in Louisiana traded surplus with Indian and French neighbors and were prime food vendors in New Orleans selling their owners' poultry, meat, and vegetables along with their own foodstuffs.

Slave cooks introduced African culinary traditions to planters' households. Mistresses read complicated recipes from English cookbooks to illiterate slave cooks, but black hands did the actual preparations. Using the choices cuts of meat, variety of garden vegetables, orchard fruits, and kitchen herbs, and imported sugar and spices from Africa, slave cooks created new combinations for planters' tables. Okra was stewed with salt and pepper and served with butter or made into a soup. Gumbo ("a West India dish," Mary Randolph noted) was made from slowly stewed lima beans, squashes, tomatoes, okra, fowl or veal knuckle, and bacon or boiled pork and served with boiled rice.[21] Whites, no less than slaves, enjoyed "hoppin' john," a combination of cooked rice and black-eyed peas or beans, fried black-eyed peas and okra, turnip greens boiled with salted bacon, cooked eggplant, fresh or pickled watermelons, and yam pies sweetened with sorghum molasses. Peppers and other seasonings made bland English dishes hotter. In coastal areas, enslaved men gathered crayfish, oysters, shrimp, crab, and fish that women added to slow simmered stews and gumbos thickened with sliced okra or powdered sassafras. Rice added to combinations of meat, vegetables, and seasonings became jambalaya. Slave women's familiarity with cooking wild game became squirrel soup, catfish curry, roast wild duck, or boiled pigeon at their masters' dinner parties. Black women taught whites how to prepare rice and create delicious rice-based dishes. Before Ralph Izard, a South Carolina rice planter wrote Thomas Jefferson with directions on cooking rice, he first "examined my cook on the subject."[22]

TOWARD SOUTHERN CUISINES

Well before 1770, distinctive southern cuisines had emerged from two centuries of colonial encounters between Native Americans, Europeans, and Africans with important Caribbean influences. What colonial Southerners ate depended on time and place, available local foods, and population diversity. Southern cooking mixed New World corn, beans, squash, wild game, fish, and fowl with European grains, alcoholic beverages, domestic animals, dairy products, and African plants and spicy seasonings. Southern dishes developed from humble one-pot stews and breads, basic fare in America, England, Europe, and Africa alike but each with distinctive ingredients, cooking methods, and seasonings. Environmental resources and cultural interactions created many southern staples like smoked hams, barbecued meats, roasted corn, hoecakes, and rice or corn and meat casseroles; signature southern dishes, like spicy gumbos, jambalaya, and hoppin' john; and prized delicacies of turtle soup and Brunswick stew. Peppers and sesame from Africa and nuts and bear oil from America added spice to bland European dishes. Hogs, cattle, wild game, and fowls thrived in the colonial South adding meat to everyone's diet. Hogs provided salt pork for seasoning boiled vegetables and lard for frying chicken, fish, and cornmeal fritters. Expanding Atlantic trade brought Caribbean sugar to planters' tables, molasses to sweeten plain folk's meals, and rum to quench everyone's thirst.

In the 18th century, ships brought European wines, Asian exotic ingredients, and cookbooks with new French recipes that turned ordinary fare into fancy dining. Planters emulated English food fashions, but their slave cooks added African touches to create high southern cuisine. Mary Randolph learned that "ochra soup" was best prepared by slowly simmering it in an "earthen pipkin." Harriet Horry had recipes for yam pudding, rice pie casserole, and "pompion chips," the latter a pumpkin marmalade using sugar and limes.[23] In the 1720s, a New Orleans nun enjoyed "Rice cooked in milk . . . and we eat it often along with sagamité, which is made from Indian corn that has been ground in a mortar and then boiled in water with butter or bacon fat. Everyone in Louisiana considers this an excellent dish."[24] Early in the century, satirist Ebenezer Cooke captured the beginnings of the South's fusion cuisine:

Pon (corn-pone) and Milk, with Mush well stoar'd
In Wooden Dishes grace'd the Board
With Homine and Syder-pap
(Which scarce a hungry dog wou'd lap)
Well stuff'd with Fat from Bacon fry'd
Or with Mollossus dulcify'd[25]

NOTES

1. Jay Anderson defines foodways as "the whole interrelated system of food conceptualization, procurement, distribution, preservation, preparation, and consumption shared by all members of a particular group," cited in James Deetz, *In Small Things Forgotten: An Archaeology of Early American Life,* 2nd ed. (New York: Doubleday, 1996), 73. Colonial settlements are food frontiers; sites of culinary change and Creole cuisines.

2. See Chapter 4 for dining furnishings and Chapter 6 for drinking.

3. John Banister, *John Banister and His Natural History of Virginia, 1678–1692,* ed. by Joseph and Nesta Ewan (Urbana: University of Illinois Press, 1970), 376, cited in Helen C. Rountree, *The Powhatan Indians of Virginia: Their Traditional Culture* (Norman: University of Oklahoma Press, 1989), 51.

4. James Adair, *James Adair's History of the American Indians*, ed. by Samuel Cole Williams (Johnson City, TN: Watauga Press, 1950), 456, cited in Theda Perdue, *Cherokee Women: Gender and Culture Change, 1700–1835* (Lincoln, NE: University of Nebraska Press, 1998), 22.

5. *Fleur de Lys and Calamut: Being the Pénicault Narrative of French Adventure in Louisiana*, ed. by Richebourg Gaillard McWilliams (Baton Rouge: Louisiana State University Press, 1974), 18, 19, cited in Daniel H. Usner, Jr., *Indians, Settlers, and Slaves in a Frontier Exchange Economy: The Lower Mississippi Valley before 1783* (Chapel Hill: University of North Carolina Press, 1992), 194, 195.

6. Adair, *History of American Indians*, 456, cited in Perdue, *Cherokee Women*, 75.

7. Ibid., 77.

8. Eron Opha Rowland, *Peter Chester*, Vol. 5 (Jackson: Mississippi Historical Society, 1925), 148, cited in Richard White, *The Roots of Dependency: Subsistence, Environment, and Social Change among the Choctaws, Pawnees, and Navajos* (Lincoln: University of Nebraska Press, 1983), 75.

9. Durand of Dauphiné, *A Huguenot Exile in Virginia, or, Voyages of a Frenchman Exiled for His Religion . . .*, ed. by Gilbert Chinard (New York: Press of the Pioneers, 1934), 123, cited in Henry M. Miller, "An Archaeological Perspective on the Evolution of Diet in the Colonial Chesapeake, 1620–1745," in *Colonial Chesapeake Society*, ed. by Louis Green Carr, Philip D. Morgan, and Jean B. Russo (Chapel Hill: University of North Carolina Press, 1988), 194.

10. Richard Frethorne, "Letter to His Father and Mother from Jamestown, 1623," in *The Records of the Virginia Company of London*, 4 vols., ed. by Susan Myra Kingsbury (Washington, D.C.: Government Printing Office, 1906–1935), 4: 58 and Jasper Dankers and Peter Sluyter, *Journal of a Voyage to New York and a Tour in Several of the American Colonies in 1679–80*, ed. by Henry C. Murphy (Brooklyn, NY: Long Island Historical Society, 1867), I: 191, 192, cited in James Horn, *Adapting to a New World: English Society in the Seventeenth-Century Chesapeake* (Chapel Hill: University of North Carolina Press, 1994), 275.

11. Devereux Jarratt, "The Autobiography of the Reverend Devereux Jarratt, 1732–1763," ed. by Douglass Adair, *The William and Mary Quarterly*, 3rd ser., 9, no. 3 (1952): 360, 361 and Dr. Alexander Hamilton, *Gentlemen's Progress: The Itinerarium of Dr. Alexander Hamilton*, ed. by Carl Bridenbaugh (Chapel Hill: University of North Carolina Press, 1948), 8.

12. William Black, "Journal" (1744), cited in Anne Elisabeth Yentsch, *A Chesapeake Family and Their Slaves: A Study in Historical Archaeology* (New York: Cambridge University Press, 1994), 160.

13. Cited in Jane Carson, *Colonial Virginia Cookery* (Williamsburg, VA: Colonial Williamsburg Foundation, 1968), xxiii, xxiv. The first Virginia cookbook was Mary Randolph, *The Virginia Housewife: Or, Methodical Cook*

(Washington, D.C.: Davis and Force, 1824). Randolph, born 1762, asserted her recipes were "written from memory, where they were impressed by long continued practices" and provides a firsthand account of the late 18th-century high cuisine in Virginia. See Mary Randolph, *The Virginia Housewife* (New York: Dover Publications, Inc., 1993 [1860]), iv.

14. Olaudah Equiano, *Narrative of the Life of Olaudah Equiano,* 2nd ed., ed. by Robert Allison (New York: Bedford/St. Martin's Press, 2005), 46.

15. Instructions of Joseph Ball, cited in Stacy Gibbons Moore, "'Established and Well Cultivated': Afro-American Foodways in Early Virginia," *Virginia Cavalcade* 39, no. 2 (1989): 73.

16. Thomas Anburey, *Travels through the Interior Parts of America, with a Series of Letters,* 2 vols. (London: William Lane, 1789), 2: 333, 334.

17. Cited in Ira Berlin, *Many Thousands Gone: The First Two Centuries of Slavery in North America* (Cambridge, MA: Harvard University Press, 1998), 69.

18. Jean-François-Benjamin de Montigny, "Historical Memoires of M. Dumont," in *Historical Collections of Louisiana,* 5 vols., ed. Benjamin E. French (New York: Wiley and Putman, 1846–1853), 5: 120, cited in Berlin, *Many Thousands Gone,* 204.

19. Hugh Jones, *Present State of Virginia,* ed. by Richard L. Morton (Chapel Hill, NC: University of North Carolina Press, 1956 [1724]), 40.

20. *South Carolina Gazette* (Charles Town), March 30, 1734, cited in Philip D. Morgan, *Slave Counterpoint: Black Culture in the Eighteenth-Century Chesapeake and Lowcountry* (Chapel Hill, NC: University of North Carolina Press, 1998), 251.

21. Okra soup recipe: "Get two double handsful of young ochra, wash and slice it thin, add two onions chopped fine, put it into a gallon of water at a very early hour in an earthen pipkin, or very nice iron pot; it must be kept steadily simmering, but not boiling: put in pepper and salt. At 12 o'clock, put in a handful of Lima beans; at half-past one o'clock, add three young cimlins cleaned and cut in small pieces, a fowl, or knuckle of veal, a bit of bacon or pork that has been boiled, and six tomatos, with the skin taken off; when nearly done, thicken with a spoonful of butter, mixed with one of flour. Have rice boiled to eat with it" (Randolph, *Virginia Housewife,* 17).

22. Letter from Ralph Izard to Thomas Jefferson, 1787, cited in Moore, "Afro-American Foodways," 80.

23. Pompion chips recipe: "Shave your Pompion thin with a plain and cut it in slips about the width of your finger, put shread of Lemon peal (peel) among it, wet you sugar with orange Juice and boil it into Syrup. Then put it in your chips and lemon Peal and let them boil till done" (Harriott Pinckney Horry, *A Colonial Plantation Cookbook: The Receipt Book of Harriott Pinckney Horry, 1770,* ed. by Richard J. Hooker (Columbia: University of South Carolina Press, 1984), 66).

24. Myldred Masson Costa, trans., *The Letters of Marie Madeleine Hachard, 1727–28* (New Orleans, 1974), 18, cited in Usner, *Indians, Settlers, and Slaves*, 207, 208.

25. Ebenezer Cooke, *The Sot-Weed Factor: Or, a Voyage to Maryland, a Satyr* (London: B. Bragg, 1708), cited in Gloria Main, *Tobacco Colony: Life in Early Maryland, 1650–1720* (Princeton: Princeton University Press, 1982), 205.

6

LEISURE

"About Seven the Ladies and Gentlemen begun to dance in the Ball-Room," recorded Philip Fithian, tutor of tidewater planter Robert Carter's children, in 1774, "first Minuets one Round; Second Giggs (Jigs); third Reels; And last of All Country-Dances. . . . But all did not join in the Dance for there were parties in Rooms made up, some at Cards, some drinking for Pleasure; some toasting the Sons of america; some singing "Liberty Songs" as they call'd them, in which six, eight, ten or more would put their Heads near together and roar, & for the most part . . . unharmonious[ly]." Charles Woodmason, itinerant Anglican minister in the Carolina back-country in the 1760s, found no pleasure in common folks' "Singing Matches" as they were "only Rendezvous of Idlers, under the Mask of Devotion. Meetings for Young Persons to carry on Intrigues and Amours." Nor have they "made any Reform in the Vice of Drunkenness. . . . Go to any Common [militia] Muster or Vendue," he sputtered, "Will you not see the same Fighting, Brawling Gouging, Quarreling as ever? . . . Are Riots, Frolics, Races, Games, Cards, Dice, Dances, less frequent now than formerly? Are fewer persons to be seen in Taverns? or reeling or drunk on the Roads?"[1]

These contrasting narratives not only reveal leisure's omnipresence in everyday life, but also how these activities performed cultural norms and marked social boundaries. Unlike modern society, play in the colonial world comingled with other life activities with little division between spectators and participants. Indian women sang corn songs as they planted, slave men and boys hunted at night, men imbibed alcoholic beverages while trading at country stores, and women exchanged news during sewing bees. People filled nonwork time with songs, dances, drinking bouts, games of chance, competitive sports, and family celebrations.

Leisure relieved hard labor, sustained communal ties through shared activities, and sanctioned temporary respites from social obligations. Differences in the uses, forms, and participants in recreational activities replicated distinctions of gender, race, and class: respectable women avoided taverns, slaves' songs satirized masters, and backcountry men brawled while gentlemen fenced. Leisure activities sometimes blurred social divisions. Natives and Europeans entertained each other with songs and dances, servants and slaves wagered on planters' birds at cockfights, neighbors celebrated after wheat harvests, and genteel young women and men displayed hot dance steps at fancy balls.

New patterns of leisure transformed inherited traditions. Moravian choral harmonies, Scots-Irish ballads, African polyrhythms, and Roman Catholic chants were maintained, but festivals specific to particular English or African villages were lost in transatlantic passages. African men played European fiddles at balls as whites danced minuets and reels. Hunting, an aristocratic prerogative in England, became a popular male pastime in the game-abundant South. Priests in mission villages tried unsuccessfully to ban Indian ball games. In the 18th century, the wealthy adopted new leisure activities modeled on European genteel culture, like tea drinking, board games, and polite conversation, and joined Woodmason in condemning common folks' rough pleasures. A few men and women consciously cultivated fashionable leisure as "a state of being in which activity is performed for its own sake or as its own end" by acquiring libraries, learning foreign languages, or developing intellectual interests. Here were seeds for declaring independence through individual pursuits of happiness.[2]

SINGING AND DANCING[3]

Native American

Music, as Pedro Menéndez de Alive's (Saint Augustine's founder) and Carlos (a Calusa cacique) recognized, was a medium of diplomacy. Invited to dine with the Florida chief, the Spanish conquistador arrived with "2 fifers and drummers, 3 trumpeters, one harp, one vihuela de arco [a violin], and one psaltery, and a very small dwarf, a great singer and dancer." The host began as "more than 500 Indian girls, from 10 to about 15 years . . . began to sing [in successive groups of 50], and other Indians danced and whirled: then the principal Indian men and women who were near the cacique sang." During the meal, Menéndez responded as "the Spaniards blew the trumpets . . . [and] played the instruments very well and the dwarf danced: 4 or 6 gentlemen . . . who had very good voices, began to sing in excellent order. . . . [and] the cacique prayed that until the Adelentado should depart, his men should always keep on singing and playing the instruments."[4] Carlos believed music secured Menéndez's allegiance; to the Spanish, music confirmed their cultural superiority.

Virginian Robert Beverley's observations on the Powhatans remind us that music is a common human expression yet creates no universal language. Virginia Indians' songs, he wrote, are "not the most charming that I have heard" and their dances are performed "without much regard either to time or figure." Participants appeared "menacing and terrible, beating their feet furiously against the ground and showing ten thousand grimaces and distortions," which surrounding villagers joined in "singing outrageously and shaking their rattles."[5] Like most Europeans, historian James H. Merrill asserts, Beverley misunderstood the importance of Native American singing and dancing for creating "communal ceremonies linking people to the invisible world, to one another, and to their common past."[6] Songs and dances were frequent evening entertainments around fires and imbedded in daily activities: greeting visitors, preparing for hunts, healing the sick, celebrating successful raids, mourning the dead, warding off witches, narrating history, courting young women, and insulting enemies.

Drums and rattles emphasized percussion in Indian music. Drums were made of wet deerskins stretched across large clay pots, attached with hoops, and were struck with sticks. They came in various sizes: handheld drums or tambourines beaten with sticks or hands and shallow wooden war drums with dried walnuts tied together at each corner that produced rattling sounds. Rattles were made from dried gourds that were filled with seeds or with different-size stones and held by wooden handles. Dancers wore leg rattles made of terrapin shells or deer horns. Drums, rattles, hand and thigh clapping, and singing accompanied

Natchez Indian dance. Dancing was central for Native Americans' social and ritual lives. Everyone participated with men and women forming separate circles around a central fire or leader and shuffling in opposite directions. Drums, rattles, and voice created dense layers of percussive sound. Etching from LePage Du Pratz, *Histoire de la Louisiane* (Paris, 1758). (Library of Congress.)

dances and created rhythmic patterns with muddled sounds. As two drummers played and sang, James Adair observed, "the dancers prance it away, with wild and quick sliding steps, and variegated postures of body, to keep time with the drums, and the rattling calabashes shaked by some of their religious heroes, each them singing their old religious songs, and striking notes *in tympano et choro* [amid music and dancing]."[7] Flageolets (flutes made from hollowed reeds, cane, or deer bones) greeted visitors and announced chiefly processions. Sonic layering from drums, rattles, and voice that natives found filled with deep meaning sounded discordant to European ears.

Most songs consisted of a series of short sections combined in various ways punctuated by guttural cries and whoops. Natchez men pursued survivors of the ill-fated de Soto expedition down the Mississippi River with rowing songs to pace their speed and boast of "deeds in war of their own or of other chiefs, the memory of which incites them to battle and to triumph."[8] Southeastern Indians' songs used a call-and-response structure with a group leader and chorus. Short choral groans punctuated priestly invocations in religious ceremonies. After killing foraging settlers, Powhatan warriors mocked the English in a four-verse song with a repeating first line, an improvised second line of insults, and a repeating chorus sung to imitate the "lamentations our people made."[9]

Patterned body movements harnessed spiritual power and created emotional and physical ties that made villagers a people. Dancing occurred often, and almost everyone participated. Dances greeted guests, placated spirits before hunts and harvests, celebrated victories over enemies, established relationships with animals, and provided temporary outlets for transgressing social norms. Circle patterns around a central drummer/singer or a fire created communal space. Dancers moved counterclockwise keeping time with their feet in alternating shuffle steps but improvised with exaggerated body postures, distended arms, and high kicks. Some dances included two circles, women inside and men outside, moving in opposite directions accompanied with rattles or drums; others featured fancy dancing as individuals entered the circle in turn, encouraged by handclapping and singing, with everyone joining in at the end. A drummer/singer began a Powhatan welcome dance, soon joined by one dancer, then others entered the circle "one after another who then dance an equal distance from each other in the ring, shouting, howling, and stamping their feet against the ground with such force and pain, that they sweat again."[10] Cherokee booger dancers wore elaborate wooden masks with exaggerated phallic noses or, after contact, grotesque caricatures of Europeans or Africans. Participants acted out sexual fantasies and expressed aggressive behavior symbolically, rendering it harmless.

Euro-American

Europeans brought diverse sacred and secular, vernacular and genteel musical traditions to the colonial South. Melody underlay European music with growing separation between folk music passed down orally by amateurs and composed notated music performed by professionals in courts and concert halls. These distinctions blurred in daily life. Dissenters sang Isaac Watts's revival hymns at home as well as in meetinghouses. Mixed audiences in colonial towns laughed together during ballad operas with their contrived plots and familiar songs. Country-dances followed French minuets at fancy balls. College student Thomas Jefferson played his violin with planter Robert Carter on the harpsichord and Governor Francis Fauquier at weekly concerts at the Governor's Palace. Although music associated with particular village festivals could not survive, all non-Native music in the colonial South was imported, strengthening cultural ties to the Old World while blending new sounds to create the first "American" music.

Ballads, narrative verses organized into four-line stanzas each sung to the same tune, a pattern known as strophic, comprised music of ordinary folk. Many ballads were already old when English and Scottish emigrants brought them to the colonial South. Some ballads narrated real events (e.g., "Chevy Chase" is about a 1388 battle between the English and the Scots), but most had universal themes of family betrayal (The Children in the Wood: "Uncle Plots Murder of Child Wards"), sanctity of marriage (The Spanish Lady: "Women Enters Nunnery after Discovering Lover is Married"), unfaithful women (Gypsy Laddie: "Lady Leaves Husband and Children for Gypsy"), or unrequited love (Barbara Allen: "William Green Dies from a Broken Heart"). Several hundred ballads circulated orally with innumerable variations as individual singers altered verses and endings. In the mid-18th century, Scot-Irish settlers carried them into the backcountry and to Appalachia where folklorists discovered them more than a century later. Ballads' timeless imagery of lords, ladies, knights in armor, faraway lands, and bloodshed provided settlers emotional respites from wresting new lives in harsh environments and folk wisdom on gender conventions and family relations. "Little Musgrave," who was seduced by Lord Arnol's wife, warned of women's sexual aggressiveness; in "The House Carpenter," a wife tempted by promises of wealth abandoned her family; and Lord Thomas in "Fair Ellender" followed his mother's advice to marry for money not love. Justice is restored in the end: Lord

Arnol murdered his wife and her lover; the house carpenter's wife drowned at sea; and Lord Thomas, "the brown girl," his bride, and Fair Ellender, his lover, all met violent deaths.

Sung without accompaniment (a cappella), ballads were suitable for work places, homes, frolics, and taverns. Their repeating phrases and refrains and simple rhyming patterns (usually the second and fourth lines) made ballads easy to remember yet allowed for individual embellishments. The strophic form flattened emotional delivery, minimized personal commentary, and provided a simple framework for telling the story. Ballad lines often alternated between different voices (narrator, female, and male), emphasized critical events and conversations, and omitted background details. Ballads' antiquity and survival into the 20th century reveal their enduring appeal as reminders of homes left behind, shared personal and community cultures, and commentaries on the human condition.

Composed ballads, another European musical tradition, became popular in the 18th century with the spread of newspapers and literacy. Also called "broadside" ballads, as they were printed on large single sheets of cheap paper and sold for a penny, these songs narrated current events. Indian wars, criminal executions, pirates, and political protests were especially popular topics. Set to familiar melodies, they often took moral positions or points of view and relied on stereotypes to convey simple messages. "The Downfal of Pyracy," attributed to teenage apprentice Benjamin Franklin, appeared only a few months after Lt. Edward Maynard killed Edward Teach, the notorious pirate Blackbeard, off the North Carolina coast in November 1718. Most of the ballad's 20 stanzas focused on the dramatic capture: "Wounded Men on both Sides fell Sir, / 'Twas a doleful Sight to see, / Nothing could their Courage quell Sir, / O, they fought courageously." Maynard and Teach had starring roles: "Teach and Maynard on the Quarter, / Fought it out most manfully, / Maynard's Sword did cut him shorter, / Losing his Head, he there did die." The tune "What Is Greater Joy and Pleasure," a popular hit, was chosen, perhaps, as ironic commentary. The original story told of faithful Elizabeth, who disguised herself as a sailor to find Robert Maynard, her fiancé, who had been impressed just before their wedding. Proving herself fearless in combat, the captain reunited the couple upon discovering her true identity.[11]

Small orchestras of violins, valveless French horns, and harpsichords at formal balls or a pair of fiddles or bagpipes for country frolics were as essential at social gatherings as food and drink. Young women and men courted at dances where patterned rhythmic movements created erotic bonds. Colonial Southerners lacked Puritan strictures against mixed couples dancing. Virginians, a clergyman observed in 1759, are "immoderately fond of dancing, and indeed it is almost the only amusement they partake of"; reportedly, they could dance almost until dawn.[12] Any packed dirt surface or room cleared of furniture would do; but in the 18th-century city, taverns and large planters' homes boasted separate ballrooms. Dances increasingly segregated along class lines as royal governors and wealthy men sponsored dress balls "by invitation only." Subscription "dancing assemblies" with formal rules and dance sequences and gentlemen's organizations, like the Tuesday Club in Annapolis or Charles Town's St. Cecilia Society, sponsored balls during the winter social season.

Popular dances in the colonial South were already hybrids from Europe, and stylistic mixing continued in the colonies. The French minuet was the most popular formal or court dance. Executing its elaborate footwork, precise movements, and measured stateliness required special training from dancing masters, who set up town studios or traveled around plantations teaching youths French and English formal dances and English and Scottish country-dances. Couples performed minuets one at a time, allowing peers to observe and judge their skill (and slaves to mock their stiff formality). One dancing demonstration gave Fithian "peculiar pleasure in the Accuracy of their performance—There were several Minuets danced with great ease and propriety; after which the whole company Joined in country-dances, and it was indeed beautiful to admiration, to see such a number of young persons, set off by dress to the best Advantage, moving easily, to the sound of well performed Music, and with perfect regularity."[13] Proficiency in dancing was an essential marker of social accomplishment and graceful gentility.

Country-dances had folk origins, but Fithian watched court versions of these dances English elites had adopted. John Playford, *The English Dancing Master* (1650), provided instructions and tunes for over 100 dances. Many were line or contra dances where women and men faced one another and created group patterns with couples sometimes moving up or down the line. The Virginia reel is a modern example. Four-couple, square set dances became all the rage after the mid-18th century. Originating in Elizabethan England, exported to France, and returning to England and the colo-

A dance instruction manual. Social dancing accompanied by stringed music included set patterns by paired couples or, as shown here, line formations. Colonials eagerly learned the latest European dances from itinerant dancing masters and from instruction manuals like John Playford, *The Dancing Master* (London), which went through many editions between 1650 and 1728. (Library of Congress.)

nies, each dance had its own particular music. Scottish reels, for example, were popular for their steady tempos and repetition. As soon as musicians began, participants knew which dance to perform. These were forerunners of modern square dancing, which has retained French names for set movements: allemande, promenade, dos-a-dos, and chassez (sashay). Once court-dances returned to the folk tradition, the association of specific music to particular dances was lost, requiring callers to direct the sequence of figures. Step and solo dancing, usually to jigs or hornpipes, were hybrids of Irish and African dance styles and allowed individuals to show off quick footwork and fancy moves until "cut out" by a competitor.

Amateur music making, "a companion which will sweeten many hours of life," Thomas Jefferson reminded his daughter, was popular. Music was part of genteel cultivation, and planters hired music masters to teach sons to play fiddles and German flutes and daughters guitars, keyboard instruments, and singing. Family members sang and made music together as evening entertainment. Men measured a women's character by her musical and dancing skills. Wealthy men cultivated their musical talents for personal enjoyment, performed for family members and friends at private concerts, and backed up visiting professionals. Thomas Jefferson, an accomplished violinist and cellist, described music as "the favorite passion of my soul." Fithian thought Robert Carter had "a good Ear for Music; a vastly delicate Taste" with "a *Harpsichord, Forte-piano, Harmonica, Guittar, Violin, and German Flutes*" at his house and an organ in Williamsburg.[14] Fiddlers entertained family members and friends in evenings, swapped music with fellow musicians, and tested skills in fiddle contests. Military units included fifers and drummers who set marching tempos, marked camp duties, and performed at public ceremonies. British commanders hired wind instrument bands to provide entertaining *harmoniemusik.* Urban merchants carried a wide assortment of musical instruments, strings, songbooks, and sheet music of the latest London hits.

By mid-18th century, professional musicians and actors from Europe entertained urban dwellers with popular music and plays from London. Varied programs satisfied audiences' diverse tastes. One evening's entertainment in Charles Town included "the opera of 'Flora or Hob in the Well,' with the Dance of the two Pierrots, and a new Pantomime Entertainment in grotesque characters, called 'The Adventures of Harlequin & Scaramouche,' with the 'Burgo-master Trick'd.'"[15] Tickets to single "benefit" performances, which paid performers, were often pricy (an evening at the theater could cost 40 shillings), but gallery seats for popular plays and other entertainment were under 2 shillings. A few professionals settled in colonial capitals and offered instruction on several instruments, court and country dancing, singing, fencing, and acting. Large rooms in taverns and public buildings provided early entertainment spaces; but by mid-18th century, colonial capitals had dedicated performance venues. In 1752, Lewis Hallam's company—direct from London—promised to bring "all the best plays, opera's, farces, and pantomimes" complete with "scenes, cloaths, and decorations [that are] all entirely new, extremely rich, and finished in the highest taste" to Williamsburg's theater.[16] Charles Town's St. Cecilia Society, founded in 1762, the first musical society in the colonial South, had its own building, well-attended concert series supported by membership dues, and auditions for violin, hautboy (oboe), and bassoon players. Monsieur Abbercrombie, a French violinist, received top billing at 500 guineas per year.

Provincial elites enjoyed the latest European music and London plays as talismans of cultural sophistication. They delighted in the music of Franz Joseph Hayden, Johann Christian Bach, Wolfgang

Amadeus Mozart, and in William Shakespeare's plays, especially *Romeo and Juliet, Hamlet,* and *Othello.* An evening at the theater included a full-length play; music, songs, and dances between acts; and a concluding "afterpiece," such as a farce. Works with familiar plots, characters, and music and spectacular scenery attracted the largest audiences. Especially popular were ballad operas, comic satires of social class, moral conventions, and gender roles, with new lyrics set to familiar tunes, and pasticcios, operas, like Thomas Arne's *Love in a Village* (1762), with song medleys set to music by well-known composers. John Gay's *The Beggar's Opera* (1728), the most popular play in the colonies, used 69 English ballad tunes, including "Our Polly is a Sad Slut!" sung to "Oh London Is a Fair Town." George Farquhar's *The Beaux' Stratagem* (1707) traced the main characters' schemes for repairing their fortunes and gradually revealed their true identities. These plays' popularity resonated with colonial Southerners, who lived in fluid but status-insecure societies where newcomers' appearances often deceived.

African and African Americans

As with Native Americans, African music and dance enriched daily life in stateless village societies and both traditions shared similar instruments, playing styles, and social uses. Drums and rattles emphasized percussion as the foundation for African music. Musicians played different-sized drums fashioned from hollowed logs with skins stretched across openings, and wedged small drums between their legs or sat cross-legged behind large kettledrums. Gourds filled with pebbles and leg and arm rattles accompanied dancers. There were many kinds of string, wind, and plucked instruments from densely populated, ethnically diverse West African societies. African banjos, first noted in 1754 in Maryland and much earlier in the West Indies, became an archetypal southern instrument after whites adopted it in the early 19th century. Slaves' fretless banjos accompanied songs at a "Negro ball," and were "made of a Gourd . . . with only four strings and played with fingers." A balafo or xylophone consisted of "an oblong box with the mouth up and stands on four sticks put in the bottom, and [a]cross the [top] is laid 11 lose sticks upon [which] he [the slave] beats."[17] Other African instruments in the colonial South included quills or panpipes, tambourines, reed flutes, mouth harps or musical bows, bells, gongs, and triangles. Few instruments physically survived the Middle Passage (an African drum found in Virginia now in the Sloane collection at the British Museum is a rare exception), but slaves used instrument-making skills to fabricate American versions from local materials.

Music and dance were part of West African daily life. "We are almost a nation of dancers, musicians, and poets," recalled Olaudah Equiano, an Igbo captured as a child in 1745, and "every great event, such as a triumphant return from battle, or other cause of public rejoicing is celebrated in public dances, which are accompanied with songs and music suited to the occasion."[18] Songs set the pace for fieldworkers and for boatmen; celebrated successful hunts and raids; narrated village histories; praised or condemned individuals; reported local happenings; marked passages of birth, puberty, marriage, and, especially, death; and welcomed distinguished visitors. Praise singers marked chiefly power, and professional musicians in state societies entertained guests and recorded rulers' accomplishments. Spectators clapped hands and shouted encouragement as musicians played and women and men performed ring dances with shuffling steps as "their hands having more of motion than their feet, and their heads more than their hands. They may dance a whole day, and ne'er heat themselves," Richard Lignon reported from the Barbados "yet, now and then, one of the activest amongst them will leap bolt upright, and fall in his place again, but without cutting a capre."[19]

African performance styles distinguished slaves' music from other aural traditions by emphasizing improvisation from layered contrasting beats that created polyrhythm and syncopation, dialog between song leaders and the group through call-and-response or antiphonal structure, poetic language rich in social commentary and metaphor, and vocal intensity marked by shouts, groans, gutturals, and falsetto voices. Songs were constructed from short musical elements that were repeated with subtle variations. While the mix of slaves from specific African societies varied over time and place, similar performance and vocal styles and instruments created new Pan–West African sounds even as slaves absorbed European fiddles and horns, ballad singing, and paired couples dancing. "Outward forms, whether song lyrics or common musical instruments, were primarily Anglo-American," historian Philip Morgan concludes about slaves' syncretistic music, "but underlying principles owed more to African sources."[20]

Contests between masters' assertions of domination and slaves' struggles for autonomy shaped slave music. Slaves extracted concessions—time off on Sundays and holidays, personal spaces in slave quarters and plantation groves, and freedom to travel—that made social gatherings possible. By the early 18th century, slave "feasts, dances, and merry Meetings upon the Lord's day" were "customary" practices in South Carolina, and Maryland slaves reportedly got "Drunke on the Lords Day beating their Negro drums by which they call considerable Number of Negroes together in some Certaine places."[21] Slave diversions were regular events. A visitor to South Carolina who stumbled upon a Saturday night slave assembly outside Charles Town discovered 60 women and men enjoying "Music, Cards, Dice," storytelling, and dancing. An English traveler in Virginia viewed a "Negro Ball" where slaves danced to a banjo, mocking, perhaps, formalized minuet steps, and sang ditties that "generally relate the usage they have received from their Master or Mistresses in a very satirical stile and manner."[22] "The Old Plantation," a watercolor recently attributed to John Rose, a South Carolina planter, captured slave recreation. The central male figure wears a head covering and performs a stick dance, concentrating his movements in his hands and upper body. Musicians play instruments possibly of Yoruba origin: a fretless four-sting banjo made from a gourd, a small drum held between the knees and with two sticks, and gourd rattles enclosed in netting that upon shaking strike shells or bones woven into the fabric to create percussive sounds.[23] Music strengthened interpersonal intimacy. Slave men courted young women with songs, mothers sang lullabies to infants, and fathers played homemade fifes as children danced.

Slave music and dance contested slaves' dehumanization even when whites observed their performances. Traders forced captives to dance and sing during the Middle Passage for physical exercise and as deterrence against shipboard rebellions. If slaves refused, an eyewitness testified, there was "a cat to flog them, and make them do it which I have seen exercised repeatedly." Their songs, he noted, were "lamentations . . . for having been taken away from their friends and relations."[24] Overseers heard laborers in tobacco and rice fields singing in unison to set the work pace, pass the time, and amuse each other (and whites, too) with clever word play. Slaves called to assist in arduous wheat harvests "will frequently come twenty, nay thirty Miles on this Occasion, [for] the Entertainments are great, and the whole Scene pleasant and diverting; but if they can get Musick to indulge this Mirth, it greatly add to the Pleasure of the Feast."[25] Music reverberated through the Virginia woods in fall evenings as work gangs arrived at plantations for communal corn shuckings. Whites watched ears fly from corn piles and

Slave recreation. This rare scene of Lowcountry slaves socializing likely depicts a wedding. The male at the center cuts a figure with a stick, while two women dance with net rattles accompanied by a gourd banjo player and a drummer. The clothes are European but several figures wear African-style head coverings. In the distance is a plantation village with mansion house, out buildings, and slave quarter. (Watercolor by John Rose, "The Old Plantation," 1785–1790. Abby Aldrich Rockefeller Folk Art Museum, Colonial Williamsburg, Williamsburg, Virginia [1935.301.3].)

enjoyed song leaders' improvised lyrics punctuated by their team's supporting responses. Slave boatmen in the Carolina Lowcountry "amused" a traveler "by singing their plaintive African songs, in cadence with the oars," and a slave on a ship from Florida to the Bahamas had a "gambee," which he played with two sticks one "split lengthwise into several clappers" rapidly rubbed against "a notched bar of wood" to produce "a hollow rattling noise, accompanied by a song in the Guinea tongue."[26]

Slave music sometimes unnerved whites. They banned slave drumming whose sounds carried for miles at night believing they were calls for rebellion. After slaves beat drums to recruit followers during the failed Stono rebellion in 1739, South Carolina legislators outlawed "using or keeping of drums, horns, or other loud instruments, which may call together, or give sign or notice to one another of their wicked designs or purposes."[27] Whites "dreaded" large slave gatherings, where one white Louisianan believed that "under pretense of Calinda, or the dance, they sometimes get together to the number of three or four hundred, and make a kind of Sabbath, which it is always prudent to avoid; for it is in those tumultuous meetings that they . . . plot their rebellions." The Maryland assembly unsuccessfully sought to suppress "tumultuous meetings of slaves" on Sundays and holidays.[28] Even when drums were banned, slaves clapped hands and struck body parts to produce syncopated rhythms, the forerunner of "pattin' Juba."

Slaves observed European music and dances, and slave musicians parleyed their talents to play for whites at country frolics, fancy balls, and dancing schools earning recognition and money. In the 1690s, a Virginia minister returned home outraged after discovering his daughter had hosted an impromptu dance that had lasted until Sunday morning. The fiddler, a local slave, left enriched with a Spanish piece of eight and several yards of ribbon and lace. Slaves learned to play violins and French horns. White youths were attracted to African-style jigs' hot dance steps. On one cold Sunday evening in January, Philip Fithian interrupted a slave dance after discovering two of his charges among the company: Ben Carter, age 18, and Harry Willis dancing with his coat off. Encouraged by his young owner, Dick, a slave in Virginia, played banjo for dances in the quarter, where "my young master himself could shake a desperate foot at the fiddle; there was nobody that could face him at a *Congo Minuet*." One English emigrant enjoyed a Virginia barbecue or hog roast where "a great number of young people . . . " enjoyed music performed by a slave fiddler and a banjo player as they "danced and drunk till there are few sober people amongst them." Black musicians played at winter balls, where whites enjoyed "Country dances" and "everlasting jigs. A couple gets up and begins to dance a jig (to some Negro tune) others comes and cuts them out, and these dances always last as long as the Fiddler can play."[29] Slaves attended militia days observing white men marching to fifes, drums, and trumpets. During the American Revolution, slaves became regimental fifers and drummers, music that announced local dances in parts of the rural South until recent times.

DRINKING AND SOCIALIZING

Colonial Southerners were awash in alcohol. No settler lived far from rural ordinaries or town taverns, backcountry farmers made small beer and hard cider, storekeepers surreptitiously sold alcohol to servants and slaves, European traders brought rum to Indian villages, and Indians living far in the South's interior obtained alcohol from Natives. Women, men, and even children drank daily as distilled spirits were believed safer than local water. Alcohol consumption rose by the late 17th century after cheap potent West Indian rum flooded colonial markets. Colonial authorities licensed taverns and ordinaries, set hours and prices, and prohibited sales to slaves and Indians in hoping—yet failing—to curb drunkenness and public disorder. By 1770, men over age 15 drank an estimated 3 pints of distilled beverages weekly. While humans have long enjoyed alcohol's mood-altering effects on their minds and bodies, culturally prescribed rules determined who, what, and where one drank. Spanish and French settlers preferred wines and Germans beer over rum; respectable English women imbibed at home not in taverns; Natives, unlike Europeans, tolerated violent drunks.

Europeans believed alcohol provided nutritious food, health from its curative powers, and pleasure by relieving labor's aches and lubricating social intercourse. Alcohol was drunk upon arising and before turning in; during meals; at all social events like weddings, funerals, dances, and frolics; and on public celebrations. Even residents of the Carolina backcountry, hardly the most loyal subjects, enthusiastically toasted the king's birthday. Strong labor, workingmen thought, required strong drink, and they expected a steady supply throughout the day. Richard Frethorne, an indentured servant in Virginia in the 1620s, attributed laborers' poor health to lack of alcohol: "For as strong beare (beer) in England doth fatten and strengthen them so water here doth wash and weaken these here."[30] Settlers planted orchards to make home-brewed hard cider (20 proof) and peach brandy, fermented small beer (2 proof), and built stills to distill whiskey from small grains. By the early 18th century, the most common beverage was rum (90 proof), which was often watered down in an inventive array of cocktails: toddy, punch, julep, sangaree, and grog. Only the wealthy imbibed imported wines as most experiments in local viniculture failed in the South's humid climate. Colonials stunned foreign visitors with their prodigious alcohol consumption. At one 1617 funeral in Virginia, the liquor bill included over 50 gallons of cider, beer, and brandy combined.

Male sociability emphasized heavy drinking in taverns, on court days and militia musters, and during horse races, cockfights, and other amusements.[31] Militia commanders provided hogsheads of liquor after musters, and candidates for political offices treated voters with food and drink at local taverns. William Byrd was pleased his generosity "entertained all the people and made them drunk and fighting all evening, but without mischief."[32] Men drank to intoxication. Ability to hold one's liquor after numerous toasts tested masculinity and institutionalized binge drinking. Getting strangers drunk was a favorite tavern game. Etiquette required returning each toast with another, and each newcomer was greeted with raised glasses. Drunkenness was a favorite topic of male humor. Seeking lodging after a court day filled with the usual "Blood[y] Battle and fractious clamour," the fictional protagonist of Ebenezer Cooke's satire of colonial Maryland arrived to "A Herd of Planters on the ground, / O'er-whelmed with Punch, dead drunk, we found."[33] Alexander Hamilton, a medical doctor, observed a drunken group stagger from a Maryland tavern: "Most of them had got upon their horses and were seated in an oblique situation, deviating much from a perpendicular to the horizontal plan[e]. . . . Their discourse was as oblique as their position; the only thing intelligible in it was oaths and God dammes; the rest was an inarticulate sound . . . interlaced with hickupings and belchings."[34]

In addition to providing travelers meals and lodgings and their horses stabling and forage, taverns were male social clubs where locals frequented often to share a pint or two; make music; exchange news; argue politics; play cards, billiards, and table games; tell stories filled with lies; transact business; and waste time generally. A Virginia minister's indictment reveals taverns' importance in men's daily lives. Taverns, he fumed, were:

> Rendezvous of the very Dreggs of the People; even of the most lazy and dissolute . . . , where not only Time and Money are, vainly and unprofitable, squandered away, but (what is yet worse) where prohibited and unlawful Games, Sports, and Pastimes are used, followed, and practiced, almost without any Intermission; namely, Cards, Dice, Horse-racing, and Cock-fighting, together with Vices and Enormities of every other Kind, and where (their inseparable Companions, or Concomitants) Drunkenness, Swearing, Cursing, Perjury, Blasphemy, Cheating, Lying, and Fighting, not only tolerated, . . . but permitted with Impunity; nay, abound to the greatest Excess.[35]

Trips to courthouses, country stores, and gristmills included visiting the nearest ordinary. Rural tavern keepers operated stores and extended credit to regulars; one could imbibe drink within or carry out alcohol. There were more taverns than churches in the Carolina backcountry, and after weekend sprees more drunks, an Anglican minister despaired, "firing, hooping, and hallowing like Indians" than worshippers at religious services.[36] Taverns were community centers where like-minded people learned the latest gossip, read newspapers, and advertised estate sales, lost objects, and slave auctions. Taverns in towns had large rooms for dances, musical performances, lectures, traveling shows, and political meetings. After Governor Lord Botetourt dissolved the Virginia General Assembly in 1769 to block protests against the Townsend Acts, a group of burgesses met at the Raleigh Tavern's Apollo Room to draw up petitions urging boycotts of British goods.

As in other areas of daily life, elite men increasingly sought to distance themselves from common folk by frequenting respectable urban ordinaries with private lodgings, renting tavern rooms for their regular use, and forming exclusive gentlemen's clubs. The Ancient and Honourable Tuesday Club of Annapolis, established in 1745, limited membership to 15 men: all large planters, professionals, and elite artisans. They met weekly in each other's homes, noted a member, to "converse, laugh, talk, smoke, drink, differ, agree, argue, philosophize, harangue, pun, sing, dance and fiddle together" but mostly to drink copiously. Humorous speeches, verses, and toasts were the order of the day: "Wishing this ancient club may always be / Promoters of facetious mirth and glee / . . . And while gay laughter furbishes each soul / Let each a bumper drink to noble Jole [i.e. Charles Cole, club president]."[37] Meetings included music, especially ribald ballad opera songs, and new compositions. Large towns had several clubs where men ate, drank, and engaged in lively conversations. A visitor to Charles Town in 1773 spent an evening at one talking about "negroes, rice, and the necessity of British regular troops being quartered in Charleston" and enjoyed "cards, feasting and indifferent wines" at another.[38] In addition to male conviviality, clubs provided newcomers with connections to local elite men, opportunities to practice gentility and demonstrate learning, and business, political, and professional contacts, while inebriated horseplay—acting up with wigs off—gave temporary releases from polite society's stiff formality.

As tavern clientele divided along class lines, authorities sought to control popular drinking habits of raucous laborers, sailors, servants, slaves, women, and prostitutes—who ate, drank, played, gambled, and danced after work at night and on weekends and holidays. Believing their behavior threatened social order, assemblies passed laws banning gaming, sales of alcohol to Indians and minors under 16, and adulteration of liquor; requiring servants and slaves to obtain owners' permission; and limiting hours of operation,

Gentlemen at leisure. Elite men formed private social clubs to drink, socialize, debate, read original compositions, make music, and satirize social conventions. Meetings began with ritual readings of minutes with tobacco pipes and a punch bowl at the ready. The inscription reads: "Long live the Tuesday Club, so wisely fram'd/ . . . long may the members stand/ and still maintain their badge of hand in hand." [See club seal at top.] (Drawing by Dr. Alexander Hamilton, *Tuesday Club Record Book.* Maryland Historical Society, Baltimore.)

Playing pool. Taverns were centers of male conviviality for drinking, gossiping, and playing games like billiards that tested one's skill and risked personal honor. Men of different classes and ages competed as spectators observed the action and wagered on the outcome. Benjamin Henry Latrobe, "Billiards at a Country Tavern," 1798, in *The Journal of Latrobe.* New York, D. Appleton and Company, 1905. (Library of Congress.)

drinking on Sundays, and credit extended to patrons. New Orleans tavern keepers were required to "report immediately to the Police Officer, all disputes and rows taking place there; . . . [and] allow no vagabonds, notorious men, nor women of ill repute to enter; [and] they shall allow no swearing nor blasphemy."[39] Constables raided disorderly houses, and courts denied licenses to disreputable men. Yet, governments needed revenues from licensing fees, tavern keepers' bonds posted for good behavior, and excise taxes on distilled spirits, and restrictive legislation did little to deter working-class carousing.

Colonial Southerners lived on scattered farms and plantations, and frequent visiting, historian Daniel Blake Smith notes, "was almost an essential activity for families that sought to maintain close ties of kinship and friendship." Ordinary planters stopped by friends' homes during trips to stores, courthouses, or mills and enjoyed a drink. Their wives visited to borrow foodstuffs and gossip over tea. William Byrd, a wealthy planter, welcomed guests to Westover or ventured out four of five days during the year and enjoyed cricket, billiards, and archery during visits with male friends. Colonel James Gordon saw his Virginia neighbors, friends, and kin or had a "full house" or "large company" of guests so often that he noted a day without company, *"which is surprising."*[40] Great planters invited peers to lavish dinners slaves prepared and served. Philip Fithian enjoyed "an Elegant Dinner" with John Turberville and two other planters' families "so that there dined today . . . besides his usual Family thirteen Persons" and including "the Waiting Men With the Carriages they were twenty." The food, however, "did not in any thing exceed what is every day at Mr. *Carters* Table."[41] After dinner, strolls through formal gardens provided pleasant conversation and river vistas. Playing instruments, singing, dancing, cards, board games, reading aloud, charades, and pantomime filled inclement days and winter evenings.

Socializing in elite families began early. Fathers carried young sons to neighbors' houses, stores, mills, taverns, courthouses, and militia musters inculcating them into the world of male sociability. Teenage boys had freedom of movement and traveled by horseback on errands and on visits to distant relatives. Women's sociability centered in homes. Daughters accompanied female relatives on family visits absorbing women's lore and bonding with female relatives and neighbors. During conversations over teacups, women shared personal stories, commented on mutual friends and family members, and created lifelong emotional bonds. More distant visits required male escorts, especially when young women traveled for extended periods to homes of aunts and cousins who organized social events for meeting peers and possible marriage partners.

Southern hospitality began in the colonial period. Isolated planters and yeoman with abundant resources welcomed travelers for company and outside news. "A stranger has no more to do but to inquire upon the road where any gentleman or good housekeeper lives and there he may depend upon being received with hospitality," historian Robert Beverley, a planter, asserted, and even "poor planters who have but one bed will very often sit up or lie upon a form or couch all night to make room for a weary traveler to repose himself after his journey."[42] Even mean backcountry homes were preferable to most rural ordinaries that often had a single room converted for eating, sleeping, and drinking.

Drinking loosened and reinforced racial divisions. Alcohol provided male slaves time outs from enslavement's psychological traumas and for domestic workers respites against abusive masters, who tolerated their waiting men's drunken sprees. Lower-class whites and slaves partied on holidays. A visitor to Maryland was surprised by "tumultuous scenes" where "100s and 100s of blacks were assembled—wonderfully interspersed with whites young and old Gaming—Fiddling, Dancing, drinking, cursing, and swearing."[43] Alcohol, cheap rum mostly, was readily available at "disorderly houses" in towns and in the countryside where slaves and poor whites lingered to drink, play cards and dice, gamble, dance, and fraternize. Slaves readily obtained hard cider and fruit brandy from plantation stores and purchased illicit alcoholic beverages from overseers, yeoman farmers, and storekeepers. Legislators' repeated efforts failed to limit slaves' easy access to taverns and the underground alcohol trade.

Slaves found their own gatherings even more enjoyable. Drink, music, dance, and simply being together allowed for free expression and humor to relieve slavery's pains. At one large slave gathering outside Charles Town, a white visitor reported, "the entertainment was opened by the men copying (or *taking off*) the manners of their masters, and the women those of their mistresses, and relating some highly curious anecdotes, to the inexpressible diversion of that company." Eighteenth-century slave populations, recalled a slave fugitive, included many Africans, who told stories of "demons, miracles, and murders" as entertainment and moral instruction for the young.[44]

Native Americans

Native American socializing was embedded in their kin-based village life. Cooperative labor, shared childrearing, and communal living created constant interactions and limited privacy. By singing, teasing, gossiping, and telling humorous stories about themselves or others, villagers created deep social ties that music, dancing, games, and rituals reinforced. Reciprocity necessitated extending hospitality to kin, strangers, and guests broadening social ties outside one's immediate village.

Indians adopted alcohol, like other aspects of European material culture, into existing social practices and ceremonies. Offering rum to honored guests was added to gift-giving rituals and toasts in treaty negotiations. Believing spiritual forces imbued all things, Natives were especially attracted by alcohol's consciousness altering effects. They consumed alcohol as quickly as possible to harness its spiritual power and achieve dreamlike states. Mourning rituals included drinking during all-night wakes. Yet, alcohol use was never indiscriminate. Many individuals abstained; some young women traded sex for liquor; and when supplies were insufficient for all, a designated individual became completely intoxicated rather than everyone merely enjoying a mild buzz.

Accounts of besotted Indians fill colonial narratives reinforcing colonials' convictions of Natives' depravity. Indians, trader James Adair asserted, are "excessively immoderate in drinking. They often transform themselves by liquor into the likeness of mad foaming bears."[45] Scholars debate why Natives in eastern North America eagerly sought alcohol, drank to inebriation and even unconsciousness, and tolerated the consequent social mayhem. Indians in the colonial South were no more genetically predisposed to alcoholism than Europeans or Africans, but unlike native peoples in Mexico or the Southwest, they had no prior experience with alcoholic beverages or with the "art of getting drunk."[46]

Inebriated Indians often engaged in antisocial behavior, assaulting or injuring one other. During "drunken Frolicks (which are always carried on in the Night)," naturalist John Lawson recorded in 1709, "they sometimes murder one another, fall into the Fire, fall down Precipices, and break their Necks, [along] with several other Misfortunes."[47] It was the alcohol, Natives explained, that controlled drunken individuals' behavior. "They have no conception that they are culpable so far as to deserve to suffer for any mischief or outrage committed by them while in that Condition," Edmond Atkin, southern superintendent of Indian Affairs, rebuked, "If complained or, or up-braided for it, they say with great composure 'that they are sorry for what has happened, But that it was not they that did it, 'twas the Rum that did it.'"[48] Alcohol loosened inhibitions tightly governing social relations in kin-based villages where there were few acceptable ways to challenge gender norms, redress grievances, or exact revenge. Men assaulted drunken women, women and men fornicated in public, and individuals expressed forbidden feelings or acted out suppressed impulses. Alcohol provided Indian men outlets for aggressive behavior when they could no longer acquire honor through hunting or warfare. As diseases depopulated villages, game disappeared from overhunting and from European livestock's competition, settlers encroached on native lands, and priests condemned ancient customs, alcohol provided solace in a collapsing world of death, poverty, displacement, and apostasy.

By the mid-18th century, some native leaders condemned alcohol abuse and appealed to colonial officials to control or even ban the rum trade. Unlike metal objects, textiles, and other trade goods, whose demand was relatively fixed, Indians consumed rum immediately, which rarely satiated their desire for more. Rampant drunkenness disrupted village harmony and created new conflicts with settlers. Indians valued personal autonomy, so controlling alcohol's consequences seemed insurmountable, but appeals to colonial authorities to ban alcohol sales were no more effective. In 1754, Hagler, Catawba headman, pointed out the source of his people's drinking problem: "If the White people make strong drink let them sell it to one another or drink it in their own Families. This will avoid a great deal of mischief which otherwise will happen from my people getting drunk and quarrelling with the White People."[49] Profits from watered-down rum were four times what was made from the rest of the Indian trade, and Natives' demand for alcohol never diminished. It became a condition of doing business; if merchants failed to supply it, Indians would not trade.

AMUSEMENTS AND HOLIDAYS

A county fair in Virginia held on St. Andrew's Day, November 30, 1737, promised horse races on a three-mile course "and several other Diversions, for the Entertainment of the Gentlemen and Ladies," including fiddle competition (bring your own instruments); cudgeling match (no left-hand play allowed); boys' races; band concert; ballad-singing contest promising songsters will "have Liquor sufficient to clear their Wind-Pipes"; wrestling match; dance contest; prize of silk stockings to the "handsomest young country Maid"; after dinner toasts to the royal family, the governor, and others; and "many other whimsical and Comical Diversion." The fair's subscribers promised "to discountenance all Immorality with the utmost Rigour" and expected participants to behave "with Decency and Sobriety." Like other highbrow diversions, "the best sort, of both Sexes," could meet and reaffirm their social status, but ordinary folk, servants, and slaves joined the throngs of contestants and spectators and bet on races' outcomes. The fair's organizers, the county's leading gentlemen and merchants, displayed their wealth by paying for prizes and expenses, exclusivity by monopolizing horse races, and intense competitiveness by risking male honor publicly. While the fair's British origins and timing on the day of Scotland's patron saint maintained Old World connections, the event itself was an invented tradition for "cultivating Friendship and innocent Mirth" among a newly settled and isolated New World people.[50]

Horses, the preferred mode of transportation and self-presentation, and horse racing became southern obsessions. Early quarter races featured two riders sprinting down straight quarter-mile tracks at breakneck speeds jockeying, whipping, and elbowing each other for advantage with their owners wagering heavily on outcomes. Every county had at least one track at the courthouse or a tavern with set races during the year, challenge races on weekends, and impromptu matches between rivals. While ordinary men and slaves cheered favorite horses and made small side bets, matches were only between men of the same rank. In 1674, James Bullock, a tailor, was fined 100 pounds of tobacco for entering a mare in a race as it was illegal "for a Labourer to make a race being a Sport only [for] Gentlemen."[51]

After 1700, the gentry preferred longer races along mile-long circular tracks and quarter racing became amusement for common folk. Subscription races had stiff entry fees and large prizes, and only wealthy planters could purchase Arabian steeds to breed horses for endurance races. Fithian described the action in one 1773 race with a purse of 500 pounds of tobacco "besides small Betts [were] almost enumerable. . . . Assembly was remarkably numerous. . . . The horses started precisely at five minutes after three; the Course was one Mile in Circumference, they performed the first Round in two minutes, third in two minutes and a-half, *Yorick* came out the fifth time round about 40 Rod before *Gift*[.] They were both, when the Riders dismounted, very lame; they [had] run five miles and carried 180 lb." By mid-century, town racing clubs organized multiday spring and fall races with established rules, trained jockeys, handicapping of horses, and purses of 50 pounds sterling or more. Often coinciding with fairs, work ceased as large crowds of whites and blacks gathered to cheer and bet on favorite horses, transact business, and enjoy dances, "puppet shows, rope dancing" and other entertainment.[52]

Cockfighting rivaled horse racing as a male pastime attracting participants across classes and races. Gentlemen placed extravagant bets on their birds trained by slave handlers, who developed special diets, conditioning regimen, and techniques for placing spurs hoping to gain advantage. On Mondays following Easter and Whitsunday (Pentecost), there were scheduled matches between cocks from rival communities. A 1768 contest involved teams of 30 cocks from 2 counties that paid 5 pounds to victors of each fight and 50 pounds for the "odd" team with the most wins, and promised an evening ball for the ladies. Other matches occurred at county fairs and court days, and enthusiasts constructed cockpits on plantations for local meets. Once news of a fight spread, a French traveler noted, men and boys "for thirty or forty miles around, attend, some with cocks, but all with money for betting, which is sometimes very considerable." Feathers and blood ensued one Carolinian recalled:

> Exceedingly beautiful cocks were produced, armed with long, sharp steel-pointed gaffs, which were firmly attached to their natural spurs. The moment the birds were dropped, bets ran high. The little heroes appeared trained to the business, and not the least disconcerted by the crowd or shouting. They stepped about with great apparent pride and dignity; advancing nearer and nearer, they flew upon each other at the same instant with a rude shock, the cruel and fatal gaffs being driven into their bodies, and, at times, directly through their heads. Frequently one, or both, were struck dead at the first blow, but they often fought after being repeatedly pierced, as long as they were able to crawl, and in the agonies of death would often make abortive efforts to raise their heads and strike their antagonists.[53]

Heavy betting on horses and gamecocks was but one aspect of men's gambling obsession. Anything could be wagered: cards, games, dice, drinking contests, trials of strength, an election, or tomorrow's weather. Ordinaries kept dice and cards for their patrons, and urban taverns owned billiard tables. Card and board games came from England. Participants learned from experienced players or from popular treatises, like Charles Cotton's *The Compleat Gamester* (1674, with many later editions) or Edmond Hoyle's books on the latest popular games such as quadrille, piquet, and backgammon. Card and board games provided evening diversions for family members and guests and were usually played for small bets. Tavern-play between men, however, put reputations and wealth on the line. The greater the stakes, the deeper the match became for participants and onlookers alike. Legislators' enthusiasm for gambling surprised a Jamestown visitor in the 1680s when a participant warned him not to wait for the contest to end, "'For,' said he, 'it is quite possible that we shall be here all night,' and in truth I found them still playing the next morning."[54]

Popular card games included whist, the ancestor of modern bridge, which required skill as well as luck; piquet, similar to modern rummy and enjoyed for its rapid play; loo, an early form of poker; and lotto with special cards like bingo but with numbers not letters. New board games were the rage especially cribbage invented in the 17th century, backgammon, and "The Royall and Most Pleasant Game of Goose," originally from Italy and similar to modern Parcheesi. All remain popular today. Lower-class men and boys preferred games of chance: all fours or seven up and put, another poker game, dice games like chance and hazard (the latter a simplified version of craps), and coin tossing, calling out "cross" (heads) or "pile" (tails).

Ball games were popular. As early as 1610, men in Jamestown reportedly spent more time playing lawn bowls, an ancient game, than planting. A century later, large planters constructed private bowling greens. Like bocce, the object was to roll earthenware balls, which were unbalanced with lead weights on one side, and hit a target ball, called a "jack." In ninepins or skittles, similar to modern bowling, balls were thrown to knock down rows of pins. Gentlemen enjoyed billiards, which was played on an oblong cloth-covered table with a low railing and six pockets (called "hazards") for its simple rules, leisurely pace, and display of skill. Play consisted of using a long cue stick to hit a hard ball through a wicket ("port"), touch without knocking over a peg ("king"), and knocking an opponent's ball into a hazard. Betting, drinking, boasting, and cheating were all part of the game. Cricket and fives (a form of handball) were other favorite gentlemen's pursuits. Quoits, or pitching horseshoes, was a common pastime on court days. As today, the goal was to throw a metal object, a horseshoe or a discus with hole in middle, to hit an iron pin or "hob" staked in the ground.

Men enjoyed competitive physical activities especially hunting and fighting as tests of endurance, skill, and honor. Unlike Europe, where hunting was a privilege of royalty and the gentry, the colonial South's abundant environment and mild climate provided, Robert Beverley reported, unrestricted enjoyment of "hunting, fishing, and fowling with which they entertain themselves a hundred ways . . . [in] the pleasure of the chase."[55] Deer, rabbits, and other small game supplemented diets of slaves, servants, and poor whites and provided time away from farmwork. On summer evening hunts on foot small dogs chased after raccoons, opossums, and foxes. Large dogs helped trap wolves, bears, and wildcats. Hunters presenting wolves' heads with cropped ears received government bounties for exterminating vermin. By the end of the colonial period, old settled areas had extensive cleared lands for planters to organize foxhunting on horseback with dog packs.

Boxing, wrestling, racing, shooting contests, and other tests of individual stamina appealed to lower-class men. Fights included set matches or spontaneous settlings of personal slights. Rules were few: "Every diabolical Stratagem for Mastery is allowed and practiced," Philip Fithian noted with disgust, including "Bruising, Kicking, Scratching, Pinching, Biting, Butting, Tripping, Throtling, Gouging [the eyes], Cursing, Dismembering [the genitals], Howling, etc." Combatants agree beforehand "whether all advantages are allowable" and usually agreed to fight "no holts [holds] barred" scrupulously following them until one man gave up or was incapacitated. Successful fighters earned local fame. One man, a British traveler reported, "a great adept in gouging . . . constantly kept the nails of both his thumbs and second fingers very long and pointed" to maintain his weapon![56]

Free men and slaves, especially in the Chesapeake, shared some leisure activities with wealthy men. Slave men accompanied owners and guests on hunts handling dogs to drive out deer or retrieving downed birds. Slave handlers raised prize gamecocks for their owners' blood matches, and slave jockeys rode blooded steeds in horse races and shared victors' laurels, testimonials to slave men's skills and planters' honor. Slaves and poor whites enthusiastically joined planters in drinking and betting at cockfights and horse races, cheered combatants at wrestling matches, and caroused during militia musters and at monthly court days. Adrenaline ran high at one North Carolina horse race where there was "betting . . . , quarrelling, wra[n]gling, Anger and swearing" between "white Boys and Negroes eagerly betting 1/-, 2/-, a quart of Rum, a drink of Grog etc., as well as Gentlemen betting high."[57]

Social gatherings of family members, friends, and neighbors marked rites of passage like christenings and weddings and seasonal events, such as Christmas, New Year's Day, and breaks in work routines. Their elaborateness varied by wealth and location—fancy dress balls in Charles Town, cabin raisings in the backcountry, and merry-making in slave quarters—but all included feasts, music, and dances that often lasted several days. Families of newlywed couples held parties at their houses. The winter lull in work extended Christmas into a festive season of several weeks, and even slaves enjoyed the week after Christmas as a general holiday. The 1765 *Virginia Almanac* anticipated the social season:

Christmas is come, hang on the pot,
Let spits turn round, and ovens be hot;
Beef, pork, and poultry, now provide
To feast thy neighbors at this tide;
Then wash all down with good wine and beer,
And so with mirth conclude the Year.

Gentry youths, the first leisured class in America, enjoyed rounds of balls in towns and dances in relatives' homes, while slaves socialized with one another on neighboring plantations. New Year's Eve marked another evening of "strong ale, good fires, and noble cheer."[58] Chesapeake planters organized riverboat races, betting on outcomes and eating, drinking, and dancing afterward. Everyone looked forward to summer fish fries with fresh catches by men and boys earlier in the day and to fall barbecues featuring roasted pork, both made merry with drinking and dancing. Cabin raisings welcomed newcomers into backcountry communities with food, drink, and dancing.

While Catholic Florida and Louisiana retained the liturgical calendar of holy days and religious processions and dramas, holidays in British colonies increasingly centered on secular celebrations. Protestants reduced the number of saints' days in favor of the weekly Sabbath. In the early 18th century, Virginians reportedly kept "no Holydays, except those of Christmas day and good Friday, being unwilling to loose (lose) their dayly labour."[59] Political events—a new governor's arrival, a new monarch's coronation, a new heir's birth, and royal birthdays—were special public occasions that reaffirmed provincial loyalties to crown and empire. Military parades, speeches, special music, trumpet blasts, drum beats, cannon fire, cheers, feasts, toasts to every member of the royal family, balls, and fireworks marked these events in colonial capitals. Fireworks honoring Queen Anne's ascension to the throne in 1702 went awry when the master of ceremonies "blew up everything at once in a great blaze and smoke. As . . . he like others had to run and he had his clothes burnt." Celebrations at county courthouses were simpler as local officials met and "in most solemn manner by Sound of Trumpet and beat of Drumm . . . testify their rejoicing by a triple Discharge of all their musquets and fire armes & other publick acclamations of Joy usuall on the like occasions."[60] One Virginia county authorized 10,000 pounds of tobacco to treat citizens celebrating the birth of James II's son.

Unlike modern societies with their adult-supervised, age-segregated activities, colonial children often participated in the same leisure activities as adults: card and board games, instrumental music and songs at family gatherings, and barbecues and balls. With no legal drinking age, male teens like adults often drank to excess. Between chores, young farm boys roamed woods and fields exploring, hunting small game, and fishing and learned to ride horses by their early teens. Children enjoyed outdoor games still played today: marbles, stickball, hopscotch, leapfrog, blindman's bluff, and hide-and-seek. Only the wealthiest families indulged children with store-bought toys on New Year's Day and on birthdays like imported dolls dressed in the latest London fashions, miniature tea sets, and toy soldiers. Most played with homemade whirligigs, cup-and-balls, spinning tops, rolling hoops, and checks (an early form of checkers).

With the possible exception of John Canoe festivals, which mixed African animal masking with English Christmas festivities, African village festivals and formal recreations were lost in the Middle Passage. In some towns, companies of slave men, who were covered under nets of bright colored calico with animal horn headdress and cows' tails on their backs and accompanied by musicians and singers, went round from house to house on Christmas or New Year's Day begging for coins or rum. Slaves created a rich informal culture on their own time. Like their music and dance, they adapted African pastimes to European forms. Slaves in Charles Town played papaw, an African dice game, while Chesapeake slaves learned English games of chance at local taverns, like huzzle cap (hustle-cap), pitch penny, trap ball, and fives. Slaves raised fighting cocks and matched birds from different plantations, and they staged their own cockfights and athletic contests where men competed in running, jumping, and tree climbing.

Native Americans

Native Americans were inordinately fond of ball and gambling games, which they played with a ferocity that astounded Europeans. Chunkey (called guicio by the Spanish), an ancient game, was played between two men using long eight-foot notched poles and small wheel-shaped discs made from polished stones or wooden hoops about six inches in diameter. One player rolled the disc; just as it stopped, both men threw their poles. Which notch came closest to or touched the stone or whether poles went through the hoop determined the score. Heavy betting between participants and their supporters increased competition's stakes and deepened its social meaning. Villages owned chunkey stones and maintained chunkey yards, which were located between town houses and sritual grounds and often enclosed by low earthen walls. In the center stood a 40-foot single pole used in another ancient ball game the Spanish called pelota. The object was to kick a tiny ball against the goal post above a notched mark or even better hit a stuffed eagle perched on a nest at the pole's top. Teams from two villages with 40 or more men each engaged in rough play with heavy betting on the sidelines. The first team scoring 11 points (2 points for hitting the nest!) won. In the colonial period, both sexes played a version of this game with women hitting the ball with their hands and men using ball sticks.

Stickball, the predecessor of modern lacrosse and field hockey, was played between two teams. The object was to drive a small leather ball made of deerskin stuffed with animal fur through a goal of upright poles or trees about three feet apart using a curved stick (shinny) or two sticks looped at one end to form a small racket laced with skin or fiber. Fields could be very large—Chickasaws needed 500 yards of bottomland—and the number of male players ranged from a few dozen to over 100. An old man (or the Great Sun for the Natchez) began the game by tossing the ball between the two teams. The first team to reach a set number of points, usually 12 or 20, won. Rules varied whether the ball could touch the ground or players' hands. Otherwise, play was a free-for-all as individuals hit, tackled, and even fought each another, suffering numerous injuries and, occasionally, death.

Sacred ceremonies, preparatory rituals, personal adornments, and prized traits of speed, stamina, and deception associated with warriors were also essential for ball players with one difference: women, children, and old men participated in pregame rituals, cheered teams from sidelines, and bet heavily on outcomes. Feasts and dances celebrated raising ball poles; and well before fall ball seasons began, village youths began training by competing in footraces, wrestling contests, and practice games. As game day approached, players consulted conjurers, avoided certain foods, and abstained from sex (except pelota players, who had sex with any women they chose for good luck). The night before games, players fasted and villagers sang and danced to raise their spirits and weaken opponents through symbolic acts of desecration. Conjurers blessed players in the morning and made inspirational speeches; these were contests of rival's spiritual power as well as of physical strength. Cherokee men underwent ritual scratching with

Choctaws preparing for a ballgame. Ballgames were sacred as well as social contests between different lineages or villages that required extensive ritual preparation. Action centered on men wearing breechclouts, feathers, and body paint, who tested their stamina and prowess, but everyone participated in pregame rituals. (George Catlin, "Ball-Play Dance, Choctaw" (1834–1835) American Art Museum, Smithsonian Institution [1985.66.428]).)

a comb of turkey leg splinters causing blood to trickle from arms, legs, breasts, and backs. Eagle feathers, animal tails, snake rattles, black and red body paint, and breechcloths completed players' uniforms.

Natives were deeply attached to ball games, as missionaries in Florida discovered when they tried to ban pelota in Apalachee in the 1670s. Spanish priests objected to ceremonies associated with the game, its violent play, and diversion from mission work. Pelota was part of their origin stories and a gift from the creator. Stickball mediated political differences between rival villages of competing chiefdoms or between two moieties or lineages within a village and served to establish new social relations. Dislocations from disease, war, and displacement strengthened stickball's importance over chunkey's individual competition. As village autonomy declined, competitive games, the "little brother of war," provided alternative ways for males to acquire prestige formerly obtained as warriors.[61]

Even today, ball games remain an important part of southeastern Indians' social and ceremonial lives.

Women and men enjoyed hidden object or shell games where small stones were placed in moccasins or under pieces of cloth. The goal was to guess where the stone was located by outwitting your opponent's misleading gestures, rapid hand movements, and distracting chants. Colonials marveled at Natives' skills of deception. Virginia Indians' "one great diversion . . . ," Robert Beverley noted, involved guessing the number of reeds, "which they know how to count as fast as they can cast their eyes upon them and can handle with a surprising dexterity."[62] These personal tests of skill and trickery were another outlet for competitive behavior between close-knit villagers who ordinarily prized cooperation and social harmony.

PLEASURABLE PERFORMANCES

Leisure for colonial Southerners was as necessary for daily life as labor. "Diversions which have no immoral Tendency, when purchased by those who can well afford it," a 17th-century Virginian observed, "unbend the Mind from severer Applications, promote a social Temper, and diffuse a general Satisfaction through the Ranks of Life."[63] Elite men and women imported new forms of leisure from Europe—court dances, gentlemen's clubs, and tea-drinking rituals—that set them above rude folk and engaged in lavish entertaining, extravagant betting, and comparative gaming to mark distinctions within elite ranks. Horse racing and cockfighting mixed men of different classes and castes yet reinforced hierarchy: common whites and slaves watched as wealthy planters risked honor and wealth. Everyone enjoyed feasting and dancing, and European, African, and Indian men all engaged in excessive drinking, obsessive gambling, and aggressive self-assertion with violence lurking just below competition between rivals. Recreation mixed highbrow with lowbrow activities. Fithian observed that Virginia gentlemen were "presumed to be acquainted with Dancing, Boxing, playing the Fiddle, and Small-Sword, and Cards," but he became alarmed when one of his pupil's "Genius seems towards Cocks, and low Betts, much in company with the waiting Boys."[64] Africans' creative incorporation of European instruments and songs into polyrhythmic performance styles created new cultural forms and became acts of resistance. As Indians' autonomy declined, traditional games continued with new purposes. For Europeans, Africans, and Indians alike, old forms of leisure were adapted to new situations as colonial Southerners performed the dramas of daily life in their fluid and culturally mixed societies.

NOTES

1. Philip Fithian, *Journal and Letters of Philip Vickers Fithian, a Plantation Tutor of the Old Dominion, 1773–1774,* January 18, 1774, ed. by Hunter Dickinson Farish (Charlottesville: University of Virginia Press, 1968), 57 and Charles Woodmason, *The Carolina Backcountry on the Eve of the Revolution,* ed. by Richard J. Hooker (Chapel Hill: University of North Carolina Press, 1953), 98.
2. Sebastian de Grazia, *Of Time, Work, and Leisure* (New York: The Twentieth Century Fund, 1962), 15.
3. Sacred music and dance is discussed in Chapter 8.
4. Gonzalo Solís de Merás, *Pedro Menéndez de Avilés: Memorial,* trans. by Jennette Thurber Connor (Gainesville: University of Florida Press, 1964), in Judith Tick, ed., *Music in the USA: A Documentary Companion* (New York: Oxford University Press, 2008), 6, 7.
5. Robert Beverley, *The History and Present State of Virginia,* ed. by David Freeman Hawke (Indianapolis: The Bobbs-Merrill Company, Inc., 1971 [1705]), 113, 114; see illustration on p. 44, lower right corner.
6. James Merrill, *The Indians' New World: The Catawba and Their Neighbors from European Contact through the Era of Removal* (New York: W.W. Norton and Co., 1989), 132.
7. James Adair, *The History of the North-American Indians,* ed. by Kathryn E. Holland Braund (Tuscaloosa: University of Alabama Press, 2005 [1775]), 153.
8. John Grier Varner and Jeannette Johnson Varner, trans. and ed., *The Florida of the Inca* (Austin: University of Texas Press, 1951), 575, 576, cited in Robert Stevenson, "Written Sources for Indian Music until 1882," *Ethnomusicology* 17, no. 1 (1973): 5.
9. William Strackey, *The Historie of Travell into Virginia Britania,* ed. by Louis B. Wright and Virginia Freund (London: Hakluyt Society, 1953), cited in Robert Stevenson, "English Sources for Indian Music until 1882," *Ethnomusicology* 17, no. 3 (1973): 402.
10. Ibid., 402, 403.
11. J.A. Leo Lemay, *Benjamin Franklin: A Documentary History,* "Printer, 1657–1731," entry for 1719, http://www.english.udel.edu/lemay/frankslin/printer.html. For details on Blackbeard, see Chapter 9.
12. Andrew Burnaby, *Burnaby's Travels through North America* (New York: A. Wessels Company, 1904), 57.
13. Fithian, *Journal and Letters,* December 18, 1773, 33.

14. Letter from Thomas Jefferson to Martha Jefferson Randolph, April 4, 1790, in Julian Boyd, ed., *The Papers of Thomas Jefferson* (Princeton, NJ: Princeton University Press, 1950–), 16: 300; Letter from Jefferson to Giovanni Fabbroni, June 8, 1778, ibid., 2: 196; and Fithian, *Journal and Letters,* March 13, 1773, 30. The "harmonica" was a glass harmonica, which consisted of a series of glass goblets tuned with different amounts of water and played by rubbing a moistened finger around the rim. After hearing one, Fithian pronounced "The music is charming! . . . The Notes are clear and inexpressibly soft, they swell, and are inexpressibly grand; and either it is because the sounds are new, and therefore please me, or it is the most captivating instrument I have Ever heard" (Fithian, *Journal and Letters,* December 22, 1773, 37).

15. *South Carolina Gazette,* February 8–15, 1735, in Tick, *Music in the USA,* 43. Quotation marks inserted. *Flora* was a ballad opera.

16. *Virginia Gazette* (Hunter), Williamsburg, VA, June 12, 1752.

17. Nicholas Cresswell, *The Journal of Nicholas Cresswell, 1774–1777,* May 29, 1774, 2nd ed. with Introduction by A.G. Badley (New York: The Dial Press, 1928 [1924]), 19 and John Harrower, *The Journal of John Harrower, an Indentured Servant in the Colony of Virginia, 1773–1776,* March 5, 1775, ed. by Edward Miles Riley (Williamsburg, VA: Colonial Williamsburg, 1963), 89.

18. Olaudah Equiano, *The Interesting Narrative of the Life of Olaudah Equiano, Written by Himself,* 2nd ed. with Introduction by Robert J. Allison (Boston: Bedford/St. Martins, 2007), 45.

19. Richard Ligon, *A True & Exact History of the Island of Barbados* (London: Humphrey Moseley, 1753), cited in Dena J. Epstein, *Sinful Tunes and Spirituals: Black Folk Music to the Civil War* (Urbana: University of Illinois Press, 1977), 26, 27.

20. Philip D. Morgan, *Slave Counterpoint: Black Culture in the Eighteenth-Century Chesapeake and Lowcountry* (Chapel Hill: University of North Carolina Press, 1998), 594.

21. Francis Le Jau, *The Carolina Chronicle of Dr. Francis Le Jau, 1706–1717* (Berkeley: University of California Press, 1956), cited in Epstein, *Sinful Tunes and Spirituals,* 38 and Russell R. Menard, "The Maryland Slave Population, 1658 to 1730: A Demographic Profile of Blacks in Four Counties," *William and Mary Quarterly* 32, no. 1 (1975): 37.

22. *South Carolina Gazette,* September 17, 1772, cited in Epstein, *Sinful Tunes and Spirituals,* 82 and Cresswell, *Journal,* May 29, 1774, 18, 19.

23. John Rose, "The Old Plantation," ca. 1785–1790, Abby Aldrich Rockefeller Folk Art Museum, Williamsburg, Virginia. The African instruments are a molo (banjo), gudugudu (drum), and shegureh (gourd rattle).

24. Testimony of James Towne, carpenter, Great Britain, Parliament, House of Commons, *Minutes of the Evidence . . . Respecting the African Slave Trade,* Sessional Papers, XXXIV (1791), cited in Epstein, *Sinful Tunes and Spirituals,* 8.

25. John Brickell, *The Natural History of North Carolina* (Dublin, 1737), 40.

26. Elkanah Watson, *Men and Times of the Revolution* (New York: Dana and Company, 1856), cited in Epstein, *Sinful Tunes and Spirituals,* 72 and Johann David Schoepf, *Travels in the Confederation, 1783–1784* (Philadelphia, PA: W. J. Campbell, 1911), cited in Epstein, *Sinful Tunes and Spirituals,* 16.

27. South Carolina, Laws, Statutes, etc., *Statues at Large,* VII (1840), 410, cited in Epstein, *Sinful Tunes and Spirituals,* 59.

28. Le Page du Pratz, *The History of Louisiana . . .* (London: Printed for T. Becket, 1774), cited in Epstein, *Sinful Tunes and Spirituals,* 32 and Jeffrey R. Brackett, *The Negro in Maryland: A Study of the Institution of Slavery* (Baltimore: John Hopkins University Press, 1889), 100, cited in Epstein, *Sinful Tunes and Spirituals,* 59.

29. John Davis, *Travels of Four Years and a Half in the United States of America during 1798, 1799, 1800, 1801, and 1802* (New York: Henry Holt and Company, 1909), 414 and Cresswell, *Journal,* July 26, 1774 and January, 7, 1775, 30 and 53.

30. Letter from Richard Frethorne to his parents, 1623, in Susan M. Kingsbury, ed., *The Records of the Virginia Company of London,* 5 vols. (Washington, D.C.: Government Printing Office, 1935), 4: 59.

31. The terms "tavern," "ordinary," and "public house" were used interchangeably. Illustration on p. 380 shows a public space in front of the county courthouse.

32. William Byrd, *Secret Diary of William Byrd of Westover, 1709–1712,* ed. by Louis B. Wright and Marion Tinling (Richmond: The Dietz Press, 1941), 234.

33. Ebenezer Cooke, *The Sot Weed Factor, or, a Voyage to Maryland* (Baltimore, MD, 1865 [1708]), 16.

34. Alexander Hamilton, *Gentleman's Progress, the Itinerarium of Dr. Alexander Hamilton, 1744,* ed. by Carl Bridenbaugh (Chapel Hill: University of North Carolina Press, 1948), 6.

35. *Virginia Gazette* (Hunter), April 11, 1751.

36. Woodmason, *Carolina Backcountry,* December 1767, 30.

37. Records of the Tuesday Club, cited by Bridenbaugh, *Gentleman's Progress,* 48a and xvii.

38. Josiah Quincy, Jr., "Journal of Josiah Quincy, Junior, 1773," entries for March 12, 15, 1773, *Massachusetts Historical Society Proceedings* 49 (1916): 450, 451. The Tuesday Club of Annapolis avoided local politics; if mentioned, club rules directed that "No answer shall be given thereto, but . . . the society shall laugh at the Member offending in order to divert the discourse" (Bridenbaugh, *Gentleman's Progress,* xvi).

39. Jack D. L. Holmes, "Notes and Documents: O'Reilly's Regulations on Booze, Boarding Houses, and Billiards," *Louisiana History* 6, no. 3 (1965): 298.

40. Daniel Blake Smith, *Inside the Great House: Planter Family Life in the Eighteenth-Century Chesapeake Society* (Ithaca, NY: Cornell University

Press, 1980), 196 and James Gordon, "The Journal of Col. James Gordon, of Lancaster County, Virginia," *William and Mary College Quarterly Historical Magazine* 11, 3rd ser., no. 2 (October 1902): 98–112, cited in Smith, *Inside the Great House*, 211.

41. Fithian, *Journal and Letters*, January 4, 1774, 47.

42. Beverley, *History and Present State of Virginia*, 167.

43. "Journal of a Traveler," June 2, 1800, cited in Morgan, *Slave Counterpoint*, 413.

44. *South Carolina Gazette*, September 17, 1772, cited in Epstein, *Sinful Tunes and Spirituals*, 82 and Charles Ball, *Fifty Years in Chains* (New York: Dover Publications, Inc., 1970 [1837]), 201.

45. Adair, *History of the North-American Indians*, 68.

46. James Boswell, *Life of Johnson*, ed. by R.W. Chapman (New York: Oxford University Press, 1980), 1022, cited in Peter C. Mancall, *Deadly Medicine: Indians and Alcohol in Early America* (Ithaca, NY: Cornell University Press, 1995), 16.

47. John Lawson, *A New Voyage to Carolina* (Champaign, IL: Project Gutenberg, n. d.), 151.

48. Edmond Atkin, *Indians of the Southern Colonial Frontier: The Edmond Atkins Report and Plan of 1755* (Columbia: University of South Carolina Press, 1954), 26, cited in Charles Hudson, *The Southeastern Indians* (Knoxville: University of Tennessee Press, 1976), 441.

49. William L. Saunders, ed., *The Colonial Records of North Carolina*, 10 vols. (Raleigh: P. M. Hale, 1886–1890), cited in Mancall, *Deadly Medicine*, 118.

50. *Virginia Gazette* (Parks), Williamsburg, VA., October 7, 1737.

51. York County Order Book, 1674, in Warren M. Billings, ed., *The Old Dominion in the Seventeenth Century: A Documentary History of Virginia, 1606–1689* (Chapel Hill: University of North Carolina Press, 1975), 319, 320.

52. Fithian, *Journal and Letters*, December 25, 1773, 24, 25 and Harrower, *Journal*, October 8, 1774, 65.

53. Francis Jean, Marquis de Chastellux, *Travels in North-America in the Years 1780, 1781, and 1782*, rev. ed., 2 vols. (London: 1828), 2: 121, 122 and Watson, *Men and Times of the Revolution*, 261, 262.

54. Durand of Dauphiné, *A Huguenot Exile in Virginia* (New York: Press of the Pioneers, 1934), cited in T.H. Breen, "Horses and Gentlemen: The Cultural Significance of Gambling among the Gentry of Virginia," *William and Mary Quarterly* 3rd ser., 34, no. 2 (April 1977): 239.

55. Beverley, *History and Present State of Virginia*, 164, 167.

56. Fithian, *Journal and Letters*, September 3, 1774, 183 and Thomas Anburey, *Anburey's Travels through the Interior Parts of North America*, Vol. 2 (Carlisle, MA: Applewood Books, n. d. [1923]), 203, 217, 218.

57. Lida Tunstall Rodman, ed., *Journal of a Tour to North Carolina by William Attmore, 1787* (Chapel Hill: University of North Carolina Press, 1922), 17, 18, cited in Morgan, *Slave Counterpoint*, 416.

58. *Virginia Almanac* (Royal), 1765, cited in Harold B. Gill, Jr., "Christmas in Colonial Williamsburg," in *Celebrating the Holidays* (Williamsburg, VA: Colonial Williamsburg Foundation, 2011), http://www.history.org/visit/christmas/hist_inva.cfm and *Virginia Almanac* (Royal), 1767, cited in Leigh Eric Schmidt, *Consumer Rites: The Buying and Selling of American Holidays* (Princeton, NJ: Princeton University Press, 1995), 109.

59. William S. Perry, ed., *Historical Collections Relating to the American Colonial Church* (Hartford, CT, 1870–1878), 1: 213, cited in Schmidt, *Consumer Rites*, 26.

60. William J. Hinke, ed. and trans., "Report of the Journey of Francis Louis Michel from Berne, Switzerland, to Virginia, October 2, 1701–December 1, 1702, Part II," *Virginia Magazine of History and Biography* 24, no. 2 (April 1916): 128 and Henry McIlwaine, ed., *Executive Journals of the Council of Colonial Virginia* (Richmond, VA: Davis Bottom, 1927), II: 250, 253–55, cited in Jane Carson, *Colonial Virginians at Play*, Williamsburg Research Series (Williamsburg, VA: Colonial Williamsburg, 1965), 198, 199.

61. Hudson, *Southeastern Indians*, 411.

62. Beverley, *History and Present State of Virginia*, 113.

63. C.C. Pearson and J. Edwin Hendricks, *Liquor and Anti-Liquor in Virginia, 1619–1919* (Durham, NC: Duke University Press, 1967), cited in Sharon V. Salinger, *Taverns and Drinking in Early America* (Baltimore: Johns Hopkins University Press, 2004), 119.

64. Letter from Fithian to John Peck, August 12, 1774, *Journal and Letters*, 161 and September 15, 1774, ibid., 190.

7

BODIES

Daily life was experienced through bodies in work and play, prayer and procreation, pleasure and pain, health and sickness, and, eventually, death and burial. Bodies embraced the physical and the spiritual. Native Americans' gods had human attributes and foibles, and Africans' ancestors watched over villages. Jews, Christians, and Muslims believed human bodies were fashioned in God's image and in bodily resurrection after death. Human consciousness of life's finite nature included anticipation of death and bodily preparations and rites to mark transitions between physical and spiritual existence. Environments shaped bodies through life-sustaining sustenance and life-shortening dangers and diseases. "All the inhabitauntes of the worlde are fourmed and disposed of suche complexion and strength of body," asserted a 17th-century English observer, "that euery [one] of them are proportionate to the Climate assigned unto them, be it hotte or colde." Migration from the Old World to the New World stressed European and African bodies as they encountered novel climates and new diseases. Arrival of Old World plants, animals, and diseases created a new world for Native Americans. Proper rituals and healing methods to restore diseased bodies and maintain health was literally a matter of life and death. As historian Joyce Chaplin concludes, "Human adaptation to climate was both physical and mental: the sinews, or fibers of the human body changed; humoral temperament became unbalanced then readjusted; susceptibility to diseases altered; bodily change created demand for different foodstuffs; temperature affected capacity for intellectual activity and military rigor."[1]

The colonial South's cultural stew and social instability turned human self-awareness about one's own body into scrutiny of the bodies of others. Adornments (tattoos, piercings, and scarifications) and accessories (wigs, jewelry, hairstyles, and head cloths) beautified bodies, confirmed old identities, and constructed new ones. In believing "physical appearance . . . is but the visible mark of an inner essence, which is expressed in behavior or culture," historian Thomas Holt notes, people inspected strangers' bodies to make comparative assessments.[2] European men gazed at Indian and African men and especially women to define colonial projects, measure their own worth, project sexual fantasies, construct new European identities, and, later, justify dispossessing Native Americans of land and Africans of freedom. Indians and blacks returned their gazes making their own opinions about the bodies of Europeans and of each other and formed new ethnic and racial identities. Individuals scrutinized bodies to discern which differences mattered: skin color, hair, nudity, smell, posture, and breast or penis size. Europeans debated whether these features were caused by environment factors and therefore changeable, or inherited traits, permanent biological markers of intelligence, moral character, and, even, human status. Once ethnocentric judgments of cultural difference became immutable racial markers (earlier for Africans; later for Indians), race became central for defining social hierarchies and determining whom had access to political power and economic opportunities. Race making and the work of race were contingent on time and place, neither predetermined nor fixed, but messy and contested in colonial Southerners' everyday lives.

OBSERVING BODIES

English scrutiny of Algonquians followed earlier Spanish accounts that viewed read external appearances as windows into inner character. Christopher Columbus' 1493 report of his voyage to the Indies noted Arawarks' naked bodies, though "well built and of handsome stature," signified their "timorous . . . guileless and so generous" nature. Englishmen made similar observations. The Powhatans, reported a minister, "are of bodie lustie, strong, and very nimble: They are a very understanding generation, quick of apprehension, suddaine in their dispatches, subtile in their dealings, exquisite in their inventions, and industrious in the labour"—prime candidates, in short, for Christian conversion.[3] Religion and culture not Indians' "olive" or "tawny" skin color were emphasized in early narratives. As long as natives remained vital informants, laborers, or potential converts for colonial projects, Europeans searched for commonalities with them and proposed scriptural or environmental explanations for human diversity. Scholars debated whether Indians were children of Adam and Eve, had scattered after Noah's Flood, were descendents of the Lost Tribes of Israel, or became darkened from the sun after migrating to the New World, but few doubted that Indians' bodily differences made them less than human. To form "a just estimate of their genius and mental powers," Thomas Jefferson concluded, "great allowance [is] to be made for those circumstances of their situation. . . . This done, we shall probably find that they are formed in mind as well as body, on the same module with the 'Homo sapiens Europaeus.'"[4]

While admiring tall, strong, and agile Indian men, Englishmen took even greater interest in semiclothed women. "They are as fine-shap'd Creatures . . . as any in the Universe," John Lawson, an Indian trader, observed with "a tawny Complexion; their Eyes very brisk and amorous; their Smiles afford the finest Composure a Face can possess; their Hands are of the finest Make, with small long Fingers, and as soft as their Cheeks; and their whole Bodies of a smooth Nature." Nor are they "so uncouth or unlikely, as we suppose them," he fantasized, nor "Strangers or not Proficients in the soft Passion." Men's sexual desires for Indian females, understandable when English women were scarce, continued in the 18th century even among married men. Native women had "very straight and well proportioned" bodies, William Byrd, a planter, noted, their "innocence and bashfulness that with a little less dirt would not fail to make them more desirable." Meeting a "dark angel" one evening, Byrd joined his companion, who "examined all her neat proportions with a critical exactness," with his own appraisal: "Her complexion was a deep copper, so that her fine shape and regular features made her appeal like a stature *en bronze* done by a masterly hand."[5] Sexual conquest had long been part of men's colonial dreams: in ravishing native women, whom they imaged as compliant and sexually insatiable, they mastered a continent.

Europeans responded to Indian resistance to conversion and land encroachments with harsh judgments about native bodies. *Sauvages* (the French term for natives) were wild men, described in medieval tales as a "hairy, naked, club-wielding child of nature who existed halfway between humanity and animality." Columbus reported stories of "Caribs," who though "no more malformed than are the others," reputedly were "very fierce and who eat human flesh."[6] When Powhatan warriors killed almost 30 percent of the colonists in the 1622 Anglo-Powhatan War, "defacing, dragging, and mangling the dead carkasses into many pieces, and carrying some parts away in derision, with base and brutish triumph," the English retaliated with a policy of extermination. Indians seemed beyond redemption: "by nature sloathfull and idle, vitious, melancholy, slovenly, of bad condition, lyers, of small memory, of no constancy or trust," as the colonial secretary approvingly cited a 16th-century Spanish historian, "the most lying and most inconstant in the world, sottish (habitually drunk)and sodaine (sodden): never looking what dangers may happen afterwards, lesse capable than children of sixe of seaven yeares old, and lesse apt and ingenious."[7] Such deficient, debased people contributed nothing to civilizing a wilderness and required pacification, expulsion, or confinement on reservations.

Africans' blackness initially and most deeply impressed English traders to West Africa. While the Spanish thought differences of skin color exemplified the diversity of God's creation, a poem by an English voyager in the 1560s made more negative assessments:

> And entering in [a river], we see / a number of blacke soules,
> Whose likelinesse seem'd men to be / but all as blacke as coles.
> Their Captaine comes to me / as naked as my naile,
> Not having witte [wit] or honestie / to cover ones his taile.

In England, "black was an emotionally partisan color," historian Winthrop Jordan notes, "the handmaid and symbol of baseness and evil, a sign of danger and repulsion." Africans' black skin colored other negative evaluations: unclothed bodies, woolly bushy hair, "Large Breasts, thick Lips, and broad Nostrils." Physical differences darkened evaluations of Africans as "people of beastly living, without a God, lawe, religion, or commonwealth," and their alleged licentiousness made them more animal than human. A few observers claimed living near the equator darkened Africans' skin, but its blackness, a "natural infection," was most often explained by the biblical story of Ham, Noah's son, who had seen his father's nakedness.[8] When Noah awoke, he cursed Canaan, Ham's son, declaring that he and his descendants would become his brothers' servants. From this brief story that seemed to account for slavery's origins, Europeans devised divine sanction for enslaving black Africans.

Africans' bodily debasement accelerated with slavery's spread. The slave trade turned humans into commodities, and historian Winthrop Jordan notes that "new slaves off the ships were described as 'well-fleshed,' 'strong-limbed,' 'lusty,' 'sickly,' 'robust,' 'healthy,' 'scrawny,' 'umblemished.'"[9] As English colonial laws gave owners almost unlimited control over enslaved Africans, killing a slave under "moderate" correction was no murder nor did rape violate antimiscegenation statutes, violence inflicted on slaves' bodies increased almost unchecked. Slave runaway notices were replete with details of physical abuse: shaved hair, lacerated backs, limps

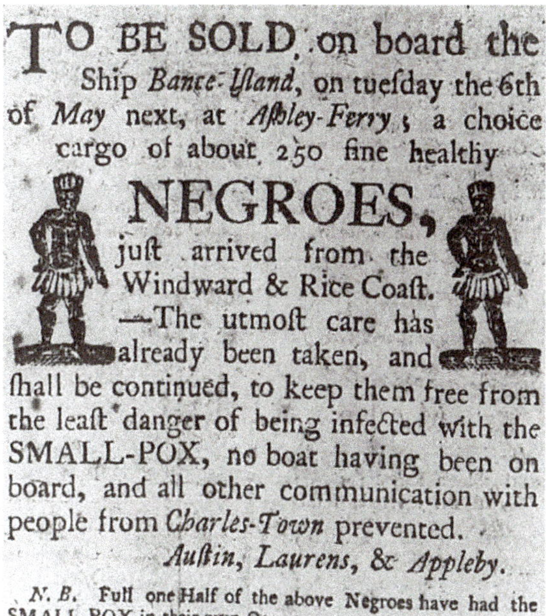

Slave advertisement. Marketplace language and images of scantily-clad Africans describe this sale of a "choice cargo . . . of fine healthy Negroes" guaranteed to be "free from the least danger of being infected with the SMALL-POX." The slave ship was named after an English trade post on Bunce Island in the Sierra Leone River, which supplied slaves from the Rice Coast to South Carolina and Georgia rice planters. (Library of Congress.)

from broken bones, branded breasts and shoulders, missing fingers and toes, and cropped ears. Whippings were the most common punishments. In South Carolina, reported a visitor, "the common Method is to tie them up by the Hands to the Branch of Tree, so that their Toes can hardly touch the ground . . . hardly a Negro but bears the marks of Punishment in large Scars on his Back and Sides." Charles Wesley, secretary to Georgia governor James Oglethorpe, recorded one female slave was whipped so severely as to require medical attention, but after recovering, her owner "repeated the whipping with equal rigour, and concluded the punishment by dropping scalding wax upon her flesh: her only crime was over-filling a tea-cup!"[10] Slaves convicted of felonies faced castrations and whippings with stripes "well laid on" and public executions by being burned at the stake, quartered and drawn, gibbeted, and hung in cages to die slowly from starvation with severed heads impaled on poles; punishments rarely inflicted on white felons. Louisiana's *Code Noir,* which banned mutilation and killing but not shackling, beating, and whipping, went unenforced on Louisiana plantations.

By mid-18th century, skin "emerged as the primary index of difference," according to historian Nancy Shoemaker, in Europeans' rankings of humanity that unvaryingly placed themselves on top, Africans on the bottom, and Indians and Asians in between.[11] If beards signified male virility to Europeans, Indian men's beardlessness denoted effeminacy. Epidemic diseases that caused catastrophic Indian mortality but left Europeans relatively unscathed seemed to prove natives' biological inferiority. Once slaves replaced indentured servants on plantations and partially acculturated to European norms, skin color remained an indelible marker of servility. Jefferson advanced "as a suspicion only, that the blacks, whether originally a distinct race, or made distinct by time and circumstances, are inferior to the whites in the endowments both of body and mind," but he minced no words on the biological origins of black bodies' deficiencies:

> The first difference . . . of colour . . . is fixed in nature, . . . [and] Is it not the foundation of a greater or less share of beauty in the two races? Are not the fine mixtures of red and white, the expressions of every passion by greater or less suffusions of colour in the one, preferable to that eternal monotony, which reigns in the countenances, that immoveable veil of black which covers all the emotions of the other race? Add to these, flowing hair, a more elegant symmetry of

> form . . . [and] other physical distinctions proving a difference of race. They have less hair on the face and body. They secrete less by the kidneys, and more by the glands of the skin, which gives them a very strong and disagreeable odour. This . . . renders them more tolerant of heat, and less so of cold, than the whites. . . . They seem to require less sleep. . . . They are more ardent after their female: but love seems with them to be more an eager desire, than a tender delicate mixture of sentiment and sensation. Their griefs are transient. . . . In general, their existence appears to participate more of sensation than reflection. . . . Comparing them by their faculties of memory, reason, and imagination, it appears to me, that in memory they are equal to the whites; in reason much inferior, . . . and that in imagination they are dull, tasteless, and anomalous.[12]

In imposing their own standards for evaluating the worth of Native American and African bodies, European colonists sharpened their own self-identities as Christians, Europeans, and whites. Once indices of difference shifted from nurture to nature, bodily differences seemingly confirmed European superiority and justified conquering natives and enslaving Africans as the natural and inevitable order of things.

Miscegenation—sexual unions between whites, Indians, and blacks—created new racial peoples that muddied the emerging categories of white, red, and black and threatened gender hierarchies. Some colonial promoters encouraged interracial marriages between European men and Indian women, and no laws banned them, to erase cultural differences by turning natives into Europeans. The most celebrated match was between Pocahontas, Powhatan's daughter, and John Rolfe, a tobacco planter. A Christian convert, Pocahontas' portrait made during a good will tour of England portrayed her wearing upper-class English clothes and accessories, a high capotain hat, pearl earrings, and indigenous facial features: the model new native. English and French traders and soldiers in Louisiana and Florida formed liaisons with native women, who provided sexual companionship, household labor, and village alliances. Young white female captives taken in frontier wars and adopted into clans took Indian husbands. Most refused to be redeemed back to civilization preferring the social equality and lightened labor of Native societies. Children of these mixed unions faced conflicted racial identities. Some became cultural brokers and Indian leaders, but most Europeans, historian Jennifer Spear notes, uniformly condemned "halfbreeds who are naturally idlers, libertines and even more rascals."[13]

Pocahontas. This portrait made during a publicity tour in England affirmed Pocahontas' cultural conversion. She wears English gentlewomen's clothes—a reply to popular images of naked savages—and sports a capotain, a fashionable tall hat. Yet, her indigenous facial features are clearly visible and she wears freshwater pearl earrings worn by high-status Native women, and includes Matoaka, her adult name, alongside Rebecca, her baptismal name. Simon Van de Passe, 1616. (Library of Congress.)

When Africans became numerous in the Chesapeake region, authorities acted to suppress *all* black–white unions. In the 1660s, interracial fornicators in Virginia faced double fines, and Maryland condemned English servant women making "shameful matches" with slave men.[14] A few decades later, all intermarriages between whites and blacks, including free blacks, became illegal, a policy enforced in Virginia until 1967 when the Supreme Court in *Loving vs. Virginia* declared all antimiscegenation statutes unconstitutional. Louisiana's 1724 *Code Noire* banned marriages between whites and blacks, whether slave or free, or holding slave women as concubines. Unlike mixed-race Indian–white children, mulattoes appeared unequivocally dark to Europeans, evidence, they thought, of the permanent stain of blackness. Mulatto children blurred the logic of racial slavery based upon maintaining clear demarcations between black and white, the enslaved and the free.

Yet, colonials sexualized slaves' bodies, even slave youths. One Virginia visitor was shocked at a dinner party to see "young boys of about Fourteen and Fifteen years Old" waiting on women at dinner with their "whole nakedness Expose'd and I can Assure you It would Surprize a person to see these d_____d black boys how well they are hung." Despite public condemnation of miscegenation, "the country swarms with mulatto bastards," observed one Virginian, but only white women charged with bearing illegitimate mulatto children faced criminal prosecution.[15] Mulatto children in Virginia were bound to servitude until age 30 despite having free mothers, and Louisiana enslaved them for the Ursuline hospital. The danger arose from black men's insatiable lust for white women, not women's own sexual desires, white men reassured themselves. But white women knew it was far more common for their husbands and sons to impregnate black women. Eighteen-year-old Ben Carter's younger brother tattled that Ben had taken Sukey, a 16-year-old slave, "into your stable, and there for a considerable time lock'd yourselves together!" Sukey, observed Philip Fithian, tutor to the Carter children, was "plump, sleek, and likely." Only in Charles Town could men joke publicly about liaisons with enslaved women. The *South Carolina Gazette* advised bachelors and widows "to wait for the next Shipping from the Coast of Guinny. Those African Ladies are of a strong, robust Constitution: not easily jaded out, able to serve them by Night as well as Day."[16] White men desired black women's bodies, yet blamed their moral lapses on black women's alleged hypersexuality and rejected their enslaved biracial offspring. Mulattoes never occupied social spaces between white and black; slaveowners' darker children remained slaves.

Indians and Africans, of course, formed their own opinions about Europeans' bodies that can only be glimpsed from European sources. Lacking body hair except on top of their heads, hirsute Europeans reminded Indians of animals as they playfully pulled men's beards!

Olaudah Equiano likened being tossed into the slave ship's hold as entering the Gates of Hell and assumed Europeans were preparing to eat him. The spiritual power inhabiting novel European goods and technology left impressions in names like "long-knives," and Equiano wondered what magic filled the ship's sails carrying him across the Atlantic. Europeans' behavior not appearance left the most lasting impressions. Did nature or nurture make them stingy not generous, violent not hospitable, arrogant not broadminded? Why did they recoil at bodily caresses and body rubbings that signified friendship? Did they enjoy forced sex more than freely receiving a woman's gift? Slaves gazed back at whites with coded body language: instead of stooped shuffling, they swaggered with upright carriages, made "down looks" avoiding facial contact to indicate hostility, closed eyes to signify rejection, gave hostile or "cut-eye" glares by moving eyes downward and across the body to mark disapproval, and "sucked teeth" or drew in air to express anger. By 1770, Indians and Africans adopted the language of race to contest European racial rankings and embrace new pan-ethnic identities as "redmen" and "blacks" that were based upon shared oppression. Race making, while originating in social experiences, increasingly was perceived as innate traits that defined mutually hostile castes of white, red, and black.

Natives and Africans often made other choices. Africans sought shelter with natives living in the interior, and villagers adopted them into their clans to rebuild their population. Natives and Africans often labored together on plantations in early Carolina and Louisiana and formed intimate relationships. Africans lived near settlement natives in the Chesapeake, outside Saint Augustine, and in the Gulf Coast. Each group had unbalanced sex ratios—a shortage of Indian men from warfare and deficit of African women from the slave trade—that facilitated male African–female Indian unions. Their children formed one of many new racial groups in the colonial South, who survived in isolated swamps, piney woods, and mountain coves. Under the one-drop rule, whites reclassified these mixed-race people as blacks and denied their native ancestry. Not until the mid-20th century, would they reclaimed their native identities.

ADORNING BODIES

Devereux Jarratt, a carpenter's son, knew a wig was "a distinguishing badge of *gentle folk.*" As a boy, "when I saw a man riding the road, near our house, with a wig on, it would so alarm my fears, and give me such a disagreeable feeling, that, I dare say, I would run off, as for my life." Yet, when first employed as a schoolteacher, acquiring a wig upgraded his rough attire. So "that I might appear something more than common, in a strange place, and be counted somebody," he recalled, "I got me an old wig, which, perhaps being cast off by the master, had become the property of his slave, and from the slave it was conveyed to me."[17] Gentleman, commoner, and slave: each understood adornments' powers to refashion individuality, alter social position, and denote ethnic and gender identities and nowhere more visibly than on colonial Southerners' skin and faces.

Fully clad Europeans fixated on extensive decorations marking Indians' and Africans' exposed bodies. Tattoos covered native women's legs, breasts, shoulders, arms, and faces in geometric patterns and designs of flowers, fruits, snakes, birds, fish, and animals highlighted, an early Virginia settler noted, with "sundry lively colours, [which] they rub it into the stampe which will never be taken away, because it is dried into the flesh where it is sered."[18] Men and women painted their shoulders and faces for practical reasons and for dressing up using dyes of black, blue, yellow, white, and especially red. The latter was made from roots and hickory nut oil or bear's grease, and they applied the red ointment liberally as protection against cold weather, sunburns, and mosquitoes. Special occasions called for colorful patterns: mourning (black), warfare (half red/half black), social dances (white), and hospitality (crimson, blue, and silver). Scarifications were male Africans' most distinctive skin embellishments. Deep incisions on cheeks or stomachs marked boys' initiation into manhood and full ethnic identity. Village leaders had more elaborate markings. The Igbo, according to Olaudah Equiano, cut foreheads down to the eyebrows that were hand-rubbed until they shrank into thick welts. "Country marks," as Europeans called them, allowed Africans to identify ethnic origins, but to Creoles they denoted "old Africans," men to be feared, yet respected.

Smooth unblemished skin separated genteel women from their social inferiors, whose outdoor labor, cooking, and washing wrinkled and roughened skin. Concerning beauty, Molly Tilghman, a Maryland teenager, wrote to her cousin, "Wisdom says it is a fading flower, but fading as it is, it attracts more admiration than wit, goodness, or anything else in the world."[19] Gloves, muffs, and tippets covered hands and necks from the cold; lip salves and cold creams protected against sunburn; scented powders and floral waters

Young Algonquian male. European artists emphasized natives' exoticism by highlighting men's muscular bodies, beardlessness, nakedness, and personal adornment including freshwater pearl necklaces and earrings, shell head ornaments, shaved "Mohawk" hair, and facial tattoos. High-status men wore more jewelry, and men painted their bodies in preparation for hunting, war, and ceremonies. Engraving by Wenceslaus Hollar, 1645. (Library of Congress.)

preserved skin; toothbrushes and dentifrices whitened teeth; and black patch appliqués emphasized skin's whiteness. Common planters' wives shared beauty tips and recipes from housewifery manuals to prepare homemade cosmetics.

Styled hair, pierced ears, and jewelry expressed masculinity, and men obsessed over keeping up with male rivals and changing fashion. Indian men spruced up by cutting some hair close and leaving other places tall to fashion the original "Mohawk." They also tied up long hair with roaches or cloth pieces and added decorative feathers, multiple earrings, copper and bone jewelry, and multicolored paint and tattoos. Silver, copper, or bone ornaments dangled from pierced ears and noses. Virginia men, according to one European, "hang through their eares Fowles legs; they shave the right side of their heads with a shell, the left side they weare of an ell long tied up with an artificial knot, with a many of Foules feathers sticking in it . . . some paint their bodies blacke, some red, with artificiall knots of sundry lively colours, very beautifull and pleasing to the eye." Indeed, concluded another, "if you see an hundred of them, you shall always observe some difference . . . either in their Painting, Tonsure of their hair, or the marks made in their Skins."[20]

European men experienced a facial style revolution from full bearded, flowing hair of the 17th century to smooth-shaved, wigged-heads of the 18th century. Once short wigs replaced courtly full-bottom wigs whose flowing manes fell onto shoulders, they became essential male accessories. William Peake, a Yorktown, Virginia, merchant, boasted of his "choice Assortment of the best hairs" and offered custom-made wigs "after the newest and neatest Fashion" in various styles, including "Live human hair . . . for Tye-wigs, Bobs, or Naturals;" stained and bleached animal hair "for Tyes or Crowns, Horse Hair, Cropp'd or Round-abouts;" and wig care products: "Steel and Iron Cards, and Brushes, and drawing Cards, pinching Tongs and Topee Irons, Wig Springs, hollow blocks, . . . [and] Peruke Bags."[21] There were wigs for every occasion and budget: toupees covering foreheads that could be brushed up into pompadours, perukes or round wigs, bag wigs with side curls, bob wigs with frizzled sides, queue attachments that went down backs, all-weather sports wigs suitable for hunting, and a lively used wig market. By mid-century, wigs were transportable markers of gentility and expressions of the self: no social aspirant could be without one.

Male slaves utilized their tightly spiraled hair's expressive possibilities while incorporating European and Indian styles. African men generally cut their hair short, but slaves typically had "bushy" hairdos styled by combing the hair forward, back, and high over their foreheads, creating the first "Afros." Young Creole men developed personal styles by shaving part or all of their hair into various patterns, close cropped in the front and long in the back, or vice versa, or braided their hair into long queues, or, occasionally, wore wigs. Frank, a "waiting lad," sported the latest "macaroni taste" with his hair "teased into side locks, and a queue."[22] Lowcountry

Stylin' hair. Male slaves used free time for personal adornment: combing and grooming hair, tying it into long queues, and shaving beards. Slaves accessorized their wardrobes with personal touches like felt hats and head coverings, long jackets, and colorful clothing. (Watercolor by Benjamin Henry Latrobe, "Preparations for the Enjoyment of a Fine Sunday among the Blacks, Norfolk," 1797. Maryland Historical Society, Baltimore.)

men often had beards, some thick and large, and others short and small, while Chesapeake men favored a smooth-shaven look. In altering facial appearances, young slave men forged personal identities that parodied whites.

Women's hairstyles and accessories displayed their social status.[23] Indian girls' hair was cut short except for a long braid lock in the back; after marriage, it was combed, rubbed with hickory oil until sleek, and braided with ornaments. African women spent hours grooming their hair in elaborate styles. After cleaning, combing, and oiling, they shaped their hair into tight pleats with shells, cloth pieces, or beads woven in; selectively cut it into different lengths to form patterns; and wrapped small clusters with fabric that curled when released. Enslaved women had little time for hair maintenance, and whites' descriptions of their unkempt "bushy" hair must have been especially humiliating. During the week, brightly colored bandanas and head wraps covered disheveled hair or protected styled hair from the sun and dirt of fieldwork. On weekends, coverings came off as slave women cleaned, brushed, plaited, and threaded their hair and taught daughters hairstyling techniques. In the 18th century, genteel women's hair became elaborate artifices, dramatic departures from an earlier style of drawing hair back from foreheads to hang in long curls about the neck or coiled up and covered with caps. New styles involved combing hair into high piles atop the head, teased into stiff curls and puffs, and adorned with combinations of false hair, lace, ribbons, feathers, artificial flowers, pompoms, and flycaps. Such artistry required professional hairdressers, but women of lesser means purchased accessories for styling their own hair. Men ridiculed women's elaborate hairstyles (yet overlooked their own obsession with wigs), but proudly displayed the results as trophies of economic and social arrival.

Earrings, necklaces, and hairpins from rare or labor-intensive materials were especially prized adornments: copper tubes, freshwater pearls, quahog shell beads, decorated conch shell disks, and European glass beads adorned Indian women, and their European sisters coveted diamonds, precious stones, and pearls. The wife of one ex-collier flaunted her husband's new wealth from tobacco planting by sporting about Jamestown in "her rough bever hatt with a faire perle hatband, and a silken suite."[24] Commoners made do with plain gold, mother of pearl, marcasite (iron pyrite), and paste (bright glass). Enslaved women wore ear bobs and drops, armbands, and bracelets made from cowrie shells, blue glass beads, brass, iron rings, and coins.

Whether Indian, African, or European, adornments were essential accessories for social performances. A Rappahannock ruler greeted visiting Englishmen wearing:

> a Crown of Deares haire colloured red, in fashion of a Rose fastened about his knot of haire, and a great Plate of Copper on the other side of his head, with two long Feathers in fashion of a paire of Hornes placed in the midst of his Crowne. His body was painted all with Crimson, with a Chaine of Beads about his necke, his face painted blew, besprinkled with silver Ore . . . his eares all behung with Braslets of Pearle, and in either eare a Birds Claw through it beset with fine Copper or Gold.

Francisque, a runaway slave in New Orleans, knew what attracted the ladies at Saturday night dances (and roused male rivals' resentments). Carrying a snuffbox and generously paying the drummers, the newcomer arrived dressed "like a Gentleman, [in] ruffled shirt, blue waistcoat, white hat, and wearing three or four handkerchiefs around his neck and elsewhere about him." "Embelishments of Dress & good Breeding" were prominent in Philip Fithian's "reconnoiter" of Elizabeth Lee, a 26-year-old "well-set maid," who:

> sits very erect; places her feet with great propriety, her Hands She lays carelessly in her lap, & never moves them but when she has occasion to adjust some article of her dress, or to perform some exercise of the *Fan*. . . . When She has a Bonnet on & Walks, She is truly elegant; her carriage neat & graceful, & her presence soft & beautiful—Her hair is dark Brown, which was crap'd up very high. & in it she had a Ribbon interwoven with an artificial Flower—At each of her ears dangled a brilliant Jewel.[25]

AILING BODIES

Thomas Hariot, an English naturalist on the expedition to Roanoke, North Carolina, predicted an ominous future for Indian bodies in a colonized New World:

> within a few dayes after our departure from every such Towne, the people began to die very fast, and many in short space, in some Townes about twentie, in some fourtie, and in one sixe score, which in trueth was very manye in respect of their numbers. This happened in no place that wee coulde learne, but where we had bene. . . . The disease also so strange, that they neither knew what it was, nor how to cure it, the like by report of the oldest men in the Countrey never happened before, time out of minde.[26]

Death inadvertently came with Europeans to the New World. In Europe, long-distance trade and warfare, overcrowded filthy cities, and close living with domesticated animals introduced many infectious diseases. People experienced horrific epidemics (the bubonic plague in the 14th century killed one-third of the population), but once exposed, their bodies developed adaptive immunities that made these diseases less lethal and mostly affecting unexposed children.

Precontact America was not disease free, as archeological evidence reveals Indians suffered from salt and protein deficiencies and childhood malnutrition that contributed to spinal disorders, respiratory problems, encephalitis, anemia, tuberculosis, dental decay, hepatitis, intestinal parasites, and venereal syphilis. While debilitating and life shortening, they were not mass killers, and native healers had effective therapies for treating them.

Centuries of biological isolation from the Siberian Alaskan ice barrier and from low population densities meant Indians had no immunities to unknown Old World pathogens and diseases. Utterly vulnerable, virgin soil epidemics of smallpox, measles, typhus, scarlet fever, plague, cholera, diphtheria, and influenza repeatedly swept through Indian villages like scythes, killing half the people in the first wave and reducing populations by 90 percent or more within a century. The number of Powhatans and other Virginia Indians dropped from over 14,000 to less than 2,000 individuals by 1700. Smallpox epidemics reduced by half the Cherokees in 1738 and the Catawbas in 1759, and Florida natives declined from 350,000 to just 1,500 after 200 years. Total Indian population in the colonial South dropped by two-thirds between 1685 and 1730, and by 1775, coastal native peoples numbered in the hundreds not thousands. "From the moment Europeans set foot in America," notes historian Colin Calloway, "hundreds of thousands of Indian people were doomed to die in one of the greatest biological catastrophes in human history."[27] Historians now estimate at least five million people lived north of Mexico at the time of European contact, five times higher than earlier estimates. Europeans mistakenly took a "widowed" land as empty wilderness.

Epidemics struck villagers already weakened from malnutrition, land encroachment, war, displacement, and the social chaos of colonization. Since everyone became sick at once, pandemics reduced subsistence activities and care for the ill, increasing mortality and weakening native resistance to European colonization. Traditional healing practices of bathing, fasting, taking sweat baths, and confining the sick made many illnesses worse and spread communicable diseases more quickly. Returning epidemics of different diseases carried off the unrecovered, suppressed autoimmune systems that increased the likelihood of succumbing to other diseases, and slowed survivors' acquiring immunities. Flight, trade, and migration spread disease beyond exploration parties and colonial settlements; most dying Indians had never seen a European.

Still, the impact of epidemics varied over space and time depending on social and human forces as well as lack of prior exposure. Densely populated farming peoples were especially vulnerable and many groups simply vanished. In 1539, Hernando de Soto saw newly abandoned villages in the Carolina upcountry, and his rampage across the South carried diseases to Mississippi Valley peoples. When the French first arrived in the 1680s, except for the Natchez, great towns had been abandoned when chiefdoms collapsed. Survivors fled to the less diseased interior, where they regrouped into small villages or were absorbed by hill people into new confederacies of Cherokees, Creeks, Catawbas, and Choctaws. Powhatans, who had been exposed to disease from Spanish friars in the 1580s, recovered. Powhatan enlarged his paramount chiefdom by adopting refugees and conquering weaker villages and posed a formidable challenge when the English arrived in 1607.

Neither Europeans nor Indians understood that pathogens caused pandemics, how they spread so quickly, or why they were so deadly, as the germ theory of disease was unknown until the late 19th century. Instead, they sought spiritual explanations: divine punishment when illness struck and God's provenance when striking down enemies. A Virginia planter despaired over extensive illnesses on his plantation in 1710, "These poor people suffer for my sins," he confessed, "God forgive me all my offenses & restore them to their health if it be consistent with His holy will." Evangelist George Whitfield excoriated Charles Town planters' material excesses in 1740 and declared that recent epidemics of smallpox and yellow fever were "Divine judgments lately sent amongst them."[28] Massive Native deaths from epidemics, in contrast, seemingly proved their biological inferiority to Europeans and inability to prosper once God had opened the New World for European civilization.

Indians believed illness originated from taboo violations, witchcraft, angry animal spirits, or unfulfilled dreams. When smallpox first struck the Cherokee, priests explained it was "sent among them, on account of the adulterous intercourses of their young married people, who . . . violated their ancient laws of marriage in every thicket, and broke down and polluted many of the honest neighbours bean-plots."[29] Shamans attributed smallpox—the deadliest killer with its painful sores, rotting flesh, and disfiguring scares—to European sorcery. They looked for invisible bullets that spread death and urged expelling missionaries and traders from villages. Shamans' ineffectual cures and mounting deaths among the old and the young left survivors bereft of elders' wisdom of the past and of children's promise of a future. Many natives lost faith in old traditions; Christianity's greater spiritual power, perhaps, provided a way out of despair.

Europeans fared little better in early settlements as many settlers arrived weak from sickness, hunger, scurvy, and Old World diseases. Unfamiliar foods, novel climates, and unhealthy environments debilitated European bodies and lead to widespread illnesses, food shortages, and premature deaths. The English located Jamestown in a swampy peninsula by the tidal James River that became fetid in summer from reduced flows of freshwater. By August 1607, one leader recorded, "Our men were destroyed with cruell diseases as Swellings, Fluxes, Burning Fevers, and by warres [wars], and some departed suddenly, but for the most part they died of mere famine . . . our drinke [was] cold water taken out of the River, which was at floud [tide] verie salt, at low tide full of slime and filth, which was the destruction of many of our men." Typhoid fever, "the bloody Fluxe" or dysentery, malnutrition, and salt poisoning made joints painful and bodies weaker and contributed to psychological withdrawal and high mortality. Jamestown settlers' alleged laziness and lethargy had physiological not moral origins. Leaving the sick untended, "their bodies trailed out of their Cabines like Dogges to be buried" brought settlers "such dispaire, as they would rather starve and rot with idlenes, then be perswaded to do anything for their owne reliefe without constraint," John Smith recorded. "There is nothing to be gotten here but sickness, and death," an indentured servant wrote, as the environment "Causeth much sickness, as the scurvy and the bloody flux, and divers other diseases, which maketh the bodie very poore and Weake," from overwork and made worse from an insufficient diet of "pease, and loblollie [or water gruel]."[30] Only 1,200 emigrants, a mere 20 percent of the 6,000 arriving in Virginia before 1625, survived.

Chronic illnesses remained high even after settlers dispersed from unhealthy tidal rivers to higher ground with fresh springs and consumed more small grains, vegetables, meat, fowl, game, and cider. Coastal residents suffered from mosquito-borne malaria carried from Europe (*Plasmodium vivax*), and in the 1690s, slaves introduced a more virulent variety (*Plasmodium falciparum*) along with yellow fever and hookworms. Observers blamed settlers' intemperate habits for frequent illnesses, "neglecting to shift their cloaths with the weather" or "eating too plentifully of some delicious fruits," but they acknowledged newcomers experienced "feavers and agues, which is the country distemper, a severe fit of which (called a seasoning) most expect, sometime after their arrival in that climate."[31] Cleared land for tobacco and rice fields, ditches, and millponds created ideal breeding grounds for malaria-carrying mosquitoes, and rice planters built their first houses near swamps to supervise their slaves closely. Ships arrived in Charles Town and other ports with fresh diseases from Europe, Africa, and the West

Indies adding to intestinal infections from poor sanitation, strewn garbage, and wandering hogs.

In the 18th century, yellow fever, smallpox, measles, and influenza epidemics became more frequent and more virulent as populations grew and became denser. Charles Town endured eight outbreaks of yellow fever before 1750. Eight smallpox epidemics struck South Carolina and the Chesapeake region between 1696 and 1763; Charles Town lost over 200 people in 1697–1698, 300 in 1737, and 700 in 1760. Growing trade spread diseases along the Atlantic coast creating overlapping intercolonial epidemics of measles in 1747–1748 and 1759 and influenza in 1748–1749, 1749–1750, and 1761.

Epidemic diseases—which struck with little warning, spread quickly, infected almost everyone, and dispatched many—terrified colonials. Yet, far more people died from endemic diseases, as already weakened bodies became susceptible to new respiratory and intestinal infections. Malaria season ran from late summer through the fall and brought cycles of fevers, chills, nausea, sleeplessness, and general debilitation. One doctor observed: "Carolina is in the spring is a paradise, in the summer a hell, and in the autumn a hospital." Sudden temperature changes during Chesapeake winters brought influenza, or "distempers," a debilitating disease that resulted in depression, "the most fatal of all Diseases in this Climate amongst the Negros and Poor People," one Virginia planter wrote in 1737. "For most colonial inhabitants," medical historian James Cassidy observes, "a considerable measure of suffering from sickness and pain at one time or another was the normal expectation" of daily life.[32] With limited human means for preventing illness or alleviating pain, submission to God's will provided a measure of comfort.

Enslavement wrecked havoc on Africans' bodies. Slave merchants filled their holds with slaves from several ports that spread African malaria, yellow fever, yaws, and dengue fever. European crewmen exposed captives to European smallpox and measles and gonorrhea and syphilis to raped women. Shipboard conditions made widespread illnesses the norm. Most captains were tight packers, who crammed 400 or more slaves into tiny spaces 6 feet long by 16 inches wide and 30 inches high, believing the largest cargoes, despite greater loss of life, produced the highest profits.[33] Slaves were stripped naked, slept on wooden benches with little bedding, men chained together, and only allowed outside twice daily. Stifling holds below decks became cesspools of disease especially fevers, dysentery, and seasickness, a nightmare few forgot. Olaudah Equiano, a child captive, remembered:

> The stench of the hold . . . was so intolerably loathsome . . . absolutely pestilential . . . [and] almost suffocated us . . . the air soon became unfit for respiration, from a variety of loathsome smells, and brought on a sickness among the slaves . . . the filth of necessary tubs, into which the children often fell, and were almost suffocated. The shrieks of the women, and the groans of the dying, rendered it a scene of horror almost inconceivable.

Dr. Alexander Garden, Charles Town's port physician, reported than when visiting newly arrived ships, "I have never yet been on board one that did not smell most offensive and noisome, with for Filth, putrid Air, putrid Dysantries . . . it is a wonder any escape with Life."[34]

Life in the colonial South scarcely improved slaves' health. All arrived debilitated, some barely alive, and were exposed to new diseases especially smallpox. Purchasers assigned adults to back-breaking tasks of clearing forests for tobacco and draining swamps for rice. Long hours of labor sometimes in standing water or rain, scanty clothing and lack of shoes, drafty dirt floor cabins, starchy protein-poor meals prepared outdoors in garbage-strewn yards, and relieving oneself nearby were formulas for bone and joint disorders, respiratory diseases, malnutrition, pellagra, and hookworm. Exposure to virulent malaria and yellow fever in African did give Africans relatively greater immunities as compared to Europeans but hardly compensated for lives of hard labor and material deprivation. Slaves' bodies, owners rationalized, withstood laboring in steamy swamps and hot fields while allegedly superior European bodies could not. Despite inadequate clothing, slaves remained in "perfect health," William Byrd, a Virginia planter, cheerily claimed, and "Negroes which are kept the barest of clothes and bedding are commonly freest from sickness."[35] Plantation graveyards and potter's fields long erased from colonial landscapes and American memory told a different story.

HEALING BODIES

Indian healers developed effective therapies for curing diseases and healing injuries through observation and specialized training, knowledge of human anatomy and medical botany, and skill in harnessing spiritual power. The sick consulted diviners to diagnose serious maladies and wounds and then priest-healers for cures. Rebalancing spiritual forces or expelling malicious spirits that brought illnesses required both physical and spiritual healing. Quarantines, special diets, and physical therapy, such as rubbing, breathing on, or scratching pain sites, brought relief. Difficult illnesses required curing rituals to restore harmony with the spirits and between patients and villagers. Priests chanted, shook rattles, and danced to exorcise evil spirits by invoking their spiritual enemies to "now come to remove the intruder" from ill bodies. Specific conditions believed to cause diseases suggested appropriate therapies. If "unlawful copulation in the night dews" brought smallpox fever, then lying bare-breasted at night might affect cures. But the best medicine was prevention: following social rules and taboos, participating in dances and ceremonies, and maintaining clean bodies through purgatives, sweat baths, and frequent bathing. Powhatans reportedly washed daily in rivers, and Choctaws, according to anthropologist Charles Hudson, purified themselves in "steam cabinets in which are boiled all sorts of medicinal and sweet smelling herbs."[36]

When the plants discovered the animals were conspiring to wage war against humans, the Cherokee recounted, "They determined to defeat the latter's evil designs. Each Tree, Shrub, and Herb, down even to the Grasses and Mosses, agreed to furnish a cure for some one of the diseases named, and each said: 'I shall appear to help Man when he calls upon me in his need.'" Indians gathered local plants thanking them with verbal formulas and gifts, and like modern pharmacies, John Lawson observed, carried "their Compliment of Drugs continually about them, which are Roots, Barks, Berries, Nuts, &ct. that are strung upon a Thread."[37] They used many plants (including sassafras and ginseng) and various barks, roots, leaves, and berries that were crushed, pulverized, or steeped to cleanse wounds, clot blood, reduce inflammation, treat common maladies (like coughs, stomach aches, and intestinal worms), and alleviate pains of asthma, rheumatism, spine, and broken bones. Other plants were prized as purgatives, enemas, expectorants, and abortifacients and for treating insect and snakebites. The Creeks used willow root bark extract, or "red root," as a purgative for malaria, rheumatism, nausea, and fever. Choctaw healers, reported a French traveler, treated wounds by sucking out blood, drawing out pus with snakeroot powder, and dressing with another root powder "to dry and heal the wound, and still other roots . . . in a solution with which the wound is bathed to help prevent gangrene."[38]

European naturalists inventoried native healing plants and adopted them into their own pharmaceutics. Like Indians, they believed that as a divine gift "every country and climate is blest with specific remedies for the maladies that are connatural to it." John Lawson admired Carolina native healers' knowledge and skills including antidotes for rattlesnake bites:

> I have seen such admirable Cures perform'd by these Savages, which would puzzle a great many graduate Practitioners to trace their Steps in Healing, with the same Expedition, Ease, and Success. . . . Amongst all the Discoveries of America, by the Missionaries . . . I wonder none of them was so kind to the World, as to have kept a Catalogue of the Distempers they found the Savages capable of curing, and their method of Cure.[39]

Early European accounts described the New World as a lost paradise promising to restore health. Long after Juan Ponce de León failed to find a "fountain of youth," or miraculous spring, in 1513, the search for wonder cures continued. Unlike Indians, Europeans prized tobacco not for supplicating spiritual helpers before councils and ceremonies but as a miracle drug. Smoking its crushed leaves, an early observer claimed, would "purgeth superfluous fleame & other grosse humors, openeth all the pores & passages of the body: by which meanes the use thereof, not only preserveth the body from obstructions; but also . . . in short time breaketh them: wherby their bodies are notably preserved in health, & know not many greevous diseases where withall wee in England are oftentimes afflicted."[40] Sassafras, ginseng, and rattlesnake root were touted for their curative powers. John Tennent, a Scots doctor living in Virginia, claimed the latter root was not only effective against snakebites but also for curing pleurisy, consumption, gout, dropsy, rabies, fevers, jaundice, smallpox, and more. While his grandiose claims proved unfounded, Indian knowledge of the healing properties of roots, bark, leaves, berries, and herbs and European herbal lore became the foundation for the lotions, syrups, salves, and drinks of Southern folk medicine that was practiced into the 20th century to treat insect bites, poisonings, burns, coughs, colds, indigestion, cuts, and sprains. Modern pharmacology uses over 300 indigenous plants whose medical effects native people first identified. Salicin found in willow bark (*miko hoyanïdja*), which the Cherokee used to relieve pain, has been synthesized as aspirin.

With few trained physicians, their exorbitant fees beyond most settlers' means, and heroic medicine's repeated bleedings, purgings, dosings, and blisterings to restore bodily humors' balance bringing uncertain results, ordinary people turned to popular treatises and folk medicine for self-medication. *Every Man His Own Doctor: Or, The Poor Planter's Physician*, published in Williamsburg in 1734 with many later editions, promised "Plain and Easy Means for Persons to cure themselves of all, or most of the Distempers, incident to this Climate; and with very little Charge, the Medicines being chiefly of the Growth and Production of this Country."[41]

Some New World maladies were believed to have environmental causes arising from "sudden changes of the weather, from heat to cold," according to a Virginia minister, or from the "Multitude of Marshes, Swamps, and great Waters, [which] send forth so many fogs, and Exhalation, that the Air is continually damp."[42] Treatment generally combined bleeding, purging, and blistering to reduce bodily excesses and herbal medicines and moderate diets to restore bodily deficiencies. For pleurisy, the *Planter's Physician* called for removing 10 ounces of blood daily, vomiting by an administration of Indian Physick (*Ipecacuania*), drinking pennyroyal water, taking a honey–linseed oil mixture, applying plaster of Indian pepper and pennyroyal, and for persistent cases, blistering the neck and arms. Applying a truss with "fresh cow dung" and poultices of swamp-lily roots and sumac berries would heal ruptures in children along with a diet of easily digested foods and drink of garden cress and quince syrup. By the 1720s, Jesuit's bark (cinchona) from South America, which contains quinine, was recognized as effective in reducing malarial fevers but was used alongside traditional remedies of bleeding, purging, and administering doses of sassafras root powder, snakeroot, and wormwood. African slaves were quarantined in pest houses on Sullivan's Island outside Charles Town to reduce danger from infectious diseases. After the mid-18th century, inoculation for small pox, which required infecting healthy bodies with pus from pustules of smallpox victims and keeping them under quarantine (with some physicians experimenting on slaves' bodies), proved effective though controversial. Patients developed mild infections with over 95 percent surviving and acquiring immunity against future attacks.

Unlike epidemics, which some people believed were divine punishments, personal behavior was blamed for endemic diseases.

Settlers' "want of timely care, . . . ignorance or obstinacy, . . . [and] especially if they live meanly, drinking too much water, and eaten too much salt meat," Hugh Jones warned resulted in "cachexy (general ill health) [that] generally ends their lives with a dropsy, consumption, the jaundice, or some such illness." Robert Beverley charged new immigrants' "own folly or excesses" for causing their "seasoning" of illness. "Timely Means" the *Planter's Physician* urged mitigated such illnesses; one cannot "hope that Heaven will assist us in our Calamities unless we endeavour, at the same Time, to at assist ourselves." To prevent quinsy, or inflamed throat, wash "your Neck, and behind your Ears, every Morning, in cold Water; nor muffle up your self too warm, either Night or Day." Not sleeping on the ground, wading in cold water, eating copious amounts of fruit, or drinking new cider prevented dysentery; and malaria's effects could be lessened by sweating "out ill digested Humours" in hot months, avoiding chilling "your Bowels too much with cold Water . . . [or] being abroad in the Rain, or in the Dews of the Night . . . sleeping on the Ground, or with your Windows, or Door open, to let the wind blow upon you."[43]

By the mid-18th century, almanacs were another source of popular medical advice. The most widely circulated publications after newspapers, they charted movements of the sun, moon, and zodiac constellations allowing readers to track celestial bodies' influences on their health. They included drawings of male bodies with 12 constellations (Taurus, Cancer, Virgo, etc.), specific body parts (neck, breast, bowels, etc.) each governed, and optimal times for bleeding. In addition to astrological medical information, they reprinted cures for common disorders and treatments for injuries. The *Virginia Almanack for 1753* included "Negro Caesar's Cure for Poisons," a concoction made of steeped plantain and wild horehound roots to be taken for three days with a "spare diet" free of fatty meats or oily foods. Caesar received a 100-pound bounty from the South Carolina legislature for his wonder cure, but made no ironclad guarantees. An illnesses lingering after three days was "a Sign that the Patient has either not been poison'd at all, or that it has been with such Poison as Caesar's Antidotes will not remedy."[44]

Family members' tender care was an essential part of healing. In the 17th century, most servants and slaves and many settlers died alone, and only falling mortality and prolonged family life in the next century made illnesses family concerns. Large planters directly managed their dependents' medical care and kept a supply of decoctions, powders, pills, and draughts on hand. Bleedings and

THE ANATOMY OF MAN'S BODY,
AS GOVERNED BY THE TWELVE CONSTELLATIONS.

♈ *Head & Face.*

♓ *Feet.*

To know where the Sign is, find the day of the month, and against the day in the 4th column, yon have the sign or place of the Moon; then find the sign here, and it will give you what part of the body it governs.

Names and Characters of the Signs of the Zodiac.

♈ (*Arie*) a Ram,
♉ (*Taurus*) a Bull,
♊ (*Gemini*) Twins,
♋ (*Cancer*) a Crab Fish,
♌ (*Leo*) a Lion,
♍ (*Virgo*) a Virgin,
♎ (*Libra*) a Ballance,
♏ (*Scorpio*) a Scorpion,
♐ (*Sagitarius*) Archer,
♑ (*Capricornus*) a Goat,
♒ (*Aquarius*) a Butler,
♓ (*Pisces*) Fish.

Doctor Johnson being asked his opinion of a certain nabob, better known by his riches, than learning. "A mere sheep, sir, with a *golden fleece*," observed the cynic.

Folk healing. Celestial bodies were believed to influence specific areas of the body and determine the best bleeding times to balance bodily humors. The symbols represent signs of the zodiac. Almanacs also included practical information: tables of rising and setting of the sun and moon, calendars marking ideal planting dates and country court sessions, and popular aphorisms. Benjamin Franklin, *Poor Richard's Almanac* [Philadelphia, 1750]. (Library of Congress.)

purging were given as preventatives against influenza and smallpox. Popular English household manuals like *The Compleat Housewife, or Accomplished Gentlewoman's Companion* included medical information and reprinted medical treatises. Female relatives and neighbors nursed the ill and helped with childbirth with the assistance of white and black midwives. Only when mothers became gravely ill were physicians called in.

If self-doctoring proved insufficient, ordinary people turned to ministers, whose reading encompassed physical as well as spiritual healing, and to surgeon-apothecaries for amputations and tooth extractions, treatment of fractures and abscesses, diagnoses of illness, and drug prescriptions.[45] Unlike physicians, whose university degrees made them similar to modern internists, surgeons and apothecaries were general practitioners trained through apprenticeships and personal experience. Without licensing regulations in the colonial South, these separate European guilds merged. Apothecaries imported a few drugs, including mercury and cinchona bark for treating syphilis and malaria, respectively, but most were of local origin. Practitioners generally called on patients in their homes, as medical facilities were limited to plantation hospitals in Carolina, a quarantine house on Sullivan's Island in Charles Town harbor, and military and charity hospitals in New Orleans established by Ursuline nuns in 1723.

Slaves' medical care mixed European and traditional African practices. Planters had an economic self-interest in safeguarding their slaves' health and personally examined injuries and supervised treating illnesses by consulting medical treatises, devising their own treatments, or calling upon British-trained physicians and skilled slaves. Lowcountry slaves often recuperated in plantation hospitals. Older children and elderly women nursed patients; black midwives delivered babies; and, occasionally, trusted slaves, such as Nassau (Landon Carter's man servant and "the best bleeder about" he boasted), treated whites.[46] Planters even hired out skilled slave doctors and midwives and, occasionally, freed slaves who devised valuable cures.

Africans shared with Europeans and Indians belief in plants' curative powers and with the latter recognition of the porous line between healing and conjuring. Native and settler lore added to slaves' stock of healing plants, and slaves sought out root doctors when ill or victimized by sorcery. Africans' knowledge of "several poisonous powders, roots, herbs and simples" and their antidotes both impressed and frightened whites (and many slaves) whose fears it could be used against them were well founded. Even trained doctors like naturalist John Bartram were convinced modern medicine was ineffective against artful slave conjurors' "dreadfull poison" for its power "either to cause Sudden death or lingering."[47] Hundreds of slaves were tried for poisoning—most were acquitted for insufficient evidence—but their victims were as often fellow slaves as whites, targets of interethnic rivalries, African–Creole tensions, or interpersonal conflicts. The traumas of enslavement and the Middle Passage, which uprooted villagers, caused deaths of the great gods and brought unimaginable sorrows, as historian Philip Morgan concludes, unleashed lesser gods' malevolence that empowered the powerless to address their misfortunes.

BURYING BODIES

Death marked the end of an individual's physical existence, but in rupturing the social fabric, it also became the occasion for defining life's meanings. High infant and child mortality, about one-third died before their 10th birthday, lowered life expectancy everywhere in the premodern world to around age 30 at birth. Once reaching adulthood, however, free individuals could expect to live until their mid-50s. Embracing death's ever-present reality, Europeans, Native Americans, and Africans had well-established cultural expectations about proper ways to die and appropriate rituals to console the living and ease transitions of the dead to a spiritual world. Death in the New World, however, became so frequent a companion that it often disrupted "good" deaths.

Diseases, wars, and social disruptions of colonization shortened lives. About one-third of European emigrants to the Chesapeake died within a few years of their arrival. Even men surviving to adulthood typically lived only until their mid-40s and women slightly less from hazards of childbearing, both dying more than 20 years *younger* than adults in New England. Only by the mid-18th century could adults expect to survive to their late 50s. Mortality remained high in the endemic disease environments of semitropical Carolina and Gulf Coast, and only about a third of French and German settlers to Louisiana arriving before 1730 survived. Epidemics, wars, and slave raids decimated native populations, which continued to fall from several million people before contact to under 200,000 by 1685 and in the hundreds in settled areas of English colonies. About one out of every six African captives died in the Middle Passage, and all arrived debilitated. In the Chesapeake, about one-quarter died in the first year, one-third in the Lowcountry, and another quarter within 10 years. One-third of Creole children died before age 4, and adult slave life spans were at least 10 years shorter than for whites.

Devout Protestants and Catholics were expected to face death with professions of faith, submissions to God's unknown purposes, and promises of a future better life. "This life here," a young planter assured his mother, is "as but going to an inn, no permanent being by God's will . . . therefore [I] am always prepared for my certain Dissolution, wch. I ca'nt be perswaded to prolong by a wish." Even a child's death must be "easily & cheerfully born, if natural affection be laid aside," he continued, as this "troublesome & uncertain terrestrial being" would now experience a "certain & happy Celestial habitation."[48] As mortality fell and family life became more settled with deeper emotional ties, containing sorrow over loss of a spouse or child, especially for women, became more difficult. Death of "the best and tenderist of husbands," a planter's widow wrote to her brother:

> is so great an affliction to me, that I han't words to express it. I know it is my duty as a christian, to bear patiently whatever happens to me, by the allotment of divine providence, and I humbly beseech Almighty God, to grant me his grace, that I may be enabled to submit patiently, to whatever trialls it may please him to lay one me . . . but that I may bear them as a good Christian, with courage and resolution, with calmness and resignation.

"Good deaths" occurred at home surrounded by family members who took special meaning in the last words of the dying. Our sister spent "her last breath in prayers for all her relations and acquaintances," a brother wrote to absent siblings, "and in blessing me and my little family, one by one, as we stood in tears around her."[49]

Prescribed prayers, collects, scripture readings, and, often, funeral sermons, historian John K. Nelson argues, placed "the reality of death in the context of the faith and teaching of the church with its proclamation of resurrection and another life beyond death." Household members held vigils over the deceased until placed in a wooden coffin and carried to the churchyard cemetery, which was surrounded by a low wall to keep wandering hogs from uprooting bodies. For common folk, a clergyman or parish clerk or lay reader, if no minister was available, read a simple burial service at graveside with family members and neighbors present. Women bore responsibility for visiting the bereaved. By the 18th century, according to a contemporary, wealthy planters established private cemeteries "in gardens or orchards, where whole family members lye interred together, in as spot generally handsomely enclosed, planted with evergreens, and the graves kept decently."[50] Before funeral services, which occurred several weeks or even months after burial, family members, neighbors, and friends gathered at homes for food and drink, which some critics thought turned into occasions of "noise feasting drink or Tumult." Funeral sermons at services for prominent individuals, paid by the family, were not eulogies, according to John K. Nelson, but reminders to listeners "on the right uses of time, true repentance, and righteous living, a call to faithful attendance upon one's religious duties, and vigorous affirmation of the promised resurrection."[51]

Indians' mortuary rituals eased separation of the dead from the living, facilitated spirits' journeys, and repaired breaks in the social fabric. Treatment of the dead varied by gender, social status, and manner of death. Clan members supervised preparing bodies and burial arrangements, honoring the dead, and mourning processes. Bodies of common people were wrapped in skins or mats and either buried with personal possessions inside houses in stake-lined graves or placed on scaffolds three feet high to ward off animal predators before final internment. Relatives praised male relatives' brave deeds and personal character. Women with blackened faces mourned with loud cries to chase ghosts off into the Western sky lest they haunt or bring sickness to the living. Proper care for the dead was essential for psychological and physical health of the living, and Indians made great effort to retrieve those killed in raids or hunts to prevent bodies from being devoured by animals or dismembered by enemies. During prolonged mourning, spouses left their hair unkempt and wore old clothes. After four annual green corn ceremonies, Creek widows—unless released by kinsmen to marry into the deceased spouse's lineage or eloping successfully—were purified, given new clothes, danced with villagers, and became eligible to remarry.

High-status men received public funeral ceremonies, pleasurable afterlives, and second burials in temples. After a short period of family mourning, priests supervised wrapping bodies in skins, blankets, or mats; placement in cane coffins with personal possessions needed for journeys to the spirit world; and processions to high scaffolds for public ceremonies where villagers, lineage members of the deceased, and allied villagers gathered. Professional mourners "cry and lament over the dead Man," John Lawson reported. Lengthy funeral orations praised the deceased's skills as a hunter, bravery in war, generosity, and noble character, "After which, he . . . bids them supply the dead Man's Place, by following his steps, who, . . . is gone into the Country of Souls, . . . and that he will have the Enjoyment of handsome young Women, great Store of Deer to hunt, never meet with Hunger, Cold or Fatigue, but every thing to answer his Expectation and Desire."[52] Speeches ended with tribal histories followed by celebratory feasts that renewed social ties and tribal alliances. Bodies were either left on scaffolds or buried taking care no earth touched the corpse to avoid pollution. Kinsmen mourned and wept in blackened faces, and villagers left offerings of tobacco, pipes, game, and food. After the flesh had dried or decomposed, bones were cleansed, hung with jewelry, and either wrapped in dressed deerskins or, among Algonquians, placed inside embalmed skins and put in baskets on raised shelves in temples alongside ancestors' remains. The Natchez, a late Mississippian mound-building culture, accorded their Suns even higher honors with the deceased dressed in fine clothes to lay in state, an elaborate procession to their personal temple, and voluntary suicides of surviving spouses, favorite servants, and other close relatives as devotional acts and to be companions in the spirit world.

Male war captives, torn from their lineages, met far different deaths. Taken in revenge raids to replace someone who had been killed, men (villagers usually adopted women and children to replace dead relatives) were stripped naked and tied to stakes. Everyone joined in or watched the contest of wills. Sharp mussel shells slowly flayed and cut off body parts that were burned and "others split the Pitch-Pine into Splinters, and stick them into the Prisoners Body yet alive . . . [and] light them, which burn like so many Torches; and . . . make him dance round a great Fire, every one buffeting and deriding him."[53] The captive sought to play his role well by deriding his torments with mocking death songs. Only stoic deaths, inured to insults, preserved warriors' honor and prevented their spirits from haunting relatives.

African burial rituals marked journeys from the physical to the spiritual world where ancestors, villagers believed, would "attend them, and guard them from the bad spirits or their foes."[54] Conceptions of the afterlife varied: the Kongo, for example, located the underworld in lake bottoms and riverbeds; among Afro-Christians, death became "passing over" the River Jordan. Each ethnic group had its own particular funerary customs, but rulers received much more elaborate rituals than common villagers. Failure to follow prescribed rites caused spirits of the deceased to linger and harm the living. Burials involved washing and wrapping bodies in fine cloths or mats; wakes marked by wailing cries of women, who shaved their heads and painted faces white and repeated the deceased's name and deeds; processions to graves; and nighttime interments. Pipes, tobacco, pots for food and drink, stools, jewelry, and other personal items were buried with the deceased or decorated graves to aid souls' journeys to the ancestors. Later, a second funeral with animal sacrifices and drumming, dancing, and feasting celebrated the deceased's successful entrance to the spirit world. Ancestors needed propitiation with ritual offerings of food and drink and nighttime visits to graves with lamentations and libations. Since persons held in servitude in Africa had been removed from their birth lineages, their spirits posed no harm, and no family members mourned their passing. But the Atlantic slave trade's casual wastage of human life, with dead bodies piled up in trade posts' dungeons and slave ships' holds and bodies dumped en masse into graves or thrown overboard without ceremony, was another one of its many barbarities.

Slaves resisted enslavement's social death by maintaining African dying rites. Some attempted suicide in the Middle Passage and refused to eat (kept alive only by force feeding) or jumped overboard hoping to evade restraining nets and recapture and drown themselves. Such deaths brought release from bondage, return to ancestors, and rebirth in homelands. Africans, especially Koromanti and Igbo, an Anglican missionary observed, believed "that when they die, they are translated to their own countrey, there to live in their former free condition." In the Lowcountry, another minister stated, slaves "frequently take their own lives out of desperation, with the hope of resurrection in their homeland, and of rejoining their people."[55]

Slave communities gathered at night to bury their dead with personal objects, like glass beads, necklaces, tobacco pipes, and the last used set of plates, glasses, and spoons; placed strings of beads and seeds on wooden coffins; decorated graves with seashells, upturned bottles, and broken pottery to free spirits to follow the deceased; and made periodic food offerings. At a private ceremony by one slave couple, the father, an African priest, added personal tokens and necessities for their infant child's homeward journey, including:

> a small bow and several arrows; a little bag of parched meal; a miniature canoe, about a foot long, and a little paddle, (with which he said it would cross the ocean to his own country) a small stick, with an iron nail, sharpened, and fastened onto one end of it; and a piece of white muslin, with several curious and strange figures painted on it in blue and red, by which, he said, his relations and countrymen would know the infant to be his son, and would receive it accordingly, on its arrival amongst them. . . . He cut a lock of hair from his head, threw it upon the dead infant, and closed the grave with his own hands. . . . the God of his country was looking at him, and was pleased with what he had done.[56]

Burials took place soon after deaths, a necessity in the South's semitropical environment. Boisterous funeral celebrations followed several weeks later usually at night when slaves could gather away from whites, and in Charles Town, noisy funeral processions marched through the streets. At these large gatherings, relatives and friends made "merry for the dead" with music, dancing, feasting, and drinking that eased the deceased's journey to the ancestors, assuaged the living's personal losses, and healed ruptures in the social fabric. In marking the final but most important transition in everyday life, a part of Africa lived on in the colonial South.

COLONIAL BODIES

Colonization altered bodies, which, in turn, became sites for new patterns of daily life. Persistently high mortality turned the paradise of European imaginings into colonial graveyards that decimated native lineages and villages. It made immigrants' lives more precarious by making marriages infrequent and shorter, families smaller, population growth slower, and religious and political institutions weaker. Death intruded on life with the pressing need to cure new illnesses, repair fissures in the social fabric, care for orphaned children, and maintain good deaths to ensure proper afterlives and assuage the living. Sick or dying workers left crops untended and increased malnutrition and planters' economic losses. Falling mortality, however, made enslaved Africans more lucrative investments than servants, speeding the transition to a slave-based plantation economy that decimated African bodies and created a social chasm between the new superrich and everyone else. Colonial Southerners' bodies *looked* different. After returning to Maryland, Alexander Hamilton, a doctor, was struck by the sickly "washed countenances of the people standing at their doors . . . for they looked like so many staring ghosts."[57]

New ways of perceiving and using bodies developed in the colonial South's cultural mix. Encountering in their everyday lives an unprecedented array of previously unseen bodies—English, Scots-Irish, German, African, and Indian—colonial Southerners considered new ideas about the origins and significance of human diversity and the meaning of their own identities. Bodies were sites for asserting new personal styles by acquiring wigs, braiding a daughter's hair, or using trade goods as jewelry. Restrained bodily movements—learning the right gestures, walking with upright posture, and dancing with controlled movements (as in a minuet)—became physical accoutrements of gentility. Social pretenders adopted upper-class styles or created new bodily poses by adopting Indian hairstyles, strutting walks, and cutting stares as forms of resistance. The appearance of the physical body and use of body language became intrinsic to everyday life, signifiers of freedom and of enslavement, the genteel and the common, and arrival of the individual self.

NOTES

1. Richard Eden, "The Life and Labours of Richard Eden," in *The First Three English Books on America*, ed. by Edward Arber (Birmingham, Eng.: Author, 1885), cited in Joyce E. Chaplin, "Climate and Southern Pessimism: The Natural History of an Idea, 1500–1800," in *The South as an American Problem*, ed. by Larry J. Griffin and Don H. Doyle (Athens: University of Georgia Press, 1995), 66.

2. Thomas C. Holt, "Of Blood and Power: An Introduction," *William and Mary Quarterly*, 3rd ser., 61, no. 3 (2004): 436. The context of the quote concerns racially mixed offspring.

3. Christopher Columbus, *The Journal of Christopher Columbus, 1493*, trans. by Cecil Jane and revised by L.A. Vigneras (London: Hakluyt Society, 1960), cited in Robert F. Berkhofer, *The White Man's Indian: Images of the American Indian from Columbus to the Present* (New York: Vintage Books, 1979), 7 and Alexander Whitaker, *Good Newes from Virginia* (London: Felix Kyngston, 1613), cited in ibid., 19, 20.

4. Thomas Jefferson, *Notes on the State of Virginia*, ed. by William Peden (Chapel Hill: University of North Carolina Press, 1959), 62. Jefferson praised male Indian bravery and oratory and attributed lower native fertility to women's physical labor, accompanying men on winter hunts, and use of abortifacients.

5. John Lawson, *A New Voyage to Carolina* (London, 1709), Project

Gutenberg Etext, July 1999, http://www.gutenberg.org/dirs/etext99/nvycr10.txt, 137; William Byrd, "The History of the Dividing Line," in *The Prose Works of William Byrd of Westover: Narratives of a Colonial Virginian*, ed. by Louis B. Wright (Cambridge, MA: Harvard University Press, 1966), 218; William Byrd, "The Secret History of the Line," in *Prose Works*, 60; see illustrations on pp. 186 and 289.

6. Berkhofer, *White Man's Indian*, 13 and Christopher Columbus, Journal, 1493, cited in ibid., 7.

7. Edward Waterhouse, "A Declaration of the State of the Colonie and . . . A Relation of the Barbarous Massacre," in *The Records of the Virginia Company of London*, 4 vols., ed. by Susan Myra Kingsbury (Washington, D.C.: Government Printing Office, 1906–1935), 3: 551, 562. Waterhouse cited Gonzalo Fernádez de Oviedo, *The Natural History of the Indians* (Toledo, 1526).

8. "The First Voyage of Robert Baker to Guinie . . . 1562, in Richard Hakluyt, *The Principal Navigations, Voiages and Discoveries of the English Nation . . . (London, 1589)*, cited in Winthrop D. Jordan, *White over Black: American Attitudes toward the Negro, 1550–1812* (Baltimore, MD: Penguin Books, 1969), 4, 5; ibid, 7; Francis Moore, *Travels into the Inland Parts of Africa* (London: Edward Cave, 1738), cited in ibid, 10; George Best, "Experiences and Reasons of the Sphere, . . . ," Hakluyt, *Principal Navigations*, cited in Jordan, *White over Black*, 15; and "Second Voyage to Guinea," (1554), in Hakluyt, *Principal Navigations*, cited in Jordan, *White over Black*, 24.

9. Ibid., 233.,

10. [Edward Kimber], "Itinerant Observations in America," *London Magazine* (July 1735), cited in Peter Wood, *Black Majority: Negroes in Colonial South Carolina from 1670 through the Stono Rebellion* (New York: W.W. Norton and Company, 1975), 279 and Charles Wesley, *The Journal of the Rev. Charles Wesley*, (London: Wesleyan Methodist Book-Room London, 1849), cited in ibid.

11. Nancy Shoemaker, *A Strange Likeness: Becoming Red and White in Eighteenth-Century North America* (New York: Oxford University Press, 2004), 127.

12. Jefferson, *Notes on the State of Virginia*, 138, 139.

13. Jennifer M. Spear, "Colonial Intimacies: Legislating Sex in French Louisiana," *William and Mary Quarterly*, 3rd ser., 60, no. 1 (2003): 95.

14. *Archives of Maryland* (Baltimore, 1883–), cited in Jordan, *White over Black*, 79.

15. Military Journal of Lt. William Feltman, entry of June 22, 1781, cited in Jordan, *White over Black*, 159 and Letter from Peter Fontaine to Moses Fontaine, March 30, 1757, cited in Philip D. Morgan, *Slave Counterpoint: Black Culture in the Eighteenth-Century Chesapeake and Lowcountry* (Chapel Hill: University of North Carolina Press, 1998), 399.

16. Philip Vickers Fithian, *Journal and Letters of Philip Vickers Fithian, a Plantation Tutor of the Old Dominion*, ed. by Hunter Dickinson Farish

(Charlottesville: University Press of Virginia, 1968 [1957]), entries for March 27, September 5, 1774, 86, 184 and *South Carolina Gazette*, 1739, cited in Jordan, *White over Black*, 146.

17. Douglass Adair, ed., "The Autobiography of the Reverend Devereux Jarratt, 1732–1763," *William and Mary Quarterly*, 3rd ser., 9, no. 3 (1952): 361, 367.

18. George Percy, "A Discourse of the Plantation of the Southern Colonie in Virginia (1606–1607)," in *Envisioning America: English Plans for the Colonization of North America, 1580–1640*, ed. by Peter C. Mancall (Boston: Bedford/St. Martin's, 1995), 123; see illustrations on pp. 51, 88, and 186.

19. Letter from Molly Tilghman to Polly Pearce, [n.d.], cited in Julia Cherry Spruill, *Women's Life and Work in the Southern Colonies* (New York: W.W. Norton and Company, 1972 [1938]), 135.

20. Percy, "Discourse," 119; John Brickell, *The Natural History of North Carolina* (Dublin: James Carson, 1737), 284; see illustrations on pp. 60 and 88.

21. *Virginia Gazette* (Hunter), Williamsburg, VA, July 25, 1751; see illustration on p. 105.

22. *South Carolina Gazette and Country Journal, (Charles Town)* August 30, 1774, cited in Shane White and Graham White, "Slave Hair and African American Culture in the Eighteenth and Nineteenth Centuries," *Journal of Southern History* 61, no. 1 (1995): 62.

23. See illustrations on pp. 105, 186, and 220.

24. Letter from John Pory to Sir Dudley Carleton, September 30, 1619, in Warren Billings, ed., *The Old Dominion in the Seventeenth Century, a Documentary History of Virginia, 1606–1689* (Chapel Hill: University of North Carolina Press, 1975), 305.

25. Percy, "Discourse," 119, 120; Testimony of Demoirité, Records of the Superior Council of Louisiana, 1766, cited in Sophie White, " 'Wearing Three or Four Handkerchiefs Around His Collar, and Elsewhere About Him': Slaves Constructions of Masculinity and Ethnicity in French Colonial New Orleans," *Gender & History* 15, no. 3 (2003): 536; and Fithian, *Journal and Letters*, entry for July 4, 1776, 130, 131.

26. Thomas Hariot, *A Briefe and True Report of the New Found Land of Virginia* (London: Theodore de Bry, 1590), 28, cited in *Documenting the American South* (Chapel Hill: University of North Carolina, 2003), http://docsouth.unc.edu/nc/hariot/hariot.html.

27. Table 2; Peter Wood, "The Changing Population of the Colonial South: An Overview by Race and Region, 1685–1790," in *Powhatan's Mantle: Indians in the Colonial Southeast*, ed. by Gregory A. Waselkov, Peter H. Wood, and Tom Hatley, rev. and exp. ed. (Lincoln: University of Nebraska Press, 2006), 60, 61; and Colin G. Calloway, *New Worlds for All: Indians, Europeans, and the Remaking of Early America* (Baltimore, MD: Johns Hopkins University Press, 1997), 33.

28. William Byrd, *William Byrd Diary, 1709–1712*, cited in Daniel Blake Smith, *Inside the Great House: Planter Family Life in Eighteenth-Century Ches-*

apeake Society (Ithaca, NY: Cornell University Press, 1980), 256 and George Whitefield, *George Whitefield's Journals, 1737–1741,* entry for January 6, 1740 (Gainesville, FL: Scholars' Facsimiles & Reprints, 1969 [1756]), 382.

29. James Adair, *The History of the American Indians,* ed. by Kathryn E. Holland Braund (Tuscaloosa: University of Alabama Press, 2005 [1775]), in American Memory, *The First American West: The Ohio River Valley, 1750–1830* (Washington, D.C.: Library of Congress, n.d.), 232.

30. Percy, "Discourse," 125, 126; John Smith, *True Relation of Such Occurrences and Accidents as Hath Hapned in Virginia,* in Philip L. Barbour, *The Jamestown Voyages* (Cambridge, 1969), cited in Karen Ordahl Kupperman, "Apathy and Death in Early Jamestown," *Journal of American History* 66, no. 1 (June 1979), 28; and Letter from Richard Frethorne to his parents, 1623, in Kingsbury, ed., *Records of the Virginia Company,* 4: 58, 59.

31. Hugh Jones, *The Present State of Virginia* (Chapel Hill: University of North Carolina Press, 1956), 84, 85.

32. Johann David Schoepf, *Travels in the Confederation [1783–1784],* trans. and ed. by Alfred J. Morrison (Philadelphia, PA: W.J. Campbell, 1911), 172, (http://www.archive.org/details/travelsinconfede00schuoft); Letter from William Byrd to Sr. Hans Sloane, 1737, cited in John Duffy, *Epidemics in Colonial America* (Baton Rouge: Louisiana State University Press, 1953), 200; and James H. Cassidy, *Medicine in America: A Short History* (Baltimore: Johns Hopkins University Press, 1991), 12.

33. See illustration on p. 115.

34. Olaudah Equiano, *The Interesting Narrative of the Life of Olaudah Equiano,* 2nd ed., ed. by Robert J. Allison (Boston: Bedford/St. Martin's, 2007), 66, 67; Edmund Berkeley and Dorothy Smith Berkeley, *Dr. Alexander of Charles Town* (Chapel Hill: University of North Carolina Press, [1969]), cited in Morgan, *Slave Counterpoint,* 444.

35. William Byrd, "A Progress to the Mines," in *Prose Works,* 349, 350.

36. Charles Hudson, *The Southeastern Indians* (Knoxville: University of Tennessee Press, 1976), 347; Adair, *History of the American Indians,* 232; Jean-Bernard Bossu, cited in Calloway, *New Worlds for All,* 32; see illustration on p. 94.

37. Hudson, *Southeastern Indians,* 159 and Lawson, *New Voyage to Carolina,* 11.

38. Bossu, cited in Calloway, *New Worlds for All,* 30.

39. Adair, *History of the American Indians,* 234 and Lawson, *New Voyage to Carolina,* 17, 166.

40. Hariot, *A Briefe and True Report,* 16.

41. Anon., *Every Man His Own Doctor: Or, The Poor Planter's Physician* (Williamsburg, VA, 1734). This treatise has long been attributed to John Tennent, but recent studies have questioned this.

42. Jones, *Present State of Virginia,* 84 and *Every Man His Own Doctor,* frontispiece, 4.

43. Jones, *Present State of Virginia,* 85; Robert Beverley, *The History and Present State of Virginia,* ed. by David Freeman Hawke (Indianapolis:

Bobbs-Merrill Company, 1971 [1705]), 162; and *Every Man His Own Doctor,* 5, 7, 12, 29.

44. Theophilus Grew, *The Virginia Almanack for the Year of our Lord God 1753* (Williamsburg, VA: William Hunter, [1752]).

45. John Wesley, founder of Methodism, published a popular medical treatise, *Primitive Physic* (Philadelphia, PA: Andrew Steuart, 1764), which went through many editions.

46. Landon Carter, *The Diary of Colonel Landon Carter of Sabine Hall, 1752–1778,* 2 vols., ed. by Jack P. Greene (Charlottesville: University Press of Virginia, 1965), cited in Morgan, *Slave Counterpoint,* 324.

47. Trial of Tom, Caroline County, Virginia, Order Book, 1740–1746, cited in Morgan, *Slave Counterpoint,* 616 and John Bartram, *Diary of a Journey through the Carolinas, Georgia, and Florida from July 1, 1765, to April 10, 1766,* ed. by Francis Harper, American Philosophical Society, *Transactions of the American Philosophical Society* 33, no. 1 (December 1942): 22.

48. Letter from William Fitzhugh to Mary Fitzhugh, June 30, 1698, cited in Smith, *Inside the Great House,* 261.

49. Letter from Mary Bland Lee to Theodorick Bland, Sr., March 1, 1748, cited in John K. Nelson, *A Blessed Company: Parishes, Parsons, and Parishioners in Anglican Virginia, 1690–1776* (Chapel Hill: University of North Carolina Press, 2001), 227 and Letter from Peter Fontaine to John and Moses Fontaine, March 2, 1756, cited in Smith, *Inside the Great House,* 278.

50. Nelson, *A Blessed Company,* 227 and Jones, *Present State of Virginia,* 97.

51. Will of William Fitzhugh, Stafford County, Virginia, December 10, 1701, *Ancestry.com,* http://boards.ancestry.com/thread.aspx?mv=flat&m=181&p=surnames.fitzhugh and Nelson, *A Blessed Company,* 229.

52. Lawson, *New Voyage to Carolina,* 135, 136.

53. Ibid., 148.

54. Equiano, *Interesting Narrative,* 51.

55. Letter from Rev. Philip Reading to Rev. Samuel Smith, October 10, 1748, cited in Morgan, *Slave Counterpoint,* 641 and Johann Martin Bolzius, "Johann Martin Bolzius Answers a Questionnaire on Carolina and Georgia," *William and Mary Quarterly,* 3rd ser., 14, no. 2 (1957): 233.

56. Charles Ball, *Fifty Years in Chains* (New York: Dover Publications, 1970 [1837]), 265.

57. Alexander Hamilton, *Gentleman's Progress: The Itinerarium of Dr. Alexander Hamilton, 1744,* ed. by Carl Bridenbaugh (Chapel Hill: University of North Carolina Press, 1975), 198.

8

BELIEFS

For most of the 20th century, the South was a stronghold of evangelical Christianity as most Southerners, black and white, according to historian Samuel Hill, shared core beliefs in "(1) the Bible as the sole reference point; (2) direct and intimate access to the Lord; (3) Christian morality defined in the terms of individualistic and interpersonal ethics; [and] (4) informal, spontaneous patterns for worship."[1] Conversion (or personal acceptance of God's promise of salvation to unworthy sinners) and baptism (a rite of passage into a new Christian life of moral uprightness) are central religious experiences for evangelical Southerners. Spiritual beliefs and practices in the colonial South, in contrast, were marked by variety not homogeneity, by transatlantic not parochial contexts, and by fluidity not rigidity. Not only were there enormous differences between Europeans, Africans, and Native Americans but also diverse practices within each of these groups. European church establishments and spiritual leadership weakened in the early decades of settlement, but after 1680, non-English emigrants and new religious movements crossed the Atlantic strengthening religious commitment and diversity. Despite the horrors of Native American population decline and African enslavement and Middle Passage, both groups retained core beliefs that gave structure and meaning for living under radically new circumstances. A few adopted some aspects of Christianity into their traditions and forged new Pan-Indian or

Pan-African religions, seedbeds for revitalization movements after the American Revolution.

Religion answers basic questions of daily life: *How shall I live? What is my relationship to the transcendent? How is spirituality expressed in everyday life?* Through sacred rituals—prayers, visions, divination, dances, and liturgies—individuals sought connection to the supernatural world and interceded spirits on behalf of themselves or their group. They not only relied on spiritual specialists, shamans, priests, and conjurers, but also followed folk practices and shared occult knowledge. Religion provided moral guidance in defining social norms and obligations with others and with the natural world that made community life possible and undergirded existing social structures. Creation stories defined collective identities and for Christians, Jews, and Muslims narrated the future as well as the past. Religion was a prism through which Europeans, Indians, and Africans encountered and sought to understand one another.

INHERITANCES

Europeans emphasized the religious gulf between themselves and peoples of North America and Africa. Certain of their faith's inerrancy, they condemned native beliefs as pagan devil-worship. Alexander Whitaker, a Virginia minister best known for converting Pocahontas, described Powhatans as "naked slaves of the divell" who "acknowledge that there is a great good God, but know him not, having the eyes of their understanding as yet blinded: wherefore they serve the divell for feare, after a most base manner, sacrificing . . . their own children to him. . . . Their priests . . . are no other but such as our English witches are." Thomas Herbert, a 17th-century English traveler, used similar language to describe Africans who "in colour so in condition are little other than Devils incarnate . . . [as] the Devil . . . has infused prodigious Idolatry into their hearts, enough to rellish his pallat and aggrandize their tortures when he gets power to fry their souls, as the raging Sun has already scorcht their cole-black carcasses."[2] Wild-men, savages, infidels, heathens, and barbarians were interchangeable descriptors for natives on both continents.

Indian and African reactions to Christianity are filtered through European accounts, but except for the Kongo kingdom's conversion to Catholicism in the early 16th century, Christianity's emphasis on a wrathful God, original sin, and hell's torments impressed few natives or Africans. Even when incorporating Christian rituals as new ways for manipulating the spirits, shamans claimed priests were malevolent demons bearing incurable diseases and pointed out the gap between Christian beliefs and settlers' deeds.

Still, similarities in spiritual beliefs allowed for intercultural dialogue. Aware of human frailty and limited in understanding many natural events, ordinary people turned to the transcendent to order the world and understand life's mysteries. Lines between the sacred and the secular were blurred compared to the modern world, and supernatural powers were believed to intervene in human affairs. Divine dispensation explained personal success or victory over enemies. Divination, witchcraft, cunning folk's spiritual power, and species shifting explained unnatural events and misfortunes like birth defects, sudden illnesses, livestock deaths, harvest failures, and hurricanes. Only in the late 17th century did educated people question Satan's power to appear in disguise, possess individuals, or empower people to work mischief or even cause death. Dreams had special significance as omens requiring interpretation. Spiritual leaders with specialized training conducted elaborate ceremonies that combined chants, prayers, sacred texts, music, and, often, sacred dance. Rituals invoked the divine, delineated liturgical calendars, reinforced moral norms, and sustained community. The landscape itself was sanctified with temples, churches, ceremonial grounds, and sacred places: healing springs, saints' shrines, mountains, lakes, and cave entrances to the underworld.

Native Americans

Indians lived in a world where nonhuman persons—the Sun, animals, plants, rivers, thunder, and more—were invested with personalities and spiritual power. This contentious world of powerful spirits required ritual precautions to avoid offense lest they caused harm yet also provided opportunities to harness their power for success in daily life. Deer hunters apologized for sacrificing lives and offered first kills or entrails. Failure to do so or wantonly killing excess game risked angering deer ghosts, who would then warn off other deer or cause hunters to contract rheumatism. "All the *Indians* hereabouts carefully preserve the Bones of the Flesh they eat, and burn them," a traveler to Carolina observed, "as being of the Opinion, that if they omitted that Custom, the Game would leave their Country, and they should not be able to maintain themselves by their Hunting."[3] The Sun, like a grandparent, was treated with respect by throwing food and meat into fires or offering prayers at sunrise and sunset. Birds were spirit helpers with traits humans emulated. Seeking to acquire the falcon's ability to kill game with single blows, Cherokee hunters applied face paint and dressed as falcons in prehunt dances. Indians' awareness of the interdependency with the natural world did *not* make them modern-day environmentalists. Their connection was spiritual not ecological and marked by uncertainty not harmony. Ritual preparation and restraint were essential to maintain delicate balance with nature and avoid misfortunes from spirits' retribution.

Creation stories used kinship language to personify relationships with spiritual beings and connected past and present with sacred places. Cherokees prayed to Corn Mother for good harvests; annually relit sacred fires, grandmother Sun's earthly allies; and supplicated Red Man and Little Red Men, his sons, for protection against storms. Supernatural animals created the world. According to the Powhatans, Great Hare made women and men. When the four Great Giants (the winds of the four directions), threatened to eat them, he retaliated by filling the world with many deer and releasing the people, assigning each man and woman to their own country. Places of spiritual power linked Ancient Time, when rules of everyday life were suspended, and Recent Time, when humans lived. Little People, mischievous invisible spirits similar to Irish leprechauns, left footprints in a cave near the head of the Oconaluftee River in the Smoky Mountains, and the game preserve of Kanati (First Hunter and husband of Salu, Corn Mother) was a cave on Black Mountain, North Carolina.

To Indians, the cosmos was filled with contending forces, and maintaining balance between them was essential to sustain harmony. The human world was precariously caught between the upperworld of sky beings that represented order, predictability, and the past and the underworld of ghosts and monsters that brought disorder, change, and the future. Upperworld beings were helpers: the Sun brought fire and the Moon fertility from rain and menstruation. Cardinal directions were paired opposites with symbolic meanings. According to anthropologist Charles Hudson, the Cherokee believed "the east was the direction of the Sun, the color red, sacred fire, blood, and life and success," while "its opposite, the west, was associated with the Moon, the souls of the dead, the color black, and death."[4] Similarly opposed were North (cold, blue, trouble, and defeat) and South (warmth, white, peace, and happiness). Categorical thinking also applied to plants (human's friends) versus animals (human's enemies); birds (upperworld), and animals (this world), and snakes (underworld); four-legged and two-legged animals; fire and water; and women and men.

Preventing misfortune required avoiding pollution from mixing elements from two different categories. Fires were extinguished with dirt not water. Two-legged and four-legged animals were never eaten together. Menstrual blood flowed outside women's bodies; best to isolate them in special huts apart from villagers. Yet things with attributes of different categories also possessed symbolic and spiritual importance. Bears are four-legged animals that can walk on two legs like men; no permission is needed to kill them. Laurel keeps its leaves all year and has healing powers. Uktena combined a body of a snake (associated with the underworld), antlers of a deer (who live in this world), and wings of a bird (an upperworld being). Cherokee feared this fabulous creature, which lived in deep river pools and in high-mountain passes, bewitched people with its eyes and tongue, and whose breath meant death. These anomalies explained imperfections in nature and warned of the dire consequences of breaking rules.

Propitiating gods and spirits with gifts was another way to avoid ill luck. Before journeys, Powhatans made burnt offerings of tobacco to the Sun for good weather and threw tobacco, puccoon (red body paint), and peak (shell beads) into swollen rivers for safe passage. Paramount chiefdoms had supreme deities that resided in temples tended by full-time priests. Okeus, the Powhatans' chief god, lived in a multiroom house 60 feet long at Uttamussak along with the sacred fire, bones of high-status persons, and valuable presents. He appeared to priests in the "forme of a personable Virginian [i.e., a Powhatan], with a long blacke locke on the left side, hanging down neere to the foote" and was represented in temples by carved painted wooden statues decorated with multicolored cloth and a fine pearl necklace.[5] Okeus sternly watched over individuals, and only priests entered his temple and conferred with him using sacred speech unintelligible to ordinary people, much like Latin in Catholic rituals. Okeus predicted the future, including, it was said, the arrival of the English. Presents avoided his displeasure and at his altar stone worshippers left tobacco; the first fruits of horticulture, gathering, and hunting; and offerings giving thanks for success. They performed sacred dances around a circle of tall posts with painted face carvings on top. Like European monarchs, the Great Sun of the Natchez combined spiritual and political power. He ruled atop a man-made mound that held his house, chief temple with the sacred fire, and ceremonial plaza for rituals and ball games.

Following well-known rules of daily life usually avoided misfortune, but when events happened for unknown reasons or crises arose when the world was out of balance, people consulted shamans and priests, who possessed extraordinary abilities to interpret and manipulate invisible forces.[6] Gifted youths underwent rigorous training by elders to acquire special knowledge, songs, prayers, and sacred objects that cured illness, interpreted dreams, uncovered meanings of thunder and bird cries, secured desired lovers, located stolen objects, predicted the future, exacted revenge on enemies, and warded off witches. Priests healed broken relationships, manipulated the weather, and brought success in hunting, war, and ball games. Indians believed souls left their bodies during sleep to visit spirits, who communicated their desires in dreams and warned of future danger. Reenacting events of dreams released their spiritual power and avoided misfortune.

By entering the spirit world through ecstatic trances, priests diagnosed causes of illnesses or misfortunes and invoked the gods for healing, restoring harmony, and knowledge of the future. In 1607, John Smith underwent a divination ritual that lasted eight hours daily for several days as Powhatan priests spread corn around him, sang, danced, and divided kernels with a sacred stick to determine what the English were up to. Smoke from "remade" or consecrated tobacco, like bread and wine in Catholic communion, brought one closer to the divine. Divination crystals—the most powerful came from Uktena's forehead and required special care and feeding with blood—brought prophetic insight and personal success. Men carried crystals and other sacred objects in medicine bags for good luck in hunting or warfare. Europeans scoffed at natives' "idolatrous adorations," yet Robert Beverley, a Virginia planter, acknowledged one conjurer's power. During a drought and without "the least appearance of rain nor so much as a cloud," a half hour of "a-pow-wowing" brought "up a black cloud into the sky that showered down rain enough on this gentlemen's corn and tobacco, but none at all upon any of the neighbors."[7] Shamans identified witches, man-killing monsters, that could change shape to appear as animals or as humans and caused unexplained illnesses and misfortunes by stealing peoples' lives to extend their own. After discovery, witches were summarily executed.

Ceremonies combined music, song, and dance to renew connectedness to the spirit world and restore social harmony. Horticulture,

The Black Drink. Before council meetings, men consumed large quantities of a dark tea made from holly leaves. High doses of caffeine acted as a stimulant, diuretic, and emetic that purified bodies and cleared minds. The artist accurately included women's roles in tea preparation, conch shell drinking vessels, and projectile vomiting, but rendered native bodies as idealized European figures. (Based on an engraving by Theodor de Bry, 1591, of a watercolor by Jacques Le Moyne, 1564. Smithsonian Institution, National Anthropological Archives, BAE GN 02860WW09-6453700.)

hunting, warfare, and ball games required prescribed personal preparations and village rites beforehand, and community feasts, music, and dances celebrated success afterward. The Green Corn Ceremony, held in late summer when corn first ripened, was farming peoples' ritual high-point. Originating in the southeastern ceremonial complex of Mississippian mound-building cultures, which only the Natchez had retained at the time of European contact, the original cycle included special feasts featuring seasonal foods at each new moon. These gradually reduced to a large annual harvest ceremony. Details varied between groups, but common features included fasting and purging to purify bodies, giving thanks for harvests, relighting sacred fires that has become polluted after a year of use, performing sacred dances and speeches, forgiving social wrongs (except murder) committed over the previous year, and closing feasts and social dances. Ceremonies confirmed the social order—priests, chiefs, warriors, and "beloved women" had privileged roles—but all participated in parts of the ritual. Women cleaned out their houses, made and served sacred medicine and food to men, presented new corn crops to priests, extinguished old home fires and relit them from the new sacred fire, and initiated sacred dances. Priests reminded the people, anthropologist Hudson observes, "that if they behaved properly they would enjoy good health, the rainmakers would be able to bring plenty of rain, and they would be victorious over their enemies; but if they failed to keep the rules they could expect drought, captivity and death from their enemies, witchcraft, and disease."[8] Recognizing human imperfections, rituals of forgiveness cleansed communities of personal resentments and injuries and restored social harmony.

Europeans

Christianity, like Native American spirituality, provided answers about the nature of the transcendent, humans' place in the world, and how to live a moral life, but its organization, beliefs, and outlook could not have been more different. A monotheistic faith based on sacred texts, Christianity was almost 1,500 years old when Europeans arrived in the New World. Formal institutions structured religious experiences and were led by full-time specialists: priests conducting sacred rites, theologians debating religious creeds, monks and nuns living apart as models of Christian life, and officials determining church policies and enforcing orthodoxy. As the wealthiest institution in Western Europe, the Catholic Church enjoyed enormous political power ruling directly over its own territories and legitimizing rulers' divine authority. Church establishments and nation-states formed an interconnected hierarchy of sacred and secular authority. Social order, all agreed, required subjects subscribe to a single faith. Catholic, Anglican, or Lutheran establishments received tax support and monopolies over liturgy, religious rites, and office holding and assistance in suppressing heresies. Ancient stone churches were villages' largest structures whose bells marked time's passage, called people to worship, and reminded them of the church's central place in their lives.

Religious turmoil of the 16th and 17th centuries spilled into the colonial South. The Protestant Reformation broke Rome's monopoly over Christianity in the West. Martin Luther's followers created a new church, Henry VIII installed himself head of an Anglican Church, and numerous dissenting faiths arose: Puritans, Presbyterians, Quakers, Anabaptists, Huguenots, Reformed, and German Pietists. Reformed Protestants "purified" worship by eliminating organs, non-Psalm hymns, stained glass, and ornamentation; substituting vernacular languages for Latin; reducing the number of saints' days; and emphasizing sermons, Bible reading, and personal piety. A Catholic Counter-Reformation revived the faith with lay confraternities and renewed devotion to the Holy Family and to Communion rites. Each group believed they possessed religious truth and debated each other (and among themselves) about the means of justification (God's grace or humans' good works), meaning of Communion (actual transformation or symbolic presence of Christ's body and blood in bread and wine), laity's role (spectacle of the Mass or priesthood of all believers), and structure of church authority (hierarchical or self-governing congregations). Religious turmoil strengthened the equation, "one church, one people, and one nation," and turned religious differences into struggles for political power at home and motives for establishing colonies abroad. The true faith's righteous defenders gave opponents no quarter, yet persecution only strengthened dissenters' convictions that they were God's chosen people whose faith was being tested.

Despite many colonial Southerners' preoccupation with securing economic profits, Christian worldviews, church establishments, and rituals framed their everyday lives. As elsewhere in the New World, converting natives to the true faith (either Catholic or Protestant) provided one rationale for colonial claims. Rituals of taking possession at first landings used religious and national symbols and language: Christian crosses, sovereigns' standards, declarations of fidelity to God and Crown, and geographic places renamed after saints and kings. On September 8, 1565, the Spanish unfurled banners of Felipe II, sounded trumpets, and exploded gunpowder as Pedro Menéndez de Avilés landed, kneeled to kiss the cross, and established Saint Augustine. He then attacked and slaughtered over 300 French Huguenots at Fort Caroline some 40 miles north.

Protestants and Indians "held similar beliefs, probably Satanic in origin," Menéndez reported to Felipe, "It seemed to me that to chastise them in this way would serve God Our Lord, as well as Your Majesty, and then we should thus be left more free from this wicked sect." James I chartered the Virginia Company in 1606, in part, for "propagating of Christian religion to such People, as yet live in darkness and miserable ignorance of the true knowledge and worship of God."[9] Since God made man in His own image and gave him dominion over the earth, spiritual power rested outside nature. Plants and animals—indeed, all of nature—were profitable commodities not spiritual beings requiring respect and reciprocity.

Indian missions waned in Virginia as the colony struggled to survive and Powhatans resisted conversion but not efforts to transplant a religious establishment necessary for maintaining social order among an unruly population of young, single men. Governors were instructed to ensure that "the true word, and service of God and Christian faith be preached, planted, and used, . . . according to the doctrine, rights, and religion now professed and established within our realme of England." Governor Thomas West, Baron De La Warr, had a 60-by-24-foot chapel constructed at Jamestown with cedar pews, pulpit, font, and chancel; a black walnut communion table; and two bells calling people to worship. Before services, the governor and other officials processed into church accompanied by "a guard of fifty Halberdiers in his Lordship's livery, [wearing] fair red cloaks."[10] Under Sir Thomas Dale's *Lawes Divine, Morall and Martiall* (1612), bells called settlers to services each workday morning and afternoon and to sermons and religious instruction on Sundays. Fines levied for missing services included loss of food rations, whippings, and six months at the galleys for the third offence, and death penalties were threatened for repeated gaming on the Sabbath, blasphemy, or church robbery.

By 1634, there were a dozen parish churches in Virginia and 50 more constructed by 1670. Ministers conducted divine services using rites prescribed in the *Book of Common Prayer* (1571), catechized settlers in Anglican doctrine, and disciplined moral transgressors. Vestries of laymen levied parish taxes; constructed and maintained churches; hired and fired ministers; purchased Bibles, prayer books, vestments, and communion chalices; controlled church finances including ministers' salaries; kept registers of baptisms, marriages, and burials; and maintained orphans, bastard children, and the poor. Two vestrymen served as churchwardens, who twice yearly presented alleged Sabbath-breakers, blasphemers, adulterers, and other religious or moral offenders to county grand jurors for possible indictment. The goal, recorded in laws, was to maintain "uniformity in our church as neere as may be to the canons in England; both in substance and circumstance, and that all persons yeild readie obedience unto them under paine of censure."[11]

Although church and state in Virginia allied to enforce morality and orthodoxy, religious establishments remained weak. Chronic shortages in the supply of clergymen—there were never more than 10 resident ministers at any time before 1670—left many parishes vacant. Nor did new church construction keep pace with the spread of settlement. Only a single brick church survives from the 17th century; like planters' homes, most were small impermanent wooden structures. Virginia's parishes, four times the size of English ones, meant most settlers lived too far away to hear church bells or attend weekly services. Few talented men served in Virginia; most were poorly trained, inattentive, or intemperate. Even the Virginia Assembly accused some ministers with "excesse in drinkeing, or riott, spendinge theire tyme idellye by day or night, playing at dice, cards, or any other unlawfull game."[12] Uninspired leadership and frequent squabbles with vestrymen weakened ministerial authority.

Lay-controlled parishes became self-governing congregations. Without ordained clergy, lay readers conducted weekly services and read printed homilies, but could not preach sermons, administer communion or baptism, or perform marriages or burials. With no resident bishop or ecclesiastical court, ministers became subordinate to large planters who sat on vestries and country courts. They haggled with ministers over salaries and used their authority to discipline unruly neighbors by accusing poor planters of gaming on Sundays and servant women of bearing bastard children. An anemic church establishment secularized Virginia society as individuals conducted personal devotions and developed their own religious beliefs—or none at all. Most settlers rarely attended services or received religious instruction, few presented their children for baptism, and the dead were buried in family plots not church yards and remembered with feasts not solemn rituals. Presentments for failing to attend services or working on Sundays declined; the Sabbath became a day of rest and recreation.

Authorities tolerated nominal Anglicans and even religious indifference but not dissenters who questioned the necessity of church establishments for maintaining social order. Dissenting Puritans in the 1640s and Quakers a decade later provided what little religious fervor existed in early Virginia. Both were suppressed either by requiring ministers to conform to Anglican doctrine and organization or by fleeing the colony. Quaker belief in equality of all before God and with one another, which extended even to allowing women preachers, threatened social hierarchy. Shocked, authorities excoriated them as "An unreasonable and turbulent sort of people . . . teaching and publishing, lies, miracles, false visions, prophesies and doctrines, which have influence upon the communities of men both ecclesiasticall and civil endeavouring and attempting thereby to destroy religion, lawes, comunities and all bonds of civil societie."[13]

Catholic church establishments were no stronger. Maryland was founded in 1634 as a haven for oppressed Catholics, but soon faced a 10-to-1 Protestant majority. Priests supervised construction of four churches but conducted services privately lest they anger Protestants. Converting local Algonquians was safer. The 1649 "Act concerning Religion" was intended to protect Maryland Catholics from persecution by making religious belief among Christians entirely a personal affair, thus, blocking creating *any* religious establishment. Maryland attracted Puritan, Presbyterian, and Quaker dissenters, but with church support entirely voluntary, most settlers remained unchurched and children unbaptized. In this secular society, one Anglican despaired, "not only many Dayly fall away either to Popery, Quakerism or Phanaticisme but alsoe the lords day is prophaned, Religion despised, and all notorious vices committed soe th[a]t it is become a Sodom of uncleaness and a Pest house of iniquity."[14] Toleration failed to lesson anti-Catholic hostility. After the Glorious Revolution of 1688 replaced Catholic Charles II with Protestant William and Mary, Maryland Protestants charged Catholics with plotting to turn the colony over to Spain or France, arrested their priests, and burned their chapels. Indifference not persecution plagued the Catholic Church in Florida and Louisiana where religious life atrophied among the small overwhelmingly male settlers, and churches remained half empty even on Easter. Despite state subsidies, contemporaries described parish churches in Saint Augustine and in New Orleans, wooden structures built in the 1720s on the towns' central plazas, as "in shambles" and "falling down."[15]

Despite weakened church establishments, settlers held Christian worldviews. Good and evil were present in the world and affected daily life. Protestant colonists believed God sometimes visited misfortunes to chastise those who had turned away from Him and Satan scored temporary victories by recruiting witches who used malevolent powers to harm others, but they never doubted God's ultimate triumph over evil. Europeans saw religious opponents—whether Muslim, Catholic, Protestant, or Nonconformist—as the Antichrist, but in the New World, the Devil was no mere apparition but present in the bodies of indigenous women and men whose priests were skilled practitioners of witchcraft. Conflicts with natives, thus, were not mere struggles over land or political power, but rather millennial contests between good and evil. God had to be on the settlers' side.

Unexplained events, or "remarkable providences," were scrutinized as signs of God's dispensations. When a Virginia planter's wife found large globs of blood in her washing bucket on April 1, 1644, her husband thought this was a "miraculous premonition and warning from God having some kinde of intimation of some designe of the Indians." Although they had never encountered hostility before, five men took up arms and thus "secured our selves against 20 savages, which were three houres that day about my house. Blessed be the name of God."[16] Goodwife Wright faced accusations of dabbling in magic after allegedly bringing sickness to those who had angered her, predicting future deaths, and claiming ability to turn back witches' curses. Belief in witches' malevolent powers was widespread with slander or causing physical injury or damage to crops or livestock the most common charges. Yet, authorities only reluctantly brought convictions and in the two-dozen trials acquitted most of the accused. Isolation from neighbors and religious indifference limited witchcraft accusations, but prudent men hung horseshoes over doors to ward off witches' harm.

Africans

If Africans and Indians discussed spirituality when they labored together on Carolina and Louisiana plantations or when native porters bearing deerskins lingered in Charleston or after Africans sought sanctuary in Native villages, they would be surprised by their overlapping beliefs. Both thought the world was alive with spirit beings that intervened in daily life for good or ill and required propitiation to secure prosperity and avoid misfortune by following taboos, offering gifts, and participating in sacred dances with drumming and singing. A supreme creator god lived in the sky, made the world, and brought gifts of rain, fertility, and sacred medicine.

More approachable were lesser spirits (northern Algonquian's *manitowuk*, Fon of Dahomey's *vodun*, and Yoruba's *orisha*) that lived in thunder, rivers, hills, and animals. They could have swapped stories about their gods' personalities and behavior and how the world had come into existence. Priestly diviners and healers—men and, sometimes, women—with extraordinary spiritual power interceded the gods on behalf of the people, led sacred ceremonies and festivals, understood plants' powers to heal sick bodies and souls, provided charms and amulets to ward off malevolent witches' curses or harm enemies, and read omens that foretold one's fate. Elders were revered as story keepers and for their wisdom. Women's spiritual power became so strong during monthly menstrual cycles, they had to be isolated in special huts.

What theological debates might have taken place! What was the nature of relationships between the spirit world and human souls? Did everyone enjoy an afterlife or just high-status people? Did life after death mirror village life or promise continuous abundance and health? Were some people reincarnated in women's wombs? Was the creator god removed from daily life or intimately involved in the people's survival? What was the relationship of ancestors and spirit animals to the living? Africans heard about the power of dreams when souls left sleeping bodies and communicated with spirits, and they learned which animals had souls and the proper rituals and taboos that ensured successful hunts. Natives marveled over Africans' spiritual powers, which protected them from new deadly diseases that accompanied Europeans, while Africans learned which plants cured New World maladies. Natives wondered, perhaps, about Africans' devotion to ancestors who protected villages, mediated spiritual matters, and guarded customs and laws. After death, one's soul or "little me" left the body to join ancestors who lived nearby and watched over the living. Failure to venerate ancestors angered them and brought illness and misfortune. "For this reason," recalled Olaudah Equiano, an Igbo captured as a boy, "they always before eating . . . put some small portion of the meat, and pour some of their drink, on the ground for them: and they often make oblations of the blood of beasts or fowls at their graves" housed in small thatched huts.[17] Burial rites speeded journeys to ancestors' embraces and kept lost souls from becoming malevolent ghosts. The living carefully prepared bodies, left food and personal possessions on graves, followed prescribed periods of mourning, and honored the deceased with music, dance, and feasts. Natives might have observed African sacred dances with drums and songs that called the gods. During ecstatic trances, gods "mounted" masked devotees' bodies in spiritual coitus as they performed the gods' personalities and became their voices.

Before mid-18th century, very few slaves became Christians. Missionary energy in converting Indians was marked by indifference toward enslaved Africans. Despite declarations from church and government leaders that baptisms did not require manumitting slaves, skeptical slaveowners continued to oppose slave conversions. They feared Christianity diverted slaves from Sunday labor, made them "proud and Undutifull" by instilling ideas of spiritual equality, or, most worrisome, facilitated plotting conspiracies under the guise of night religious gatherings. Planters remained unconvinced by a Carolina missionary's plea that converted slaves would "do better for their Masters profit than formerly, for they are taught to serve out of Christian Love and Duty."[18] Laws requiring Catholic masters to instruct their slaves in the faith went unenforced. Few Africans found solace in their oppressor's Anglicanism with its formal services, lengthy sermons, prolonged instruction, and emphasis on Bible reading. Muslims and shamans mocked baptism for requiring converts to renounce publicly "any design to free yourself from the Duty and Obedience that you owe to your Master while you live." A group of Virginia converts after realizing that "baptism did not change their status . . . grew angry and saucy" and allegedly planned an uprising.[19] Unlike Catholic friars, who studied Indian religions for parallels with Christianity and used sounds and images to convey the faith, Anglican ministers never learned African languages or moderated rote memorization for indoctrinating their beliefs.

Islam's emphasis on literacy, knowledge of the Qur'an, and individual spiritual discipline of daily prayers, dietary laws, and Ramadan fasts aided Muslims in maintaining religious practices. North African merchants brought Islam to West Central Africa in the ninth century, and its influence spread with expansion of sub-Saharan trade and conversion of urban merchants and local rulers. Captives from wars between Muslim and non-Muslim states in Senegambia and Sierra Leone were traded to Atlantic slavers, and several thousand Mandingo, Mande, and Wolof Muslims were shipped to coastal Carolina and Georgia and to Louisiana. Ayabah Suleiman Diallo, a Jolof merchant from a family of Muslim clerics, was kidnapped in 1730 and ended up in Maryland. Literate in Arabic but not English, he continued prostrating himself in daily prayers despite local whites' mocking. Charles Ball, a Georgia slave, remembered a Muslim on a Lowcountry plantation in the early 19th century "who prayed five times every day, always turning his face to the east, when in the performance of his devotion."[20] Non-Muslim slaves sought Muslim slaves' prized amulets of Qur'anic inscriptions encased inside sealed pouches.

REVITALIZATIONS

In 1763, John Marrant, a free black teenager, reputed party man, and virtuoso violinist and French horn player, passed by a large meetinghouse in Charles Town as a large crowd streamed in. His companion noted "a crazy man was hallooing" inside, none other than the Rev. George Whitefield, the famous evangelist then barnstorming the colonies. The merry pranksters proposed Marrant blow his French horn to disrupt the meeting:

> So we went and with much difficulty got within the doors. I was pushing the people to make room, to get the horn off my shoulder to blow it, just as Mr. Whitefield was naming his text, and looking round, and, as I thought directly upon me, and pointing with his finger, he uttered these words, "*Prepare to meet thy God, O Israel.*" The Lord accompanied the word with such power, that I was struck to the ground, and lay both speechless and senseless near half an hour. When I was come a little too, I found two men attending me, and a woman throwing water in my face and holding a smelling-bottle to my nose; and when something more recovered, every word I heard from the minister was like a parcel of swords thrust into me, and what added to my distress, I thought I saw the devil on every side of me. I was constrained in the bitterness of my spirit to halloo out in the midst of the congregation, which disturbing them, . . . they carried me as far as the vestry, . . . Mr. Whitefield . . . being told of my condition he came immediately, and the first word he said to me was, "JESUS CHRIST Has got thee at last."

Doctors could not cure Marrant's soul sickness. Four days later, Whitefield returned to pray and after "a considerable time, and near the close of his prayer, the Lord was pleased to set my soul at perfect liberty, and being filled with joy I began to praise the Lord immediately; my sorrows were turned into peace, and joy, and love. The minister said, 'How is it now?' I answered, 'all is well, all happy.'" Eschewing his old life, which had been "devoted to pleasure and drinking in iniquity like water," Marrant became an itinerant preacher to the Cherokees and, later, a Methodist minister to black loyalist refugees and Native Americans in Nova Scotia.[21]

Marrant's conversion was part of a transatlantic, intercolonial religious movement called "The Great Awakening" that swept across the colonies in the mid-18th century. Evangelicals challenged a reviving Anglican establishment, whose institutional presence with new parishes and ordained ministers strengthened over the previous half century. Anglican faith grew gradually from studying Scriptures and the catechism, listening to reasoned sermons, accepting one's place in society, and performing acts of benevolence. Evangelicals' emotional preaching, in contrast, sought immediate individual conversions, new births that were sharp breaks from old sinful lives into new lives of personal piety and membership in voluntary Christian communities. During the 18th century, non-English emigrants poured into the colonial South bringing new faiths that increased religious diversity and intensity. By 1760, many of these dissenters joined awakeners in validating religious experiences of women, youths, slaves, and Indians; questioning social hierarchy; and condemning religious establishments.

Anglicans

The Church of England's renewal arose from adapting to an expanding but scattered rural population. The Virginia Assembly authorized new parishes as settlements spread, and the Crown created new church establishments in Maryland (1692), South Carolina (1706), North Carolina (1715), and Georgia (1732). The Society for the Propagation of the Gospel in Foreign Parts (SPG), a London missionary organization founded in 1701, funded Anglican ministers and missionaries to proselytize the unchurched. Between 1700 and 1774, Virginia parishes doubled to 95 with almost 90 percent supplied with ministers, and there were 30 new parishes in Maryland, 20 in South Carolina, and 8 in Georgia. Unlike England's single-church parishes and village centers, the colonial South's large parishes required multiple congregations so every parishioner had access to divine services. By 1774, there were over 250 congregations in Virginia, as mushrooming parish levies funded ambitious building programs that replaced 17th-century frame and log structures with brick mother churches near parish centers and built new, framed clapboard chapels in outlaying areas. Church spires dominated town skylines, and churches and chapels, many named for saints, marked rural landscapes.

Vestrymen specified the size, building materials, and furnishings to local contractors and craftsmen, who followed well-known styles. About a third of new churches in Virginia and Maryland were made from local bricks laid in alternate courses of headers (short side) and stretchers (long side), known as Flemish bond, which created variegated textures for otherwise unadorned exteriors except for architectural treatments around windows, doors, and cornices. Rectangular buildings, about twice as long as wide, sufficed in small parishes, but larger congregations adopted central Greek cross (Christ Church, 1730s, Lancaster County, Virginia) or Latin cross or crucifix (Burton Parish Church, 1711, Williamsburg, Virginia) plans to add seating. A few churches had multistory tower entryways (Newport Parish Church [St. Luke's], 1680s, Isle of Wight County, Virginia) or towering steeples (Burton Parish's soared 100 feet high). St. Michael's Church (1752–1761), whose 184-foot tower and steeple composed of 5 sections still dominates Charleston's skyline, bespoke rice planters and merchants' great wealth. Its 8 tower bells called worshippers, who passed through a 4-columned portico with a decorated frieze into a 60-by-130-foot nave with balconies on 3 sides. With a cost of over 60,000 pounds sterling, it was the largest church building in the colonies.

Parishes were inclusive communities—every resident, even freethinkers, belonged. Worshippers mingled outside until parish clerks called them to divine services, and gentlemen noisily entered en masse during opening calls to worship. As parishioners passed through west doors facing east toward Jerusalem, they entered spaces of refinement, symmetry, and reflection. Large clear-glass windows flooded interiors with light reflecting against white smooth paneled or plastered walls. Low screens set off chancels on east ends with communion tables. Decorated altar pieces were set on walls with large tablets on either side inscribed with the Ten Commandments and the Lord's Prayer and, above, the royal coat of arms. Humble folk, servants, and slaves sat on wooden benches in the back, common planters in middle pews, men on one side of center aisles and women opposite, and magistrates and gentry in enclosed pew boxes in the front. High pulpits dominated interiors; some comprised three levels with clerks' desks on floors, mid-level reading desks, and preaching stations above topped by wooden sounding boards suspended from ceilings. Leather-bound Bibles and prayer books, chandeliers, silk table coverings, and overstuffed pulpit cushions completed the sacred ensemble. At a glance, congregants glimpsed their community's social hierarchy and competition for prestige. They recalled squabbles over pew assignments in the new church—several rising planters had felt slighted—and how the wealthiest families insisted on constructing balconies with private windows so they could enjoy divine services apart from the herd.

Anglicanism was a religion of the Word, whose tenets were instilled through a liturgy prescribed in *The Book of Common Prayer* (1662); a lectionary, or annual calendar of readings from *The King James Bible* (1611); learned sermons on moral behavior; and instruction in creeds and doctrines as set down in the Anglican catechism. Parish clerks assisted ministers as services moved through set sequences of confessions, creeds, collects (intercessory prayers), responses, Psalms, and readings from the Old and New Testaments. Clerks announced hymns with texts based on the Book of Psalms and sung to familiar tunes. Worshippers stood, kneeled, and sat as they sang, responded (*"Lord, hear our prayer"*), and prayed for God's blessings on their community:

> Almighty and everlasting God, by whose spirit the whole body of the Church is governed, and sanctified: Receive our supplications, and prayers which we offer before thee for all estates of men in thy holy church, that every member of the same in his vocation, and ministry, may truly, and godly serve thee, through our Lord and Savior Jesus Christ, Amen.[22]

Parishioners followed services in personal prayer books or memorized movements and responses. Urban churches hired professional organists who trained choirs in harmony singing.

Ministers, garbed in distinctive black gowns and white surplices, or loose outer vestments, ascended pulpits to begin sermons, the service's high point. Reading from prepared texts and delivered in a restrained uninflected style with little eye contact with the congregation below, sermons expounded, according to historian John K. Nelson, "a 'reasonable' faith, moral conduct, benevolence, acceptance of the social order and one's attendant duties, and obedience to all in authority." Philip Fithian, a Presbyterian, thought them brief: "seldom under and never over twenty minutes, but always made up of sound morality, or deep studied Metaphysicks."[23] Holy Communion was celebrated only four times annually and required silver plate, often wealthy planters' gifts: flagons for holding consecrated wine, cups to serve to communicants, and patens or plates

Anglican high pulpit. Anglican church interiors modeled social hierarchy. High pulpits with sounding boards that projected the voice elevated ministers above their parishioners, who were seated according in boxed pews to conserve heat. Prominent families sat apart in balconies shown on the left. Photograph, Christ Church, 1732, Lancaster County, Virginia. (Library of Congress.)

for wafers. Few took communion either because they associated it with Catholicism or feared their unworthiness made participation sacrilegious.

Church rituals marked the life cycle's passages. In settled areas, white parents (and a few slaves) brought infants to church for baptism; masters provided religious instruction to servants; children learned to read from the Bible; individuals publicly affirmed Anglican tenets at "initiations," or confirmations; and only Anglican ministers performed legal marriage rites and buried the dead with Anglican rituals. Faith was instilled gradually through weekly attendance at divine services and reasoned sermons not from sudden conversions or charismatic preaching. Shorn of saints' days and village rituals, divine service on the Sabbath marked each week's beginning and the church calendar the major holidays of Advent, Christmas, Epiphany, Lent, and Easter, when local residents gathered as a community. Fithian noted on one Easter Sunday "all the Parish seem'd to meet together High, Low, black, White all came out—After Sermon the Sacrament was administered, but none are admitted except communicants."[24]

Parish and county consecrated a unified vision of order and hierarchy. Divine service and church architecture reproduced society in miniature, and sermons reminded parishioners of Christian virtues of obedience, charity, and goodwill to all. Robert Rose, a Virginia minister, was remembered as a model Anglican for "the great goodness of his heart. Humanity, benevolence, and charity ran though the whole course of his life. . . . In his friendship he was warm and steady; in his manner gentle and easy; in his conversation entertaining and instructive."[25] All household heads regardless of personal beliefs supported the church with taxes, and vestrymen had civil responsibilities to aid the poor and the infirm, police public morality, and maintain religious orthodoxy. Anglicans tolerated diverse personal religious beliefs and even moderate religious dissent as long as unity of parish, county, and residential community remained intact.

This Anglican model of inclusive religious life, realized most fully in old settled parishes, attenuated on the frontier. Multicongregational parishes made parsons local itinerants, who conducted services at main churches twice monthly and less often at outlaying chapels as poor roads hindered travel. Clerks filled in for absent ministers, but their short services of scripture readings, prayers, and printed homilies attracted small audiences. Formal liturgy and reasoned sermons suited gentry's tastes but did not reach common folks' hearts. Devereux Jarratt, an artisan's son who became an Anglican preacher, described his parish minister in tidewater Virginia as "but a poor preacher . . . very unapt to teach or even to gain the attention of an audience." When Jarratt moved to the frontier, he found, "no minister of any persuasion, or any public worship, within many miles. The Sabbath day was usually spent in sporting; And whether this was right or wrong, I believe, no one questioned." Immigrants who came as indentured servants, convicts, and redemptioners joined the throngs of unchurched laborers and backcountry squatters. Charles Woodmason, an SPG missionary, found "Not the least Rudiments of Religion, Learning, Manners or Knowledge" in backcountry Carolina as settlers were "Neither of one Church or other or of any denomination by Profession, not having . . . even seen a Minister—heard or read a Chapter in the Scriptures, or heard a Sermon in their days."[26]

Dissenters

Anglican growth occurred as the colonial South became more diverse in religion. Eager to encourage frontier settlement, Carolina proprietors, Georgia trustees, and Virginia governors recruited French Huguenots, German Lutherans and Pietists, Scottish Presbyterians, and English Quakers. Jews settled in Charles Town and Savannah, and Catholics experienced modest growth in Maryland and New Orleans. Dissenters were required to pay parish levies, use Anglican ministers for marriage rites, and were often disfranchised and barred from office holding, but otherwise were unmolested as long as they maintained meetinghouses with settled ministers who took prescribed oaths. Dissenters, authorities learned, made obedient subjects, and religious diversity did not necessarily disrupt social order. Religious life among non-Anglicans varied markedly not only from different beliefs and ritual practices but also from migration patterns, extent of institutional support, and Anglo-American connections. Intercolonial and transatlantic institutions sustained Presbyterians, Lutherans, Quakers, Catholics, and Jews by maintaining contacts with dispersed congregations, supervising ordination and ministerial supply, settling theological disputes, and providing financial support for distant coreligionists. Economic and political aspirations tempted Huguenots and individuals from other religious groups to become Anglicans. European Pietists' heartfelt religion created holy communities apart from the world, models evangelicals adopted during their revivals.

Non-Anglicans created different ideals of religious life with independent meetinghouses, private chapels, or synagogues that were sustained by members' voluntary contributions not tax levies, lay leaders not ordained ministers, and personal piety not outward conformity. For dissenters, religious buildings were vital as places of fellowship and for sustaining their small communities. Despite religious toleration, each group faced challenges maintaining core beliefs, whether Calvinist, Catholic, Quaker, or Jewish; traditional liturgies with varying emphases on sermons, ceremonies, music, or testimonies; and mother tongues of French, German, Latin, or Hebrew. With priests, ministers, and rabbis in short supply, laity, like vestrymen, assumed greater responsibility for administering congregational affairs and oversaw construction of religious buildings, hired and supported ministers, supervised members' moral behavior, and modeled devotional life.

Presbyterians

Fleeing deteriorating economic conditions and Anglican persecution, over 100,000 Scots-Irish Presbyterians emigrated to the colonial South before the American Revolution and traveled the Great Wagon Road from Philadelphia to Maryland in the 1730s and to the Shenandoah Valley a decade later. By the 1750s, their American-born children and new emigrants poured into up-country Carolina and Georgia. About 20,000 Gaelic-speaking Presbyterians from Scotland's Western Highlands moved to the Cape Fear River Valley in North Carolina. Many arrived in groups—Presbyterian congregations from Ulster, clansmen led by tacksmen, Highland clan chiefs' military leaders and leasing agents, and extended families—and settled near one another.

As Reformed Protestants, Presbyterians emphasized a powerful sovereign God, Word over ritual and ceremony, an educated ministry, personal discipline, catechetical instruction, and Bible reading. Anglican landlords' discrimination and Irish Catholics' hostility forged Scots-Irish identities as members of God's elect, who had fled hostile lands to the Promised Land in the New World. Local church sessions of pastors and elders punished moral offenders and adjudicated conflicts between members, and regional presbyteries enforced orthodox doctrine. Backcountry emigrants appealed to the Donegal Presbytery in Pennsylvania for ministers but often waited a decade or more. The Rev. John Campbell, the first Gaelic-speaking minister, arrived in Cape Fear Valley 25 years after the first settlers. Lay elders led weekly services and itinerant ministers visited frontier settlements conducting services with lengthy sermons, prayers, and Psalm hymns; administering sacraments of baptism and communion; performing marriages and burials; and providing catechetical instruction. Early meetinghouses, like the Presbyterians' faith, were unadorned and hewed from local materials with small windows and lacked decoration or pulpits creating austere interiors. In settlements where civil authorities were weak, churches assumed disciplinary functions as sessions heard charges for sex offences, false testimony, unethical business dealings, family discord, Sabbath-breaking, and blasphemy and arbitrated civil disputes between members.

Annual Holy Fairs, or outdoor revivals, relieved the severity of backcountry Presbyterian faith and daily life. A tradition adopted

Outdoor communion. Scots Presbyterians brought outdoor Holy Fairs to the southern backcountry. Several days of fasting, preaching, prayer, and confession culminated in Holy Communion. This image captures the dramatic moment as the minister blesses the elements of bread and wine, symbols of Christ's body and blood, before distribution to seated congregants who had received Communion tokens. ("A Communion Gathering in the Olden Time," in Samuel *Miller, Presbyterian Reunion: Memorial Volume, 1837–1871* (New York: De Witt C. Lent & company, 1870. Courtesy Wabash College Library, Crawfordsville, Indiana.)

from Scotland and Ulster, these four-day sacramental festivals were held outdoors in the late summer or fall and gathered scattered people to fast, pray, hear preaching, sing Psalm hymns, confess sins, renew covenant vows, convert sinners, and give thanks to God. Led by local and itinerant preachers, "The Assembly was large . . . " reported one chronicler of a 1740s Virginia revival, "It appeared as one of *the Days of Heaven* to some of us; . . . a most glorious Day of the Son of Man." Faithful members and new converts received communion tokens admitting them to the festivals' high point: the ritual of the Last Supper. Seated along long cloth-covered tables enclosed by a fence, elders carried the elements to the ministers, who broke bread (symbolic of Christ's body broken on the Cross) and poured wine into cups (representing Christ's blood shed for remission of sins) and distributed them down rows of the assembly. Two thousand people reportedly attended a 1755 communion in Virginia; at another, a pastor rejoiced as "Believers were more quickened, and sinners were much alarmed."[27] Shorn of religious pageantry, evangelical Presbyterians created new seasonal rituals that gathered the faithful from dispersed frontier communities, healed breaches between neighbors, and extended the faith to the unchurched. When Separate Baptists and Methodists swept through the South in the late 18th century, they drew on Presbyterian models of outdoor rituals and redeemed communities, ironically wooing many former Presbyterians into these new faiths.

Lutherans

Germans' diverse faiths were nourished and transformed in the colonial South. Virginia's Hebron Church, the oldest Lutheran church in continuous use in the United States, was founded in the 1720s by skilled miners Governor Alexander Spotswood had imported to develop his Virginia iron works. Most Germans arrived from the religiously diverse Palatinate in southwest Germany that included Catholics, Lutherans, German Reformed, and Radical Pietists like Moravians, Mennonites, and Dunkers. Religious persecution and resentments against church establishments motivated some emigrants, but most left in small groups of family members or villagers seeking inexpensive land near their coreligionists. Maryland Germans created ethnic enclaves and built three-dozen Lutheran and Reformed churches by 1776. Denominational associations in Philadelphia supplied ordained ministers, who maintained services in German and traditional rites marking milestones of baptism, marriage, and burials. Newcomers settled near other Germans strengthening ties of religion and ethnicity.

Germans in the Shenandoah Valley and especially in the Carolinas were too dispersed and too diverse to create homogeneous religious communities or establish German schools. They held services in homes, barns, public buildings, or fields for decades before constructing church buildings. With only occasional visits from itinerant Lutheran, Reformed, and Moravian ministers, "irregular," nonordained preachers served many rural communities. Henry Muhlenberg, Lutheran patriarch, condemned one local pastor as possessing "neither the necessary shell nor the kernel neither the mediate nor the immediate gifts, for the important office [of pastor]."[28] Familiarity with religious diversity in their homeland and in Pennsylvania, where many initially settled, and intermarriage between Germans weakened denominational attachments. Lutherans and Reformed shared meetinghouses, attended services conducted by itinerant ministers of other faiths, and learned each other's hymns. Lay leaders simplified rituals, dropped liturgical calendars, and stopped enforcing church discipline. Pietism, which sought to revitalize Palatinate Lutheran and Reformed churches through individual faith experiences, Bible study, personal morality, and ecumenical cooperation strengthened in the backcountry and gave greater emphasis on religious experience over liturgies and creeds and expanded laity's roles over ecclesiastical authority. Churches became community centers for an ethnic German population living in scattered backcountry settlements.

Roman Catholics

Catholics in Maryland and Louisiana followed different paths of renewal. After Indian missions collapsed with John Ingle's rebellion in Maryland in 1645, local priests focused on settlers' spiritual needs. Jesuits acquired land and slaves to support themselves, and local Catholics gathered at their chapels for weekly Masses, confessions, feasts, and holy days and for baptisms, marriages, and burials. Itinerant Jesuits visited wealthy Catholics, whose private chapels also served neighbors and held mass, preached sermons, catechized, heard confessions, administered sacraments, and visited the sick. Devotions, including daily prayers, Bible reading, fasts on Fridays and during Lent, rosaries for reciting creeds and prayers, devotional books, and religious images sustained religious piety and created personal relationships between the faithful and God. Intermarriage, godparentage (sponsoring a child for baptism), guardianships for Catholic orphans, and church bequests sustained Catholic communities and religious practice despite Protestant hostility. After 1750, private chapels became parish churches and Catholic life acquired a more public character with weekly masses, celebrations of liturgical holidays, new rituals such as adoration of the Blessed Sacrament and devotion to the Sacred Heart, and new organizations like schools and female devotional societies.

On July 17, 1734, a remarkable procession of Ursuline nuns wended through New Orleans' muddy streets as they moved to their new convent. Rank ascended front to back: town inhabitants led; then convent orphans, students, and confraternity members of the Children of Mary; a young girl dressed "in a robe of cloth of silver with a long train" representing St. Ursula, the convent's patron; nine nuns with mother superior and assistant superior behind the canopy sheltering the reserved sacrament; and finally, parish priests. Files of soldiers marched alongside playing fifes and drums as the procession passed the governor and the intendant. "Almost all the people of both the upper and the lower classes of the city" attended, noted a chronicler, and "no one got out of order in spite of the mud and the singing of the children."[29] New Orleans' Ursuline Order (1727) and Children of Mary (1730) confraternity were products of the French Counter-Reformation, which emphasized women's religious devotion and personal piety. Ursuline nuns opened a female school and took in orphan, destitute, and abused women regardless of social rank or, remarkable for a slaveholding society, color. They sponsored the Children of Mary, a female confraternity dedicated "to serve the Blessed Virgin, to honor her not by their prayers alone, but also by their morals, and by all the conduct of their lives." Like nuns, members pledged to "have a special zeal for visiting the sick, the relief of the poor and the instruction of their children and their slaves."[30] Within a decade, one-third of free women in New Orleans belonged and included women of color alongside wives of wealthy planters, administrators, and artisans. In locating themselves between the laity and the priests in the procession, the nuns linked the holy and the profane, made visible women's agency, and asserted primacy of spiritual universalism over social and racial hierarchies.

Jews

Small Jewish communities in Charles Town and Savannah adopted ancient faiths to new social conditions. For almost the first time, Jews lived in tolerant societies and faced little overt persecution, though not escaping popular anti-Semitism, and, like Catholics and dissenters, were banned from officeholding. Religious life depended on voluntary affiliation. Despite their small numbers (under 200 in Charles Town), immigrants included acculturated Sephardim originally from the Iberian Peninsula and Ashkenazim from Central Europe, who reportedly were "a great deal more strict in their way, and rigid Observers of their Laws." Synagogues became centers for community life. In Savannah in the 1730s and Charles Town two decades later, Jews rented meetinghouses for Shabbat services and holy days of Passover, Rosh Hashanah, Yom Kippur, Sukkot, and Purim. Lay leaders hired chazzans as readers and singers; acquired prayer books, Torahs and Arks to house them, and circumcision kits; purchased land for cemeteries; disciplined members; dispensed aid to the poor; and assisted in supplying kosher meat to maintain dietary laws. Sephardim worship rites prevailed with men in prayer shawls swaying as they intoned passages from the Torah in Hebrew and chanted prayers aloud; women sat in separate sections or in galleries. Jews utilized transatlantic connections with other Jews for business connections, marriage partners, and material support (London Jews sent over 40 settlers to Savannah in 1733 and, later, religious books, a Torah scroll, and Hanukkah menorah) while acculturating to English ways. They wore gentile clothing and men shaved their beards and formed friendships and business partnerships with their English neighbors. "The Englishmen, nobility and common folks alike treat the Jew as their equal," a Protestant pastor marveled, and "They drink, gamble and walk together with them; in fact, let them take part in all their fun."[31]

Huguenots

About 500 Huguenots, French Calvinists who had resettled in England after fleeing persecution, arrived in Carolina before 1700 and built one of the earliest churches in Charles Town and 3 rural congregations. Within two generations, they lost their distinctive religious and ethnic identities and acculturated into Anglo-Carolina society. Huguenots' youthfulness, material aspirations, and small numbers gave them advantages in acquiring land and slaves, becoming naturalized British subjects, and holding political offices. They were the SPG's most successful missionary project. Anglicans included rural Huguenot churches in Anglican parishes, provided French translations of the *Book of Common Prayer,* and offered their ministers Anglican reordination. With little material or institutional support from London Huguenots or help in recruiting ministers and attracted by the colony's tolerant Anglicanism and lay-controlled parishes, wealthy individuals drifted into Anglican churches and married into Anglican families. By 1750, even Charles Town's large Huguenot Church, which earlier had defiantly rejected conformity, was a memorial church (a status it retains today) without an active congregation. Anglicanism absorbed other dissenters as congregations adopted their neighbors' English language and Anglo-colonial ways. George Samuel Klug, Hebron Lutheran Church's long-serving pastor, lived on glebe lands, purchased slaves, and assisted the local parish rector; Samuel, his son, attended the College of William and Mary and became an Anglican minister.

Moravians

In 1753, an advance party of Moravians left Bethlehem, Pennsylvania, to found Wachovia on 100,000 acres of land in the North Carolina Piedmont. Tracing their origins to John Hus, a Bohemian reformer martyred in 1415, and reconstituted as the *Unitas Fratrum* (Unity of Brethren) under Count Nicholaus von Zinzendorf's protection in 1722, Moravian religion was more a way of life than doctrine. Emulating Christ's love of humanity and crucifixion to atone mankind's sins, Moravians established a kingdom of God on earth based on the Bible and on surrendering individual will to serve God and others. Community governance and religious rituals bound members together. As a theocracy, church leaders controlled the economy and leased land and developed farms, mills, and artisan shops. Leaders admitted new members, decided one's occupation, and even chose marriage partners using the Lot to consult God's will by selecting scriptural passages or tokens marked yes, no, or blank from a bowl. Choirs grouped individuals by age, gender, and marital status and were the most vital social institution. Adolescents, for example, moved into boys and girls choirs, lived and ate together, attended their own services with special music, and "[tried] to live as a House of God in proximity to Jesus in love and harmony with one another." Weekly church services, daily choir devotions, monthly communion (participation required examination by church elders), love feasts, or communal meals, and a festival calendar that included Christmas, Easter, events in Moravian history, and special days for each choir renewed commitments to live as brothers and sisters in Christ. Music was an essential part of worship ("In the Bible one sees how God speaks to Men," Zinzendorf wrote, "and in the song book how Men speak to God.") and included composed hymns and choral anthems. Trombone quartets played German chorales and announced members' deaths by playing "O Sacred Head Now Wounded" from church bell towers that radiated through the community.[32]

Separate Baptists

On May 11, 1771, 1,200 people, the largest gathering in the colony's history, converged at Blue Run Church in Orange County, Virginia, to celebrate 6 years of Baptist evangelism. Persecution had not silenced itinerant preachers, nor had ridicule slowed conversions among yeoman, women, and youths. One preacher stirred outpourings of enthusiasm that set "the Christians all a fire with this love of God, [the] assembly praising of God with a loud voice. Brother Waller to exhorting till he got spent. Then Br[other] Marshall and E[lijah] Craig both broke loose to gether, the Christians shouting." Preaching continued for three days; on Sunday before "4 or 5,000 souls," a witness recalled, "The Lord of a truth was among us. My hard heart seem[ed] to open and let Jesus in." May was peak planting time, yet a thousand people appealed for more preaching.[33] This meeting birthed the Baptist church that would become the South's largest denomination in the next century.

Unlike the Calvinist Regular Baptists, who saw themselves as members of God's elect whose educated ministers conformed to toleration laws, Separate Baptist preachers were called directly by God, proclaimed universal salvation, and used vivid language to reach people wherever they gathered. They challenged church establishments by denying states had authority over ministers' qualifications or where they could preach and insisted self-governing congregations should be free from government supervision separates. In 1765, Samuel Harris, a Separate Baptist itinerant from North Carolina, arrived in Virginia where he and his party were greeted by a mob armed with sticks, whips, and clubs. Per-

Dissenter meetinghouse. Mennonites, a German Pietist sect, probably built this plain log cabin meeting house. The roughly finished interior and wooden benches bespoke dissenters' egalitarian faith and communal ideal. Separate Baptists rebuilt the meetinghouse in the late 18th century and added weatherboarding by the mid-19th century. (Photograph, 1936, Mill Creek [Maucks] Meeting House, Page County, Virginia. Library of Virginia, Virginia Historical Inventory, PA 240.)

severing, "great crowds" soon heard Harris's sensational preaching, and he encouraged converts "in whom he discovered talents to commence the exercise of their gifts." Lay leaders continued revivals by meeting in private homes and tobacco houses where "great numbers were awakened and several converted." Harris returned for three years preaching in homes, barns, and fields; at one night meeting, the "floor [was] covered with persons struck down under conviction of sin."[34]

Separate preachers balanced condemnations of moral complacency with messages of God's redemption of every individual from sin and with new rituals that forged supportive communities. Baptist preachers decried frivolity—drinking, fighting, card playing, dancing, and fiddle playing—and sought to create religious anxiety that led "awakened" hearers to new births and personal relationships with God. Conversions were prolonged physical struggles between God and Satan for control over bodies and souls. "Deep impression upon my soul had a very considerable influence upon my exterior appearance," James Ireland recalled, and the "wild vivacity that flashed in my eyes, and natural cheerfulness . . . was entirely gone; my eyes appeared solemn and heavy, my flesh began to pine away. My ruddy cheeks and countenance had vanished, whilst my head was often hanging down like a bulrick [bullock?] under the internal pressure of my guilty state." When a friend arrived to carry him to a dance, Ireland recognized in his companion his former convivial self-centeredness. I had "never beheld such a display of pride in any man . . . as I beheld in him at that juncture, arising from his deportment, attitude and gesture. He rode a lofty elegant horse, and exhibited all the affectation possible, whilst his countenance appeared to me as bold and daring as Satan himself, and with a commanding authority called upon me if I were there to come out." Shocked by Ireland's appearance, his friend renounced his wicked ways and sought "God through Jesus Christ for pardon."[35]

Shared conversion experiences created emotional bonds between believers as rituals marked each phase of sinners' progress toward conversion: "soul sickness," public confession of sins, acceptance of Jesus as personal savior, renouncing frivolous social pastimes, river baptisms, receiving the "right hand of fellowship," embracing "brothers" and "sisters" in Christ, night love feasts, and foot washings. Everyone—women and men, slaves and free—participated in meetings with prayers, scripture readings, sermons, and, especially, singing. Hymns, free paraphrases of the Psalms and New Testament texts and spiritual songs, and new compositions by Isaac Watts (an English Nonconformist) and Charles Wesley (an Anglican Methodist) were especially popular. They became the foundation for southern evangelical hymnody and 19th-century camp meeting songs. Leaders called or "lined out" verses for the largely illiterate worshippers, who sang each line unaccompanied to a popular tune. This method slowed the tempo and encouraged individual elaboration of notes, a singing style that continued in black and white rural congregations into the 20th century. Songs expressed a joyful personal spirituality of a powerful God (Watts: "I Sing the Almighty Power of God"), freedom from sin and death (Watts: "Alas! And Did My Savior Bleed" and Wesley: "Love Divine, All Love's Excelling"), praising God (Watts: "Come, Ye That Love the Lord" and Wesley: "Sing We to Our God Above"), new life (Watts: "Am I a Soldier of the Cross" and Wesley: "A Charge to Keep I Have"), and promise of heavenly home (Wesley: "Come, Let us Join Our Friends Above"). Charles Woodmason, an Anglican itinerant minister, condemned these songs as "not only execrable in Point of Versification, but withal full of Blasphemy Nonsense, and Incoherence."

Many, including Watts's "Oh God, Our Help in Ages Past" and "Joy to the World," remain popular today.[36]

The laity, not ordained ministers, sustained early Baptist and Methodist congregations. Witnessing followed conversions, as women and men encouraged friends and family members to be saved. In Virginia, three-fourths of women joined either as individuals or or in female mother–daughter–sister groups. Small property owners and slaveowners comprised two-thirds of early members; the rest were young men and women living with parents or married women with children. Recent converts with particular "gifts" became community "exhorters." Lewis Craig traveled from house to house conversing "on religious subjects; sometimes telling his own experience, sometime reading, praying, and singing." His preaching "being new and strange, made great noise, and brought people together who catch the seriousness one from another." "Presents," or free will offerings, not compulsory taxes, supported ministers, whose authority came from the laity who ordained them by "prayer and a Laying on of hands."[37] Men donated land, materials, and labor to build modest 20-by-40-foot meetinghouses. Like members' homes, they were fashioned from rough-hewn planks with unadorned interiors and benches for seats. Local origins of ministers, lay leaders, and small groups made Baptism and Methodism grassroots movements.

Baptist congregations embraced neighborhoods of believers, not entire counties, whose members were expected to behave in "Christian conversation" with one another. Avoiding gentry-dominated country courts, church deacons supervised each member's moral conduct—swearing, drunkenness, and failure to attend meetings—and mediated differences between members like disputed horse trades. Women and blacks watched over their respective groups. One man, whom justices of the peace had acquitted of stealing money, came to Ireland: "The hand of man could not find me out," the thief confessed, "but the hand of God hath reached me, and I believe I should assuredly go to hell, were I to conceal this act of injustice from you . . . the pride of my heart, for the sake of my reputation, would have led me to conceal [the theft]." Urging him to go to the man he had wronged, the confessed thief implored God for pardon, "then looked the man in the face and begged for his forgiveness and pardon." Public confession restored members to full fellowship; obstinate offenders faced expulsion. Humility and cooperation, not individual pride and self-assertion, were central to evangelical life.[38]

Charismatic itinerant leaders and emphasis on personal religious experiences threatened Anglican ministers and state officials. One Virginia justice accused Baptists of uttering "many indecent and scandalous Invectives & Reflections against the Church," and, therefore, they "cannot reasonably expect to be Treated with common decency or respect." Church and state were part of an indissoluble social fabric; the duty of each individual, William Bradley (a justice of the peace) reminded Nathaniel Saunders (a Baptist preacher), is "to obey Every ordinance of man for the Lord's Sake and that the Magistrate Dos not Bar[e] the Sword of Justice in vaine." A parish rector and county sheriff asserted their formal learning and political authority to demand members of a crowd listening to Ireland choose "either the preacher or the law." They chastised: you "have been deceived by him [Ireland], if you will confess it by coming over from the side where he is, to our side, we will take that act as your concession, and the law will not be in force against you." Ireland retorted: "they had heard nothing preached but the Gospel of Christ" and triumphantly recounted how magistrates were "much mortified at seeing the ill will they had gotten from their neighbors and their ignorance being . . . exposed before the congregation." The Baptist model of voluntary self-governing communities had triumphed over inclusive but hierarchically ordered societies.[39]

Mission Indians

Turning Indians into Christians was a prominent motive for European colonization, but only in Spanish Florida were the personnel and financial resources provided for effective missions. The Reconquest, a seven-century crusade to oust "infidel" Moors from the Iberian Peninsula, and the Inquisition, which sought to repress heresy, forged Castilian identity as defenders of Catholic orthodoxy. Convinced of Christianity's inerrancy, they expected Indians to embrace the true faith that would convert them from savagery to civilization. Geopolitics and imperial goals influenced missionaries' success. In Florida, conversions made natives laborers and warriors and priests informants. Christian Indians fought against English and French incursions strengthening the strategic but isolated colony. Indian converts in Carolina, however, threatened to disrupt merchants' lucrative deerskin and slave trade and slow land seizures. The few SPG ministers who attempted missionary work had dismal results. Jesuits in French Louisiana fared little better among Mississippian and Gulf Coast peoples, as planters sought land and traders economic partnerships with powerful interior nations. Although Christian converts were sparse in the colonial South, Christianity accompanied the demographic, economic, and political disruptions cascading across native communities and altered spiritual traditions.

Dedicated to winning new souls for Christ through vows of piety, poverty, celibacy, and even martyrdom, Franciscans, a mendicant brotherhood founded in 1209, arrived in Florida in 1573 and established missions in Guale and Timucua villages along the Atlantic coast from Saint Augustine to present-day Savannah. Presents of food and material goods established reciprocity and won native confidence. Men constructed missions (*doctrinas*) with churches (*iglesias*), typically 35 by 60 feet, friars' housing (*conventos*), and cookhouses, all set apart by enclosures. One or two priests lived at each mission and conducted daily prayer services and Sunday masses; catechized neophytes in Catholic doctrine, prayers, rituals, hymns, and playing European musical instruments; gave deathbed baptisms; and visited outlying villages. Priests assiduously inserted themselves into daily life with gifts, showy vestments, silver vessels, bright paintings, statues of saints and the Holy Family, and the rich pageantry of the mass, festivals, and religious processions with candles, incense, chants, and images. Neophyte boys assisted in mission routines by ringing bells and serving at mass. Targeting children and high-status individuals, friars hoped, would convert families and entire villages. Some learned native languages and debated shaman over fine theological points. Gabriel Díaz Vara Calderón, Bishop of Cuba, visited 36 mission villages in 1674–1675, which stretched north from Saint Augustine to Port Royal Sound, South Carolina, among the Guale and west across central Florida to the Timucua, the Apalachee, and the Apalachicola (Lower Creeks) on the Chattahoochee River. Administering confirmation rites to over 13,000 converts, he thought them "clever and quick to learn . . . not idolaters, and they embrace with devotion the mysteries of our holy faith."[40]

Catholic converts became *gente de razón* ("people of reason") only by adopting Spanish names, diet, clothing, housing, material culture, labor standards, gender roles, and sexual preferences—in short by utterly rejecting all former ways of living. According to directives in the "Royal Orders for New Discoveries" (1573), native Catholics were to "live in a civilized manner, clothed and wearing shoes . . . [and] given the use of bread and wine and oil and many other essentials of life—bread, silk, linen, horses, cattle, tools, and weapons, and all the rest that Spain has had." Yet, old ways continued. Shocked by neophyte women in traditional attire, "naked from the waist up and the knees down," Bishop Díaz ordered they cover up with fabric made of Spanish moss. Natives resisted European monogamy and sexual restraint and abandonment of ancient rituals. A Castilian Timucuan catechism (1612) posed questions for Confession: "Have you shown some part of your body to arouse in some person desires of lust or excite them? Have you desired to . . . do some lewd act with some man or women or kin? Have you had intercourse with someone contrary to the ordinary manner?" Friars banned pelota, the sacred ball game, because of its allegedly idolatrous symbols and use of magic and replaced ball poles in village plazas with crosses. When persuasion failed, friars burned sacred images and medicine bundles and punished idolatry, polygamy, moral offences, and running away with stocks, incarceration, and whips, which, one padre asserted, were "so necessary to their good education and direction."[41]

Indian responses ranged from conversion to rejection. Some native leaders in Florida embraced missionaries as sources for European goods, intermediaries with colonial authorities, pacifiers for intervillage conflicts, and allies against Indian rivals or European enemies. Settlement Indians on the margins of colonial settlements accepted Christianity as a way to rebuild personal lives and communities in a world broken by population losses and shamans' powerlessness. The Rev. Alexander Whitaker, an earnest Anglican who believed Indians were educable, adopted Pocahontas, Paramount Chief Powhatan's daughter and English captive, as his special project. Under his tutelage, she was taught English and catechized in Anglicanism, learned to eat with knives and drink from cups, and performed for settlers on Sundays. In April 1614, just before marrying John Rolfe, a Virginia planter, she was baptized and renamed Rebecca. Pocahontas's motives are unknown, as she left no personal accounts, but her conversion and marriage brokered several years of Anglo-Powhatan peace, elevated her as cultural mediator gaining knowledge for surviving a changing world, and produced children who might have allegiance to both cultures. It also confirmed, in the English mind, the prospect of saving natives from savagery and making them into Englishmen.

More natives resisted conversion. In 1561, the Spanish captured Paquiquino, son of a chiefly family living along the James River, and took him to Mexico where he was baptized, renamed Don

Luis de Velasco, educated, and apparently converted to Catholicism. After 10 years, he convinced 8 Jesuits to return with him to his native village. Abandoning them upon arrival, Luis returned an apostate with a war party that killed the Jesuits and burned the mission. In Florida, labor exploitation, tribute payments, corporal punishments, polygamy bans, political interference, and epidemic diseases led to individual runaways and to village rebellions by Guales (1576, 1597, 1645, and 1680s), Timucuas (1656 and 1665), Apalachees (1565 and 1647), and Apalachicolas (1675 and 1681). Juanillo, heir of head Guale *mico* (ruler), explained the continuing hold of old ways:

> We who are called Christians, experience only hindrances and vexations. They take away from us our women, allowing us but one. . . . They prohibit us from having our dances, banquets, feasts, celebrations, games and wars, in order that, being deprived of these, we might lose our ancient valor and skill. . . . They deprive us of every visage of happiness which our ancestors obtained for us, in exchange for which they hold out the hope of the joys of Heaven.[42]

Even native communities ravaged by disease, dislocation, and war did not completely reject older spiritual practices even when shamans were unable to propitiate angry gods. They rejected missionaries' demands to abandon every aspect of their culture. Settlement Indians, coastal Carolina refugees huddled around Fort Christanna, North Carolina, for example, resisted missionaries' intrusiveness by melding old village rituals into new Pan-Indian ones. One exasperated clergyman reported they were so "intractable and unwilling to be Civiliz'd that they will not [th]emselves nor let their children learn to wear decent apparrel to be instructed in anything of Literature or be either taught Arts or Industry. They are wholly addicted to their own barbarous and Sloathful Customs and will only give a laugh w[he]n pleased or grin w[he]n displeas'd for an Answer."[43] Eager to redeem Indians from control of hated Catholic rivals and secure more slaves, Carolina-Yamasee armies raided Guale missions in the 1680s and Apalachee and Timucua missions in 1704. Many alienated converts joined in attacking their old villages, plundering missions, and torturing friars. Two years later, the Florida missions were but a memory: up to 10,000 Christians were enslaved and a few hundred sought refuge near Castillo de San Marcos at Saint Augustine or moved west to Pensacola and Mobile.

Many natives pursued middle courses accepting aspects of Christianity that aided their lives while rejecting the rest. Since priests escaped deadly diseases accompanying Europeans and old healing rites proved ineffectual, Christians were thought to possess greater spiritual power. Baptism, perhaps, was a new water sorcery offering protection and praying to Jesus, Mary, and the saints added new spirit helpers. Psalm singing continued after missionaries left, and the Guale adopted new rituals, like the Day of the Dead in early November that replaced mortuary gifts, and men wore religious medals instead of shell gorgets. Indians listened politely to missionaries' tiresome sermons, but left unconvinced, noting the gap between Christian ideals and colonials' deeds. Silence, missionaries discovered, did not mean assent. Old ceremonies, like sweat baths and war dances, continued away from prying whites' eyes even as natives participated in Christian rituals. Uneven conversions left villages divided into traditionalist and Christian factions with converted children ridiculing elders. An afterlife, a vague concept in most traditions or limited to high-status persons but promised to all Christians, became a more prominent belief as did unregenerates' condemnation to hell's torments. Here were seeds for new syncretic faiths that emerged by 1800 and promised cultural revitalization and physical survival in a changing world.

African American

Despite the loss of African systems of religious belief, village rituals, and priestly castes in the Middle Passage, few enslaved Africans embraced their masters' faith with conversions limited to less than 5 percent of the adult slave population. An SPG minister in South Carolina explained his lack of success from "the Fondness they have for their old Heathenish Rites, and the strong Prejudice they must have against Teachers from among those, whom they serve so unwillingly." Continued imports divided slave communities by ethnicity, African-born versus Creole, and degree of acculturation, so "enslaved Africans turned to their gods and deployed their religious convictions in ways that gave structure and meaning to the present," a recent study concludes, "and challenged the total authority over their persons being claimed by Europeans."[44] Yet, Protestant and Catholic proselytizing planted seeds for a later African American Christianity that incorporated African worship styles, spoke to conditions of enslavement, trained black religious leaders who carried Christian messages into slave quarters, and provided both early condemnations and defenses of slavery. By 1800, religious changes were revolutionizing slave culture.

Encouraged by the SPG, Anglican ministers convinced some masters to bring slaves, mostly acculturated domestics, to divine services, where they sat apart from white parishioners on benches and in balconies and received instruction in the creeds, Lord's Prayer, and Ten Commandments. Newly arrived Africans' limited English conversions; in one Virginia parish, 30 to 40 slaves attended services but accounted for less than 5 percent of baptisms. Targeting American-born slave children as likely converts, Anglicans opened schools in Charles Town and Williamsburg; their literate graduates became missionaries to slaves and Indians. Before baptism, Anglicans required slaves to accept enslavement as God's will, obey earthly masters, and seek only future rewards in Heaven. Even George Whitefield—an Anglican evangelist who condemned slaveholders' materialism, inhumanity toward slaves, and indifference over slaves' religious condition—separated spiritual from temporal equality. He acquired slaves to provision his orphanage and lobbied to introduce slaves into Georgia. Accommodating the church to slavery softened planter opposition to black conversions and refashioned slaveholders as humane paternalists not economic exploiters.

Slaves in Catholic colonies found more opportunities for conversion. As with Indians, Catholics sought parallels between Catholicism and indigenous rites and worship styles: ritual richness with images (statues and paintings), blessed objects (candles, holy water, rosaries, medallions, and food), processions with music and dancing, calendars of feasts and saints' days, and ritual practices of fasting and praying to lesser spirits (Mary, Joseph, and the saints) to intercede before a supreme male god. Church membership offered religious protection through participation in the mass, and sacraments of marriage and infant baptism strengthened black families. Slaveowners and slaves served as godparents for black children and formed reciprocal ties in ritual brotherhoods. Slaves on Jesuit farms in Maryland became at least nominal Catholics, and in Louisiana, mass baptisms of slaves and free blacks occurred at Easter and Pentecost. The Ursuline Convent in New Orleans instructed black girls in the faith and accepted black females as members. In 1693, the Spanish governor offered runaways religious sanctuary in Florida if they converted to Catholicism. In the 1730s, fugitives included Catholic Angolans recently imported in large numbers to South Carolina. From 1738 until the Spanish evacuation in 1763, Gracia Real de Santa Teresa de Mose (a free black town just north of Saint Augustine) buffered British attacks, provided laborers and soldiers for the Spanish, and became a haven for Carolina runaways.

More slaves responded to evangelical preachers' emphasis on personal experience over doctrinal creeds and to an inclusive Christianity that promised universal salvation. Biracial crowds attended itinerants' outdoor meetings, and preachers interpreted slaves' physical responses as validations of their ministries. Crying, dancing, singing, shouting, jerking, and fainting, which participants interpreted as marking the Holy Spirit's presence, echoed African ecstatic trances. Slaves' "Ear for Music, and a kind of extatic Delight in *Psalmody*" transfixed many evangelicals. One evening, Samuel Davies "awakened about two or three a-clock in the morning, [as] a torrent of sacred harmony poured into my chamber. . . . In this seraphic [i.e., angelic] exercise, some of them spend almost the whole night."[45] Radical awakeners validated blacks' emotional conversions and encouraged whites to accept their physical outbursts as genuine workings of the Holy Spirit. At one large meeting of several hundred whites and blacks, Francis Asbury, an Anglican evangelist and Methodist founder, reported "I was obliged to stop again and again, and beg of the people to compose themselves. But they could not; some on their knees, and some on their faces, were crying mightily to God all the time I was preaching. Hundreds of Negroes among them, with the tears streaming down their faces."[46] From religious egalitarianism and witnessing the cathartic conversions of blacks and whites came stinging denunciations of slavery as violations of Christian humanity.

Evangelicals welcomed black converts, who joined whites in prayer services, song fests, river baptisms, love feasts, foot washings, and sacramental fairs. John Todd, a Presbyterian revivalist, opened a school for blacks, and his congregation had 200 slave members. Attending meetings defied owners' authority and increased violence against Baptists and Methodists. Patrollers attacked one group of slaves listening to James Ireland and sent them "flying in every direction."[47] Black men became exhorters testifying to fellow slaves about their rebirth and organized night gatherings where slaves sang, prayed, read the Bible, and led their own funerals. Early black ministers like Harry Hosier, who accompanied Francis Asbury on his travels, became literate, spread Christianity to slaves after the American Revolution, and challenged root doctors as slave communities' spiritual leaders. Deacons not only watched over black Baptist members' conduct and heard charges of male drunkenness, female sexual improprieties, and disobedience against masters, but also interposed church authority to strengthen slave marriages and mediate disputes between slaves and, occasionally, between slaves and owners. Separate Baptists validated black women who "became possessed" with the spirit by allowing them to witness locally and become deacons over black female members.

Christianity's evolution in slave quarters grafted new spiritual ideas onto African ritual styles. Lowcountry participants in ring shouts sang call-and-response praise songs as they went counterclockwise shuffling their bare feet (to avoid dancing, which was forbidden by the church) but moving hands and upper bodies accompanied by the beat of a broom and singers' polyrhythmic hand-clapping and foot-stamping. The dance and song tempo gradually increased to an ecstatic pitch to call upon the Holy Spirit, whose presence soothed slavery's hurts, healed community divisions, and promised justice, a day of Jubilee when all people will become free.

For most slaves, similarities in spiritual beliefs and practices across West and West Central Africa melded into new Pan–African American traditions: good and evil forces affected daily life, power of song and dance to call down the spirits, and the presence of ancestors who watched over the living. Passed down to their American-born slave children, these remained core beliefs into the 20th century. Sacred dances supplicated lesser spirits for assistance even after planters banned drums. In 1665, a Virginia minister condemned slaves' "*Idolotrous Dances*, and *Revels*" on Sundays and their requests on weekdays to "use their Dances as a *means to procure Rain*."[48] By honoring ancestors and propitiating benevolent lesser gods, individuals sought spirit helpers to endure slavery's travails. "Many of them believed there were several gods; some of whom were good, and others evil, as they prayed as much to the latter as to the former," recalled Charles Ball, a fugitive slave. Like Native Americans and some Europeans, slaves "uniformly believe in witchcraft, conjuration, and the agency of evil spirits in the affairs of human life" and undoubtedly exchanged practices with one another.[49]

Only in Louisiana did root work become a religious cult. Dahomey slaves from the French West Indies brought Damballa, a snake god that governed male sexuality. He was worshipped with animal sacrifices, spirit possession, music, dancing, and feasting. Elsewhere, slaves consulted "root doctors" after sudden illnesses or deaths to discover who was responsible for their misfortunes and acquire charms to turn back their power. Sanctified objects, the original "mojo hand," warded off oppressive overseers, wooed young women, or injured those who caused harmed. Root cellars, shallow holes dug into dirt cabin floors and lined with wood, protected prized sacred objects. Planters saw slave poisonings behind unexpected illnesses, but victims were more often rival slaves than whites. Male and female conjurers, who unleashed objects' spiritual power, gained status among the enslaved, and even some whites consulted slave doctors for antidotes to illnesses.

Storytellers recalled times when "flying Africans" possessed so much magic they turned themselves into birds and returned to Africa. Suicide, an unthinkable act in most West African societies, provided escape from a world of evil white spirits. In the early 19th century, a group of Africans appalled by numerous deaths from digging canals to drain North Carolina swampland found release:

> At night they would begin to sing their native songs, and in a short while would become so wrought up that, utterly oblivious to the danger involved, they would grasp their bundles of personal effects, swing them on their shoulders, and setting their faces towards Africa, would march down into the water singing as they marched till recalled to their senses only by the drowning of some of the party.[50]

NEW FAITHS IN A NEW LAND

By 1770, transatlantic religions and pan-ethnic faiths made colonial Southerners more divided in religious beliefs and practices than ever, yet had also laid foundations for southern evangelical religion. Experimental religion challenged inherited faiths as preachers validated individuals' new births as authentic workings of the spirit. Personal transformations became centerpieces of religious experiences that were later institutionalized in camp meetings and annual revivals. Individual choice governed religious life and institutional loyalties as relationships with God and personal piety counted more than material goods or social prestige. An emotional faith of the heart ("getting happy with the Lord") supplemented a reasonable faith of the mind. Ministers' roles expanded to include not only Bible-based preaching but also missionary outreach and itinerancy to reach the unchurched and provide pastoral care marking life transitions of baptism, marriage, and burial. Laity acquired new roles as vestrymen, exhorters, moral guardians, responsive worshippers, and leaders of self-governing congregations. A new piety challenged gentry sociability, popular leisure, old taboos, ancient gods, polygamy, and magic. Traditional gods of Africa and Native America did not die but shared spiritual power with a Christian god and spirit helpers. African worship styles infused evangelical emotionalism. Ecumenical ministers shared pulpits and meetinghouses, new songs, and Holy Fairs and embraced emotional preaching and physical worship. These practices also sharpened denominational differences and the gulf between Christians and non-Christians. Shared beliefs and worship styles lessened class but not caste divisions. By 1800, religious freedom and voluntary congregations toppled church establishments' hierarchical order, but evangelical egalitarianism waned and endorsed a racial hierarchy of dominant whites, enslaved blacks, and dispossessed natives.

NOTES

1. Samuel S. Hill, "Religion," in *The New Encyclopedia of Southern Culture,* Vol. 1: *Religion,* ed. by Samuel S. Hill (Chapel Hill: University of North Carolina Press, 2006), 15.

2. Alexander Whitaker, *Good Newes from Virginia* (London: Felix Kyngston for William Welby, 1613), cited in Robert Berkhofer, *The White Man's Indian: Images of the American Indian from Columbus to the Present* (New York: Vintage Books, 1978), 19 and Thomas Herbert, *Some Years Travels in Divers Parts of Africa . . .* (London: R. Everingham, 1677), cited in Winthrop Jordan, *White over Black: American Attitudes toward the Negro, 1550–1812* (Baltimore: Penguin Books, 1968), 24.

3. John Lawson, *A New Voyage to Carolina* (London, 1709), Project Gutenberg Etext, July 1999, http://www.gutenberg.org/dirs/etext99/nvycr10.txt, 42.

4. Charles Hudson, *The Southeastern Indians* (Knoxville: University of Tennessee Press, 1976), 132.

5. Samuel Purchas, comp. and ed., *Purcas His Pilgrimage . . . ,* 3rd ed. (London: William Stansby, 1617), cited in Helen C. Rountree, *The Powhatan Indians of Virginia: Their Traditional Culture* (Norman: University of Oklahoma Press, 1989), 131; see illustration on p. 44.

6. See illustration on p. 94.

7. Robert Beverley, *The History and Present State of Virginia* (Indianapolis: Bobbs-Merrill Company, 1971), 110, 106. Healing and medicine are considered in Chapter 7.

8. Hudson, *Southeastern Indians,* 372, 373.

9. Letter from Menédez to Felipe II, October 15, 1565, cited in David J. Weber, *The Spanish Frontier in North America* (New Haven: Yale University

Press, 1992), 63 and "Virginia Company Charter, 1606," cited in Perry Miller, *Errand into the Wilderness* (New York: Harper & Row, Publishers 1964 [1956]), 101.

10. Miller, *Errand*, 106 and William Strachey, cited in Jon Butler, *Awash in a Sea of Faith: Christianizing the American People* (Cambridge, MA: Harvard University Press, 1990), 39.

11. William Waller Hening, ed., *The Statutes at Large: Being a Collection of All the Laws of Virginia*, 13 vols. (Charlottesville: University of Virginia Press, 1969 [1819]), cited in James Horn, *Adapting to a New World: English Society in the Seventeenth-Century Chesapeake* (Chapel Hill: University of North Carolina Press, 1975), 384.

12. Hening, *Statues at Large*, I: 158, cited in ibid., 385.

13. Hening, *Statues at Large*, I: 532, 533, cited in ibid., 394.

14. Letter from Rev. John Yeo to Archbishop of Canterbury, 1676, cited in Horn, *Adapting to a New World*, 388. Protestants seized control of Maryland during the Puritan Commonwealth and repealed the Toleration Act in 1654 leaving Catholics without legal protection. Churches were even scarcer in Carolina with only a French Huguenot and an Anglican church in Charles Town before 1700.

15. James D. Kornwolf, *Architecture and Town Planning in Colonial North America*, 3 vols. (Baltimore: Johns Hopkins University Press, 2002), 1: 87, 330.

16. Joseph Frank, ed., "News from Virginny, 1644," *Virginia Magazine of History and Biography* 65, no. 1 (1957): 86, 87, cited in Horn, *Adapting to a New World*, 381.

17. Olaudah Equiano, *The Interesting Narrative of the Life of Olaudah Equiano, Written by Himself*, 2nd ed., ed. by Robert J. Allison (Boston: Bedford/ St. Martin's, 2007), 51.

18. Frank J. Klingberg, eds., *The Carolina Chronicles of Dr. Francis Le Jau, 1706–1717*, entry for December 11, 1712, cited in Betty Wood, *Slavery in Colonial America, 1619–1776* (Lanham, MD: Rowman & Littlefield, 2005), 105 and Letter from Le Jau to the Secretary of the Society for the Preservation of the Gospel, September 18, 1711, *Carolina Chronicles*, cited in Albert J. Raboteau, *Slave Religion: The "Invisible Institution" in the Antebellum South* (New York: Oxford University Press, 1978), 103.

19. Edgar Legare Pennington, *Thomas Bray's Associates and Their Work among the Negroes* (Worcester, MA: The American Antiquarian Society, 1939), cited in Raboteau, *Slave Religion*, 123.

20. Charles Ball, *Fifty Years in Chains* (New York: Dover Publications, Inc., 1970 [1837]), 165.

21. John Marrant, *Narrative of Marrant* (1785), "Black Loyalists: Our History, Our People," *Canada's Digital Collections*, http://blackloyalist.com/canadiandigitalcollection/.

22. *The Book of Common Prayer* (1662), cited in John K. Nelson, *A Blessed Company: Parishes, Parsons, and Parishioners in Anglican Virginia, 1690–1776* (Chapel Hill: University of North Carolina Press, 2001), 11.

23. Ibid., 5 and Letter from Philip V. Fithian to John Peck, August 12, 1774, in Philip Vickers Fithian, *Journal and Letters of Philip Vickers Fithian: A Plantation Tutor of the Old Dominion, 1773–1774,* ed. by Hunter Dickinson Farish (Charlottesville: University Press of Virginia, 1957), 167.

24. Fithian, *Journal and Letters,* entry for April 3, 1774, 89.

25. Ralph Emmett Fall, ed., *The Diary of Robert Rose* (Verona, VA: McClure Press, 1977), cited in Nelson, *A Blessed Company,* 149.

26. Devereux Jarratt, "The Autobiography of the Reverend Devereux Jarratt, 1732–1763," ed. by Douglass Adair, *The William and Mary Quarterly,* 3rd ser., 9, no. 3 (1952): 364, 368 and Charles Woodmason, *The Carolina Backcountry on the Eve of the Revolution: The Journal and Other Writings of Charles Woodmason, Anglican Itinerant,* ed. by Richard J. Hooker (Chapel Hill: University of North Carolina Press, 1953), "Journal," entry for July 2, 1767, 23.

27. Samuel Davies, *The State of Religion among the Protestant Dissenters in Virginia* (Boston: S. Kneeland, 1751) and John Gillies, ed., *Historical Collections Relating to Remarkable Periods of the Success of the Gospel* (Glasgow: Robert and Andrew Foulis, 1754), cited in Leigh Eric Schmidt, *Holy Fairs: Scottish Communions and American Revivals in the Early Modern Period* (Princeton, NJ: Princeton University Press, 1989), 57. Rural Huguenots experienced a Calvinist revival in the 1710s and resisted church leaders' Anglicization. They mixed religious enthusiasm and folk religion: prophesying future events, speaking in tongues, raising people from the dead, millennialism (Christ's imminent return to earth), and Sabbatarianism (worshipping on Saturdays). Anglican and civil authorities suppressed the heresy.

28. Cited in Kenneth W. Keller, "The Outlook of Rhinelanders on the Virginia Frontier," in *Diversity and Accommodation: Essays on the Cultural Composition of the Virginia Frontier,* ed. by Michael J. Puglisi (Knoxville: University of Tennessee Press, 1997), 108.

29. "Délibérations du Conseil," cited in Emily Clark, *Masterless Mistresses: The New Orleans Ursulines and the Development of a New World Society, 1727–1834* (Chapel Hill: University of North Carolina Press, 2007), 59, 64.

30. "Premier Registre de la Congrégation des Dames Enfants de Marie," cited in Emily Clark, " 'By All the Conduct of Their Lives': A Laywomen's Confraternity in New Orleans, 1730–1744," *William and Mary Quarterly,* 3rd ser., 54, no. 4 (1997): 778.

31. Eli Faber, *A Time for Planting: The First Migration, 1654–1820* (Baltimore: Johns Hopkins University Press, 1992), 17, 60.

32. Daniel B. Thorp, *The Moravian Community in Colonial North Carolina: Pluralism on the Southern Frontier* (Knoxville: University of Tennessee Press, 1989), 18, 78.

33. John S. Moore, ed., "John Williams's Journal," *Virginia Baptist Register* 17 (1978): 798–801 and Robert B. Semple, *A History of the Rise and Progress of Baptists in Virginia,* rev. and ed. by G. W. Beale (Richmond, VA: Pitt

and Dickinson,1894), 68–70. Separate Baptists condemned Regulars for worldliness and for baptizing members before receiving the experience of salvation.

34. B.C. Holtzclaw, "Elder John Wiley," *Virginia Baptist Register* 1 (1962): 11, 12 and Semple, *Rise and Progress of Baptists*, 22, 24.

35. James Ireland, *The Life of the Rev. James Ireland . . .* (Winchester, VA: J. Foster, 1819), 83–85.

36. Woodmason, *Carolina Backcountry*, 97. Hymn titles from *The Methodist Hymnal: Official Hymnal of the Methodist Church* (Nashville, TN: Methodist Publishing House, 1964).

37. Semple, *Rise and Progress of Baptists*, 24, 25 and Chestnut Grove Baptist Church, Minutes, January 9, 1773, in "Baptist Churches," vertical files, Orange County Historical Society, Orange, Virginia.

38. Ireland, *Life*, 97, 98.

39. Letter from William Green to Nathaniel Sanders, February 7, 1767, cited in Lewis P. Little, *Imprisoned Preachers and Religious Liberty in Virginia* (Lynchburg, VA: J.P. Bell and Co., 1938), 78–81; Letter from William Bradley to Sanders, ca. 1770, cited in ibid., 206, 207; and Ireland, *Life*, 132–34, 156–59.

40. Lucy L. Wenhold, ed. and trans., *A 17th Century Letter of Gabriel Díaz Vara Calderón* (Washington, D.C.: Smithsonian Institution, 1936), cited in Weber, *Spanish Frontier*, 105.

41. "Ordenanzas de su Majestad para los nuevos descubrimientos, conquistas y pacificaciones," (July 13, 1573); Wendhold, *Letter of Gabriel Díaz;* Jerald T. Milanich and William C. Sturtevant, eds., *Pareja's 1613 Confessionario* (Tallahassee: Division of History, Archives and Records Management, Florida Department of State, 1972); and unnamed Franciscan testimony (1681), cited in Weber, *Spanish Frontier*, 106, 109, 113.

42. Maynard Geiger, *The Franciscan Conquest of Florida* (Washington, D.C.: Catholic University of America, 1937), cited in James Axtell, *The Indians' New South: Cultural Change in the Colonial Southeast* (Baton Rouge: Louisiana State University Press, 1997), 27.

43. Letter from Richard Ludlam to the Secretary, March 22, 1725, SPG, cited in James H. Merrell, *The Indians' New World: Catawbas and Their Neighbors from European Contact through the Era of Removal* (New York: W.W. Norton and Company, 1999), 99, 100.

44. Thomas Secker, "Sermon," 1741, in Frank J. Klingberg, *Anglican Humanitarianism in Colonial New York* (Philadelphia: Church Historical Society, [1940]), cited in Raboteau, *Slave Religion*, 121 and Sylvia R. Frey and Betty Wood, *Come Shouting to Zion: African American Protestantism in the American South and British Caribbean to 1830* (Chapel Hill: University of North Carolina Press, 1998), 35.

45. Letters of Samuel Davies, June 28, 1751 and March 2, 1756, citied in Dena J. Epstein, *Sinful Tunes and Spirituals: Black Folk Music to the Civil War* (Urbana: University of Illinois Press, 1977), 104.

46. Frances Asbury, *The Journals and Letter of Francis Asbury,* cited in Epstein, *Sinful Tunes,* 106.

47. Ireland, *Life,* 135, 136, 165.

48. Morgan Godwin, *The Negro's and Indian's Advocate* (London, 1680), cited in Raboteau, *Slave Religion,* 65, 66.

49. Ball, *Fifty Years in Chains,* 164, 165.

50. John S. Bassett, *Slavery in the State of North Carolina* (Baltimore: Johns Hopkins University Press, 1899), cited in Michael A. Gomez, *Exchanging Our Country Marks: The Transformation of African Identities in the Colonial and Antebellum South* (Chapel Hill: University of North Carolina Press, 1998), 120.

9

DISORDER

Colonial Southerners lived in an unruly, often violent, world. For a third of the years between 1609 and 1763, colonists were at war. Promoters' dreams of recreating their homelands' institutional and hierarchical order proved impossible on the western edge of European civilization with its goals of conquest, trade, and settlement and its combustible mix of people. Spanish explorers rampaged through indigenous communities, and English and other settlers dispossessed Native Americans, captured Indians, enslaved Africans and their descendents, and attacked their European rivals' colonies. Warriors' resistance to intruders escalated violence between native communities, as each jockeyed for advantage by forging alliances with other Indians and with Europeans. Ordinary male settlers, loosened from traditional social controls and established institutions, asserted personal autonomy over free and enslaved women and demanded economic opportunities and political participation from governments dominated by privileged men. Some women challenged patriarchal authority by violating gender norms of submissive behavior. Servants and slaves resisted conditions of servitude by running away, destroying property, injuring their owners, and, occasionally, rebelling. In this society of newcomers from many different places, who lived in dispersed settlements and in unfamiliar environments and whose economy exploited natives and Africans, disorder and violence was embedded in everyday life.

The 15 stories below written as imagined newspaper articles exemplify the disorder of everyday life and negotiations over autonomy, economic opportunities, gender roles, collective rights, religion, and freedom. Arranged chronologically, they include *state violence* (warfare between Europeans and Indians, suppression of slave rebellions, attacks on European rivals' colonies, and conflicts between Indian societies); *disorderly* servants, slaves, women, and settlers; and *uprisings* by Indians (Powhatan, Yamasee, and Natchez), settlers (Nathaniel Bacon, John Coode, and Regulators), and Africans (Stono).[1] Omitted are conflicts and deviant behavior that are part of every human society—personal quarrels, assaults, homicides, and the like—in favor of examples arising from the colonial condition. Elite men, determined to preserve order and privilege at all costs, responded with restrictive or punitive legislation, court actions, oaths of fealty, incarcerations, executions, warfare, militias, alliances, and divide-and-rule policies. Colonial capitals at Saint Mary's City, Annapolis, Jamestown, Williamsburg, New Bern, Charles Town, Savannah, Saint Augustine, and New Orleans with their imposing public buildings not only were stages for reaffirming central authority but also became targets for widespread disorder.

ETHNIC CLEANSING TO RID VIRGINIA OF POWHATAN PROBLEM

JAMESTOWN, VIRGINIA, 1622. Virginia governor Sir Francis Wyatt announced a new policy of ethnic cleansing abruptly ending efforts to incorporate Powhatans into English settlements through trade, tribute payments, labor, and Christian conversion. According to Edward Waterhouse, press secretary, the change is retaliation for warriors' coordinated attacks on outlying settlements led by Opechancanough, paramount werowance, who had succeeded Powhatan four years earlier. In a written statement, Waterhouse noted the new policy's benefits:

> our hands, which before were tied with gentleness and faire usage, are now set at liberty by the treacherous violence of the Savages . . . So that we, who hitherto have had possession of no more ground than their waste, and our purchase at a valuable consideration to their owne contentment, gained; may now by right of Warre, and law of Nations, invade the Country, and destroy them who sought to destroy us; whereby wee shall enjoy their cultivated places.[2]

Surprise attacks began on Friday morning, March 22, when Powhatan men arrived to trade, eat, and labor on frontier tobacco plantations along the James River. Without warning, warriors slaughtered and mutilated everyone they could reach with pick-axes and iron hatchets, women and children included, and fought armed men with bows-and-arrows and muskets. Reportedly up to 400 settlers died that week, almost a third of the entire English population. Casualties would have been even higher but for timely warnings by several Natives living near Jamestown, and settlers quickly swarmed to eight fortified places for security. Opechancanough's intensions were clear: drive the English entirely from Virginia.

Powhatan assaults came just as the once struggling colony's prospects appeared bright. With reliable food reserves and high tobacco prices, immigration soared, and new plantations dispersed settlement up the James River to the Fall Line. Opechancanough, while reportedly concerned about squatters appropriating Native lands and plans to resettle Powhatan children in English households so they would become civilized Christians, repeatedly assured Governor Wyatt of his friendship. Even the untimely death of Nemattanew, a war captain and prophet, known as "Jack-of-the-Feathers" to the English, who reportedly was immortal and possessed magic ointment that made warriors invulnerable to bullets, had not shattered peace.

Since the Powhatans and the English can never live in harmony, the new policy of "perpetual enmity" adopts Captain George Percy's actions in a 1610 attack on the Paspahegh during the First Anglo-Powhatan War. Taking their village by surprise, his men killed 65 inhabitants, burned houses and cornfields, and seized the chief's family. On their return to Jamestown, they tossed his children overboard and shot them in the water. Rebuked by the governor for sparing the chief's wife, she was run through with a sword. With 1,500 muskets and pistols recently arrived from England, Governor Wyatt organized militias in all 8 counties and ordered every able-bodied man, servants included, be armed and trained. New taxes were proposed to fund frontier patrols from a chain of forts along the James River. Swift conquest was a much easier way to pacify natives than "civilizing them by faire meanes," Waterhouse explained, and "victory of them may bee gained many waies [ways]; by force, by surprise, by famine in burning their Corne, by destroying and burning their Boats, Canoes, and Houses, by breaking their fishing Weares [weirs], by assailing them in their huntings, . . . and by pursuing and chasing them with our horses, and blood-Hounds . . . and Mastives to teare them."[3] Summer and fall raids killed inhabitants indiscriminately and survivors were either enslaved on plantations or driven inland to their enemies who completed their destruction. Truce parleys provided other opportunities for killing unsuspecting natives by poisoning their leaders.

NATHANIEL BACON'S SUDDEN DEATH ENDS REBEL ATTACKS ON JAMESTOWN

Accomac County, Virginia, 1676. Nathaniel Bacon, rebel leader, died unexpectedly on October 20, 1676, apparently from dysentery, Governor William Berkeley's spokesperson announced. Bacon's death, he supposed, would end recent uprisings against His Majesty's Government that had resulted in Jamestown's burning a month earlier. Bacon became the governor's adversary almost since his arrival two years ago by repeatedly demanding the governor issue him a military commission as head of an army to attack frontier Indians. Governor Berkeley refused to abdicate his authority over Anglo-Indian relations. At first, the governor favored Bacon, a Cambridge University graduate and second cousin, with a coveted appointment to the Council of State. With family funds, Bacon purchased a frontier plantation with slaves and seemed well on his way to joining Berkeley's privileged inner circle.

Their falling out began in September 1675 with a planter's disputed debt to a Doeg Indian on the Potomac River. Militiamen raided the Doeg village but mistakenly killed 14 Susquehannocks, allies of Maryland's proprietor. This ignited retaliatory fighting across the Maryland–Virginia frontier that reportedly resulted in deaths of over 300 colonists and many more Natives. Bacon's irregular forces—allegedly recruited from the "discontented rabble" of free laborers, leaseholders, indentured servants, and African slaves—sought to exterminate all Natives.[4] After the Occaneechee (Virginia's allies) attacked the Susquehannocks, Bacon's men ambushed and slaughtered them further unsettling Berkeley's Indian policy established after the Third Anglo-Powhatan War. In 1646, he had crushed the Powhatan Confederacy and forced them to cede all land south of the York River. For 30 years, small dependent villagers were trade partners, day laborers, and buffers against interior hostile natives. The governor proposed raising taxes to construct a chain of 9 forts with a force of 1,000 rangers to patrol the frontier, but he refused to wage war against peaceful Indians.

Bacon escalated his demands by attacking Berkeley's right to rule. For over a decade, low tobacco prices hit small planters hard, yet taxes rose to pay officials excessive salaries (starting with Berkeley's annual salary of 1,000 pounds, more than 300 times what a common planter cleared in a good year). Berkeley lavished large land grants, Indian trade monopolies, and lucrative offices on favored friends, who became richer at everyone else's expense. Bacon's followers pleaded the "cause of the oppressed" in the name of "Religion and Justice" and "the Publick good" against selfish actions of Berkeley and his inner circle and demanded to know:

> by what Caball and mistery the designes of . . . those whom wee call great men have bin transacted and caryed on, but let us trace these men in Authority and Favour to whose hands the dispensation of the Countries wealth has been commited; let us observe the sudden Rise of their Estates composed with Quality in which they first entered this Country . . . And lett us see wither their extractions and Education have not bin vile. And by what pretence of learning and vertue they could soe soon into Imployments of so great Trust and consequence, let us consider their sudden advancement and let us also . . . see what spounges have suckt up the Publique Treasure and wither it hath not bin privately contrived away by unworthy Favourites and juggling Parasites whose tottering Fortunes have bin repaired and supported at the Publique chardg.

They condemned Berkeley's peaceful Indian policy as benefiting a few traders but overlooking Natives' deprivations on frontier settlers that discouraged ordinary men from acquiring land when the population was steadily increasing. There was no difference between the "Foreign" and the "protected and Darling Indians," Bacon asserted, as *all* Natives "have bin for these Many years enimies to the King and country, Robbers and Theeves and Invaders." The best policy would be "to ruin and extirpate all Indians in Generall."[5]

The governor expressed shock by the uprising. In a remonstrance read in every country court, Berkeley called upon "God [as] Judge of al things in heaven and Earth to Witness," that he did not "know of any thing . . . wherein I have acted unjustly, corruptly or neglegently in distributing Equal Justice to all men, and taking all possible care to preserve their properties and to defend them from their Barbarous Enimies." Reminding settlers of over three decades of service to Virginia, Berkeley declared Bacon and his followers, "the lowest of the people," traitors "to his Sacred majestie and the country." Recognizing the precariousness of one who "Governes a People wher[e] six parts of seaven at least are Poore, Endebted, Discontented, and Armed," Berkeley called for elections to a new general assembly.[6] Meeting in June 1676, burgesses named Bacon as commander of an anti-Indian force of 1,000 men and ordered selling abandoned Indian lands to settlers, enslaving Indian captives, eliminating property requirements for suffrage, electing parish vestries, requiring freemen's assent for county levies and ordinances, curtailing plural officeholding, reducing the governor's power over county courts, and pardoning all rebels. Poorer men were promised lower taxes and opportunities for owning frontier land, and established planters received greater control over county courts.[7] With Bacon's death, Berkeley vowed to round up all rebels; his supporters captured various "rebels" and hung 23 of them until an investigative team from England halted proceedings. Virginia entered an era of uneasy peace.

KATHERINE WATKINS, WIFE OF HENRY WATKINS, INVESTIGATED FOR MISCEGENATION

Henrico County, Virginia, 1681. Tongues wagged at reports of unruly behavior by Katherine Watkins, wife of Quaker Henry Watkins of Henrico County. According to details leaked from an examination of Watkins by William Byrd and John Farrar, gentleman justices of the peace, conducted at the home of the Captain Thomas Cocke, the complainant swore that on Friday, August 12, 1681, John Long, a mulatto slave belonging to Cocke, raped her. As she was returning home from Cocke's plantation, Long sprang from behind a tree, threw Watkins down, stopped up her mouth with a handkerchief, "tooke up the said Katherine Coates [i.e., petticoats], and putt his yard into her and ravished her." Humphrey Smith corroborated Watkins's story, as he saw her "Mouth . . . torn and her lipps swell'd" and the bloody handkerchief. Long also told Smith that Henry Watkins warned Long to "keepe of[f] his plantation or else he would shoote him." Other deponents told a different tale. Katherine Watkins was present when Cocke's slaves and laborers were drinking cider after a long day cutting weeds in the orchard. She "dranke cupp for cupp with them" and soon became "much in drinke" with "a very high Colour in her face . . . that had turned her brains." Flirting, she took Jack, a mulatto, "about the neck and Kissed him . . . and putt her hand on his codpiece[penis], at which he smil'd." With another slave, she "took up the taile of his shirt (saying) Dirke thou wilt have a good long thing," and embraced Mingo, a slave, "about the Necke and fling on the bedd and Kissed him and putt her hand into his Codpeice."[8]

Locals were much divided whether this case will come to trial and its outcome. Some believed William Watkins should file for divorce because his wife's adulterous behavior violated his marriage and sullied his reputation. As a Quaker, however, he was unlikely to do so. Others, citing a 1662 statute requiring double fines "if any Christian shall committ Fornication with a negro man or women," believed Katherine should be punished.[9] Without a mulatto bastard child, her defenders replied, can we believe servants' tales over a free white woman even though a Quaker? No one seemed surprised that John Long apparently was never tried for raping a white woman, as the sexual incident seemed consensual. This changed 10 years later when Virginia banned all interracial unions, but only imposed harsh penalties when white women bore bastard mulatto children. Such children born to slave women were slaves by law, a boon to their owners, but black men who violated white women threatened patriarchal authority and should be hanged.

PROTESTANT ASSOCIATION OUSTS CATHOLIC GOVERNOR AND DECLARES LOYALTY TO KING WILLIAM AND QUEEN MARY

Saint Mary's City, Maryland, 1689. In a "Declaration of the reason and motive for the present appearing in arms of His Majesties Protestant Subjects," released July 25, 1689, the so-called Protestant Association affirmed their allegiance to King William and Queen Mary, the new Protestant monarchs, and called for ending Maryland's Catholic government under Proprietor Charles Calvert, Lord Baltimore. Organized by John Coode, an Anglican clergyman and tobacco planter, the association raised a militia of 700 men, who reportedly were ready to march on Saint Mary's City, demand Governor William Joseph's resignation, and petition the king to declare Maryland a royal province. Reputable sources report uprising leaders are immigrants, successful tobacco planters, county officeholders, and assemblymen from the western shore counties of Charles, Calvert, and Saint Mary's. For some time, they have grumbled about abuses by proprietary authority in vetoing of acts of the lower house of the General Assembly, monopoly of provincial offices by the Calvert's Catholic friends and exclusion of worthy Protestant planters, and neglect of the Protestant Church of England in favor of privileges extended to the Roman Catholic Church. After a suspected antiproprietor conspiracy in 1681, John Coode was warned to "keepe a Guard upon your Tongue."[10]

Tension between Protestant planters and Catholic officials—Protestants outnumber Catholics 20 to 1—escalated after Governor William Joseph's arrival last fall. His inaugural speech to members of the assembly on November 14 forcefully asserted the proprietor's authority: "There is no power but of God and the Power by which we are Assembled here is undoubtedly Derived from God, to the King, and from the King to his Excellency the Lord Proprietary and from his said Lordship to Us." Excoriating assemblymen for the prevalence of "Drunkeness, Adultery, Swearing, Sabboth breaking, etc," in the colony, he called for new oaths of fidelity to the Lord Proprietor and a service every June 10 of "General Thanksgiving to Almighty God for the Infinite Blessing" in the birth of an heir to Charles II, England's Catholic-leaning monarch. There can be no division between the people and the proprietor, he warned, and "who ever shall endeavour to Divide the hearts of the People from my Lord, or my Lord from the People, let him . . . be Declared a Traitor to Our God, King, Lord and People."[11]

Accounts from England in early 1689, unconfirmed for several months, reported a coup by William of Orange and Mary, Charles II's Protestant daughter, and that Parliament had confirmed their accession to the throne after they pledged cooperation with Parliament and religious toleration for Protestant dissenters and Catholics. At the same time, there were rumors (later discredited) of a Catholic Indian conspiracy involving thousands of Senecas gathering to attack outlying plantations and turn Maryland over to French "Papists." Dissident settlers from Massachusetts and New York overthrew the detested Dominion of New England, which had consolidated every colony north of Pennsylvania and abolished representative assemblies. Governor Joseph said nothing. To many Protestants, his silence confirmed Catholic disloyalty. Confronted by the association militia, a small loyalist band surrendered without resistance on August 1, 1689, ending the proprietary government. Two years later, the Crown vindicated their bloodless coup and declared Maryland a royal province, although the proprietor retained his landholdings; barred Catholics and Quakers from holding office; and established the Anglican Church. The lower house wrested control of government finances from the governor and claimed much the same powers in Maryland as Parliament had in Britain. Planters' power was secured.

CHEROKEE ATTACKS ON CREEKS WEAKEN YAMASEE-LED UPRISING IN CAROLINA

Charles Town, Carolina, 1716. Yamasee hopes of expanding their pan-Indian alliance against Carolina settlers suffered a major setback when news came that in January 1716, Cherokee warriors had killed a dozen Creek emissaries at Toogaloo, Cherokee County, who were arriving for a peace parley with Carolina authorities and Cherokee headmen. George Chicken, head of the Carolina expedition, reported his hopes for maintaining Cherokee neutrality in the Yamasee-led conflict had weakened when Cherokee leaders reminded him that without waging war with their Creek adversaries, they "should have no way in getting Slaves to buy ammunition and Clothing and that they were resolved to get ready for war."[12] The recent murders not only renewed hostilities with the Creeks, who now faced over 4,000 Cherokee warriors, but also blocked continued Creek participation in the pan-Indian rebellion begun by the Yamasee and their kinsmen and joined by the Catawba and numerous coastal people. While the Cherokee agreed Carolina traders' behavior had been unscrupulous, they disagreed that the economic partnership only enriched the English and left natives impoverished or that Carolina settlers in the upcountry threatened the still distant Cherokee homeland.

The Yamasee's unexpected murder of Indian traders on Good Friday, April 15, 1715, ended a three-decade alliance with the English. Guns and power had allowed warriors to kill more deer, which their wives processed into skins, and seize more slave captives from rival villages to exchange for cloth, clothing, iron goods, jewelry, weapons, and rum. Their Savannah River homeland was a vital buffer between English Charles Town and Spanish Saint Augustine, whose rivalry enhanced Yamasee leverage in trade and in catching runaway slaves. Carolina merchants offered the best-quality trade goods and highest slave prices: a single captive "brings a Gun, ammunition, horse, hatchet, and a suit of Cloathes."[13] Yamasee warriors had joined Lower Creeks and Savannahs in raids on Guale missions in the 1680s and participated in Governor James Moore's expedition to Spanish Florida in 1702 with its rich harvest of a thousand Apalachee and Timucuan captives. The Yamasee had been Carolina's staunchest ally in the Tuscarora War

(1711–1713) and had comprised the largest native contingent on both expeditions into North Carolina. Nine hundred Yamasee, Cherokee, Creek, and Catawba warriors joined 30 militiamen under Captain James Moore, Jr., in burning Nooherooka (the main Tuscarora village), where hundreds of villagers died in the flames, 166 captives were executed, and almost 400 women and children were enslaved. Survivors fled to the Iroquois or to the Virginia mountains.

Without warning, the Yamasee turned against their old allies and trade partners two years later. An English witness reported their delight in executing Indian commissioner Thomas Nairne by loading him "with a great number of pieces of wood, to which they set fire, and burnt him . . . so that he suffered horrible torture, during several days, before he was allowed to die."[14] Warriors from the Yamasee, Catawba, Lower Creek, other Piedmont and coastal peoples and fugitive slaves made coordinated attacks that burned plantations near Port Royal and killed 400 colonists and came within 12 miles of Charles Town. The Yamasee reportedly seethed with hatred toward arrogant traders for enslaving free Indians, cheating them on trades, humiliating warriors with demeaning tasks, debauching native women, and appropriating houses and food. Yamasee wants created huge debts, but with sources of deer and slaves depleted, they could never be repaid. Squatters and their cattle herds encroached on cornfields, and Carolina planters coveted Yamasee land for rice cultivation. Driving the English out might avoid the fate of Westos, Savannahs, and Tuscaroras, who once had been slavers but soon became enslaved.

Recognizing the Carolinians' superior firepower, warriors relied on hit-and-run tactics and coordinated attacks on vulnerable targets. Stunned Carolina authorities, which in earlier conflicts had armed natives with English weapons to fight each other, had to deal with fighters "Lying Sculking in the Bushes and Swamps that we do not know where to find them nor could follow them if we did So that we may as well go to War with Wolfs and Bears."[15] Fearing the Spanish in Florida and the French in Louisiana supported the pan-Indian uprising, colonial leaders armed and paid 600 whites, 400 slaves, and 100 free Indians and pleaded for outside military assistance. Arms arrived from England and Massachusetts, and Virginia sent 300 men and promised an arms embargo. Tuscarora guides led attacks on the Catawba eliminating them from the conflict, but the Cherokee decision to resume war against the Creeks was the turning point. Success on the ground came when militiamen adopted Native guerilla tactics and pursued a policy of mass destruction by slaughtering women and children, leveling villages, and burning cornfields. Defeated Yamasee and their black allies fled to Florida under Spanish protection, where they joined local natives, Guale, Apalachee, mission Indians, Lower Creeks, and African runaways from Carolina. Their descendents became the Seminole. For Carolinians, war assured the colony's survival and marked a transition from an economy based on trade in Indian slaves to one based on clearing swamps for rice cultivation with enslaved Africans.

BLACKBEARD, NOTORIOUS PIRATE, CAPTURED OFF NORTH CAROLINA COAST

James River, Virginia, 1719. Lieutenant Robert Maynard returned to Virginia with the head of the notorious pirate, Edward Teach, aka "Blackbeard," swinging from the bowsprit of the sloop *Pearl.* Captain and crew claimed the 100-pound sterling reward offered by Governor Alexander Spotswood of Virginia for Teach and 10 pounds each for the 15 prisoners. Teach was killed after furious hand-to-hand combat on November 22, 1718, in the treacherous waters of Ocracoke Inlet, North Carolina. After receiving fire upon approaching the blackguard's sloop, the *Adventure,* Maynard hoisted the king's colors. Blackbeard boasted, "Damnation seize my soul if I give you quarters, or take any from you" and fired a broadside at the *Pearl* and disabled the *Ranger.* Maynard ordered his men below decks with pistols and swords ready as they reached the pirate ship, but were met with hand grenades, bottles filled with powder and small shot, slugs, and lead. Seeing no one, Blackbeard and 14 crewmen jumped aboard the *Pearl* only to be surprised by Maynard's force of 12 men. "The sea was tinctured with blood round the vessel," an eyewitness recalled, and Maynard and Blackbeard dueled to the finish with pistols and swords. When the pirate died from 25 wounds, his men begged for quarter. Teach was as fearless in death as he was fearsome in life, as his

> cognomen (nickname) of Blackbeard [came] from the large quantity of hair which, like a frightful meteor, covered his whole face. . . . This beard was black, which he suffered to grow of an extravagant length; as to breadth it came up to his eyes. He was accustomed to twist it with ribbons, in small tails, after the manner of our ramilies wigs, and turn them about his ears. In time of action, he wore a sling over his shoulders with three brace of pistols hanging in holsters like bandoliers, and struck lighted matches under his hat, which,

appearing on each side of his face, his eyes naturally looking fierce and wild, made him altogether such a figure, that imagination cannot form an idea of a fury, from hell, to look more frightful.[16]

Governor Spotswood congratulated Maynard and his men for eliminating the arch pirate, who had been molesting the South

Blackbeard. As fearsome in appearance as he was in life with a full beard, drawn sword, a half-dozen loaded pistols, and lighted candles in his hair, the notorious pirate prepares to board a ship with his men shown in the background. Engraving by Benjamin Cole in Charles Johnson, *General History of the Pirates* [London, 1725]. (Library of Congress)

Atlantic for two years, capturing coastal sloops and slave ships. The pirates even blockaded Charles Town for several weeks holding hostages, including a council member, until they received a chest of medicines. Since the ending of hostilities between Britain, France, and Spain in 1713, merchant trade between Virginia, Carolina, and the West Indies greatly enlarged tempting ex-privateers into piracy. The Outer Banks' numerous coves, shallow inlets, and sandbars provided ideal bases for pirate raids, eluding capture, and recruiting honest seamen. Strong government action was required to protect private property; pirates refusing the king's pardon or anyone harboring them would receive no quarter. After learning that Governor Charles Eden of North Carolina, the colony's secretary, and a few merchants and planters protected Teach and shared in his plunder, Governor Spotswood decided firm measures were necessary. Maynard seized 80 hogsheads of sugar from government stores in Bath, North Carolina.

In an exclusive interview, Caesar, a Negro member of Teach's crew awaiting trial in Williamsburg, insisted they were not "Enemies to Mankind" as Governor Spotswood claimed, but experienced seamen who had fought for the king and the country in the Royal Navy or on privateers raiding French and Spanish ships in the Caribbean.[17] Peace brought unemployment and falling wages. Joining in pirate adventures might be a hard life but far preferable to the abuse, stinting of rations, low pay, long hours, and harsh discipline of the navy and merchant marine. Pirate ships were true democracies, he asserted, as men elected officers, shared risks and plunder equitably, determined their own rules, settled disputes among themselves, and might even captain a captured ship. How proudly Teach's men had walked Charles Town streets, as frightened residents dared not lay a hand on them! A dangerous life but few seamen live to old age, and what memories of all-night debaucheries! They only took what was necessary to "live well" and punished only masters who abused their men—or so Caesar averred. The *Protestant Caesar* from Boston was burned only as retaliation for several pirates who had recently been hanged there. Never underestimate a pirate's fearlessness: Caesar was prepared to blow up the *Adventure,* as soon as Maynard's men boarded. "Nor were we bloody murderers"—all Charles Town hostages were released unharmed (but relieved of 1,500 pounds sterling in gold and valuables)—and captured crews were marooned not forced to walk the plank. Caesar accepted the gallows calmly, never expecting justice from authorities.

LOUIS CONGO, FREED AFRICAN, APPOINTED PUBLIC EXECUTIONER

New Orleans, Louisiana, 1725. Louis Congo will be the new public executioner effective immediately the Superior Council announced. Congo arrived four years ago from Cabinda, Angola, on *le Néréide,* part of a cargo of almost 400 slaves belonging to the Company of the Indies. He struck a hard bargain before accepting the position, Attorney General Fleuriau reported, demanding freedom for himself and his wife, a plot of land outside New Orleans sufficient for supporting his family, full rations of wine and drink, and compensation for his services. Congo proved up to the task by breaking Coussot, a condemned man, on the wheel, and others await execution. Since Louisiana became a penal colony of unruly and overwhelmingly male settlers, including *engagés* (indentured servants), criminals, soldiers, and paupers, "Fear of punishment is the only thing which can control the evil ones," a government spokesperson said. "We must always uphold the sword of justice, even more in this colony than anywhere else because of the quality of the people who have been sent by force to work. One cannot hope that they can change enough for all of them to behave." The government hopes Congo will enforce proper discipline among Louisiana's soldiers, whom Governor Jean-Baptiste LeMoyne de Bienville described as nothing but "a band of deserters, of smugglers, and of rogues, who are even ready, not only to abandon their flag, but to turn their arms against their country."[18] Council published a schedule of fees (payable in tobacco): iron collar, 5 pounds; flogging, 10 pounds; hanging, 30 pounds; and breaking on the wheel or burning alive, 40 pounds. Congo demanded council protection from retribution by Indians and by slaves.

NATCHEZ–BAMBARA ALLIANCE DESTROYED; LOUISIANA SECURED

New Orleans, 1730. The long-feared combination of Native uprising and servile rebellion erupted in the Fort Rosalie settlements north of New Orleans along the Mississippi River on November 28, 1729. The conflict began when a Natchez delegation arrived at the fort with promised provisions while warriors visited the 40 inhabitant households asking to borrow guns for hunting, promising a share of meat in return. Gunshots at the fort signaled the start of general fighting. Almost 250 settlers, including Fort Rosalie Commandant Sieur de Chepart, died, about 10 percent of Louisiana's European population. Over 50 women and children were taken prisoner. Some 200 slaves joined the Natchez and reportedly assisted in planning the attacks and resisted recapture.

Diplomacy had settled earlier low-intensity conflicts between the French and the Natchez. Several murders and raids on outlaying plantations in 1722 ended when Governor Jean-Baptiste Le Moyne de Beinville led an army of 600 soldiers and Indian allies and demanded the heads of 5 lesser chiefs and a free black living with them as retribution. Tensions grew when the Company of the Indies granted two concessions to develop tobacco plantations with a mixed labor force of *engagés* and African and Indian slaves. They escalated with Chepart's arrival in 1728 accompanied by 280 slaves, mostly Bambara men imported from the Senegal River, which signaled his intension to turn land around the trade post into tobacco plantations. He demanded the Natchez move White Apple village without compensation, assuming their reduced condition—just 5 villages and 1,800 people—assured peaceful compliance. Natchez Suns, their sacred leaders, agreed but requested a delay until corn harvest, clearly stalling to plan an uprising. "Before the French came amongst us, we were men, content with what we had, we walked with boldness every road," an elder recalled, "But now we go groping, afraid of meeting thorns, we walk like slaves, which we shall soon be . . . Is not death preferable to slavery?"[19] To augment their forces, the Natchez promised Bambaras freedom if they joined, aware, perhaps, of their warrior reputations. There was already much intercourse between them. Some Bambara men (and French laborers and soldiers, too) had Natchez wives, encouraged resistance to French demands, and guided raids on outlying plantations. Natchez exchanged provisions with Africans living in maroon settlements in the outback for stolen plantation goods. With settlers numbering only 1,700 amidst 3,800 African slaves and 15,000 natives, Native-African collaboration could destroy Louisiana.

Determined to prevent this outcome, Governor Étienne Boucher de Périer provided presents, goods, and guns to Choctaw warriors in the east to crush the Natchez, their ancient foe. Five hundred Choctaw warriors and French soldiers besieged the Natchez and reaped much glory and booty, killing many, slowly torturing captives, including a Bambara conspirator, and selling slaves to the French for export to West Indies sugar plantations. The governor armed a small band of slaves and promised them freedom if they destroyed Chaouachas, a village of only 30 warriors as "examples made by our blacks [that] had held the other little nations below the river in respect." Hiring natives to catch slave runaways and army deserters and freed black militiamen to attack natives will keep them enemies. "The greatest misfortune which . . . would inevitably lead to its total loss would be a union between the Indian nations and the black slaves," the governor recognized, "but happily there has always been a great aversion between them which has been much increased by the war." Choctaw torture of the Natchez's Bambara allies "has inspired all the Negroes with a new horror of the Savages, but will have a beneficial effect in securing the safety of the Colony."[20]

A century later, Natchez became the main trade center for Delta cotton planters. Thousands of shackled slaves hauled from the Seaboard South turned rich Delta soil into prosperous plantations, making their owners rich. Submerged Native enclaves survived, palimpsests in landscapes with Native place names: Natchez, Mississippi, Yazoo, Tombigbee, Coosa, Pascagoula, Opelousas, Ouachita, and Arkansas.

THREE NEGRO SLAVES CHARGED WITH MURDERING FUTURE PRESIDENT'S GRANDFATHER

Spotsylvania County, Virginia, 1732. Turk and Dido, slaves of Ambrose Madison, and Pompey, belonging to Joseph Hawkins, seized on August 22, 1732, on "Suspition of Poysoning," were charged with murder after Madison died five days later.[21] Madison, a rising planter in his mid-30s, had recently moved his family, slaves, and possessions from King and Queen County to Mount Pleasant, a princely 5,000-acre domain in western Spotsylvania County. Governor William Gooch sent commissions to the justices of the peace to convene a special court of oyer and terminer ("hear and decide") held to hear slave crimes. Unlike free settlers, whose capital offences were heard by the General Court in Williamsburg, local officials acted swiftly to prosecute slave offenders, who lacked rudimentary rights that even convict servants enjoyed such as securing independent counsel or calling witnesses. Slaves received harsher punishments, including execution, than inflicted on whites convicted of similar crimes.

The trial took a single day. On September 6, 1732, the court found Pompey guilty and ordered him hanged the next day. He was the first slave executed in Virginia for murdering a white man. Turk and

Dido were taken to the public whipping post where each received 29 lashes "well-laid on" as accessories to the alleged crime. Both were punished before large crowds to serve as deterrents, justices hoped, against future offensive behavior. The two slaves remained at Mount Pleasant where Francis Madison, a widow, will manage the property until James, her son, comes of age in 10 years.

Hawkins, an overseer on property adjoining Madison, speculated about the alleged murderers' motives. For 10 years, Madison had sent overseers and slaves to develop Mount Pleasant, so Pompey, Turk, and Dido likely knew each other. Madison's 29 slaves (10 adult men, 5 adult women, and 14 children) included Africans and Creoles, and Turk and Dido possibly were husband and wife. Perhaps, they were angry that forced migration to the backcountry ended contact with family and friends in King and Queen County, or they feared Madison's arrival marked tightened control over their lives. Turk, it is rumored, was a captured Muslim on a personal jihad, and Pompey and Dido possibly resented imposed nonsensical names that mocked their real identities. At least one of the conspirators possessed an African's knowledge of plants' powers to destroy and had lived in Virginia long enough to learn when particular plants were most potent.

Madison, already a successful planter, merchant, and county court justice, was a man on the make, neighbors from King and Queen recalled, who dreamed of becoming one of Virginia's leading men. Marrying James Taylor's daughter assured him of almost 10,000 acres of the best backcountry land, and Madison wasted no time developing it. In three years, the value of the "Buildings, workes and mprovements" at Mount Pleasant, all the results of his overseers' and his slaves' hard labor, were worth 340 pounds sterling.[22] A man who bickered with English merchants over prices and litigated with neighbors over property boundaries could be a demanding master.

All agreed: taking unwilling or resentful slaves to an unpopulated frontier was dangerous.

BLACKSMITH THREATENS POPULAR EX-GOVERNOR ALEXANDER SPOTSWOOD

Orange County, Virginia, 1736. Alexander Spotswood, late governor of Virginia, demanded the Orange County justices immediately remove William Hockings, blacksmith and ferry keeper at Germanna. The ferry house, Spotswood charged, was "a constant place of Drunkenness and a continual resort for my servants and workman with other loose and prolifigate [proliferous] persons," which diverted his joiner, shoemaker, and tailor from their work. Even worse was the ferry keeper's insolent behavior. On one occasion, Hockings rode up to the mansion house and "carried his vulgar rudeness towards me to such an insufferable height," Spotswood fumed, "as to come and insult me at the door of my own dwelling House before all my family, telling me that though I had been Governor, he would not now value me as such." If Spotswood attempted to beat him, Hockings threatened, "it should be the last white man I ever should strike." In a final insult, Hawkins rode into the public highway and "dared and dared me again to come there and strike him declaring he did not value life more than the dirt under his feet."[23]

Shocked by Hocking's public abuse of such an important personage as himself, Spotswood confronted him three days later at the ferry house. Demanding the ferry keeper settle his accounts and remove himself and his family, Hockings agreed to meet Spotswood, but only "if I came without any stick, if I had one, than he should then have another. Now no man can imagine," Spotswood sputtered to the court, "that I who pay for above 130 tithes in these two parishes, could be unprovided with means to correct such a fellow for his abusive behavior or want power to force as bloody minded a wretch as he pretended to be off my land."[24] Reminding the court of his recent generosity to the county in offering use of his dwelling house for the first county court the previous year and his generous terms for a seven-year lease of a ferry site at Germanna, in addition to many years of service to the colony and numerous offices from the Crown, Spotswood demanded the justices summarily expel Hockings from his property without a hearing. The court complied that very day, yet paid Hockings for his services as ferry keeper. Peace returned to Germanna, but Spotswood's dream of an ordered society where elite men presided uncontested over grateful dependents of wives, children, servants, slaves, yeoman, and the poor was shaken.

SLAVES' FLIGHT TO FLORIDA THWARTED; "ALL REBELS CAPTURED," GOVERNOR DECLARES

Saint Paul's Parish, South Carolina, 1739. Charles Town residents were stunned by news of a long-feared general slave uprising when "On the 9th of September last at night a great number of Negroes arose in rebellion, broke open a store where they got arms, killed twenty-one white persons, and were marching the next morning in a daring manner out of the province, killing all they met, and burning several houses they passed along the road." By chance, Lieutenant Governor William Bull was returning to Charles Town after a court meeting in Beaufort when he spied a large band of reportedly 100 blacks, who had "halted in a field, and set to dancing, Singing and beating Drums, to draw more Negroes to them."[25] Sounding the alarm, men from Willtown Presbyterian Church (as it was Sunday morning) grabbed their guns and rushed to the scene on horseback where over 100 militiamen joined them.

Firing into the rebels, they killed at least 14 immediately, while the rest fled. Within a few days, many were rounded up and summarily shot, and planters "Cutt off their heads and set them up at every Mile Post they came to."[26] At least 60 more slaves were shot, hanged, or gibbeted alive, and 30 more remained at large. As slaves attacked over a dozen households along the King's Highway (now U.S. Route 17) during the night burning homes and wantonly murdering men, women, and children, over 30 other slaves hid their masters as the rebels approached or defended them with arms. The governor promised them monetary rewards and freedom to those who had risked their lives. The rebels marched south undoubtedly enticed by Florida governors' promises of freedom to runaways. When 70 slaves escaped the previous year, the Spanish governor refused to return them to their English owners. With nine slaves for every white person in the Lowcountry, regular night patrols and new laws restricting slaves' access to guns and ability to assemble and travel were essential for white security.

Planning began onboard the ship carrying us across the Atlantic Ocean, one of the slave rebels recalled. Whites called us "Angolans," but we are Kongo soldiers, trained in small arms and hit-and-run tactics, unfortunate losers in battles, and marched in coffles to the port of Cabinda on the Atlantic coast. Sharing a common faith—we have been a Catholic nation for over two centuries—and language, pidgin Portuguese used in trade, we spoke often about reclaiming our liberty. After landing on Sullivan's Island in Charles Town harbor, several of us were sold to Lowcountry planters, who sent us to work the rice swamps. Under the task system, once our work stint was finished, the rest of the day was our own: time enough to plan an escape. We heard about the Florida governor's offer, but knew we faced a dangerous 200-mile journey through swamp, marsh, and all-white Georgia settlements.

Indian slave catchers also barred our way to freedom and religious sanctuary.

Our opportunity came unexpectedly when we were drafted for arduous road work digging drainage ditches 15 feet wide and 6 feet deep along the Stono River to prevent flooding. Long hours of weekend labor in the hot sun and stinging mosquitoes wore heavily, and the guns, ammunition, and rum at Hutchinson's store supplied all we needed. About 20 of us broke in Saturday night and surprised 2 white men, Robert Bathurst and John Gibbs. We killed them and left their heads on the front steps to prevent a general alarm. Well-armed, we headed south along the Pon Pon Road attacking many houses and killing the whites, but spared Mr. Wallace, a tavern keeper, "for he was a good man and kind to his slaves." Shouting "Liberty!" we "marched on with colors displayed, and two drums beating" to encourage others to join us.[27] By early morning, we paused and sent recruiters to nearby plantations; soon our numbers swelled to almost a hundred. Exhausted, we "set to dancing, Singing and beating Drums," which was part of our military preparations. With no opposition from whites and many slave civilians in our ranks, we were unprepared when the militia suddenly arrived. We returned fire but were hopelessly outnumbered and scattered. Some returned home hoping their absence went undetected, while small soldier bands fled into the woods to continue fighting. We took courage from one brave fellow, who "came up to his master. His master asked if he wanted to kill him. The Negro answered he did, at the same time snapping a pistol at him, but it misfired and his master shot him through the head."[28]

CAPTAIN FRANCISCO MENÉNDEZ, FREE BLACK LEADER OF MOSE, TURNS BACK GEORGIA INVADERS

San Augustín, La Florida, 1741. Residents of Gracia Real de Santa Teresa de Mose, a free-black town north of San Augustín, again proved their loyalty to Governor Manuel de Montiano during the recent siege of Castillo de San Marcos by an English Indian force of over 1,000 men led by James Oglethorpe, Governor of Georgia. Captain Francisco Menéndez's militia of free blacks fulfilled their promises to be "the most cruel enemies of the English" and to spill their "last drop of blood in defense of the Great Crown of Spain and the Holy Faith."[29] The seven-month siege ended July 1740 after the freedmen recaptured their village, seized by British forces in

May, and Montiano later commended them for their bravery. For over four decades, land north of San Augustín was a zone of low-intensity conflict: English-Yamasee armies invaded Florida in 1702 and 1728, failed to capture the fortress, but laid waste to Guale, Timucua, and Apalachee villages and enslaved thousands of Christian Indians. Georgia's founding in 1732 and posting 700 Highland Scots on the St. John's River, a mere 20 miles from San Augustín, challenged Spanish sovereignty over Florida and the security of Spain's treasure fleets.

Since forming their first militia in 1683, blacks demonstrated their value as laborers, domestic servants, herders, linguists, artisans, sailors, and soldiers in the sparsely populated colony. After raids into Carolina in 1686 returned with slaves, the governor provided religious sanctuary to Catholics and rebuffed English demands

Saint Augustine. The Florida settlement's multiethnic character includes the town and fortress Castillo de San Marcos; two native villages, remnants of once extensive missions; and the "Negroe Fort," Gracia Real de Santa Teresa de Mose, a free black community founded in 1738. Natives and free blacks worked for the Spanish, resulting in considerable racial mixing between Spanish and black men and native women. William Roberts, "Plan of the Town and Harbour of St. Augustine," 1762. (Library of Congress.)

to reclaim their property. The next year, eight men, two women, and a child arrived by boat and requested baptism. Men went to work building the Castillo, and women became domestics in Spanish households. Unlike chattel slavery in Carolina, where laws stripped slaves of any protections, under Spanish law, slaves had rights of property ownership and self-purchase, access to courts, protection from separation of family members, and membership in the Catholic Church including benefit of marriage and other sacraments. In 1693, Charles II granted freedom to runaways, whose numbers increased with growing turmoil in Carolina. Many rice planters' newly imported Angolans were Catholic ex-warriors from the Kongo in Central Africa, and in 1715, the Yamasee's African allies, including Menéndez (a Mandingo), fled to Florida. Governor Antonio de Benavides appointed him captain of a black militia in 1726, and seven years later, a royal edict commended blacks for their bravery against the Carolinians and forbade reenslaving fugitives during peacetime. Finally, in 1738, Governor Montiano granted them unconditional freedom and established Mose as walled self-governing town under Menéndez's leadership.[30]

Blacks soon built their own houses and a church, planted crops, and celebrated religious holidays. New fugitives arrived, some on their own, including 23 who came by boat in 1738; others returned with Yamasee-black bands that periodically plundered Carolina and Georgia plantations. They intermarried with each other and served as witnesses at weddings and godparents for each other's children. Some men married native women in nearby villages, and other fugitives settled in Florida's interior with Indians or in maroon settlements where they cultivated rice, corn, sugarcane, and peanuts. These black *cimarrones* became part of a new mixed Native African people, the Seminoles. A century later, they would be the last holdouts to the U.S. government's policy of forcible Indian removal to the West.

MAJOR GENERAL JAMES GRANT TO LEAD NEW INVASION OF CHEROKEE COUNTY

Charles Town, South Carolina, 1761. Major General James Grant of the British Army led a third expedition into Cherokee country to avenge last year's killing of 30 British and colonial soldiers at Fort Loudon in Cherokee country. Adopting European siege tactics, Cherokee warriors had forced the garrison to surrender with loss of many lives and large gunpowder stores. General Jeffrey Amherst,

British colonial commander, rebuffed Cherokee peace overtures and ordered Grant's army of 2,800 men—half regular forces evenly divided between Scots and colonial recruits, plus 700 Carolina militiamen and a like number of Native allies—to crush the Cherokee. Fearing rumors of a united pan-Indian and slave conspiracy against the English, Grant declared he would succeed where earlier invasions had failed. Warriors' repeated ambushes in hilly Cherokee country had forced South Carolina governors William Henry Lyttelton and William Bull to retreat and sign treaties.

Lured by promises of generous pay and land bounties, backcountry Carolinians rushed to join volunteer units. Unlike British Regulars, whose red uniforms provided ready targets for Cherokee warriors, militiamen wore dull homespun and carried 10-pound muskets and cartouches with bullets, gunpowder, and flint. They had little military training (a regular soldier could fire five rounds per minute) and, as freemen, would not submit to British officers' harsh discipline, including hanging for desertion, but they understood Indian warfare. Rangers, special frontier forces, adopted Indian guerilla tactics of quick hit-and-run raids and ambushes behind forest cover and even dressed like Indians wearing hunting shirts not breeches and carrying tomahawks. Gentlemen from Charles Town's leading families rushed to serve as officers resplendent in their deep-green designer uniforms. Colonials resented arrogant British commanders who enjoyed better accommodations while men were "severely Flogg'd, hors'd and hang'd!"[31] Recruits deserted (along with some regular troops) in droves. Defeating the Cherokee might leave colonists more divided than ever.

Cherokees were Carolinians' long-term trade partners and allies, but they also maintained contacts with Virginians, the French, the Spanish, and their Native allies playing different sides against each other to maintain the balance of power, preserve Cherokee autonomy, and ensure negotiations remained on Cherokee terms. "Trade with all; entangling alliances with none" was their policy. When war between the British and the French resumed in 1754, many leaders counseled armed neutrality or forging alliances with the French or the Creeks to avenge English traders' chicanery and block settlers from encroaching on Cherokee land and game preserves. Still, in 1755, they allowed construction of Fort Loudon, deep inside Cherokee country. Several hundred warriors served with British and colonial forces attacking Shawnee raiders in western Virginia, and over 400 men joined Brigadier-General John Forbes's expedition against the French in the upper Ohio country

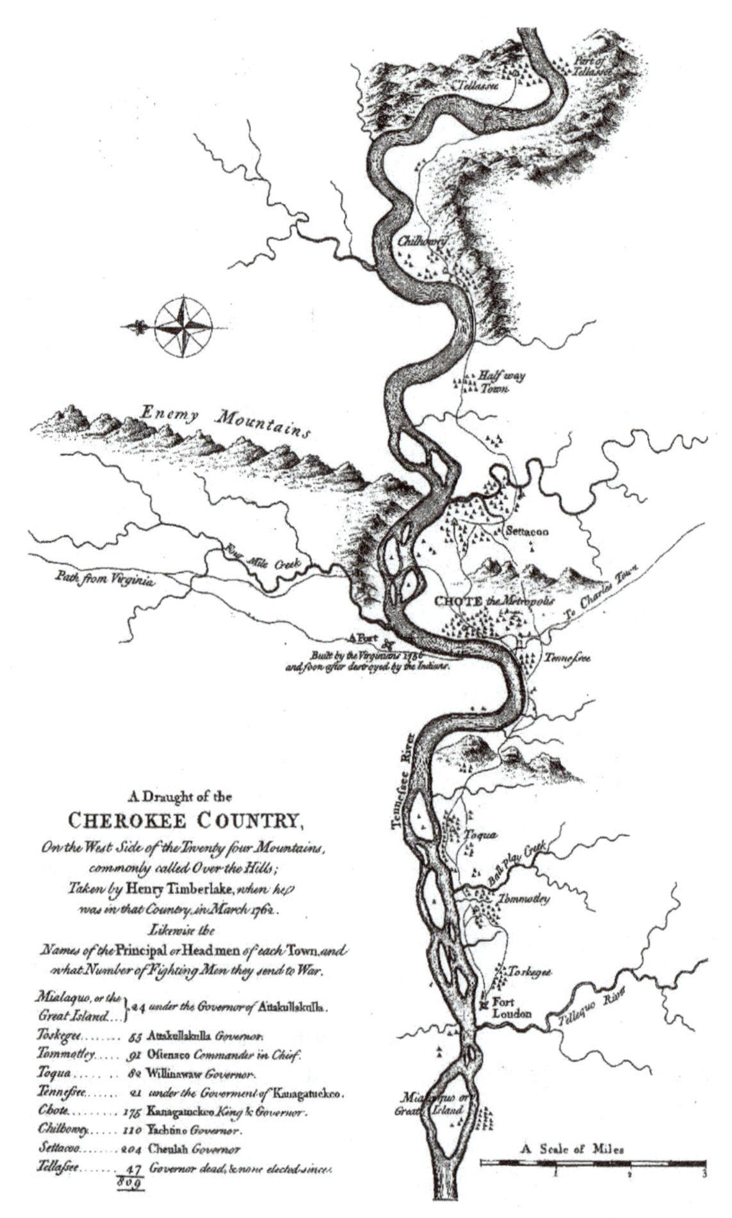

A map of Cherokee country. Maintaining the Cherokee alliance was vital for British strategic control over the southern interior. Henry Timberlake, a Virginian, mapped Cherokee villages along the Tennessee River, the number or warriors in each one, and location of Fort Loudon (bottom), built in 1755 and seized by the Cherokee five years later. After peace in 1761 the map was an instrument of imperial control. Henry Timberlake, "A Draught of the Cherokee Country," 1762, in Thomas Jeffreys, *A General Topography of North American and the West Indies* [London, 1768], No. 64. (Library of Congress.)

in 1758. Mutual distrust soon turned allies into enemies just as Cherokee conjurors had warned. British commanders treated the Cherokee with hostility, and they resented being treated as conscripts, not as autonomous warriors. When warriors failed to receive promised pay, some raided outlying settlements instead. Colonials retaliated by murdering over 30 warriors returning home in fall 1758. With Virginia authorities paying 10-pound (sterling) bounties plus plunder for enemy Indian scalps, whites professed inability to discern Cherokee from Shawnee. Cherokee raids on backcountry settlements continued in retribution.

Grant's invasion did not go entirely as planned. While soldiers laid waste to Cherokee villages and cornfields and caused great suffering, they killed far more women and children than warriors. Grant boasted in his report "fifteen [out of forty] towns and all the plantations in the country have been burnt—about 1,400 acres of corn, beans, pease, etc., destroyed; about 5,000 people, including men, women and children drove into the woods and mountains to starve."[32] Unable to resupply guns and gunpowder from the French, warriors ceded territory and avoided open battles. With bloodshed on both sides and no Creek or Chickasaw allies joining the fray, most Cherokee leaders sought peace in 1761. Three years of fighting left Cherokees devastated but unconquered.

GOVERNOR WILLIAM TRYON IN SHOWDOWN WITH BACKCOUNTRY FARMERS

Hillsborough, North Carolina, 1768. Tensions rose to fever pitch as Governor William Tryon arrived in Hillsboro, the principal town in backcountry North Carolina, with 1,400 militiamen to preserve order at the Orange County Court's September meeting. Met by almost 4,000 discontented farmers, who styled themselves "Regulators," or advocates for honest local government, Tryon calmed the crowd by releasing 3 of their leaders, who had been fined for "inciting the populace to rebellion."[33] Edmund Fanning, the unpopular court clerk, received only a nominal one-penny fine for excessive fee charging but resigned his office. This was not the first trouble in the upcountry. In March 1768, after a sheriff had seized a farmer's horse, saddle, and bridle for nonpayment of taxes, 70 Regulators tied him up and fired into Fanning's Hillsborough home. Thoroughly frightened, Fanning wrote the governor, a close friend, that Orange County "is now . . . the very nest and bosom of rioting and rebellion—The people are . . . meeting, conspiring, and confederating by solemn oath and open violence to refuse the payment of Taxes and prevent the execution of Law." Unless stopped, the Regulators, he feared, would haul local officers before them "to be arraigned at the Bar of their Shallow Understanding and to be punished and regulated at their Will."[34] Only Tryon's timely arrival maintained order among unruly backcountry settlers.

The Regulators, for their part, insisted their grievances concerned corrupt local officials, unfair taxes, and land jobbing by wealthy men. Thirty residents signed a petition to the General Assembly pleading for relief, believing they have been "continually Squeez'd and oppressed by our Publick Officers both with Regard to their fees as also in the Laying on of Taxes as well as in Collecting together with Iniquitous appropriations." Their remote frontier location limited earnings from crop sales and without money to pay levies, "On your breadth depends the Ruin or Prosperity of thousands of poor Families, and tho' to Gentlemen Rowling in affluence, a few shillings per man, may seem trifling, yet to Poor people," who faced seizure of household goods for back taxes, "Good God Gentleman, what will come of us when these demands come against us?"[35] Newly arrived outsiders with connections to the governor and eastern planters grasped for offices—Fanning was county register, superior court judge, sheriff, militia colonel, county assemblyman, and borough representative to the assembly—and unjustly enriched themselves with excessive fees at poor men's expense:

When Fanning first to Orange came,
He look'd both pale and wan:
An old patch'd coat upon his back,
An old mare he rode on.

Both man and mare wa'nt worth five pounds,
As I've been often told;
But by his civil robberies,
He's laced his coat with gold.[36]

High poll or head taxes fell most heavily on the poor. Tryon Palace, begun in 1767 as the new government seat, was only the latest financial boondoggle. Cost overruns for this "truly elegant and noble" building—the assembly tripled the initial 5,000-pound appropriation—increased the already exorbitant poll of 6 shillings per adult worker levied to pay for recent Indian wars and for Tyron's new militia raised to suppress the Regulators.[37] Without means to pay usurious taxes, the poor suffered from unscrupulous sheriffs who seized household and farm goods essential for poor men's livelihoods, pocketed fees, and, allegedly, received kickbacks by selling seized goods below their actual value.

Unelected local officials affected every property holder's daily life. Governors selected new justices of the peace for county courts from lists of nominees sitting justices had provided, creating a self-perpetuating oligarchy. Justices appointed all other local officials: registers, clerks, coroners, constables, road overseers, inspectors, sheriffs, and more. Petitioners supplicated justices' approval for new roads, gristmills, and ordinary licenses, and the court set prices for drink and lodging at taverns. Clerks collected fees to record wills, deeds, and estate inventories. Courts set local levies to pay their salaries, erect public buildings, and maintain ferries. Sheriffs received a portion of county taxes, parish levies, and court fees they collected, and constables were paid for serving warrants. Many of these officers were inexperienced men unworthy of respect. After complaints of allowing "quarrel and dance and Riot" in his house on Sundays, one justice replied: "I'll be damned if any body can hurt me . . . for I am part Judge in Court part Judge in Hell and Part Judge in heaven."[38] All Regulators demanded were honest office-holders, who protected liberty by keeping taxes low, and justice where responsible officials acted for the community's good and not to enrich their pockets. Tryon insisted on order and obedience whatever the cost. Seven Regular leaders were hanged after their military defeat at Alamance on May 16, 1771.

MOB ATTACKS BAPTIST PREACHER; JUSTICES DIVIDED ON CONTINUING BAPTIST PERSECUTION

CAROLINE COUNTY, VIRGINIA, 1771. Itinerant Baptist preachers were again met with violence from leading citizens and local government officials in Caroline County. In the latest incident, the parish minister disrupted Brother James Waller's service by whipping him across the mouth. During prayer, Waller "was Violently Jerked off of the Stage, [they] Caught him by the Back part of his Neck, Beat his head against the ground . . . [and] Carried him through a Gate . . . where a Gentleman [the sheriff] Give him . . . Twenty lashes with his Horse Whip." This was but the latest popular "contention between . . . advocates and opposers" of Baptists with tacit approval or even active participation of clergymen, sheriffs, and justices of the peace. Five years ago, Sheriff Benjamin Healy pulled Samuel Harris down as he was preaching and dragged him about by the hair and leg until friends rescued him. Mobs with clenched fists hauled David Thomas from services and threatened him and another Baptist preacher with guns. In a neighboring county, several "miscreants" stood on a table and urinated on James Ireland while he was preaching and threatened to blow up the jail where he was incarcerated.[39] Elsewhere, officials arrested Baptists for disturbing the peace, for failing to attend Anglican services, or for refusing to seek preaching licenses as required by the Toleration Act.

Persecution, authorities discovered to their dismay, only strengthened Baptists' fervor, as newly converted preachers fired up with religious enthusiasm relished martyrdom. After Allen Wiley and Elijah Craig were charged with being "Vagrant and Itinerant Persons and for Assembling themselves Unlawfully at Sundry Times and Places . . . and for Teaching and preaching Schismatick Doctrines," justices demanded they post 50-pound bonds with securities for 3 months good behavior or face incarceration. They chose jail as a matter of principle. Craig reportedly preached "through bars to the people who resorted to the prison, till he was confined to the inner dungeon where there was no opening save a hole in the door through which he received his bread and water." After his beating, Waller proclaimed "the Lord stood by him . . . & pour'd his Love into his Soul without measure," as "the Bretheren & Sisters Round him Singing praises . . . so that he Could Scarcely feel the stripes . . . Rejoicing . . . that he was Worthy to Suffer for his Dear Lord & Master."[40]

Virginia's recent religious disorders, observers contended, arose from Baptists' abrasive attacks on Anglican clergymen, whom they charged as ineffectual and lacking in religious zeal, Baptists' defiance of toleration laws, and their questioning of justices' authority. Peace can return, traditionalists insisted, only through public professions of faith, securing proper licenses to preach at set times and places, and desisting in moral condemnations of their social superiors. "I think I could Live, in Love & Peace, with a good Man of any of the various Sects Christians," a justice asserted, "Nor do I perceive any necessity for differing or quarreling with a Man, because he may not Think exactly as I do."[41] Rule of law and religious establishments sustained interdependent communities whose members were determined by residence and birth. All household heads—regardless of their personal religious beliefs—must pay taxes to support the Church of England, as the vestry with county courts' support had public responsibilities for the unfortunate and the vulnerable, for policing public morality, and for maintaining religious orthodoxy. Baptists, in contrast, believed communities arose from voluntary actions based upon shared experiences and popular participation and where participating in common rituals created moral obligations that bound people together. Their singular practices "united them together in affection, and [they] called each other brother in consequence."[42] This Baptist vision of voluntary self-governing communities proved incompatible with Anglican's inclusive but hierarchical ordering of society.

SINEWS OF COMMUNITY ORDER

The colonial South never descended into a Hobbesian war of each against all, as settlers formed new communities by adapting old structures to changing circumstances. Family and kin ties—central for maintaining social order in Native American, West African, and European societies—were gradually reconstituted despite unsettlement from migration, disease, colonization, and violence. Associations including clans, neighborhoods, and ethnic clusters; formal institutions such as warrior societies, social clubs, courts of law, councils, representative assemblies, and churches; and shared rituals connected individuals to wider networks of obligations.

By the 1720s in the Chesapeake and several decades later in the Lowcountry, Africans who survived the horrors of the Atlantic slave trade and seasoning in the colonial South found marriage partners and established families. As their American-born children reached adulthood, ethnic differences lessened in plantation communities as kinship and friendship networks strengthened. Slaves reached accommodations with owners over labor hours and customary rights that enlarged slaves' personal and social time. Native Americans who recovered from epidemics and warfare responded by removing themselves from European settlements, absorbing Native refugees, forming regional confederations, seeking strategic alliances with Europeans and Native chiefdoms, maintaining gendered divisions of labor and matrilineal family organization, and continuing veneration of old gods with traditional dances and rituals.

Persistent native-settler violence sharpened the chasm between civilization and savagery, as whites remembered frontier conflicts as "Ravages, Depredations, Scalpings, and Ruin."[43] The shift from servant to slave labor reduced the number of servants, potential recruits for class rebellion, and new laws codified white-male privileges while stripping almost all rights from free and enslaved blacks. Armed men, including servants, on occasion, served in county militias under gentleman officers to attack native villages and bands of alleged slave rebels. Monthly patrols visited slave quarters to break up "unlawful assemblies of slaves, servants, or other disorderly persons . . . or any other strolling about . . . without a pass."[44] Authorities pursued divide-and-rule policies that encouraged intertribal wars and pitted slaves and natives against one another and in Louisiana against settlers. Warfare dispossessed natives from their homelands and allowed ordinary men to acquire backcountry land.

In English settlements, local county courts, parishes, and militias provided institutional foundations for strengthening social bonds, securing private property, and maintaining order. Courts protected private property, facilitated recovery of debts, curbed interpersonal violence, and strengthened male patriarchy over free women, servants, and slaves. Widened property ownership enlarged adult white men's independence and reduced class tensions by broadening civic participation with elected representatives to provincial assemblies, right to petition assemblies, and participation in local government. Men signed petitions to provincial assemblies that expressed local needs: damning rivers for fish weirs, establishing new counties, clearing hogs from town streets, or protesting religious establishments. While justices, vestrymen, and militia officers were self-perpetuating oligarchies of wealthy land and slaveowners, they opened up local leadership posts to upwardly mobile planters. County courts needed property owners' active participation as petit and grand jurors, witnesses, and sureties to carry out their responsibilities. Threatened property losses from seizures for nonpayment of taxes or personal debts or bonds posted to deter future misconduct became powerful forces for maintaining rights and obligations. Monthly court days, weekly divine services, and quarterly militia musters created shared rituals and established temporal rhythms that extended community beyond kin and neighbors while reinforcing authority of law, church, and arms. Large crowds of men from all social ranks flocked to monthly court days to enjoy male conviviality of drinking, boasting, gossiping, trading, and, perhaps, witness the mighty made humble by the court.

Courthouse, Chowan County, Edenton, North Carolina, 1767–1773. Older county courts gradually replaced plain wooden courthouses with handsome brick structures fashioned in the latest Georgian style. Monthly court days and the quarterly militia musters held on courthouse greens were high points of male conviviality with taverns supplying abundant alcohol and fiddlers, gamesters, orators, cockpits, and race courses providing pleasurable entertainment. (Library of Congress.)

County courts connected local communities to provincial and imperial authority. Assemblies in Maryland, Virginia, and North Carolina created new parishes and counties in response to settlers' initiatives, and rituals prescribed by a distant parliament invested local leaders with authority. In exchange for broad powers

Courthouse interior, Chowan County. Courthouses' spatial ordering symbolized the rule of law and social hierarchy. The presiding justice sat in a pedimented high chair on a raised section surrounded by other gentlemen justices. The King's Attorney, the accused and his counsel, and jurymen sat below with witnesses and spectators on benches in the rear. Most property owners brought business before the court. Photograph by Frances Benjamin Johnson, 1930s. (Library of Congress.)

of home rule, the metropolis required assurances no rebellions in the empire's peripheries threatened the homeland's political and religious stability. Virginia county justices swore allegiance to the Crown, "Subscribed the Test" of conformity to the doctrines and discipline of the Anglican Church, and took oaths of "a Justice of the Peace and of a Justice of the County Court in Chancery":

> You shall swear, That well and truly you will serve our Sovereign Lord the King, and his People, . . . that you will do equal Right to all Manner of People, Great and Small, High and Low, Rich and Poor, according to Equity, and good Conscience, and the Laws and Usages of this Colony and Dominion of Virginia, without Favour, Affection, or Partiality. So Help you God.[45]

Common men with business before the court or serving as witnesses or on juries also "took the oath." Justice was promised through rule of law, but, according to historian Rhys Issac, mediated by "gentlemen justices, bewigged and dressed in their fine coats and waistcoats, seated on the raised 'bench,'" who promised discernment and respect for local custom in making decisions that affected ordinary settlers' well-being and livelihood.[46]

Yet, everywhere social order remained contingent and negotiated. Rebellious colonists periodically challenged officials who sought to enrich themselves at the expense of community well-being. Candidates for seats in provincial assemblies disdained soliciting voters but understood the importance of providing generous supplies of food and "strong Liquors to the People" so they became "merry with Drink" on race days, militia musters, and, especially, polling days. Scots-Irish Presbyterians in the backcountry remained alienated from eastern planters and church establishments. Members of different ethnic and religious groups distrusted one another and competed for land and offices. Authorities in Florida and in Louisiana ruled without assemblies and relied on military force to curb disorder even as they were contemptuous of common settlers and soldiers. Predictably, a settler described Louisiana as "a country . . . without religion, without justice, without discipline, without order, and without police."[47]

Dependents—women, propertyless men, and servants—posed even greater threats to social order. Justices heard breeches of private order such as slander, fighting, brawls, marital discord, breaking and entering, and assault and battery. Grand juries of property owners assembled twice yearly to bring charges for alleged breeches of moral conduct especially adultery, fornication, bastardy, miscegenation, gambling on the Sabbath, failure to attend church services, and blasphemy. By mid-18th century, justices increasingly failed to prosecute the last three offenses, but came down hard on sexual offences as endangering patriarchal authority. Without threat of property losses, justices imposed imprisonment and corporal punishment, including public whippings, brandings, or humiliating time in stocks, and added extra time to runaway servants and apprentices' indentures. Elite men learned, grudgingly at times, that ethnic and religious diversity, not homogeneity, was the norm of community life in the colonial South and that expanding male household heads' political participation combined with repressing women, servants, and slaves best secured a tenuous public order.

NOTES

1. For additional examples, see Chapter 1: Hernando de Soto , 1539-1543 (state violence), Menéndez's destruction of French settlement at Saint John's, 1565 (colonial warfare), and Chapter 8: destruction of Florida missions, 1702–1706.

2. Edward Waterhouse, "A Declaration of the State of the Colony and Affaires in Virginia," in *The Records of the Virginia Company of London,* 4 vols., ed. by Susan Myra Kingsbury (Washington, D.C.: Government Printing Office, 1933), 3: 556, 557.

3. Ibid., 557.

4. William Sherwood, "Virginias Deploured Conditions," in *The Old Dominion in the Seventeenth Century: A Documentary History of Virginia, 1606–1689,* ed. by Warren M. Billings (Chapel Hill: University of North Carolina Press, 1975), 276.

5. Nathaniel Bacon, "Proclamations of Nathaniel Bacon," *Virginia Magazine of History and Biography* 1, no. 1 (January 1893): 56, 57.

6. William Berkeley, "Declaration and Remonstrance," May 29, 1676, in Billings, *Old Dominion,* 271 and William Berkeley, cited in Alan Taylor, *American Colonies: The Settling of North America* (New York: Penguin Books, 2001), 148.

7. In January 1677, 1,100 royal troops arrived in Virginia to quell the rebellion, which had ended by the time they arrived. They halted further executions and plundering of rebels' estates. Berkeley was recalled, a committee investigated the cause of the rebellion, and the king annulled the June 1676 laws.

8. "Katherine Watkin's Case, 1681," in Billings, *Old Dominion,* 161–63.

9. "An Act Defining the Status of Mulatto Bastards, December 1662," in ibid., 172.

10. Cited in Aubrey C. Land, *Colonial Maryland: A History* (Millwood, NY: KTO Press, 1981), 84, 88.

11. "William Joseph's Address to the Assembly, November 14, 1688," in *The Glorious Revolution in America,* ed. by Michael G. Hall, Lawrence H. Leder, and Michael G. Kammen (Chapel Hill: University of North Carolina Press, 1964), 159, 160.

12. George Chicken, "Letter from Carolina in 1715," cited in Allen Gallay, *The Indian Slave Trade: The Rise of the English Empire in the American South, 1670–1717* (New Haven: Yale University Press, 2002), 337.

13. Thomas Nairne, cited in Taylor, *American Colonies,* 230.

14. Letter from Charles Rodd to his employer, London, cited in Gallay, *Indian Slave Trade,* 328.

15. Cited in Colin Calloway, *New Worlds for All: Indians, Europeans, and the Remaking of Early America* (Baltimore: Johns Hopkins University Press, 1997), 103.

16. Charles Johnson, *A General History of the Robberies & Murders of the Most Notorious Pirates* (New York: Lyons Press, 1998 [1724]), 55, 57, 60.

A ramilies wig has a long plait behind tied with a bow at the top and the bottom.

17. Ibid., 54. Caesar was one of Teach's crewmembers who hanged, but the interview is my invention.

18. "Deliberations of the Superior Council of Louisiana," 1725, cited in Gwendolyn Midlo Hall, *Africans in Colonial Louisiana: The Development of Afro-Creole Culture in the Eighteenth Century* (Baton Rouge: Louisiana State University Press, 1992), 131 and Bienville, cited in Taylor, *American Colonies*, 387.

19. Antoine Le Page Du Pratz, *History of Louisiana* (London: T. Becket and P.A. De Hondt, 1763), cited in Daniel H. Usner, Jr., *Indians, Settlers, and Slaves in a Frontier Exchange Economy: The Lower Mississippi Valley before 1783* (Chapel Hill: University of North Carolina Press, 1992), 71.

20. Letter from Périer to Ministry of the Colonies, 1730, cited in Hall, *Africans in Colonial Louisiana*, 102 and Périer, "Mouvements des Sauvages . . .," 1731, cited in ibid., 102–4.

21. Spotsylvania County Order Book, 1730–1738, entry for September 6, 1732, 151, Library of Virginia, Richmond, VA.

22. Ann L. Miller, *The Short Life and Strange Death of Ambrose Madison* (Orange, VA: Orange County Historical Society, 2001), 54.

23. Complaint, Alexander Spotswood to Orange County Court, August 17, 1736, Orange County Court House, Clerk's Office, Orange, Virginia, Misc. Records, Box 352.

24. Ibid.

25. Letter from William Bull to Board of Trade, October 5, 1739, cited in Peter Charles Hoffer, *Cry Liberty: The Great Stono River Slave Rebellion of 1739* (New York: Oxford University Press, 2010), 106 and James Oglethorpe, "An Account of the Negroe Insurrection in South Carolina," 1739, cited in ibid., 108.

26. "A Rangers' Report of Travels with General Oglethorpe, 1739–1742," cited in Peter Wood, *Black Majority: Negroes in Colonial South Carolina from 1670 Through the Stono Rebellion* (New York: W.W. Norton and Company, 1975), 317.

27. "An Account of the Negroe Insurrection," cited in Hoffer, *Cry Liberty*, 87, 96.

28. "A Rangers' Report of Travels with General Oglethorpe, 1739–1742," cited in Hoffer, *Cry Liberty*, 116.

29. Letter from Manuel de Montiano to the king, February 16, 1739, cited in Jane Landers, "Gracia Real de Santa Teresa de Mose: A Free Black Town in Spanish Colonial Florida," *American Historical Review* 95, no. 1 (October 1990): 18.

30. The British captured Menendéz in 1741 when he was working on a Spanish prize ship. Once discovered as the leader of Mose's black militia, he received 200 lashes, was taken to the Bahamas, and reenslaved. Ten years later, how we do not know, he was back in Mose.

31. Henry Laurens, *The Papers of Henry Laurens*, ed. by Philip M. Hamer and George C. Rogers, Vol. 3 (Columbia: University of South Carolina,

1972), cited in Tom Hatley, *The Dividing Paths: Cherokee and South Carolinians through the Revolutionary Era* (New York: Oxford University Press, 1995), 135. To be "horsed" was receiving a severe flogging while elevated on a man's back.

32. James Grant, "Journal of Lt. Colonel James Grant, Commanding an Expedition Against the Cherokee Indians," cited in Hatley, *Dividing Paths,* 156; see illustration on p. 60.

33. Cited in Hugh T. Lefler and William S. Powell, *Colonial North Carolina: A History* (New York: Charles Scribner's Sons, 1973), 233.

34. Letter from Edmund Fanning to Governor William Tyron, April 23, 1768, cited in ibid., 232.

35. Petition of citizens of Orange and Rowan counties to the General Assembly, 1768, cited in ibid., 230, 231.

36. Arthur Palmer Hudson, "Songs of the North Carolina Regulators," *William and Mary Quarterly,* 3rd ser., 4, no. 4 (1947): 477.

37. Cited in Lefler and Powell, *Colonial North Carolina,* 228.

38. Deposition of Joseph Dillard, September 1, 1755, cited in A. Roger Ekirch, *"Poor Carolina": Politics and Society in Colonial North Carolina, 1729–1776* (Chapel Hill: University of North Carolina Press, 1981), 171.

39. John Williams Journal, May 10, 1771, cited in Rhys Isaac, *The Transformation of Virginia, 1740–1790* (Chapel Hill: University of North Carolina Press, 1982), 162; Letter from D.T. to Nathaniel Saunders, cited in Garnett Ryland, *The Baptists of Virginia, 1699–1926* (Richmond, VA: Baptist Board of Missions and Education, 1955), 80, 81; and James Ireland, *The Life of the Rev. James Ireland* (Winchester, VA: J. Foster, 1819), 131, 132.

40. Orange County, Virginia, Orange County Court, Order Book, 7, 1763–1769, entry for July 28, 1768, 514 and Williams Journal, May 10, 1771, cited in Isaac, *Transformation of Virginia,* 163.

41. Letter from William Green to Nathaniel Sanders, February 7, 1767, cited in Lewis P. Little, *Imprisoned Preachers and Religious Liberty in Virginia* (Lynchburg, VA: J.P. Bell and Co., 1938), 78–81.

42. Ireland, *Life,* 53.

43. George Milligen, *A Short Account* (1763), cited in Hatley, *Dividing Paths,* 128.

44. William Walter Hening, ed., *The Statutes at Large: Being a Collection of All the Laws of Virginia* (Charlottesville: University of Virginia Press, 1969 [Richmond, VA, 1809–1823), cited in Isaac, *Transformation of Virginia,* 106.

45. Orange County Court, January 21, 1735, Barbara Vines Little, *Order Book One* (Orange, VA, 1990), 1 and William H.B. Thomas, "Orange County Be it Remembered . . .," *Orange County Bicentennial Commission, Bicentennial Series,* no. 1 (Orange, VA: 1975), 3, 4. Vestrymen also took "the oaths appointed by law" swearing their allegiance to the Crown and against Popery and subscribing themselves "to be conformable to the doctrine and discipline of the church of England."

46. Isaac, *Transformation of Virginia,* 91.

47. H.R. McIlwaine and John Pendleton Kennedy, eds., *Journals of the House of Burgesses of Virginia 1619–1776* (Richmond, VA: Colonial Press, E. Waddey Co., 1905–1915), cited in Isaac, *Transformation of Virginia,* 112 and Louisiana settlers, cited in Taylor, *American Colonies,* 386.

10

IDENTITIES

> In the South they are fiery, voluptuary, indolent, unsteady, independent, zealous for their own liberties, but trampling on those of others, generous, candid, without attachment or pretension to any religion but that of the heart.
>
> —Thomas Jefferson, 1785

In attributing these southern character traits "to that warmth of their climate which unnerves and unmans both body and mind," Jefferson also affirmed that southern distinctiveness arose from colonial experience.[1] His list of distinguishing attributes describes at best only white male property owners, but raises important final questions for this survey of daily life in the colonial South. Did colonial Southerners share an identity *as southerners* by 1770, and, if so, what were its distinguishing lineaments?

In creating new societies in the colonial South, women and men, slaves and free people, gentry and commoners, European immigrants, Africans, and Native Americans refashioned their individual and collective selves. Contact with Native Americans and the presence of enslaved Africans in the colonial South heightened Euro-American self-identity as being Christian, civilized, and, eventually, white. Widespread property ownership among white men stigmatized social dependency, and material wealth created elite styles that distinguished gentry (and pretenders to high status) from rude folk. New racial and class divisions redefined gendered ideals of lady-hood. Population diversity sharpened some ethnic divisions while the mixing of people created new forms of community for Africans, Indians, and Euro-Americans. Processes of identity formation were often unintended or forged under coercive conditions, yet outcomes altered how ordinary people understood who they were. In making the colonial South, settlers remade themselves and laid foundations for new *southern* identities.

SLAVERY AND FREEDOM

> These two words, *Negro* and *Slave,* being by custom grown Homogeneous and convertible; even as *Negro* and *Christian, Englishman* and *Heathen,* are by the like corrupt custom and Partiality made *Opposites.*
>
> —Morgan Godwyn, 1680[2]

Unfree labor created the colonial South. Indentured servants, convicts, Indian slaves, enslaved Africans, and soldiers did the backbreaking work clearing planting ground; cultivating and harvesting crops; constructing roads, buildings, and other improvements; building fortifications; and defending outposts from Native American and from European challengers. Most workers were single men in their teens and 20s who labored to enrich well-connected men: large landowners, company shareholders, and government officials.

Political power and perceived physical differences determined those whose will—and, perhaps, even life itself—was dependent upon other men. Indian environmental knowledge and powerful warriors limited exploiting Natives at first, and European servants, even the most degraded, possessed some legal rights to challenge abusive masters. From the first, Europeans saw Africans differently. Their dark skin symbolized baseness, evil, and danger. To Europeans, as Godwyn notes, Africans were uncivilized heathens and even manlike apes. Black captives' isolation and powerlessness facilitated their reduction to slavery. As indentured servants became increasingly scarce after 1670 in the Chesapeake and African captives readily available from slave traders, blacks' legal status as slaves became fixed: lifetime servitude, inherited servile status without rights, and chattel property. Slaves could not testify in courts against white persons, gather in public, own personal property, travel without permission, or legally marry—rights whose denial defined freedom for whites. Escaping servitude, a possibility for black servants earlier in the 17th century, was drastically curtailed, and free blacks became vilified anomalies in a society based on racial slavery.

As lines between white freedom and black slavery became sharper, racial attitudes hardened. In reducing Africans to degraded slave status, Africans themselves became degraded in white colonists' eyes and all the more reason to keep them enslaved. Freedom became a white man's prerogative, as ordinary men claimed access to land, political participation, legal rights, and, most importantly,

A tobacco wharf. Great planters marketed tobacco at river landings near their mansion houses. One slave is rolling a large tobacco hogshead onto an England-bound ship, while a slave carpenter seals a hogshead after it has been weighted and inspected. The slave on the left brings a drink to a seated ship captain. The contrasting dress and posture—whites' fine clothes and gestures of hospitality versus barefoot slaves wearing only short pants and working—visualize the gulf between freedom and slavery. Cartouche, Joshua Fry and Peter Jefferson, "A Map of the Most Inhabited Part of Virginia," 1751. (Library of Congress.)

recognition as social equals to planter grandees. Long before the science of race provided allegedly irrefutable proof of blacks' innate inferiority, ordinary men understood the currency of white skin. But the price of white freedom constructed on enslaving blacks was high. Slave societies, William Byrd noted in 1736, were nurseries of brutality: "Another unhappy Effect of Many Negros is the necessity of being severe. Numbers make them insolent, and then foul Means must do what fair will not."[3] Violence, especially toward blacks, was deemed necessary so whites could be free.

LIBERTY AND DEPENDENCE

> Like one of the Patriarchs, I have my Flocks and my Herds, my Bond-men and Bond-women, and every Soart of Trade amongst my own Servants, so that I live in a kind of Independence on every one but Providence.
>
> —William Byrd, 1726[4]

Acquiring sufficient property to support independent living preserved personal liberty and avoided dependency on other men's wills. Before marrying, men acquired resources to support dependent spouses and children. Desperate to promote the struggling colony's economic development and encourage population growth, the Virginia Company shifted from corporate to private property in 1618 and to fee simple landholdings without encumbrances. Free immigrants received "headright" grants of 50 acres each and similar amounts for every free person or servant they imported to Virginia. In the 18th century, settlers could acquire 100 acres of piedmont or backcountry land for 5 to 10 pounds sterling, and Maryland and Carolina proprietors offered land on generous terms to attract settlers. Land- and slaveholdings defined colonial societies' social ranks: planter grandees with thousands of acres and scores of slaves, the "middling sort" with hundreds of acres and a few slaves, and yeomen with small tracts worked by family members. Men without land—laborers, itinerant artisans like coopers and shoemakers, and the poor—had precarious lives with only unfree laborers (servants and slaves) ranking below them. Planter William Byrd's boasted independence, however, depended on markets as much as Providence. The Atlantic economy set prices for export crops, the lifeblood of the colonial South's economy. English factors and Scots storekeepers extended credit to great planters and to small farmers, respectively, facilitating purchases of the latest consumer goods. Pursuit of higher living standards and comfort risked long-term independence if prices unexpectedly fell.

Property ownership defined men's public roles. Voting required modest land- or leaseholdings and ensured participation in male electoral conviviality where gentlemen's friends solicited ordinary men's support. Property owners jealously guarded their liberty, defined as freedom from arbitrary seizure of property, by upholding the rule of law. Local courts protected men from property losses (including slaves) arising from trespass, theft, flight, or usurious taxes. Justices demanded that men convicted of assaults, slander, and unruliness risk their property to preserve social order. Only one's peers, men with property or leaseholds, sat on juries and passed judgments on their neighbors' behavior. In the mid-17th century, when Africans were still scarce in the Chesapeake, even free blacks who owed land had access to courts to defend their property rights. With slavery's spread by the end of the century, however, membership in the property-owning class became another white men's privilege.

Property defined gender relations, as only men could legally own real estate. Even women's personal property like household furnishings or slaves, and earned income belonged to husbands upon marriage. First fathers, then husbands defined women's social status. Planters' daughters enjoyed leisured childhoods but were trained in social graces to become husbands' agreeable companions and domestic managers. As planters' wives, they supervised household labor of servants and slaves, cared for small children and daughters, and organized hospitality expected of elite households. Yeomen's daughters assisted mothers in household production including gardens, poultry, dairy, food preservation and preparation, and caring for small children, an apprenticeship for becoming future husbands' goodwives and for fulfilling domestic responsibilities. Only poor and unfree women routinely performed field labor that was codified into laws collecting head, or poll, taxes on each tithe, defined as *every* male but only *unfree* females 16 years or older. Slaves dominated field labor by the early 18th century, and white female servants became domestic workers. As enslaved women did more of the tedious planting, hoeing, and harvesting work, gender roles became racialized. Only white women could enjoy running their own households as their husbands' dependents. White women were ladies, and black women only drudges.

OLD ETHNICITIES AND NEW PEOPLES

> We are desirous that he [Alexander Cameron, deputy superintendent of Indian Affairs] may educate the boy [Cameron's son] like the white people, and cause him to be able to read and write, that he may resemble both white and red, and live among us when his father is dead.
>
> —Oconostota, Cherokee headman, 1768[5]

Huddled on the edge of a vast continent, European settlers' emotional distancing of themselves from Indians and from Africans, in part, masked inner fears over potential falls from civilization. What would happen to overseas Europeans if Natives indigenized provincials or if importing Africans turned colonies into a "New Guinea"? Authorities harshly punished men who fled squalid Jamestown in the early decades of settlement and "went over to the Indians." Colonists who had lived with Natives seemed to look like them. After three years of captivity, one Virginia boy had "grown so like both in complexion and habite to the Indians that I only know him by his tongue to be an Englishman," and after John Marrant (a free black who claimed to have lived with the Cherokees for several years) returned, his family failed to recognize him.[6] Some white female captives refused to be "redeemed" back to civilization despite treaty agreements and preferred native society's gender equality and lighter labor. Civility, perhaps, was only a thin veneer barely covering the savage within.

Colonial Southerners, unlike West Indies planters, aimed to create provincial outposts of their homelands in the New World that initially incorporated indigenous peoples. But only in Spanish Florida did priests make concerted efforts to "reduce" natives to Christian civility. Whenever Indians resisted encroachment, settlers judged them as obstacles to progress and enemies of civilized society. Native Americans' relatively scanty attire revealed to Europeans' gazes no innocent children of nature but barbarous men and sensual women. Ravages of epidemic disease and drunken comportment elicited no sympathy but proofs of natives' alleged biological inferiority that justified settlers' contempt. Defeating natives reaffirmed colonists' divine role as bearers of European Christian civilization to a New World heathen wilderness.

Saltwater slaves' alien appearance also frightened settlers, who increasingly feared for their safety as Africans began arriving by the boatload. What "publick danger . . . should arise," William Byrd

Taking possession. This early European image of Florida emphasizes New World abundance in animals (turkey, peacocks, and deer) and plants (squash and grapes) and contrasts superior European technology (large ocean ships) with naked Natives. Early maps of the colonial South, like the encounter, were oriented from the Atlantic into the interior. Engraving by Theodor de Bry, 1591, of watercolor by Jacque Le Moyne, 1564. (Library of Congress.)

prophesized, if a enslaved "Man of desperate courage amongst us . . . might . . . kindle a Servile War . . . and tinge our Rivers as wide as they are with blood"? Special laws and harsh punishments were essential, whites reasoned, to "restrain the disorders, rapines and inhumanity, to which they [i.e., slaves] are naturally prone and inclined." Otherwise, colonial dreams would turned into social nightmares, anticivilizations of black over white and heathens over Christians. Even slavery's purported opponents, like Thomas Jefferson, found blacks so inferior in innate "endowments both of body and mind" that they could not envision a society where blacks were free.[7] By thoroughly rejecting "savage" natives and inhumanely disciplining "barbaric" slaves, settlers constructed racialized "others" that simultaneously created "whites," whose innate superiority made them natural rulers over allegedly inferior blacks and Indians.

Rigidly constructed racial castes proved permeable, as migration and mixing of people blurred racial and ethnic divisions in daily life.[8] Miscegenation, or interracial sex between whites and other races, became rife despite laws banning it. The resulting mulatto population had an ambiguous status in a society built on racial slavery. Courts levied heavy fines on white servant women impregnated by black partners, added additional time to their contracts, and bound out their free children until age 31. Mulatto children born to slave women raped by masters or their sons remained their owners' property. Authorities in Spanish Florida and French Louisiana created complex hierarchies of social status based on various degrees of racial mixture. White fathers faced few restrictions on freeing mulatto children, the origins of New Orleans' "free people of color." In English settlements, however, all mulattoes, whether free or enslaved with at least one-sixteenth black ancestry, were classified as "blacks," the beginnings of the South's one-drop rule of racial assignment.

No laws prohibited unions between whites and Indians; promoting intermarriage, in fact, could serve colonists' economic, religious, and diplomatic purposes. Children of European traders and native women, called "half-breeds" by colonial Southerners, automatically became members of matrilineal native villages and were raised by their mothers and her relatives. Biracial children's cultural loyalties were often divided, but their identities became matters of personal choice. In 1768, Oconostota, a Cherokee war chief, promoted an English education for the son of Alexander Cameron, deputy superintendent of Indian Affairs, as training to lead the Cherokees in increasingly turbulent times. After the American Revolution, some mixed blood sons, whose fathers' trade connections enabled them to acquire wealth including slaves, became tribal leaders who sought to preserve their peoples' independence and homelands against encroaching Americans.

Ethnogenesis, or creation of new ethnic identities, were inevitable consequences of colonization not only for indigenous peoples but also for African, British, and European immigrants. Indians often adopted newcomers, runaway servants and slaves, female war captives, and survivors of epidemic diseases and warfare into their communities to replace lost kinsmen and rebuild their population. Seminoles, for example, were a postcontact people. Reduced by disease, slave raiders, and destruction of the Spanish missions, Creek bands moved to swamps in the Florida peninsula by the mid-18th century. They lived as farmers and cattle herders and absorbed remnant Florida natives. From their Spanish name *cimarron* (or runaway) came the English "Seminole." Nearby were maroon settlements of escaped slaves from Carolina, and new arrivals augmented their numbers. Called *estelusti* by the Seminoles, blacks maintained separate villages, introduced rice cultivation, and spoke an Afro-Seminole Creole—a mix of Gullah, Spanish, English, and Muskogee (Creek). In the 1830s, black and red Seminoles fiercely resisted the U.S. government's Indian removal policies. It was a war for freedom.

Various African, Indian, and European mixtures created more new people. Unbalanced sex ratios, a shortage of Indian men from warfare and deficit of African women in the slave trade, encouraged unions between African men and Indian women. While some biracial couples lived in native villages, other families—especially nontribal natives of African or white ancestry and triracial mixes—sought refuge in isolated swamplands, piney woods, and mountain coves. Under the one-drop rule, whites classified all mixed-race people as "blacks" and denied their claims of Native ancestry. Only in the late 20th century did some biracial peoples receive recognition as Virginia Monacans, North Carolina Lumbees, South Carolina Brass Ankles, Appalachian Melungeons, and Louisiana Redbones. Even today, many struggle to resolve the meanings of their multiracial identities.

Slaves arrived in mixed cargoes as members of many different ethnic groups—Igbo, Mandingo, Fon, Wolof, Mende, Kongo, and many more—and shipboard mixes varied markedly over time and place. Valued only as commodities, bereft of lineage ties, and utterly isolated, most captives willed themselves into staying alive. Masters imposed new nonsensical names to strip away personal identities. Robert "King" Carter, a large slaveowner, directed his overseer to take "care that the negros both men and women, always go by the names we give them." Mutually unintelligible languages, different ritual markings, and worshipping different gods in different ways created ethnic divisions in many slave communities. High mortality and scarcity of women stunted forming families, and as long as the slave trade remained open, African saltwater slaves outnumbered American-born Creoles. Slowly captives "became Africans in America," historian Ira Berlin observes. Common work routines, common Creole languages, more surviving children and fewer saltwater Africans, and, above all, shared oppression of enslavement transformed "a jumble of African nationalities" and "created new African American cultures."[9]

Not that all African ethnic connections were lost. Skills in rice cultivation, net fishing, reed and grass basket making, cattle herding, and soldiering became part of African American culture. Slaves carefully observed whites and learned when to strike back and when resistance was futile. They pressed to limit slavery's terms without openly challenging the system by contesting labor hours, garden and foraging rights, and visiting and socializing privileges with their owners and overseers. They shared sacred dances and healing rituals and acquired amulets and magic hands to ward off witches and overseers or secure lovers. If drums were banned, rhythmic hand clapping and foot tapping made percussive music. Some Lowcountry parents named children for the day of their birth, an African practice, or after relatives. They adopted newly arrived children into their families as fictive kin. They gathered secretly to bear sorrows and share celebrations. The large Lowcountry slave population, who mostly lived apart from whites, spoke Gullah, a Creole language that mixed English and African pidgin with its own syntax and grammar. Blacks become a people not by retaining the old but by creating new connections to places and new cultures that varied with local conditions across the South.

European immigrants to the colonial South also became new people. Some ethnic enclaves like Carolina Huguenots and Piedmont Virginia Germans quickly acculturated to Anglican ways, while for charter generations of other religious groups, differences trumped shared languages and cultural traditions. Germans remained divided into Catholics, Lutherans, and pietistic sects, and lowland, highland, Gaelic-speaking, and Ulster Scots formed separate communities. Ethnic labels mattered. Backcountry "cohees" insulted tidewater "tuckahoes." Calling an adversary a "*Lubber*, or a *thick-Skull*, or a *Buckskin*, or a *Scotchman*" started fistfights.[10] Ethnic differences waned as rural folk shared common lives of farm homesteads, open-range herding, and community self-sufficiency and became fluent in English. Later generations, who moved to upland Carolina, Georgia, Kentucky, and Tennessee, replicated their ancestors' adaptability and pioneering experiences. By the early 19th century, many backcountry Scots-Irish Presbyterians and German Lutherans became Baptists and Methodists as they moved south and west and became Appalachian southerners. Even the Moravians, who continued to live apart, adopted southern racial attitudes by segregating black members into separate churches.

REFINEMENT AND RUDENESS

> He [a tobacco inspector] is rather Dull, & seems unacquainted with company for when he would, at Table, drink our Health, he held the Glass of Porter fast with both his Hands, and then gave an insignificant nod to each one at the Table, in Hast, & with fear, & then drank like an Ox.
>
> —Philip Vickers Fithian, 1774[11]

Atlantic commerce in goods and ideas brought English ideals of elite consumption and genteel behavior that solidified an upper-class solidarity across colonial America. Alexander Hamilton, a Maryland physician, dined in gentry homes and socialized in gentlemen's clubs as he traveled up the coast to New England in 1744, an experience Josiah Quincy, a Boston gentlemen, replicated in reverse 30 years later on a trip to the southern colonies. Wealthy planters emulated Anglican high styles by building great Georgian houses with bright airy interiors, wearing the latest London and Paris fashions, learning measured minuet steps, playing in contrapuntal stringed quartets, and practicing polite conversation and upright deportment. The nervous tobacco inspector, a guest at planter Robert Carter's table (significantly, Fithian could not recall his name), was so untutored in the art of genteel behavior he became an object of condescension, even ridicule.

Designed spaces and formal institutions provided arenas for elite performances. The gentry processed through ordered plantation landscapes with river views, tree-lined approaches, and formal gardens. Planned capitals at Annapolis (1694), Williamsburg (1699), Savannah (1734), and New Bern (1768) modeled hierarchical order. The balanced arrangement of the Capitol, Governor's Palace, Court House, and College at Colonial Williamsburg still attracts throngs of admiring modern visitors. Planters' sons established friendships at the College of William and Mary, founded in 1699, and marriages between children of wealthy families solidified an interconnected provincial elite. Newspapers—the *Virginia Gazette* was the first in 1736 and every English southern colony had at least one by 1763—created a body of shared information concerning the latest London news, colonial politics, recent social events, newly imported goods, and new ideas. Gentlemen's clubs—most towns had several that met at taverns or in private homes on different days of the week—provided male conviviality and conversation apart from women and ordinary men. The female world of gentility centered in private homes with social visits, tea ceremonies, and polite conversation.

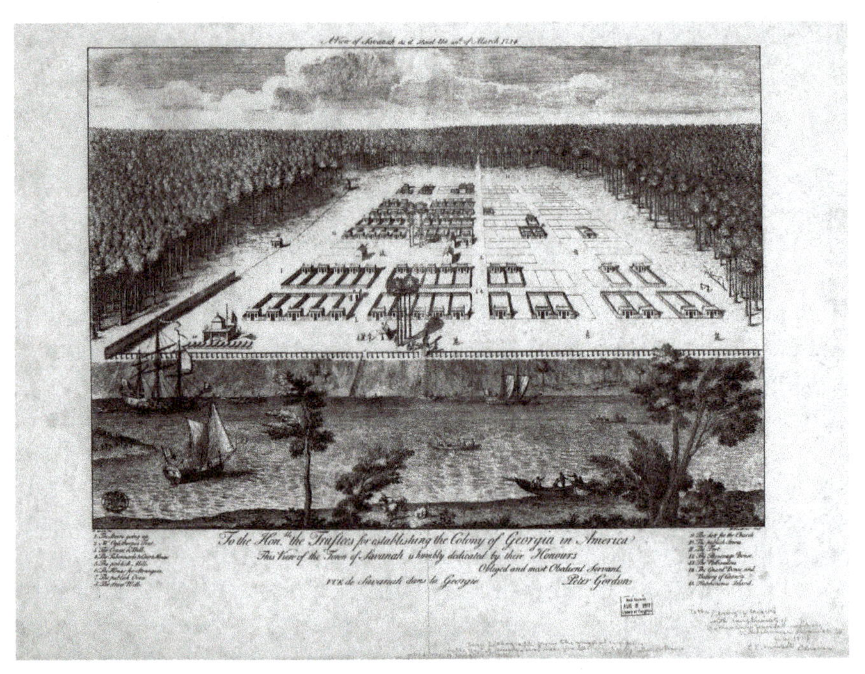

Transforming Wilderness. This 1734 plan of Savannah imposes European rationality on the New World forest. Situated on a high bluff above the Savannah River, town streets are laid out in rectangular modules with uniform building lots around four large open squares that still exist today. A palisade encloses the town, ships ply the river, and livestock on Hutchinson Island in the foreground displace native animals. Engraving by P. Fourdrinier after plan by George Jones, "A View of Savannah as It Stood the 29th of March 1734." (Library of Congress.)

Proper manners, easy conversation, and "good breeding" became hallmarks of southern elites and for those aspiring to join their ranks.

Competitive displays of learned politeness played so perfectly as to seem natural, perhaps, masked status anxiety. As prices for popular consumer goods fell, middling-rank emulators purchased gentility: tea sets, matched furniture, finer clothes, and dancing lessons. Pressured to keep up with the latest fashion, elite men often blamed their wives and daughters' extravagance for their own need to reaffirm newly acquired status and reputation. Some bet ruinously on horses, cocks, and cards to one-up rivals. Like modern plutocrats, great planters asserted their apparent indifference to financial insecurity through ostentatious display.

The "poor sort," often in the company of servants and slaves, celebrated antigentility. They favored ruleless fights over ritualized duels. "When you do fight," Charles Woodmason, an Anglican minister in backcountry Carolina, satirically advised, do not "act like Tygers and Bears as these Virginians do—Biting one another's Lips and Noses off, and *gowging* one another—that is, thrusting out one anothers Eyes, and kicking one another on the Cods [penises], to the Great damage of many a Poor Women."[12] Competitions of fighting, toasting, and binge drinking were just as much about male honor and reputation as gentlemen's extravagant betting. Slaves and poor whites gathered in the backwoods and at dockyards and unlicensed tippling houses for biracial carouses that often included white as well as black women. Assertive in-your-face behavior became hallmarks of southern lower-class self-expression that transgressed polite society's rigid racial and gender boundaries.

RECREATION AND REDEMPTION

> If a stranger went amongst them . . . [and] behaved decently, had a good face, a good coat and a tolerable share of good-nature, would dance with the women and drink with the men, with a little necessary adulation—of which . . . they are very fond—with these qualifications he would be entertained amongst them with the greatest friendship.
>
> —Nicholas Cresswell, 1777[13]

Colonial Southerners of all ranks enjoyed a good time: dancing, singing, drinking, barbecues, and socializing generally. Skill in executing jigs and reels' fast steps, playing traditional fiddle tunes, and singing British and newly composed ballads were prized. During warm months, hunting and fishing, cockfights, and horse races mixed men of different classes and races. Intimate indoor pursuits—playing cards and board games, telling stories, and making music—with male and female family members and friends filled inclement times. White children learned to ride horses that became lifelong pleasures in this rural society. Fithian, the Carter children's tutor, fretted over 18-year-old Ben Carter's "unconquerable Love for Horses" after he declared "he should be more fond & careful of a favourite Horse than of a *wife*."[14] Southerners' love of outdoor sports, their pleasure in making music, and penchant for ostentatious display continues today.

In the late colonial era, an emotional religion of the heart increasingly challenged sensual pleasures. Baptists preached about forgiveness of sin and transformed lives. Establishing personal relationships with God, inculcating piety in daily life, and maintaining cooperative relations with neighbors had more value than mere pursuit of profits and prestige. Inspired lay leaders and preachers came from common folk, who looked to the laity not elites for validation. Self-governing congregations enforced norms of behavior. Ordinary men and women usually excluded from civil society had voice in church meetings and over fellow members' personal conduct. Experimental religion encouraged emotional expression and inculcated moral conduct but uncritical examination of society. After 1800, few Baptists or Methodists challenged southern gender and racial hierarchies.

COSMOPOLITANS AND PROVINCIALS

> We should, as this house [in Georgia] now doth, join in most hearty congratulations on the conclusion of the peace with France and Spain, as an event most happy and glorious to his Majesty and the arms of Great-Britain, and, as your Excellency [Governor James Wright] justly observes, [is] particularly beneficial to the southern colonies.
>
> —*Georgia Gazette,* November 24, 1763[15]

Many a colonial Southerner joined Benjamin Franklin in toasting Britain's conquest of Canada, "not merely as . . . a colonist, but as . . . a Briton."[16] Protestant victory over Catholic France and Spain had been a joint Anglo-American one as both sides contributed men and treasure to secure the North American continent. How proud to be a Brit—a member of the world's greatest empire, whose provincial assemblies preserved self-governance and rule of law that secured property and protected liberty. How bright future economic opportunities seemed with a continent now open for settlement. Personal ties connected the English and the colonials. Great planters, like William Byrd II, were cosmopolitans as comfortable in metropolitan London as in provincial Virginia or Charles Town. They sent their sons to England not just for theological, legal, or medical training unavailable in the colonial South, but more importantly to become educated gentleman. As historian Daniel Smith notes, "learning was an integral part of the life style of the cultured gentry."[17] At the bottom of the white social order, workers in the seafaring Atlantic community also acquired cosmopolitan outlooks. Seamen's reputations for "living well" and their tales of distant lands and dangerous adventures provided livelihoods for some women as prostitutes and captured poor men's and slaves' imaginations.

During the 18th century, third- and fourth-generation settlers were developing new provincial identities. While maintaining religious ties, charter generations abandoned many local and regional traditions from their homelands to become overseas Europeans, but only later Virginians and Carolinians. In 1705, planter Robert Beverley published *The History and Present State of Virginia,* the first history of a British colony by a native, which traced Virginia's story based on personal observations, public records, and published and unpublished accounts. Here was a southern story worth telling. "I wonder nobody has ever presented the world with a tolerable account of our plantations," Beverley informed his readers, but this would be no European narrative of Virginia, as "there's none of 'em either true or so much as well invented." Its authenticity, he told readers, derived from the author's personal identity: "I am an Indian [North American] . . . but I hope the plainness of my dress will give him the kinder impression of my honesty."[18] Greater personal contact with England initially revealed the gulf between metropolitan accomplishment and provincial backwardness. As the crises with Britain intensified after 1763, some colonials responded by decrying English corruption and celebrating American innocence.

SOUTHERNERS ALL

> No foreign dish shall fire my heart, Ragoust or Fricassee,
> For they can ne'er such sweets impart, as good, boiled Hominy.
> —Thomas Jennings, Annapolis Hominy Club, 1760s[19]

A colonial South developed before there could be self-conscious southerners. Religion, ethnicity, language, province, and, above all, attachments to places-building new homes in a new and changing land—defined southerners' identities before the American Revolution. Almost every marker of future southern distinctiveness arose from the colonial South's ethnic and racial diversity and geographic variety. Dynamic tensions arose from paired opposite traits that in the 19th century became hallmarks of southern identity. Rigid racial castes, yet much racial mixing; enslaving many, yet male self-assertiveness; raucous fun, yet religious piety; biblical literalism, yet many ghost tales; personal independence, yet moral conformity; hospitality and sociability, yet suspiciousness and violence; and market plantation agriculture, yet backwoods farm isolation. Only by first becoming colonials could settlers later become southerners and, eventually, Americans.

Creative tension arising from the intermingling of Europeans, Natives, and Africans was another dynamic for creating southern identities. In language, south English dialects become the basis for Lower South English; immigrants from northern England, Scotland, and Ulster developed Upper South English; and African American English developed as a mix of British and African influences. (Linguists debate the extent of each region's contribution in the latter's origins and its impact on white southern speech.) In music, British narrative ballads and uninflected a cappella singing met African polyrhythm, percussion, and improvisation to make southern music. Field hollers, spirituals, camp meeting songs, and string bands in the 19th century became the basis for blues, black and white gospel, country and western, and rock 'n' roll in the next. In food, blending Native, African, and English ingredients and cooking methods created southern cuisine from grits ("good, boiled hominy") to barbecue to jambalaya. In recreation, southerners' love of outdoor sports and good times thrives in the popularity of horse racing, hunting, college football, and NASCAR. Peoples who disappeared or moved away left palimpsests of place names, graveyards, and burial mounds on southern landscapes. The colonial South's diversity is heard in southern speech: *bayou* (Choctaw); *catalpa* (Creek); *opossum, raccoon,* and *persimmon* (Powhatan); *saddle horse, sawbuck,* and *spooks* (German); *goober, yam, gumbo,* and *juke* (West African); and *y'all* (Southern). Rural isolation and oral traditions preserved regional southern identities from the Outer Banks English to Shenandoah Valley Mennonites, Eastern Band Cherokees, Lowcountry Gullah people, Appalachian Southerners, Louisiana Cajuns, and East Texas Germans. But the colonial South's continuing impact in the making of southerners remains present in the informal culture of everyday life: how southerners form attachments to family and home, worship and play, make music, and bury the dead.

As people of Diaspora, colonial Southerners longed for places left behind or for returns to times before colonization even while making and (re)making new homes in an ever-changing, ever-expanding colonial South. A "contrapuntal narrative" of "movement and place; fluidity and fixity," which historian Ira Berlin believes describes the making of African Americans, also made white and Indian southerners, who too can be characterized by "a malleable, flexible cultural style" and by "a passionate attachment to place."[20] In the 21st century, plaintive verses from colonial ancestors still echo from rural churches as southerners relive in song the costs of arrivals and the hopes of future possibilities:

"Idumea"
And am I born to die,
To lay this body down ?
And must my trembling spirit fly
Into a world unknown.
—Isaac Watts, 1707[21]

"Sweet Prospect"
On Jordan's stormy bank I stand,
And cast a wishful eye,
To Canaan's fair and happy land
Where my possessions lie.
—Samuel Stennett, 1787[22]

NOTES

1. Letter from Thomas Jefferson to Marquis de Chastellux, Paris, September 2, 1785, *Electronic Text Center,* Charlottesville, University of Virginia Library, http://etext.virginia.edu/toc/modeng/public/JefLett.html. Independence was the only trait common to both sections. Jefferson's southern traits were listed as paired opposites to northern attributes: "cool, sober, laborious, persevering, independent, jealous of their own liberties, and just to those of others, interested, chicaning, superstitious and hypocritical in their religion."

2. Morgan Godwyn, *Negro's and Indians Advocate, Suing for Their Admission into the Church* (Whitefish, MT: Kessinger Publishing, 2003 [London, 1680]), 36.

3. Letter from William Byrd to the Earl of Egmont, July 12, 1736, in "Colonel William Byrd on Slavery and Indentured Servants, 1736, 1739," *American Historical Review* 1, no. 1 (October 1895): 89.

4. Letter from William Byrd II to Charles, Earl of Orrery, Virginia, July 5, 1726, in "Virginia Council Journals 1726–1753," *Virginia Magazine of History and Biography* 32, no. 1 (January 1924): 27.

5. John P. Brown, *Old Frontiers: The Story of the Cherokee Indians from Earliest Times to the Date of Their Removal to the West, 1838* (Kingsport, TN: Southern Publishers, 1938), cited in Theda Perdue, *"Mixed Blood" Indians: Racial Construction in the Early South* (Athens: University of Georgia Press, 2003), 33.

6. Byrd to Egmont, 89 and Ralph Hamor, "A True Discourse of the Present State of Virginia" (London: Iohn Beale, 1615), cited in Camilla Townsend, *Pocahontas and the Powhatan Dilemma* (New York: Hill and Wang, 2004), 40.

7. Byrd to Egmont, 89; Thomas Cooper and David J. McCord, eds., *The Statutes at Large of South Carolina,* 10 vols. (Columbia, SC: A.S. Johnston,

1836–1841), 1696 code misdated 1712, cited in Winthrop Jordan, *White over Black: American Attitudes Toward the Negro, 1550–1812* (Baltimore: Penguin Books 1968), 110; and Thomas Jefferson, *Notes on the State of Virginia,* ed. by William Peden (Chapel Hill: University of North Carolina Press, 1955), 143.

8. See illustration on p. 351.

9. Letter from Robert Carter to Robert Jones, October 10, 1727, cited in Ira Berlin, *The Making of African America: The Four Great Migrations* (New York: Penguin Books, 2010), 49, 74, 77.

10. Philip Vickers Fithian, *Journal and Letters of Philip Vickers Fithian: A Plantation Tutor of the Old Dominion, 1773–1774,* ed. by Hunter Dickinson Farish (Charlottesville: University Press of Virginia, 1968 [1957]), entry for September 3, 1774, 183.

11. Ibid., entry for July 12, 1774, 138.

12. Charles Woodmason, "A Burlesque Sermon," in *The Carolina Backcountry on the Eve of the Revolution,* ed. by Richard J. Hooker (Chapel Hill: University of North Carolina Press, 1953), 158.

13. Nicholas Creswell, *Journal of Nicholas Cresswell, 1774–1777,* 2nd ed. (New York: Dial Press, 1927), 270.

14. Fithian, *Journal and Letters,* entry for September 15, 1774, 190.

15. *Georgia Gazette* (Savannah, GA.), November 24, 1763.

16. Benjamin Franklin, cited in Alan Taylor, *American Colonies: The Settling of North America* (New York: Penguin Books, 2001), 437.

17. Daniel Blake Smith, *Inside the Great House: Planter Family Life in Eighteenth-Century Chesapeake Society* (Ithaca, NY: Cornell University Press, 1980), 93, 94.

18. Robert Beverley, *The History and Present State of Virginia,* ed. by David Freeman Hawke (Indianapolis: Bobbs-Merrill Company, Inc. 1971 [1705]), 3, 4.

19. Theodore L. Chase, "Records of the Hominy Club of Annapolis," *American Historical Record* 1 (1872), cited in Anne Elisabeth Yentsch, *A Chesapeake Family and their Slaves: A Study in Historical Archaeology* (Cambridge: Cambridge University Press, 1994), 156.

20. Berlin, *Making of African America,* 18.

21. Isaac Watts, "Idumea" (1707), liner notes, in Anonymous 4, *American Angels: Songs of Hope, Redemption, & Glory* (Los Angeles: Harmonia Mundi, 2003), 17.

22. Samuel Stennett, "Sweet Prospect" (1787), in Anonymous 4, *American Angels,* 18.

APPENDIX:
MAPS AND TABLES

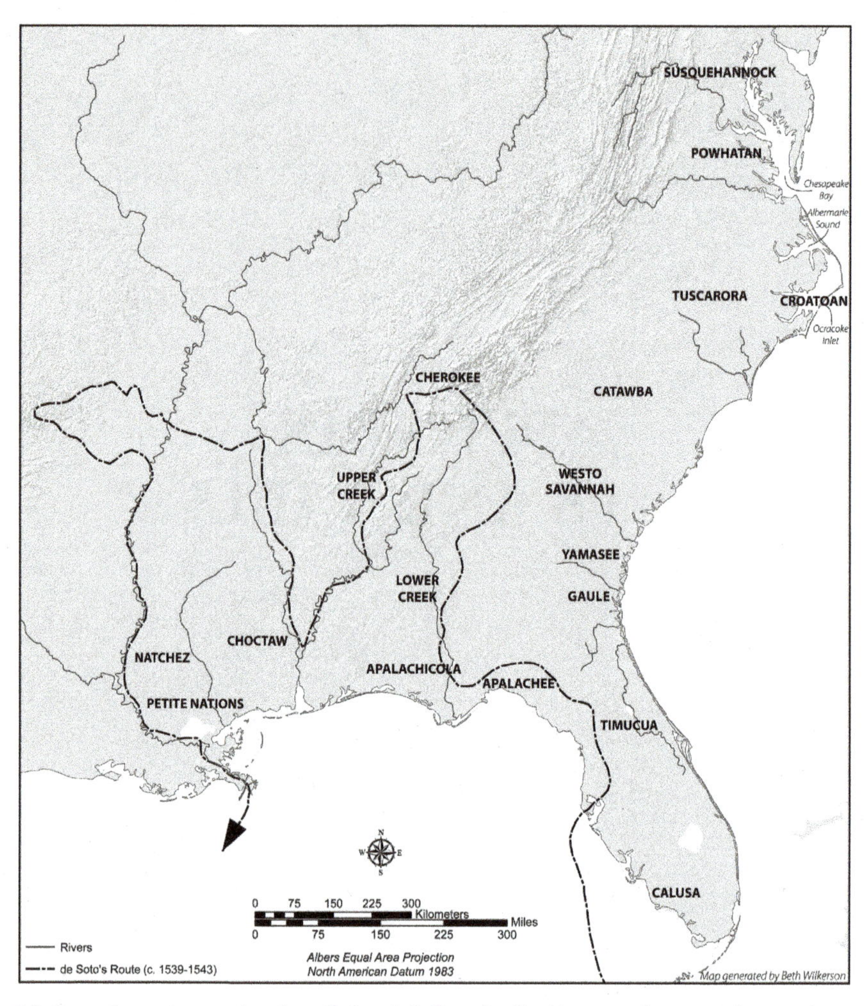

Native Americans in the Colonial South. Indian traders and warriors utilized a network of long-distance trails throughout the Southeast. Locations are approximate as groups moved, declined in population, and/or became part of new societies.

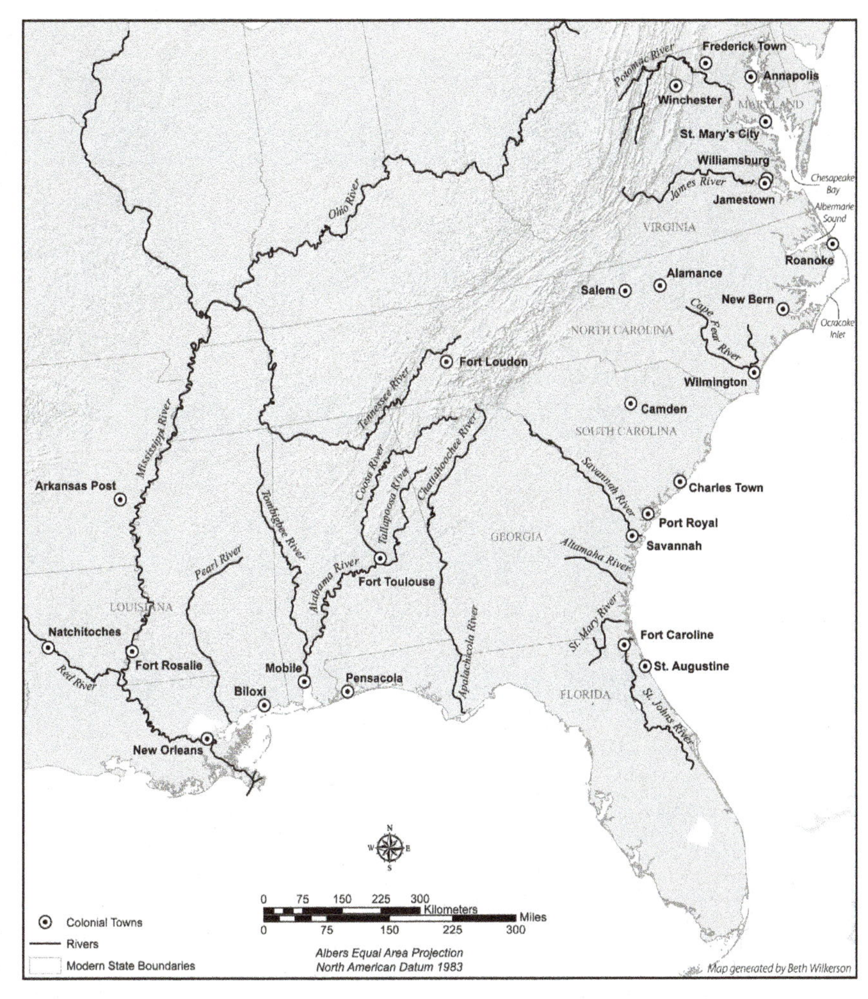

The Colonial South. (U.S. Department of the Interior, *National Atlas of the United States* [Reston, VA], http://www.nationalatlas.gov/index.html.)

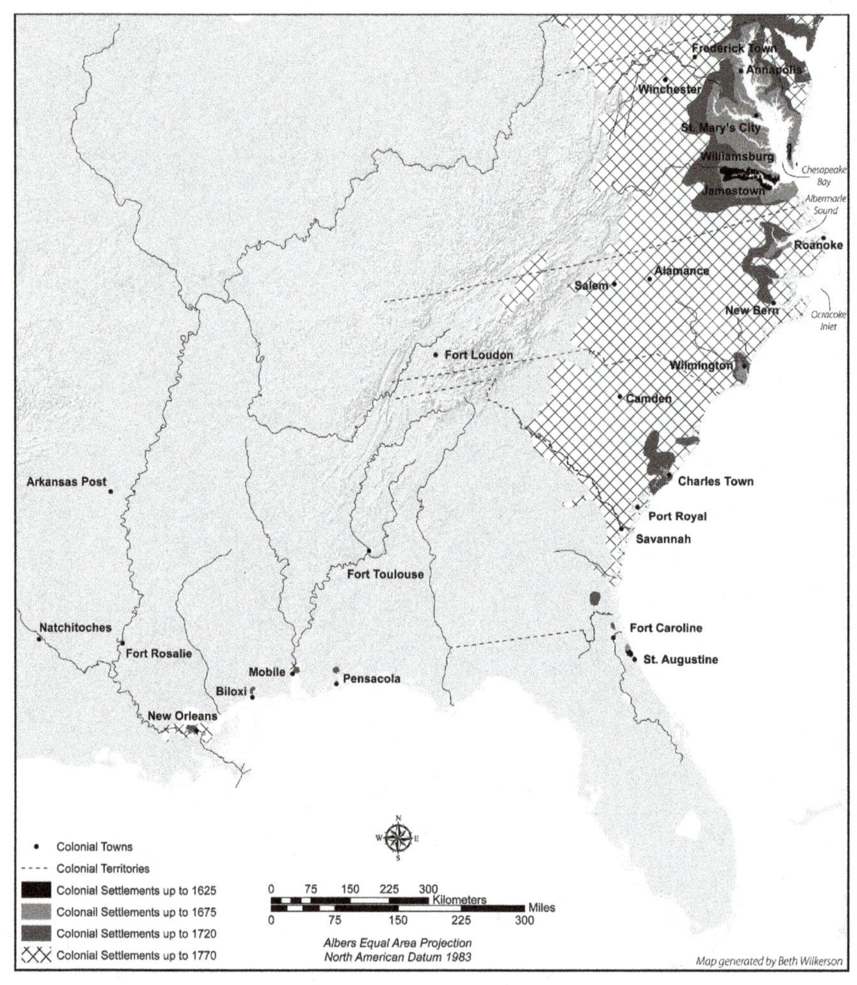

Expansion of European Settlement, 1625–1750. Before 1700, European settlers were confined to the shores of the Chesapeake Bay and to widely scattered outposts along Albemarle Sound, Wilmington, Charles Town, Saint Augustine, and New Orleans. Even after settlers poured into the backcountry of Maryland, Virginia, and the Carolinas, native peoples still dominated the vast southern interior. (Herman R. Friis, "A Series of Population Maps of the Colonies and the United States, 1625–1790," *Geographical Review* 30, no. 3 [July 1940]: 463–470.)

Table 1
Estimated White and Black Population, 1630–1770

	1630	1650	1670	1690	1710	1730	1750	1770
Maryland	—	4,504	13,226	24,024	42,741	91,113	141,073	202,599
Virginia	2,500	18,731	35,309	53,046	78,281	114,000	231,033	447,016
North Carolina	—	—	3,850	7,600	15,120	30,000	72,984	197,200
South Carolina	—	—	200	3,900	10,883	30,000	64,000	124,244
Georgia	—	—	—	—	—	—	5,200	23,375
Kentucky and Tennessee	—	—	—	—	—	—	—	16,700
Total	2,500	23,235	52,585	88,570	147,025	265,113	514,290	1,011,134

Source: Bureau of the Census, *Historical Statistics of the United States, Colonial Times to 1970,* Vol. 2 (Washington, D.C.: Government Printing Office, 1975), 1168.

Table 2
Estimated Southern Population by Race and Region

Region	Race	1685	1715	1745	1775
Virginia	Red	2,900	1,300	600	200
	White	38,100	74,100	148,300	279,500
	Black	2,600	20,900	85,300	186,400
	Total	**43,600**	**96,300**	**234,200**	**466,200**
North Carolina	Red	10,000	3,000	1,500	500
	White	5,700	14,800	42,700	156,800
	Black	200	1,800	14,000	52,300
	Total	**15,900**	**19,600**	**58,200**	**209,600**
South Carolina	Red	10,000	5,100	1,500	500
	White	1,400	5,500	20,300	71,600
	Black	500	8,600	40,600	107,300
	Total	**11,900**	**19,200**	**62,400**	**179,400**
Florida	Red	16,000	3,700	1,700	1,500
	White	1,500	1,500	2,100	1,800
	Black	—	—	—	3,000
	Total	**17,500**	**5,200**	**4,100**	**6,300**
Creeks/ Georgia/ Alabama	Red	15,000	10,000	12,000	14,000
	White	—	—	1,400	18,000
	Black	—	—	100	15,000
	Total	**15,000**	**10,000**	**13,500**	**47,000**
Cherokees	Red	32,000	11,200	9,000	8,500
	White	—	—	—	2,000
	Black	—	—	—	200
	Total	**32,000**	**11,200**	**9,000**	**10,700**
Choctaws/ Chickasaws	Red	35,000	20,800	14,500	16,300
	White	—	—	100	100
	Black	—	—	—	—
	Total	**35,000**	**20,800**	**14,600**	**16,400**
Natchez/ Louisiana	Red	42,000	15,000	5,000	3,700
	White	—	300	3,900	10,900
	Black	—	100	4,100	9,600
	Total	**42,000**	**15,400**	**13,000**	**24,200**

(Continued)

Table 2 (*Continued*)

Region	Race	1685	1715	1745	1775
East Texas	Red	28,000	17,000	12,000	8,300
	White	200	300	900	1,500
	Black	—	—	200	600
	Total	**28,200**	**17,300**	**13,100**	**10,400**
Totals	Red	190,900	87,100	57,800	53,600
	White	46,900	96,500	219,700	542,200
	Black	3,300	31,400	144,600	374,400
	Total	**241,100**	**215,000**	**422,100**	**970,200**

Source: Reprinted from Gregory A. Waselkov, Peter H. Wood, and Tom Hatley, eds., *Powhatan's Mantle: Indians in the Colonial Southeast,* revised and expanded edition by permission of the University of Nebraska Press. © 1989, 2006 by the Board of Regents of the University of Nebraska.

BIBLIOGRAPHY

GENERAL WORKS

Alden, John Richard. *The First South.* Baton Rouge: Louisiana State University Press, 1961.

Armitage, David, and Michael J. Braddick. *The British Atlantic World, 1500–1800.* New York: Palgrave Macmillan, 2002.

Boles, John B., ed. "Forum: Redefining and Reassessing the Colonial South." Special issue of *Journal of Southern History* 73, no. 3 (August 2007).

Boles, John B. *The South through Time: A History of an American Region,* 2nd ed. Upper Saddle River, NJ: Prentice-Hall, 1999.

Bridenbaugh, Carl. *Myths and Realities: Societies of the Colonial South.* New York: Atheneum, 1970.

Craven, Wesley Frank. *The Southern Colonies in the Seventeenth Century, 1607–1689.* Baton Rouge: Louisiana State University Press, 1949.

Greene, Jack P., *Pursuits of Happiness: The Social Development of Early Modern British Colonies and the Formation of American Culture.* Chapel Hill: University of North Carolina Press, 1988.

Greene, Jack P., and Philip D. Morgan, eds. *Atlantic History: A Critical Appraisal.* New York: Oxford University Press, 2009.

Greene, Jack P., and J.R. Pole. *Colonial British America: Essays in the New History of the Early Modern Era.* Baltimore: Johns Hopkins University Press, 1984.

Hawke, David Freeman. *Everyday Life in Early America.* New York: Harper and Row, 1988.

Hoffman, Paul E. *A New Andalucia and a Way to the Orient: The American Southeast during the Sixteenth Century*. Baton Rouge: Louisiana State University Press, 1990.

McGiffert, Michael, ed. "Forum: The Future of Early American History." Special issue of *William and Mary Quarterly*, 3rd ser., 50, no. 2 (April 1993).

Nash, Gary B. *Red, White and Black: The Peoples of Early North America*, 4th ed. Upper Saddle River, NJ: Prentice-Hall, 2000.

Pillsbury, Richard, ed. *Geography: The New Encyclopedia of Southern Culture*, Vol. 2, Charles Reagan Wilson, gen. ed. Chapel Hill: University of North Carolina Press, 2006.

Silver, Timothy. *A New Face on the Countryside: Indians, Colonists, and Slavery in the South Atlantic Forests, 1500–1800*. Cambridge: Cambridge University Press, 1990.

Taylor, Alan. *American Colonies: The Settling of North America*. New York: Penguin, 1991.

Vickers, Daniel, ed. *A Companion to Colonial America*. Malden, MA: Blackwell, 2006.

Wolf, Stephanie Grauman. *As Various as Their Land: The Everyday Lives of Eighteenth-Century Americans*. Fayetteville: University of Arkansas Press, 2000.

Wright, Louis B. *The Cultural Life of the American Colonies, 1607–1763*. New York: Harper and Row, 1957.

HISTORIES OF COLONIES

Maryland

Earle, Carville V. *The Evolution of a Tidewater Settlement System: All Hallow's Parish, Maryland, 1650–1783*. Chicago: University of Chicago Press, 1975.

Land, Aubrey C. *Colonial Maryland: A History*. Millwood, NY: KTO Press, 1981.

Main, Gloria L. *Tobacco Colony: Life in Early Maryland, 1650–1720*. Princeton, NJ: Princeton University Press, 1982.

Virginia

Billings, Warren M., John E. Selby, and Thad W. Tate. *Colonial Virginia: A History*. Millwood, NY: KTO Press, 1986.

Horn, James. *A Land as God Made It: Jamestown and the Birth of America*. New York: Basic, 2005.

Isaac, Rhys. *The Transformation of Virginia, 1740–1790*. Chapel Hill: University of North Carolina Press, 1982.

Kupperman, Karen Ordahl. *The Jamestown Project*. Cambridge, MA: Harvard University Press, 2007.

Morgan, Edmund S. *American Slavery, American Freedom: The Ordeal of Colonial Virginia.* New York: Oxford University Press, 1975.

Parent, Anthony S., Jr. *Foul Means: The Formation of a Slave Society in Virginia, 1660–1740.* Chapel Hill: University of North Carolina Press, 2003.

Rutman, Darrett B., and Anita H. Rutman. *A Place in Time: Middlesex County, Virginia, 1650–1750.* New York: W.W. Norton and Company, 1984.

North Carolina

Ekirch, A. Roger. *"Poor Carolina": Politics and Society in Colonial North Carolina, 1729–1776.* Chapel Hill: University of North Carolina Press, 1981.

Lefler, Hugh T., and William S. Powell. *Colonial North Carolina: A History.* New York: Charles Scribner's Sons, 1973.

South Carolina

Olwell, Robert. *Masters, Slaves, and Subjects: The Culture of Power in the South Carolina Low County, 1740–1790.* Ithaca, NY: Cornell University Press, 1998.

Ver Steeg, Clarence L. *Origins of a Southern Mosaic: Studies of Early Carolina and Georgia.* Athens: University of Georgia Press, 1975.

Weir, Robert M. *Colonial South Carolina: A History.* Millwood, NY: KTO Press, 1983.

Georgia

Coleman, Kenneth. *Colonial Georgia: A History.* Millwood, NY: KTO Press, 1976.

Davis, Harold E. *The Fledgling Province: Social and Cultural Life in Colonial Georgia, 1733–1776.* Chapel Hill: University of North Carolina Press, 1976.

Jackson, Harvey H., and Phinizy Spalding, eds. *Forty Years of Diversity: Essays on Colonial Georgia.* Athens: University of Georgia Press, 1984.

Florida

Milanach, Jerald T., and Susan Milbrath, eds. *First Encounters: Spanish Explorations in the Caribbean and the United States, 1492–1570.* Gainesville: University Press of Florida, 1989.

Proctor, Samuel, ed. *Eighteenth-Century Florida and Its Borderlands.* Gainsville: University Press of Florida, 1975.

Proctor, Samuel, ed. *Eighteenth-Century Florida: Life on the Frontier.* Gainesville: University Press of Florida, 1976.

Weber, David J. *The Spanish Frontier in North America.* New Haven, CT: Yale University Press, 1992.

Louisiana

Clark, Emily. *Masterless Mistresses: The New Orleans Ursulines and the Development of a New World Society, 1727–1834.* Chapel Hill: University of North Carolina Press, 2007.

Conrad, Glenn R., ed. *The French Experience in Louisiana.* Lafayette: Center for Louisiana Studies, University of Southwestern Louisiana, 1995.

Usner, Daniel H., Jr. *Indians, Settlers, and Slaves in a Frontier Exchange Economy: The Lower Mississippi Valley before 1783.* Chapel Hill: University of North Carolina Press, 1992.

Backcountry

Beeman, Richard. *Evolution of the Southern Backcountry: A Case Study of Lunenburg County, Virginia, 1746–1832.* Philadelphia: University of Pennsylvania Press, 1984.

Crane, Verner W. *The Southern Frontier, 1770–1732.* New York: W. W. Norton and Company, 1981 [1929].

Ferling, John. *Struggle for a Continent: The Wars of Early America.* Arlington Heights, IL: Harlan Davidson, 1993.

Hofstra, Warren. *The Planting of New Virginia: Settlement and Landscape in the Shenandoah Valley.* Baltimore: Johns Hopkins University Press, 2004.

Mitchell, Robert D. *Commercialism and Frontier: Perspectives on the Early Shenandoah Valley.* Charlottesville: University Press of Virginia, 1977.

Moore, Peter. *World of Toil and Strife: Community Transformation in Backcountry South Carolina, 1750–1805.* Columbia: University of South Carolina Press, 2007.

Puglisi, Michael J., ed. *Diversity and Accommodation: Essays on the Cultural Composition of the Virginia Frontier.* Knoxville: University of Tennessee Press, 1997.

NATIVE AMERICANS

Axtell, James. *After Columbus: Essays in the Ethnohistory of Colonial North America.* New York: Oxford University Press, 1988.

Axtell, James. *The European and the Indian: Essays in the Ethnohistory of Colonial North America.* New York: Oxford University Press, 1981.

Axtell, James. *The Indians' New South: Cultural Change in the Colonial Southeast.* Baton Rouge: Louisiana State University Press, 1997.

Calloway, Colin. *New Worlds for All: Indians, Europeans, and the Remaking of Early America.* Baltimore: Johns Hopkins University Press, 1997.

Gallay, Allen. *The Indian Slave Trade: The Rise of the English Empire in the American South, 1670–1717.* New Haven, CT: Yale University Press, 2002.

Galloway, Patricia. *Choctaw Genesis, 1500–1700.* Lincoln: University of Nebraska Press, 1995.

Hann, John H. *Apalachee: The Land between the Rivers.* Gainesville: University Press of Florida, 1988.

Hann, John H. *A History of the Timucua Indians and Missions.* Gainesville: University Press of Florida, 1996.

Hatley, Tom. *The Dividing Paths: Cherokee and South Carolinians through the Revolutionary Era.* New York: Oxford University Press, 1995.

Hudson, Charles. *The Southeastern Indians.* Knoxville: University of Tennessee Press, 1976.

Hudson, Charles, and Carmen Chaves Tesser, eds. *The Forgotten Centuries: Indians and Europeans in the American South, 1521–1704.* Athens: University of Georgia Press, 1994.

Josephy, Alvin M., Jr. *America in 1492: The World of the Indian Peoples before the Arrival of Columbus.* New York: Vintage, 1993.

Merrell, James H. *The Indians' New World: Catawbas and Their Neighbors from European Contact through the Era of Removal.* New York: W.W. Norton and Company, 1999.

Milanich, Jerald T. *Florida Indians and the Invasion from Europe.* Gainesville: University Press of Florida, 1995.

Richter, Daniel K. *Facing East from Indian Country: A Native History of Early America.* Cambridge, MA: Harvard University Press, 2001.

Rountree, Helen C. *Pocahontas' People: The Powhatan Indians of Virginia through Four Centuries.* Norman: University of Oklahoma Press, 1990.

Rountree, Helen C. *Pocahontas, Powhatan, Opechancanough: Three Indian Lives Changed by Jamestown.* Charlottesville: University of Virginia Press, 2005.

Rountree, Helen C. *The Powhatan Indians of Virginia: Their Traditional Culture.* Norman: University of Oklahoma Press, 1989.

Saunt, Claudio. *A New Order of Things: Property, Power, and the Transformation of the Creek Indians, 1733–1816.* Cambridge: Cambridge University Press, 1999.

Steele, Ian K. *Warpaths: Invasions of North America.* New York: Oxford University Press, 1994.

Townsend, Camilla. *Pocahontas and the Powhatan Dilemma.* New York: Hill and Wang, 2004.

Usner, Daniel H., Jr. *American Indians in the Lower Mississippi Valley: Social and Economic Histories.* Lincoln: University of Nebraska Press, 1998.

Waselkov, Gregory A., Peter H. Wood, and Tom Hatley, eds. *Powhatan's Mantle: Indians in the Colonial Southeast,* rev. ed. Lincoln: University of Nebraska Press, 2006.

White, Richard. *The Roots of Dependency: Subsistence, Environment, and Social Change among the Choctaws, Pawnees, and Navajos.* Lincoln: University of Nebraska Press, 1983.

Wright, J. Leitch, Jr. *The Only Land They Knew: The Tragic Story of the American Indians in the Old South.* New York: Free Press, 1981.

EUROPEAN SETTLERS

Bailyn, Bernard, and Philip Morgan, eds. *Strangers within the Realm: Cultural Margins of the First British Empire.* Chapel Hill: University of North Carolina Press, 1991.

Bridenbaugh, Carl. *Cities in the Wilderness: Urban Life in America, 1625–1742.* New York: Capricorn Books, 1964 [1938].

Butler, Jon. *The Huguenots in America: A Refugee People in New World Society.* Cambridge, MA: Harvard University Press, 1983.

Carr, Louis Green, Philip D. Morgan, and Jean B. Russo, eds. *Colonial Chesapeake Society.* Chapel Hill: University of North Carolina Press, 1988.

Dolan, Jay P. *The American Catholic Experience: A History from Colonial Times to the Present.* Garden City, NY: Doubleday and Company, 1985.

Faber, Eli. *A Time for Planting: The First Migration, 1654–1820.* Baltimore, MD: Johns Hopkins University Press, 1992.

Horn, James. *Adapting to a New World: English Society in the Seventeenth-Century Chesapeake.* Chapel Hill: University of North Carolina Press, 1994.

Kulikoff, Allen. *Tobacco and Slaves: The Development of Southern Cultures in the Chesapeake, 1680–1800.* Chapel Hill: University of North Carolina Press, 1985.

Leyburn, James G. *The Scotch-Irish: A Social History.* Chapel Hill: University of North Carolina Press, 1962.

Miller, Kerby A. *Emigrants and Exiles: Ireland and the Irish Exodus to North America.* New York: Oxford University Press, 1985.

Roeber, A.G. *Palatines, Liberty, and Property: German Lutherans in Colonial British America.* Baltimore: Johns Hopkins University Press, 1993.

Tate, Thad W., and David L. Ammerman, eds. *The Chesapeake in the Seventeenth Century: Essays on Anglo-American Society and Politics.* New York, W.W. Norton and Company, 1979.

AFRICANS AND AFRICAN AMERICANS

Berlin, Ira. *Generations of Captivity: A History of African-American Slaves.* Cambridge, MA: Harvard University Press, 2003.

Berlin, Ira. *Many Thousands Gone: The First Two Centuries of Slavery in North America*. Cambridge, MA: Harvard University Press, 1998.

Breen, T.H., and Stephen Innes. *"Myne Own Ground": Race and Freedom on Virginia's Eastern Shore, 1640–1676*. New York: Oxford University Press, 1980.

Chambers, Douglas B. *Murder at Montpelier: Igbo Africans in Virginia*. Jackson: University Press of Mississippi, 2005.

Gomez, Michael A. *Exchanging Our Country Marks: The Transformation of African Identities in the Colonial and Antebellum South*. Chapel Hill: University of North Carolina Press, 1998.

Hall, Gwendolyn Midlo. *Africans in Colonial Louisiana: The Development of Afro-Creole Culture in the Eighteenth Century*. Baton Rouge: Louisiana State University Press, 1992.

Hall, Gwendolyn Midlo. *Slavery and African Ethnicities in the Americas: Restoring the Links*. Chapel Hill: University of North Carolina Press, 2005.

Hoffer, Peter Charles. *Cry Liberty: The Great Stono River Slave Rebellion of 1739*. New York: Oxford University Press, 2010.

Kay, Marvin L. Michael, and Lorin Lee Cary. *Slavery in North Carolina, 1748–1775*. Chapel Hill: University of North Carolina Press, 1995.

Landers, Jane. *Black Society in Spanish Florida*. Urbana: University of Illinois Press, 1999.

Mariners' Museum. *Captive Passage: The Transatlantic Slave Trade and the Making of the Americas*. Washington, D.C.: Smithsonian Institution Press, 2002.

Morgan, Philip D. *Slave Counterpoint: Black Culture in the Eighteenth-Century Chesapeake and Lowcountry*. Chapel Hill: University of North Carolina Press, 1998.

Smallwood, Stephanie E. *Saltwater Slavery: A Middle Passage from Africa to American Diaspora*. Cambridge, MA: Harvard University Press, 2007.

Walsh, Lorena S. *From Calabar to Carter's Grove: The History of a Virginia Slave Community*. Charlottesville: University Press of Virginia, 1997.

Wood, Betty. *Slavery in Colonial America, 1619–1776*. Lanham, MD: Rowman and Littlefield, 2005.

Wood, Betty. *Slavery in Colonial Georgia, 1730–1775*. Athens: University of Georgia Press, 1984.

Wood, Peter H. *Black Majority: Negroes in Colonial South Carolina from 1670 through the Stono Rebellion*. New York: W. W. Norton and Co., 1974.

Wood, Peter H. *Strange New Land: Africans in Colonial America*. New York: Oxford University Press, 1996.

Wright, Donald R. *African Americans in the Colonial Era: From African Origins through the American Revolution*, 2nd ed. Wheeling, IL: Harlan Davidson, Inc., 2000.

ECONOMICS AND LABOR

Berlin, Ira, and Philip D. Morgan, eds. *Cultivation and Culture: Labor and the Shaping of Slave Life in the Americas.* Charlottesville: University Press of Virginia, 1993.

Carney, Judith Ann. *Black Rice: The African Origins of Rice Cultivation in the Americas.* Cambridge, MA: Harvard University Press, 2001.

Carr, Lois Green, Russell R. Menard, and Lorena S. Walsh. *Robert Cole's World: Agriculture and Society in Early Maryland.* Chapel Hill: University of North Carolina Press, 1991.

Clemens, Paul. *The Atlantic Economy and Colonial Maryland's Eastern Shore: From Tobacco to Grain.* Ithaca, NY: Cornell University Press, 1980.

Gray, Lewis C. *History of Agriculture in the Southern United States to 1860,* 2 vols. Gloucester, MA: Peter Smith, 1958 [1933].

Innes, Stephen, ed. *Work and Labor in Early America.* Chapel Hill: University of North Carolina Press, 1989.

Smith, Abbot Emerson. *Colonists in Bondage: White Servitude and Convict Labor in America, 1607–1776.* New York: W. W. Norton and Company, 1971 [1947].

Walker, Melissa, and James C. Cobb, eds. *Agriculture and Industry: The New Encyclopedia of Southern Culture,* Vol. 19, Charles Reagan Wilson, gen. ed. Chapel Hill: University of North Carolina Press, 2008.

WOMEN, FAMILIES, AND GENDER

Berkin, Carol. *First Generation: Women in Colonial America.* New York: Hill and Wang, 1996.

Brown, Kathleen M. *Good Wives, Nasty Wenches, and Anxious Patriarchs: Gender, Race, and Power in Colonial Virginia.* Chapel Hill: University of North Carolina Press, 1996.

Clinton, Catherine, and Michele Gillespie, eds. *The Devil's Lane: Sex and Race in the Early South.* New York: Oxford University Press, 1997.

Fischer, Kristen. *Suspect Relations: Sex, Race, and Resistance in Colonial North Carolina.* Ithaca, NY: Cornell University Press, 2002.

Jordan, Winthrop D., and Sheila Skemp, eds. *Race and Family in the Colonial South.* Jackson: University of Mississippi Press, 1987.

Kierner, Cynthia A. *Beyond the Household: Women's Place in the Early South, 1700–1835.* Ithaca, NY: Cornell University Press, 1998.

Morgan, Edmund. *Virginians at Home: Family Life in the Eighteenth Century.* Williamsburg, VA: Colonial Williamsburg, 1952.

Perdue, Theda. *Cherokee Women: Gender and Culture Change, 1700–1835.* Lincoln: University Nebraska Press, 1998.

Pesantubbee, Michelene E. *Choctaw Women in a Chaotic World: The Clash of Cultures in the Colonial Southeast.* Albuquerque: University of New Mexico Press, 2005.

Smith, Daniel Blake. *Inside the Great House: Planter Family Life in Eighteenth-Century Chesapeake Society*. Ithaca, NY: Cornell University Press, 1980.

Spruill, Julia Cherry. *Women's Life and Work in the Southern Colonies*. New York: W.W. Norton and Company, 1972 [1938].

MATERIAL CULTURE

Carson, Cary, Ronald Hofman, and Peter J. Albert, eds. *Of Consuming Interests: The Style of Life in the Eighteenth Century*. Charlottesville: University Press of Virginia, 1994.

Crowley, John E. *The Invention of Comfort: Sensibilities and Design in Early Modern Britain and Early America*. Baltimore: Johns Hopkins University Press, 2001.

McGiffert, Michael, ed. "Material Culture in Early America." Special issue of *William and Mary Quarterly*, 3rd ser., 53, no. 1 (January 1996).

Archaeology

Deagan, Kathleen, and Joan K. Koch, eds. *Spanish St. Augustine: The Archaeology of a Colonial Creole Community*. New York: Academic Press, 1983.

Deetz, James. *Flowerdew Hundred: The Archaeology of a Virginia Plantation, 1619–1864*. Charlottesville: University Press of Virginia, 1993.

Deetz, James. *In Small Things Forgotten: An Archaeology of Early American Life*, rev. ed. New York: Doubleday, 1996.

Ferguson, Leland. *Uncommon Ground: Archaeology and Early African Americans, 1650–1800*. Washington, D.C.: Smithsonian Institution Press, 1992.

Hume, Ivor Noël. *Here Lies Virginia: An Archaeologist's View of Colonial Life and History*. Charlottesville: University Press of Virginia, 1994 [1963].

Hume, Ivor Noël. *Martin's Hundred*. New York: Knopf, 1982.

Kelso, William, with Beverly Straube. *Jamestown Rediscovery, 1994–2004*. [Richmond]: Association for the Preservation of Virginia Antiquities, 2004.

Singleton, Theresa A., ed. *The Archaeology of Slavery and Plantation Life*. Orlando, FL: Academic Press, 1985.

Singleton, Theresa A., ed. *"I, Too, Am America": Archaeological Studies of African-American Life*. Washington, D.C.: Smithsonian Institution Press, 1999.

Yentsch, Anne Elisabeth. *A Chesapeake Family and Their Slaves: A Study in Historical Archaeology*. Cambridge: Cambridge University Press, 1994.

Clothing

Baumgarten, Linda. *Eighteenth-Century Clothing at Williamsburg*. Williamsburg, VA: Colonial Williamsburg Foundation, 1986.

Kidwell, Claudia, and Margaret Christman. *Suiting Everyone: The Democratization of Dress in America*. Washington, D.C.: Smithsonian Institution Press, 1974.

McClellan, Elizabeth. *Historic Dress in America, 1607–1800*. Philadelphia: George W. Jacobs and Company, 1904.

Warwick, Edward, Henry C. Pitz, and Alexander Wycoff. *Early American Dress*. New York: Benjamin Blom, 1965.

Food

Booth, Sally Smith. *Hung, Strung, and Potted: A History of Eating in Colonial America*. New York: Clarkson N. Potter, 1971.

Carson, Jane. *Colonial Virginia Cookery*. Williamsburg, VA: Colonial Williamsburg Foundation, 1968.

Edge, John T., ed. *Foodways: The New Encyclopedia of Southern Culture*, Vol. 7, Charles Reagan Wilson, gen. ed. Chapel Hill: University of North Carolina Press, 2007.

Gabaccia, Donna R. *We Are What We Eat: Ethnic Food and the Making of Americans*. Cambridge, MA: Harvard University Press, 1998.

Hooker, Richard J. *Food and Drink in America: A History*. Indianapolis: Bobbs-Merrill Company, 1981.

Houses and Furnishings

Adams, Annmarie, and Sally McMurry, eds. *Exploring Everyday Landscapes: Perspectives in Vernacular Architecture*. Knoxville: University of Tennessee Press, 1997.

Calvert, Karin. *Children in the House: The Material Culture of Childhood, 1600–1900*. Boston: Northeastern University Press, 1992.

Kornwolf, James D. *Architecture and Town Planning in Colonial North America*, 3 vols. Baltimore: Johns Hopkins University Press, 2002.

St. George, Robert Blair, ed. *Material Life in America, 1600–1800*. Boston: Northeastern University Press, 1988.

Thompson, Eleanor, ed. *American Home: Material Culture, Domestic Space, and Family Life*. Hanover, NH: University Press of New England, 1988.

Vlatch, John, ed. *By the Work of Their Hands: Studies in Afro-American Folklife*. Charlottesville: University Press of Virginia, 1991.

RECREATION

Byrnside, Ronald L. *Music in Eighteenth-Century Georgia*. Athens: University of Georgia Press, 1997.

Carson, Jane. *Colonial Virginians at Play.* Williamsburg, VA: Colonial Williamsburg, 1965.

Crawford, Richard. *America's Musical Heritage: A History.* New York: W.W. Norton and Company, 2001.

Epstein, Dena J. *Sinful Tunes and Spirituals: Black Folk Music to the Civil War.* Urbana: University of Illinois Press, 1977.

Housewright, Wiley L. *A History of Music and Dance in Florida, 1565–1865.* Tuscaloosa: University of Alabama Press, 1991.

Millar, John Fitzhugh. *Country Dances of Colonial America.* Williamsburg, VA: Thirteen Colonies Press, 1990.

Rice, Kym S. *Early American Taverns: For the Entertainment of Friends and Strangers.* Chicago: Regnery Gateway, 1983.

Salinger, Sharon V. *Taverns and Drinking in Early America.* Baltimore: Johns Hopkins University Press, 2004.

Schmidt, Leigh Eric. *Consumer Rites: The Buying and Selling of American Holidays.* Princeton, NJ: Princeton University Press, 1995.

Struna, Nancy. *People of Prowess: Sport, Leisure, and Labor in Early Anglo-America.* Urbana: University of Illinois Press, 1996.

Talley, John. *Secular Music in Colonial Annapolis: The Tuesday Club, 1745–56.* Urbana: University of Illinois Press, 1988.

RELIGION

Ahlstrom, Sydney E. *A Religious History of the American People,* Vol. 1. Garden City, NY: Image Books, 1975.

Bonomi, Patricia U. *Under the Cope of Heaven: Religion, Society, and Politics in Colonial America.* New York: Oxford University Press, 1986.

Butler, Jon. *Awash in a Sea of Faith: Christianizing the American People.* Cambridge, MA: Harvard University Press, 1990.

Frey, Sylvia R., and Betty Wood. *Come Shouting to Zion: African American Protestantism in the American South and British Caribbean to 1830.* Chapel Hill: University of North Carolina Press, 1998.

Hill, Samuel S., ed. *Religion: The New Encyclopedia of Southern Culture,* Vol. 1, Charles Reagan Wilson, gen. ed. Chapel Hill: University of North Carolina Press, 2006.

Kidd, Thomas, S. *The Great Awakening: The Roots of Evangelical Christianity in Colonial America.* New Haven, CT: Yale University Press, 2007.

Nelson, John K. *A Blessed Company: Parishes, Parsons, and Parishioners in Anglican Virginia, 1690–1776.* Chapel Hill: University of North Carolina Press, 2001.

Raboteau, Albert. *Slave Religion: The "Invisible Institution" in the Antebellum South.* New York: Oxford University Press, 1978.

Ray, Celeste, ed. *Ethnicity: The New Encyclopedia of Southern Culture,* Vol. 6, Charles Reagan Wilson, gen. ed. Chapel Hill: University of North Carolina Press, 2007.

Schmidt, Eric. *Holy Fairs: Scottish Communions and American Revivals in the Early Modern Period.* Princeton, NJ: Princeton University Press, 1989.

Sobel, Mechel. *Trabelin' On: The Slave Journey of an Afro-Baptist Faith.* Princeton, NJ: Princeton University Press, 1979.

Thorp, Daniel B. *The Moravian Community in Colonial North Carolina: Pluralism on the Southern Frontier.* Knoxville: University of Tennessee Press, 1989.

Upton, Dell. *Holy Things and Profane: Anglican Parish Churches in Colonial Virginia.* New Haven, CT: Yale University Press, 1997.

BODIES

Cassidy, James H. *Medicine in America: A Short History.* Baltimore: Johns Hopkins University Press, 1991.

Crosby, Alfred W. *The Columbian Exchange: The Biological and Cultural Consequences of 1492.* Westport, CT: Greenwood Press, 1972.

Duffy, John. *Epidemics in Colonial America.* Baton Rouge: Louisiana State University Press, 1953.

Godbeer, Richard. *Sexual Revolution in Early America.* Baltimore: Johns Hopkins University Press, 2002.

Grasso, Christopher, ed., "Sexuality in Early America." Special issue of *William and Mary Quarterly* 3rd ser. 60, no. 1 (January 2003).

Holt, Thomas C., ed. "Forum: Purity of Blood and the Social Order." *William and Mary Quarterly,* 3rd ser., 61, no. 3 (July 2004): 435–520.

Mancell, Peter C. *Deadly Medicine: Indians and Alcohol in Early America.* Ithaca, NY: Cornell University Press, 1995.

McGiffert, Michael, ed. "Constructing Race: Differentiating Peoples in the Early Modern World." Special issue of *William and Mary Quarterly,* 3rd ser., 54, no. 1 (January 1997).

Rutman, Darrett B., and Anita H. Rutman. *Small Worlds, Large Questions: Explorations in Early American Social History, 1600–1850.* Charlottesville: University Press of Virginia, 1994.

Shryock, Richard Harrison. *Medicine and Society in America, 1660–1860.* New York: New York University Press, 1960.

White, Shane, and Graham White. *Stylin': African American Expressive Culture from Its Beginnings to the Zoot Suit.* Ithaca, NY: Cornell University Press, 1998.

IDENTITIES

Berkhofer, Robert. *The White Man's Indian: Images of the American Indian from Columbus to the Present.* New York: Vintage, 1979.

Breen, T. H. *Puritans and Adventurers: Change and Persistence in Early America.* New York: Oxford University Press, 1980.

Breen T.H. *Tobacco Culture: The Mentality of the Great Tidewater Planters on the Eve of Revolution.* Princeton, NJ: Princeton University Press, 1985.

Butler, Jon. *Becoming American: The Revolution before 1776.* Cambridge, MA: Harvard University Press, 2000.

Carson, Cary, ed. *Becoming Americans: Our Struggle to Be Both Free and Equal, a Plan of Thematic Interpretation.* Williamsburg, VA: Colonial Williamsburg Foundation, 1998.

Chaplin, Joyce E. *An Anxious Pursuit: Agricultural Innovation and Modernity in the Lower South, 1730–1815.* Chapel Hill: University of North Carolina Press, 1993.

Holloway, Joseph, ed. *Africanisms in American Culture.* 2nd ed. Bloomington: Indiana University Press, 2005.

Jordan, Winthrop. *The White Man's Burden: Historical Origins of Racism in the United States.* New York: Oxford University Press, 1974.

Jordan, Winthrop. *White over Black: American Attitudes toward the Negro, 1550–1812.* Baltimore: Penguin Books 1968.

Montgomery, Michael, and Ellen Johnson, eds. *Language: The New Encyclopedia of Southern Culture,* Vol. 5, Charles Reagan Wilson, gen. ed. Chapel Hill: University of North Carolina Press, 2007.

Perdue, Theda. *"Mixed Blood" Indians: Racial Construction in the Early South.* Athens: University of Georgia Press, 2003.

Shoemaker, Nancy. *A Strange Likeness: Becoming Red and White in Eighteenth-Century North America.* New York: Oxford University Press, 2004.

Sobel, Mechal. *The World They Made Together: Black and Whites Values in Eighteenth-Century Virginia.* Princeton: Princeton University Press, 1987.

Vaughan, Alden T. *Roots of American Racism: Essays on the Colonial Experience.* New York: Oxford University Press, 1995.

Wood, Amy Louise, ed. *Violence: The New Encyclopedia of Southern Culture,* Vol. 19, Charles Reagan Wilson, gen. ed. Chapel Hill: University of North Carolina Press, 2011.

INDEX

About the Author

JOHN T. SCHLOTTERBECK is A.W. Crandall Professor of History, DePauw University, Greencastle, Indiana. He has published essays and given conference papers on various topics on Virginia history and consulted with public historians on interpreting slavery at historic house museums.

Recent Titles in
The Greenwood Press Daily Life in the United States Series

Immigrant America, 1870–1920
June Granatir Alexander

Along the Mississippi
George S. Pabis

Immigrant America, 1820–1870
James M. Bergquist

The Progressive Era
Steven L. Piott

African American Migrations
Kimberley L. Phillips